A HISTORY OF GERMAN LITERATURE
1760–1805

A HISTORY OF GERMAN LITERATURE
1760–1805

Werner Kohlschmidt

Translated by

Ian Hilton

Senior Lecturer, Department of German
University College of North Wales, Bangor

HOLMES & MEIER PUBLISHERS
New York

Published in the United States of America in 1975
by Holmes & Meier Publishers, Inc.
101 Fifth Avenue, New York, N.Y. 10003

Printed in Great Britain

Library of Congress Cataloging in Publication Data

Kohlschmidt, Werner, 1904–
 A history of German literature, 1760–1805.
 Translation of Vom Sturm und Drang zur Klassik, the 3d part
of v. 2 of Geschichte der deutschen Literatur von den Anfängen
bis zur Gegenwart.
 Bibliography: p.
 Includes index.
 1. German literature—18th century—History and criticism.
I. Geschichte der deutschen Literatur von den Anfängen bis
zur Gegenwart. Bd. 2. II. Title. PT311.K55   830'.9'006
74–32062
ISBN 0–8419–0195–3

Contents

Publishers' Note

This book is the first part of a multi-volume English translation of *Geschichte der deutschen Literatur von den Anfängen bis zur Gegenwart* (A History of German Literature from the Beginning to the Present Day), which is being published in four volumes by Reclam Verlag, Stuttgart. Volume II of the German edition, by Werner Kohlschmidt, Professor of German Literature at the University of Berne, was the first to be published, in 1965, under the title of *Vom Barock bis zur Klassik* (From Baroque to Classicism).

The translation of the series as a whole is being sponsored by the Macmillan Press and is under the supervision of the General Editor, Professor K. Spalding.

The present volume corresponds to the third part of the German Volume II (*Vom Sturm und Drang zur Klassik*). A translation of the first two parts, *Der Barock* and *Die Aufklärung*, will follow.

Translator's Note

Titles of German poems and of lesser-known plays and prose writings have been left in their original German form, but with well-known works the English titles are given at their first mention, where this is felt desirable. German quotations have been left in the original in the text itself, but translated into English as footnotes.

A few footnotes have also been provided as explanatory comment for the additional guidance of the reader where this is considered helpful. Individuals from other countries referred to in the text by way of comparison (e.g. Shaftesbury, Watteau) are not commented on in the footnotes. A small Glossary of literary terms and a Chronological Table are provided at the end of the book for the benefit of the reader.

I wish to express my sincere thanks to Professor K. Spalding for his encouragement and assistance throughout; to Mr D. Nunn for his help on points of translation; and to Mrs M. Ll. Williams for her typing of the manuscript.

IAN HILTON

Bangor, 1973

PART I

Poetry as the Mother Tongue of the Human Race

1 *Aesthetica in Nuce:* Hamann and Herder

The phenomenon compartmentalised between Rationalism and Classicism, and known in literary history as the 'Storm and Stress' movement, was of diverse origin and, when it did appear, not at all so straightforward and unambiguous as its title would suggest. There was an interplay of such varied influences as that of Rousseau and of Pietism, Old Norse romanticism and the modern English novel, Spinoza and Shaftesbury. And the freedom to indulge in all these influences was due entirely to that same Enlightenment which was parodied time and again in the writings of figures like Voltaire and Wieland as the wretched bowdlerising of the Ancients, or was seen as mere imitation when contrasted with the omnipotence of original genius. Pietism had supplied not only the mystic-pantheistic element, but also the sincerity of introspection, which led to a completely modern psychology; there was, however, no tolerance shown towards Rationalism, although the new movement claimed it for itself in unlimited measure, particularly as a right to subjectivity.

And yet it was the Enlightenment which, in the final analysis, to a considerable extent attacked itself in this literary movement. For in advocating the claims of Nature and human rights, it sponsored, too, the rights of the Individual, of originality and creative genius. And as far as the forms it took were concerned, we only need remember here the strange amalgam of liberal-minded philanthropy and mysticism in freemasonry, or the hybridism of modern science, quackery and alchemy which the century of Enlightenment had produced, to recognise the common factors in these opposing trends. The 'Storm and Stress' or *Geniebewegung* contains therefore just as much continuity as revolution.

Indeed, the revolutionary element was frequently more a matter of gesture and self-interpretation on the part of this pronouncedly youthful movement than its very essence. Moreover, it appeared with quite varying degrees of severity and mildness, as absolute creative genius in the case of Klinger and Bürger or with the still clear affiliation to the classical tradition as in the case of the *Göttinger Hainbund*; in highly political form as in the case of Schubart and the young Schiller under the motto *in tyrannos*; as social criticism with Lenz, Wagner or the young Goethe of the Gretchen-tragedy (seen as a drama of infanticide), or radically Ego-orientated as in *Werther*; theocentrically motivated as in the case of Hamann and Lavater or in the philosophy of Friedrich Jacobi, anthropocentrically as predominantly in Herder. These differences, even contradictions, can only be mastered if the all too broad concept of the 'Storm and Stress' is more precisely defined by that of *Geniebewegung*, which tends to link the starting point and the goal of this historical phenomenon, and which centres less on gesture and attitude than on a common established idea.

Furthermore, in its historical origins the term 'Storm and Stress' was not consciously promoted by its leading representatives – as happened, for example, with Romanticism and with Naturalism and Symbolism – but occurred only towards the end of the Movement, and even then in an erroneous way. It was the title of a drama by Klinger, who brought it with him in 1776 to Weimar. He and Lenz had been attracted by the new position of Goethe, their erstwhile companion, and hoped to establish a kind of Muses' Court of original geniuses there. As we know, this project was to remain unsuccessful, even though the young Duke Karl August was inclined to lead a lax and unrestrained mode of existence. For it was just this very thing that Goethe, conscious of his new responsibilities as mentor, no longer wanted in Weimar. *Wirrwarr*, the original title of Klinger's spectacle on the ways of genius, no longer found a place in Goethe's way of thinking after the time of *Werther*. Accordingly, at the suggestion of the Swiss self-styled 'apostle of genius', Christoph Kaufmann, who had also arrived on the scene, the drama was furnished with the title *Sturm und Drang*, which literary historians have adopted as the designation for the style and the age.

With Lessing, Johann Elias Schlegel and Gerstenberg, and with the later Klopstock too, Enlightenment aesthetics had by definition already abandoned the limitations, rules and prejudices of the Gottschedian period. It was a process which had basically begun as early as 1740 with the appearance of the Swiss Bodmer and Breitinger. But it had suffered a certain retrogression at their own hands, especially as Bodmer grew old. Yet we must recall that among the Swiss, and among Lessing, Möser, Gerstenberg and Schlegel there had already taken place a new evaluation of the non-classical tradition, the Old German and the Old Nordic, as well as a revaluation of Shakespeare, and in connection with this a relaxing over the question of the theory of imitation, which was noticeable even in the case of Winckelmann who was fascinated by classical antiquity. All this was evolution, not yet revolution. But it directly prepared the way for a code of aesthetics which started from counter-rationalistic presuppositions and reached revolutionary conclusions.

Johann Georg Hamann (1730–88) must be hailed as the real inaugurator of this new mood. Without him even Herder, the leading aesthetician of the 'Storm and Stress', cannot be historically understood. Hamann's background was petit-bourgeois. His father was a barber-surgeon. In order to be able to afford his wide and intense studies of theology, classical and modern languages and philosophy, Hamann was forced to take up positions as tutor early on as a means of existence; then he entered the world of trade and commerce and later became a minor official with the General Excise and Customs Administration, and subsequently Superintendent of the Customs Warehouse. We may well ask why it was that this remarkably gifted and original mind did not enjoy more material success in his everyday life at a time when class already no longer signified any insuperable barrier. Certainly he had a 'thick' tongue, he stammered. But that hardly hindered others, such as Gellert, for example, in their climb to the top. What was socially more precarious in tiny Königsberg was the fact that he openly entered into a so-called marriage of conscience with an uneducated girl who bore him several children; it was a union which he obstinately refused to legalise. This was something that Goethe could afford to do as Minister, even Lichtenberg as a scholar of international repute. But the petit-bourgeois citizen and minor official from Königsberg could not. Given these circumstances, his intellectual achievements were all the more remarkable. The man who was celebrated by the young generation as the 'Magus of the North'[1] could not play the role of prophet entirely naturally in the limited confines of his home town, especially after he had engaged in polemics with its most famous university scholar, Kant himself. Whatever importance, in fact, Hamann the writer enjoyed beyond the local confines of Königsberg made not the slightest difference.

Hamann himself has given an exact account of his inner development, in a pietistic way, without extenuation. His youthful errors, his conversion in London in 1758 – it is all revealed in his own description. It was an entirely personal development that was not at all in keeping with the normal bourgeois code; and 'free marriage' and freelance writing, which served as a second source of income, were merely its external symptoms. In *Gedanken über meinen Lebenslauf* (*Thoughts on my Life*) (1758) there is presented in radical self-critical fashion the figure of a man who 'amid the turmoil of all my shattering passions', and from the wilderness and desolation of the heart, could suddenly on reading Deuteronomy one evening identify himself with Cain:

> Ich fühlte auf einmal mein Herz quillen, es ergoß sich in Tränen, und ich konnte es nicht länger – ich konnte es nicht länger meinem Gott verhehlen, daß ich der Brudermörder, der Brudermörder seines eingeborenen Sohnes war.[2]

We are reminded of Kierkegaard, who had much in common with Hamann and who could say of his precursor: 'With all his life and soul, to the last drop of blood, he is concentrated in a single word, in the passionate protest of a highly gifted genius against a system of human life.' At all events, in Hamann's case, the conversion first allowed comfort and tranquillity to triumph over melancholy and then certainly led him to maintain a lifelong view of history that was based directly on God. It did not effect a change in his character. Hamann himself critically maintained that his character had a two-fold basis, 'in doing everything or nothing. The middle path is my antipathy; sooner one of the

---

[1] A title given him by C. F. von Moser. (*Translator's note*)

[2] All at once I felt my heart well up, it gushed forth in tears and I could no longer – I could no longer conceal from my God that I was the fratricide, the murderer of His only begotten Son.

extremes.' And he also bluntly called himself 'the most odd amalgam of opposites'. That very fact however was the clearest predestinatory sign of Storm and Stress 'genius'. Both those Hamannian utterances would have served for Werther just as well.

His individual style also corresponds to this self-characterisation. Hamann did not really write a 'book' at all in the proper sense of the word. His true essence lay in being a writer of fragments, admittedly in the grand manner. All the ideas, the conjectures, meditations, rhapsodies in prose, which he fused together in his writings, were based on the consciousness of a mission that was pietistically orientated, but which also allowed the 'Magus of the North' to find an existential symbol in Socrates: 'With me it is a question of tempests which one can hear raging . . .' And he characterised his compulsion to express himself as an 'interest sealed in my bones like a burning fire, that I can not bear it and am nearly consumed'. Small wonder then that his style which derived from such overwhelming feeling is 'sibylline' (except in the letters). It is a style full of exclamations, socratic questions, anacoluthic sentences, the fascination of which consists not in the ability to convince by means of logic, but in the compulsion to fill in the omissions or explore the inferences. It has a stuttering ring to it, but it was designed that way. In Pietism too, people would often write somewhat in that fashion, as for instance the correspondence between Lavater and Susanne von Klettenberg demonstrates. The young Goethe had likewise adopted it (in secularised form) in his letters dating from the pre-*Werther* period. Hamann was fully conscious of the inner form of his sibylline style, which he himself characterised as 'mimetic': 'In my mimetic style there rules a stricter logic and a closer bond than in the ideas of lively minds.' And: 'The clarity of certain books is often their deception and shortcoming.' In this way he defended himself against the criticism of being alogical in the outward form, and in fact claimed an inner logic. It was not the alogicality caused by the degree of immediacy, the illusion of pietistic stuttering. It was a form pedagogically intended, socratically conceived so to speak, a permanent, compelling dialogue with the reader. The language here broke away from the convention of Rationalism. Creative genius demanded freedom from it, too: 'Whoever exceeds the rules of his craft or casts them aside, is not naked and bare as a conse-

quence.' It served only to provide validity for that which was new,
that which was still unusual. Consequently, Hamann's sibylline
style must in no way be called irrational in the mystic sense,
although he did deliberately shatter the frontiers of rational
thinking.

Following on his writings that stemmed from his journey to
England (there were the *Brocken* and *Biblische Betrachtungen
eines Christen*, in addition to his autobiography) and which were
predominantly concerned with the (awakened) Self, and after his
return to Germany, came the *Sokratische Denkwürdigkeiten*
(*Socratic Memorabilia*) (1759). This treatise was the product of
a single sustained effort and was really concerned with creative
genius. The *Sokratische Denkwürdigkeiten* were conditioned by
a particular personal situation. Hamann's friend Behrens, a busi-
nessman from Riga, had, with the assistance of Kant, attempted
to win back to the Enlightenment the man who had been converted
in London. The *Denkwürdigkeiten* were Hamann's reply. In this
Hamann saw himself compelled to provide a foundation for his
opposition – originating from London – to Rationalism through
an anthropological conception of genius, which also led now to a
consciously existential opposition, extending even into the sphere of
the language he intended to use. For the *Denkwürdigkeiten* were
not to be a biography of Socrates, but were to illustrate in the
figure of the great Greek philosopher what constituted genius.
And as the first step in this process, the public was hoaxed right
from the outset in the Dedication as 'Nobody, the Well-known',
and was presented with the settled ranks of the Sophists, standing here for those of the rationalistic intellectuals, in antithesis
to socratic genius. This genius was 'ignorant', not from stupidity,
but feeling:

> Die Unwissenheit des Sokrates war Empfindung. Zwischen
> Empfindung aber und einem Lehrsatz ist ein größerer Unter-
> schied als zwischen einem lebenden Tier und anatomischen
> Gerippe desselben.[3]

Such statements anticipated both Herder and the young Goethe.
The entire later 'Storm and Stress' drew on this contrast of the-

---

[3] The ignorance of Socrates was sensitivity. But between sensitivity and a
theoretical proposition there is a greater distinction than between a living
animal and its anatomical skeleton.

oretical proposition and life. And Hamann also, a little later, not surprisingly extended the problem of ignorance to the area of aesthetics by relating it to Homer, Aristotle and Shakespeare:

> Was ersetzt bei Homer die Unwissenheit der Kunstregeln, die ein Aristoteles nach ihm erdacht, und was bei einem Shakespeare die Unwissenheit oder Übertretung jener kritischen Gesetze? Das Genie ist die einmütige Antwort.[4]

All this was consciously aggressive, anti-rationalistic, because there was an absolute religious basis involved. The contempt with which the Rationalist was addressed in the 'Peroration' as 'a reasonable, useful, agreeable man in the world' meant a final annihilation of a rationalist way of thinking which was justifiable only as a means of self-criticism, but not as a universally valid philosophy. Such rationalism was questioned yet again in the sequel *Wolken* in the context of its quest for autonomy, to which Hamann opposed the freedom which was reserved for the Spirit ('of the Lord') alone.

A few years later in 1762 there appeared *Kreuzzüge des Philologen*, with *Aesthetica in nuce* (*Aesthetics in a Nutshell*) as its chief item. This had been preceded in 1761 by the literary polemic[5] couched in the form of *Abaelardi Virbii chimerische Einfälle*. The year 1762 also produced a controversy over Christian Ludwig von Hagedorn's theory of art, which was given expression in *Leser und Kunstrichter nach perspektivischem Unebenmaße* (*Reader and Critic*). In these treatises Hamann's (pietistic) theology clearly developed into a doctrine of aesthetics in its own right, at the centre of which an irrational view of language grew more and more manifest alongside the irrational theory of genius. As the famous passage in *Aesthetica in nuce* put it:

> Poesie ist die Muttersprache des menschlichen Geschlechts; wie der Gartenbau älter als der Acker: Malerei – als Schrift: Gesang – als Deklamation: Gleichnisse – als Schlüsse: Tausch – als Handel. Ein tieferer Schlaf war die Ruhe der Urahnen; und

---

[4] What for a Homer replaces ignorance of the rules of art which an Aristotle devised after him, and what for a Shakespeare replaces the ignorance or transgression of those critical laws? Genius is the unanimous answer.

[5] With Moses Mendelssohn. (*Translator's note*)

ihre Bewegung ein taumelnder Tanz . . . Sinne und Leidenschaften reden und verstehen nichts als Bilder. In Bildern
besteht der ganze Schatz menschlicher Erkenntnis und Glückseligkeit.[6]

Quite certainly this equating of primitive language and poetry,
of sensuality and imagery as their immediate expression was
far removed from the rationalistic evolutionary theory of language
deriving from convention. The very opening words show that he
considered himself to be engaged on a kind of revolutionary
Augean task. Thus there appeared in this 'Rhapsody in Cabbalistic Prose' a sentence which would inevitably provoke a Lessing or a Mendelssohn: 'Do not therefore venture forth into the
metaphysics of the fine arts, without being accomplished in the
ways of orgies and eleusinian mysteries.' Similarly, in addition to
orgies and mysteries, the letter to the 'rabbi' (Mendelssohn) also
contains the demand, echoing the Bible: 'Verily, verily, we must
become children, if we are to receive the spirit of truth.' It is a
demand which again anticipated a basic theme of the 'Storm and
Stress'. The cue now, therefore, was an outspoken anti-intellec-
tualism. And in keeping with this was the radical reproach aimed
at the art critics of the Enlightenment for having got rid of real,
true nature through their philosophical abstractions, and for the
fact that as a result of this their theory of imitation was in a
sorry way: 'Your mendacious philosophy has cast nature aside,
and why do you urge us to imitate?' The restoration of
nature and of genius lay, therefore, along the same path. Dead
Hellenism and dead nature, defunct language and dead philosophy, which had replaced sensual mythology – all that was the
work of the Enlightenment and its *bels esprits*. As the deliberately provocative introduction to *Leser und Kunstrichter* put it:

Wer Willkür und Phantasie den schönen Künsten entziehen
will, stellt ihrer Ehre und ihrem Leben als ein Meuchelmörder

---

[6] Poetry is the mother-tongue of the human race: as gardening is older
than farming, painting older than writing, singing than declamation,
parables than inferences, bartering than commerce. A deeper sleep was the
rest of our ancestors and an ecstatic dance their movement . . . Senses
and passions speak and understand nothing but images. The whole treasure
of human knowledge and happiness consists in images.

nach und versteht keine andere Sprache der Leidenschaften als der Heuchler ihre.[7]

Hence the bias in the literary sphere for Homer against Voltaire, for Luther against Montaigne and Bacon, for Rousseau against Mendelssohn. Hence the outspokenness later in favour of Goethe's *Götz*, which Hamann called the 'dawn of a new dramaturgy'. Fragmentary and 'sibylline' as Hamann's form was, his deductions were of one piece and were to form a basis for a new view of poetry and language in line with that of the nascent 'Storm and Stress'. Language as an expression of sensual originality and wealth of imagery, which existed before thought, creative genius that was not limited in its freedom, nature as a yardstick, but not the 'beautiful nature' of the Enlightenment – it was all an early revaluation of values,[8] which, expressed as it was in original form, had to have the consequences it did.

Johann Gottfried Herder (1744–1803) was born in the little East Prussian town of Mohrungen, the son of the sexton. The family was, therefore, of limited means. The boy's rare talent became evident early on to the minister at the Mohrungen church, Trescho, a man who was active and ambitious in the field of literature. He employed Herder as a copyist for his works. Through the good offices of a benefactor, he took the courageous step of going to Königsberg to study. As a sixeeen-year-old Herder registered as a student of theology there, assiduously attended the lectures of Kant, and became a friend and student of Hamann. With his young and lively mind Herder wished to extend his studies as widely as possible, and it was Hamann again who introduced him to English and Italian. Herder was not only exceptionally active and receptive, but also possessed inexhaustible energy. His quest – already envisaged at that time – for universal culture was combined with a tremendous sensitivity and a pedagogical élan, which were later to make him the brilliant, scintillating member of society at the Weimar Court. Admittedly in his sensitivity there lay too the seeds of embitterment which oppressed his later life.

When he was no more than twenty, he came as a teacher to the

---

[7] He who wants to abolish caprice and fancy from the fine arts is like an assassin plotting against their honour and their life, and understands no other language of passion than that of hypocrites.

[8] An allusion to a phrase by Nietzsche. (*Translator's note*)

Cathedral School in Riga, a position which was combined with
the duties of minister. Here he won early literary fame with
Über die neuere Deutsche Litteratur. Fragmente (*Fragments on
Recent German Literature*) (1766–67) through his flexible and
direct utilisation of recently acquired motifs and subject matter.
In the *Fragmente* he dealt with topics which had only just come
to his notice – and always with the freshness of the first impression, and partly with breathtaking conjectures, flashes of insight and appraisals. Also dating from this period were the
Kritische Wälder (*Critical Groves*) (1769), in which he took
issue with aesthetes of the first rank like Lessing and Winckelmann, but also with second-rate ones like Riedel and Klotz. In
this period of early development it was not so much a question of
establishing his reputation, as of promoting the cause as such,
which is revealed in the distrustful anonymity of Herder's early
works. He shied away from publicising his name and office. The
feeling that he had been tied down much too early and encum-
bered with responsibilities, as well as his own inclination to gain
experience of the world, in fact drove him away from Riga after
only five years. And it was in this very move, in this inner unrest
of his, in the driving urge for drastic action, that Herder was
already early on a creative genius in the 'Storm and Stress' sense
of the term – as a leader of which movement he was destined
to emerge within a matter of years. The famous voyage to France,
which led him in 1769 to Paris and Nantes, and in the following
year *via* Holland back to North Germany, determined the next
phase of his life. The product of that trip was the *Journal meiner
Reise im Jahr 1769* (*Journal of my Voyage of 1769*); it was a
grand attempt within the framework of this experience to translate the experience itself into the focal point of a pedagogic
Weltbild, undertaken on the basis of English empiricism and
sensualism, which he had passionately assimilated during his
years in the east German towns. At the same time he continued
to stimulate his ideas by a broadening of his investigations into
aesthetics, as his studies and sketches for the work entitled
Plastik testified. In Hamburg in 1770 he became personally
acquainted with Claudius and Lessing and then undertook a
further educational journey, this time to take up the post of
tutor to the Prince of Eutin. This was to settle his destiny in a
two-fold way. In the Darmstadt Court circle he met Caroline

Flachsland, to whom he became engaged. She was an extraordinarily talented girl, orphaned at an early age, and without her intellectual encouragement and assistance his later life would have been unthinkable. At the same time this journey led him, in his search to find a cure for an eye complaint, to Strassburg in the August of 1770, where his and the twenty-one year old Goethe's paths crossed. In a unique teacher-pupil relationship there began that association out of which the long-standing friendship at Weimar was later to develop. For the meeting – described in such detail in Goethe's *Dichtung und Wahrheit* (*Poetry and Truth*) – survived even Herder's Bückeburg period, which commenced in 1771 and was the most strongly pietistically orientated of his development (*Die älteste Urkunde des Menschengeschlechts* (*Oldest Document of the Human Race*) (1774–76) and *An Prediger, Fünfzehn Provinzialblätter* (*To Preachers: Fifteen Provincial Letters*) were the theological testimony to this). During the time he was Court Preacher at the tiny *Residenz* of Schaumberg-Lippe, where he assumed the position of the prematurely deceased Thomas Abbt, to whose memory he dedicated the *Torso*, Herder both started a family, and, in the literary sphere, produced the essays *Über den Ursprung der Sprache* (*On the Origin of Language*) (1771), the *Briefwechsel über Ossian und die Lieder alter Völker* (*On Ossian and the Songs of Ancient Peoples*) and *Shakespeare*. The last two pieces formed the stimulating part of the contents of *Blätter für deutsche Art und Kunst* (*On German Character and Art*), which appeared in 1773 and constituted the real manifesto of the 'Storm and Stress'. After plans for a Chair at the University of Göttingen had failed to materialise, he became Superintendent-General in Weimar at Goethe's suggestion three years later and entered an atmosphere which offered him sufficient scope and associates of equal stature.

What he had to offer the generation of *Stürmer und Dränger* was an astonishing diversity of interests and at the same time a homogeneous approach. Here he resembled his mentor Hamann: he had a broadly directed outlook, already deriving at that time from a conception of universal literature, scattering liberally both cryptic and obvious ideas for further investigation. In keeping with his disposition he was likewise predominantly a fragmentist and hence took delight in the pointed comment, even to the extent of paradox; he was well-read, interested in everything to a greater

degree than Hamann, his form more elastic and freer than
Hamann's. No less passionate, yet more comprehensible as a
pedagogue, Herder was the very best person to point the way towards conquering the Enlightenment in the realms of philosophy,
language and poetry, but above all towards the awakening of a
new sense of history which was founded on empathy and no
longer on dogmatic categorisation.

The *Fragmente* already touched upon a multitude of themes,
the majority of which suggested the stimulus of Hamann. The fact
that they represented a critical disputation with the Berlin
Literaturbriefe brought them in line with the thinking contained
in *Kreuzzüge des Philologen*. The line taken by Herder also
echoed Hamann's:

> Die Literaturbriefe waren im Anfang ein Zeitvertreib eines
> kranken Offiziers, nachher des kranken Publikums und oft auch
> kranker und ermüdeter Verfasser . . . Daher ist auch unsere
> Zeit um so viel reicher an Journälen, als sie an Originalwerken
> arm wird.[9]

Such a declaration manifested Rousseauistic ideas. It led to the
development of the idea of a history of literature, which aimed at
the arousing of ambition in the various peoples through competition, with the ultimate intention of influencing the present. This
idea was utopian in its vision. But Herder was aiming at a communal, collective work which alone could realise his 'dream'. The
basis of it would be language, which was taken in the full Hamannian sense to be a language of image and metaphor, and not a language governed by rules; an expression of human sensitivity, and not
a creation of philosophy or of God. This last point went beyond
Hamann (and the 'Magus' understood and later censured it). In
this connection Herder's strong sense of historical genesis already
found expression in his conception of the ages of language. Here
was to be found that oft-quoted superb sentence about Luther:
'He it is, who has awakened and set free a slumbering giant, the
German language.' Compared with Luther, Erasmus was, in Herder's view, merely the 'finest pedant the world has perhaps seen'.

---

[9] In the beginning literary letters were a means of passing the time for
a sick officer, later a sick public and often also sick and weary writers . . .
Hence our age is all the richer in journals, as it is destitute in original
works.

It was not Erasmus's Humanism based on the Ancients however, but rather the Enlightenment that was seen as the epitome of linguistic impotence and decadence:

> Kommet her, ihr neuen schönen Geister, ihr französierenden Witzlinge, ihr prosaisch poetischen Stolperer, ihr berühmten Wochenschriftsteller, ihr gelehrten Weisen im akademischen Paragraphenstil, ihr erbaulichen Redner im Kanzelstil. Versucht es doch, aus euren reichen Vorratskammern ein Buch unseres Jahrhunderts zu suchen, das in Absicht der Schreibart die Würde der Bibelübersetzung des Luthers erreichte.[10]

In the same context Herder's metaphor of language as 'the sublime gothic edifice, which it was in Luther's time' was years ahead of the somewhat negative rehabilitation of the Gothic concept as expressed in Goethe's essay on the Strassburg Minster. This high estimation of Luther and, in the same way, of the 'gothic' sublimity of the Hohenstauffen period naturally had, as mentioned, its counterpart, namely contemporary language seen as a 'new-style building, cluttered with strange ornamentation'. Herder's purpose was therefore exactly like that of Hamann, and was aimed at a conception of the history of language, which led from the poetic sensuousness of the Old German period up to its perversion and atrophy (at the hands of the Enlightenment). Here was the starting point for the counter-movement as found thematically and linguistically in Goethe's *Götz*, in the reappraisal of the folk song, of dialect, right up to the deliberate irreverence of the later 'Storm and Stress'. Naturally, the *Fragmente* plunged ahead with a detailed look at the relationship of imitation and originality. Against a poetry that was misconceivedly aiming for gracefulness Herder, here in agreement with Winckelmann, urged 'Do not rob them [the Greeks] of what they have invented, but rather seize upon the art of invention, composition and form!' This led to the ideal of 'imitate thyself'. Quite clearly this was nothing other than the replacement of imitation by originality, the reverse of the traditional significance of the terms. Indeed

[10] Come hither, you new fine spirits, you francophile wags, you prosaically poetic blunderers, you renowned writers of the weeklies, you wise men skilled in academic pedantry, you edifying pulpit preachers: Just try from your rich store to find one book from our century which equals the dignity of Luther's translation of the Bible in the very style of writing.

Herder took issue here in productive fashion even with Edward Young's influential *Conjectures on Original Composition* (1759). On the other hand, his basic theme turned equally determinedly into a negative criticism of the Latin influence on the development of German language and thought. The cultural theme of the *Reisejournal* was herewith already presaged. First, however, he pursued his personal difference of opinion with Winckelmann in the *Kritische Wälder*; in the first *silva* it was in relation to the history of art, in the second with specific reference to the *Laokoon*. Here he continued Lessing's theory of the 'pregnant' moment (which the creative artist had to choose for himself) characteristically into a theory of the 'eternal' moment, and on the strength of the polemic directed against Klotz and Riedel arrived at an aesthetic viewpoint of the arts based on the senses, which he was later to expand in the *Plastik*. Herder argued that as far as poetry was concerned, sight did not belong solely to painting, nor hearing solely to music, nor the tactile sense solely to sculpture, but that rather poetry entailed the interplay of all three senses. The thoughts of the English writers or of Diderot also played some part of course here. Yet the principle of the combined sensual qualities simultaneously did correspond to Hamann's thought, particularly with the emphasis on the senses and passions in the as yet uncorrupted area of language.

The *Reisejournal* broadened the propositions of the Riga period to a thoroughly modern utopian vision of education, whose specific demands both anticipate and fascinate. The aim here lay in the call for the 'use of all one's senses':

> Oh, gebt mir eine unverdorbene, mit Abstraktionen und Worten unerstickte Jugendseele her, so lebendig als sie ist, und setzt mich dann in eine Welt, wo ich ihr alle Eindrücke geben kann, die ich will; wie soll sie leben! [11]

Rousseau and yet not Rousseau. To start from scratch, from what was natural and original, was Rousseauistic. What was not Rousseauistic was the educative method which Nature itself did not practise, but rather Man, the pedagogue, who knew that he was

[11] Oh, give me a youthful soul, unspoilt and unchoked with abstractions and words, as lively as it ever is, and set me then in a world where I can provide it with all the impressions that I want to impart; how it will live!

in fact enraptured by Life. He was an Emile, who was spared
the detours and was directed straight to the very centre. Yet
Herder's point of departure was one in common with Rousseau,
namely an attitude that was contrary to the promotion of civil-
isation. The 'ink-slinging age' of Karl Moor was here turned
into painful self-criticism:

> Ich wäre nicht ein Tintenfaß von gelehrter Schriftstellerei, nicht
> ein Wörterbuch von Künsten und Wissenschaften geworden,
> die ich nicht gesehen habe und nicht verstehe; ich wäre nicht
> ein Repositorium voll Papiere und Bücher geworden, das nur
> in die Studierstube gehört ...[12]

(namely, if education had been a true universal education). Faust's
complaint in his opening monologue has a similar ring. It was
part of the self-awareness of a generation, an awareness which
merely found a particularly early and sensitive expression in
Herder. In his case too it related to a sweeping *apologia* for
experience in general and his own personal adventure. The
original experience was the voyage, the sea, the storm, the
solitude, the vast heavens. It was originality experienced in a
wealth of new revolutionary ideas. What a difference when compared to Hamann's account of England! Herder questioned the
whole universe. The aspects covered relate as much to 'natural
science' as to culture. Unlike Hamann's approach, the pedagogic
Eros revealed itself differently too, in the attempt, so full of vitality,
to translate his own excitement to the field of education: for
Herder, education had to be alive and realistic. It had to develop
a 'journal of human knowledge', it had to be a 'natural history
of the human soul'. Above all it had to be organic:

> Man kann nie das Folgende genießen, wenn man das Vorherge-
> hende nicht genossen hat . . . Man kann nie das Vor-
> hergehende völlig zurücknehmen (auch in Verbesserung), ohne
> das Gegenwärtige zu verlieren.[13]

[12] I would then not have become an inkwell for learned penmanship, not
a dictionary of arts and sciences, which I have not seen and do not understand; I would not have become a repository for papers and books, which
really only belong to the study.
[13] One can never enjoy what follows if one has not enjoyed what has gone
before . . . One can never fully recall what has gone before (even in
amended form) without losing the present.

Herder was later to pass on to Goethe this idea of evolution already passionately embraced so early. It was developed in the latter's work in the profound symbol of the Homunculus in *Faust II*. With Herder it was based on the conception of the various ages of man, which he translated in terms of history, language, philosophy and art. The demands of education too were here to correspond to this measuring of human development, beginning with the 'Realklasse',[14] progressing through the 'class' of the heart and concluding only then with the third 'class' of abstraction. The second stage comprised the teaching of history ('the living history of all ages'). The path led, therefore, from nature to philosophy, not *vice versa*.

Much that the *Reisejournal* had only just touched upon amid the flood of questions posed, Herder continued or at least integrated into his prize-essay *Über den Ursprung der Sprache*. Here the theme was prescribed (by the Berlin Academy) and in this very fact lay the compulsion not to digress. All the same Herder remained true to himself; in style, in the way in which he plumbed the waters of a chosen theme dynamically for every possible sounding, sometimes almost chancing beyond the limits, and then finally in the conclusions reached. These hovered between Hamann and the Rationalist theory of convention whereby language was seen as the product of a socio-human consensus. For Hamann, language was in its origins a divine dictate; for the Rationalists it was symbolic.[15] Herder could accept as bedrock neither the one nor the other. For him it was a human and not a divine issue, but at the same time not a human issue devised by man when he had reached the stage of dealing with abstractions. Consequently Herder considered language rather as the primitive sound of natural man from the very beginning, man who is still continually feeling, sensitive and passionate (in the first sentence the beginning of language is considered as at the level of animal sounds and cries). Such language transmitted 'an immediacy through its very accents', and 'in all primitive tongues there are still preserved traces of these natural sounds first used'. However, such language, Herder felt, could never find adequate and true phonetic expression through written form.

[14] The natural environment of the child being the subject of study. (*Translator's note*)

[15] i.e. mechanistic. (*Translator's note*)

Hebrew knows no phonetic script because these sounds were so differentiated that 'they could not be written'. This immediacy of primitive speech is indestructible. Children, women, people of tender feeling, in other words, 'people aware of the senses' remain receptive to the primitive sounds: 'The word has gone and it is the sound of emotion that rings out.' But all that occurred at a still pre-human stage of development. The really human language is moulded differently from those 'sounds of emotion', which child and animal have in common. Whence then does this quite different language come, if it does not appear directly divinely inspired as Hamann would have it? The instincts of the animal do not yet lead on to human language. The gift to man that furthers language is a quite different natural endowment, namely reason: reason, however, is not seen as an isolated addition to man's impulses, but rather as 'the mode of organisation of all his powers'. The crucial point that distinguished Herder from the Rationalists is this: it was not autonomous reason, but rather 'reflection' (Besonnenheit) that was accepted as the characteristic of a definitely human power:

> Ist nämlich die Vernunft keine abgeteilte, einzeln würkende Kraft, sondern eine seiner Gattung eigne Richtung aller Kräfte: so muß der Mensch sie im ersten Zustande haben, da er Mensch ist.[16]

This is something quite different from the concept of Reason as understood by the Berlin or Königsberg Enlightenment. Sense impressions and reason were for Herder 'merely designations of one single power'. This line of approach represented no longer a dualistic philosophy, but was ultimately a monistic definition pointing the direction towards the 'Storm and Stress'. Language had its origin in the consciousness itself of this power of 'reflection'. Language was more than animal sounds; for Herder, it was a 'dictionary of the soul', a 'key to man's inner being'. Herder's own position was herewith defined *vis-à-vis* the theological hypothesis of divine origin, and the Rationalists' theory of language as a system of sign communication, as well as Rousseau's concept of language originating from animal sounds:

---

[16] If, then, reason is not a separate, individually active faculty, but is rather a direction of all faculties characteristic of man, man must have had it in the first stage in which he was man.

Das Ziel Wahrheit ist nur ein Punkt! Auf den hingestellet, sehen wir aber auf allen Seiten: warum kein Tier Sprache erfinden kann, kein Gott Sprache erfinden darf, und der Mensch, als Mensch, Sprache erfinden kann und muß.[17]

The characteristic 'Storm and Stress' image which Herder employed for this process was the panentheistic reinterpretation of Prometheus's stealing of fire: the creation of language as the igniting of the divine spark in the human soul.

The sections that followed were a description of the oldest language in its original state, this time expressly attuned to Hamann's thesis that 'poetry is older than prose'. Man in the earliest times was a sensual being and therefore his language, too, had to live, move and sing. Here written language is connected with the theory of the senses contained in the preliminary studies for *Plastik* and *Kritische Wälder*. Between sight as the 'coldest' sense, and touch, hearing has its place as 'the intermediate sense'. But not one of the senses remains divorced from feeling. Old and uncivilised languages are hence 'strongly sensitive and heartfelt', bold, metaphorical, rich in synonyms, though not logical. Even abstractions depended on 'sound and feeling' and became fewer the more original the language, just as grammar was absent too.

The second part of the prize-essay set out the 'natural laws' for the growth of language. Firstly on the basis of the progression of the powers of man as a free-thinking, active being. The free use of the senses was a prerequisite. Then from the standpoint of man as a Σῷον Πολιτικόν, i.e. from the point of view of family and race. Here too as in the *Reisejournal*, Herder was at variance with Rousseau, who started with the child and not the mother, whose 'natural law' is teaching as well as nursing. Finally, the differentiation of the 'herd' into peoples, of the one language into national tongues. The categories contained in the later *Ideen* were already appearing here: climate, atmosphere and water, food and drink, custom and habit vary and lead to dialect, Herder argued. There finally emerged from all this the hypothesis of one grand continuum right from the origin of the human race to the

[17] The goal of truth is just a single point. Once we stand on that point, we are enabled to look in all directions and recognise why no animal can invent language, no God may, and why man, as man, can and must invent language.

differentiation of languages, which thereby took on another more precise function – namely that of transmitting a 'sense of tradition from people to people', a new consciousness on the basis of one's own language, which thus becomes history in a more profound sense.

The essay – hastily compiled in Strassburg in a matter of days in December 1770 – provided in its concluding paragraphs a testimony to a realistic psychology ('real hard data from the human soul') and a description of language in express contrast to the 'philosophical novels' of Rousseau and others. Indeed, it was such that later neither Wilhelm von Humboldt nor Jacob Grimm in their respective treatments of the same theme could forbear to refer back to it. But more important still was its significance for the history of literature, its very character a thrilling compendium of a new sensuous self-awareness and its relation to man's original genius.

The biogenetic picture, which lay at the root of all Herder's aesthetics at that time, was then subsequently concentrated in his own philosophy of history, *Auch eine Philosophie der Geschichte zur Bildung der Menschheit* (*Another Philosophy of History*) (1774), which incorporated and expanded the seeds and ideas contained in the *Reisejournal* and his philosophy of language. This treatise was a product of his 'exile' in Bückeburg. As such it contained both elements pertaining to that Bückeburg period, namely the pietistic and the sensualistic. The latter element here had the function of producing as great an anti-rationalistic effect as the former. Their connection lay in the concept of evolution, which went right back to the story of Genesis. The origin was the Creation, which contained all the seeds of evolution. Everything that was to follow developed from these seeds implanted in man. But the curve on the graph was not a rising but a falling one, diametrically opposed to the historical optimism of the Enlightenment. Even Christianity recognised a progressive concept of history – the eschatological one of the Creation, the Fall of Man and the Salvation of all. But since this religious educator transferred the process of evolution to the human plane, the eschatological viewpoint remained outside his consideration. On the other hand, specific attacks on the spirit of the century of Enlightenment as embodied in the most extreme form in his ruler, Count Wilhelm von Lippe (who aped Frederick the Great), now grew into a kind of expression of public protest against the Age of Reason. Hamann's accusation against its 'mendacious philosophy' was resurrected by Herder, his disciple. For him it was that very philosophy which caused the destruction of 'that original, silent, eternal and patriarchal tree of life', from which mankind proceeded. Herder equated it with the pastoral life, in which complete harmony with nature still reigned. That was the childhood stage of mankind. Phantasy and reverence were the order of life. The Orient provided the setting. The scene of the next stage was Egypt and the neighbouring area of the Phoenicians. Here law and order, justice, industry, a system of weights and measures developed. These were the schooldays of mankind, to which the Phoenicians contributed world-wide trade. The next age – that of the Greeks – was the beautiful age of youth: 'Everything was youthful pleasure, grace, sport and love!' The manhood of the human race was attested in Roman virtue and intelligence, symbolised in discipline. What remained for the modern age was clear, if the process was taken to its logical conclusion. It would be decadence, if rejuvenation through the unexhausted powers of the North had not been granted to Mankind, which had already reached maturity in antiquity, – a 'true, new blossoming of the human soul'. God as the helmsman of history then created the age of Christendom. The Middle Ages, the Dark Ages in the eyes of the Enlightenment, were in reality 'solid, cohesive, noble and splendid', all of which escaped the comprehension of the 'Enlightened' world. The Reformation and Humanism had seen the dawn of a new era, when thought, culture and philosophy had taken giant strides forward. But thereupon it proceeded irresistibly towards analysis and mechanistic hypothesis, to 'reasoning, which penetrated to the very foundations of society, which in earlier times had stood and borne the weight'. The very word *verräsonieren* was coined by Herder in this context. For what was taking place here was a process in which mankind was being debilitated:

> Das liebe, matte, ärgerliche, unnütze Freidenken, Ersatz für alles, was sie vielleicht mehr brauchen – Herz! Wärme! Blut! Menschheit! Leben! [18]

[18] Nice, dull, annoying, useless freethinking, substitute for everything that is perhaps needed more – heart, warmth, blood, humanity, life!

We soon find ourselves in a region very close to Goethe's Odes. The 'Storm and Stress' call for total feeling sought to express itself in opposition to the hated regulated bourgeois life of the age emasculated through 'philosophy'. Here again, however, the philosophy of history developed into the pedagogic propositions of the *Reisejournal*: 'Paper culture' is replaced by the deed. The illusionary confidence of those believers in progress, who felt the Golden Age to be near, was lashed with biting irony. At all events Herder was sure of himself when he described the facts of this development. On the other hand he was not sure of himself when it came to the significance of this evolutionary process permitted by God. A simple return to the origins seemed out of the question. Enlightenment in itself was not decadence, in Herder's eyes, but the interpretation of it by his age was, and the mere recognition of the essential difference between the two is of importance. However, the reverence of power, and of unity and intensity that had been lost, in conjunction with an abhorrence that he had acquired from Hamann of the destructive role played by philosophical consciousness in the course of history remained unequivocal in this 'system', which was once again expressed in the manner of a writer of fragments.

2 The Ossianic World and Shakespeare

The area of literary evaluation, too, was affected by the philosophical insights into language and history, as advanced by Hamann and Herder. There was indeed need of examples and proof for the early ages so full of strength and sensuousness of perception and expression, for the decisive function of imagination and originality characterised by its wealth and energy. Quite certainly they could not be found in classical antiquity as the Enlightenment understoood it, much less in French Classicism, not to mention Voltaire. And least of all in the German tradition from Opitz to Gottsched. The mature Lessing had already advanced beyond these models and he was joined by Johann Elias Schlegel and the Baron von Gerstenberg, who were hardly aware of their being precursors of the 'Storm and Stress'. For these a new world opened up at the very height of the Enlightenment: the world of Shakespeare and old Nordic and Celtic poetry of early times, which had first been introduced, in fact, by Klopstock. It was in these areas that one looked, first tentatively and then with increasing determination, for values that equalled the achievements of the Ancients. The discovery of an indigenous old Germanic tradition began in the midst of the Rationalistic Age. Firstly with Gottsched, who drew no conclusions from it, then Bodmer, whose rediscovery, above all, of the *Minnesang*[1] coincided with his interest in English imaginative poetry. Klopstock's bardic period, too, fitted in programmatically, so to speak. The immediacy and the inventiveness of that past age still did not allow a distinction to be drawn between old Germanic and old Celtic, not even when Macpherson appeared on the scene in England and his allegedly

[1] *Vide* Glossary.

Gaelic bard Ossian became fashionable. By the time the forgery – which was characterised by an enormously subtle understanding for current tastes – was recognised as such in England, it had crossed to the Continent and continued its triumphal march *via* Herder and subsequently Goethe's *Werther*, even reaching Napoleon. Its very impetus was increased through the effect exerted by another English book, namely Thomas Percy's *Reliques of Ancient English Poetry* (1765). The result in Germany was not only interest in that vague mythology extending from Klopstock to Macpherson's translation, but also the concrete discovery of those values of expression and feeling which had lain untapped in old folk poetry in general, above all in the *Volkslied* and *Volksballade*. It now unleashed a lyrical effusion that at last seemed to do justice to the cult of creative genius after a long and sterile period of imitating the Ancients. It led *via* Herder and Bürger to Goethe's Odes and early ballad poetry, and at the beginning of the following century was still to fascinate the Romantics and invite them to continue in the same strain.

Hand in hand with all this went the development of the new Shakespeare image, the historical significance of which has been demonstrated in Gundolf's very fine book. Folk poetry was for the most part anonymous. Even the names that were known could scarcely be grasped in their historical context, or, as in the case of Ossian, it was the myth of the figure that remained in man's consciousness. The need for a comprehensible incarnation of poetic genius remained unappeased. In Shakespeare, however, (Shakespearean criticism was still somewhat dormant), there was felt to be at one's disposal a positive counter-symbol to classical antiquity, and this symbol was then subsequently taken in the 'Storm and Stress' to represent the epitome of Nordic genius, a model of originality.

Both these very themes – Ossian and Shakespeare – Herder had brought to Goethe's attention in Strassburg, and, what is more, he had given them memorable treatment in two essays in 'dithyrambic prose' for Gerstenberg's *Schleswiger Literaturbriefe*. But just then these *Literaturbriefe* ceased publication and so Herder resolutely combined his 'rhapsodies' with Goethe's *Von deutscher Baukunst* and Möser's *Vorrede zur Osnabrückischen Geschichte* to form that manifesto of the 'Storm and Stress' concept of art and history, which bore the title *Von deutscher*

B

Art und Kunst. An inorganically added piece on Gothic architecture was merely a rehash from the Italian. Herder's contributions were loaded with ingenious anti-rationalistic dynamite.
Nowhere else did he keep closer to Hamann's style than in his
Shakespeare essay. The mode of expression employed in these
'Rhapsodies' in which he hammered away at point after point,
arbitrarily selected, suppressing what was non-essential in
the sentence, conjuring forth the main points in larger than
life-size terms with untiring interjections and exclamations,
his choice of vocabulary and word-formations containing unprecedented nuances – this mode of expression achieved here
an extraordinary suggestiveness. This was true of all parts
of speech, but perhaps especially so in the case of the dynamic
verbal language. Here it was possible to 'pour forth sensations
to the full', 'stammer', 'hear and perceive with an inner ear',
'feel with an immediacy and precision', but also to 'over-refine'.
'Fortreißen', 'fortfühlen', 'einfühlen', 'eindichten', 'zusammen-
dichten' are certainly introduced here as verbs,[2] not to mention the innumerable participles with the same level of meaning
and importance which appear as dynamic epithets. In the case of
the latter, namely the adjectival formations, the combination and
accumulation of words created the same effect:

Ossian so kurz, stark, männlich, abgebrochen . . .[3]

Or again, in relation to the Skaldic poems:

Der Geist, der sie erfüllet, die rohe, einfältige, aber große,
zaubermäßige, feierliche Art . . .[4]

It is felt possible to trace *ab ovo*, so to speak, a dionysiac joy in
language everywhere. Everything expresses movement, a grop-
ing and listening for new possibilities of expression – everything
confidently original. The noun compositions and compounds are
no less fascinating, where the vocabulary of energy and immediacy, of ('inner') feeling, of rapture and bliss, but also that of
nuance and intermediate shades of response can attain full expression, in the sense in which it was said of Klopstock that he

[2] 'carry away by emotion', 'absorbed by empathy', 'enclose in poetic form',
'condense by means of poetry'.

[3] Ossian so short, strong, manly, abrupt . . .

[4] The spirit which fills them, the rough, simple but mighty, magical,
solemn nature . . .

produced 'fine nuances, often intermediate shades of feeling' together with the full flood of emotional outpourings in his writings. And highly characteristic was the devaluation of the word
'beautiful', which Herder denigrated almost to the level of a
synonym for 'artificial', 'regular', 'useful' by connecting it with
the classical *bon goût*.

The *Auszug aus einem Briefwechsel über Ossian und die Lieder
alter Völker* was based right from the outset on a passionate bias
in favour of originality. The German translation of Macpherson
by the Jesuit Michael Denis (whose *nom de guerre* was the 'bard
Sined') had been completed in hexameters. For the 'Storm and
Stress', however, that was a *crimen laesae majestatis* against the
original, the allegedly genuine bard Ossian:

> Ihnen wollte ich nur in Erinnerung bringen, daß Ossians
> Gedichte Lieder, Lieder des Volks, Lieder eines ungebildeten
> sinnlichen Volks sind . . .[5]

Songs, however, are something other than a fine flowing epic. One
has to feel one's way into their style, otherwise one destroys them.
Characteristically Herder leapt directly to Shakespeare to furnish
proof for this assertion and showed by example from the latter's
songs the senselessness of translating them into epic verse. The
empathic translator has to be 'flexible', Herder argued, he must
have 'an inner feeling for the sensuous qualities in form, sound,
tone, melody, all those dark and ineffable impressions which flood
our soul when we hear the poem sung'. The translator is then seen
as a trustee of original genius, in this instance the genius of the
folksong, which has 'the miraculous power of being the rapture,
the mainspring, the eternal hereditary and joyful song of the
people'. But what is folksong? (Including Ossian's Skaldic poetry?)
Herder heaps up a pile of epithets to define it: wild, lively, unhindered, sensuous, strong, dynamic, hence full of 'leaps and
sallies', and hence alogical too in the scholastic sense. The decisive thing is the ear as an organ for rhythm, tone, melody:

> Nichts ist stärker und ewiger und schneller und feiner als die
> Gewohnheit des Ohrs![6]

[5] I merely wanted to remind you that Ossian's poems are songs, folk-
songs, songs of an uncultured, sensuous people . . .

[6] Nothing is more powerful and lasting, quicker and finer than the habit
of listening!

All this found verification in the old English and old Scandinavian ballads which Herder knew of from Percy's and other collections, quite apart from Ossian and Shakespeare too. And it was also put to the test in Herder's own translations, excellently so, for example, in that of the old Scottish ballad *Edward, Edward*. But Herder did not romantically narrow the limits of his subject to the past. He took just as seriously as original compositions in this genre pieces that were composed in his own day, such as Ewald von Kleist's *Lied eines Lappländers* or Goethe's *Sah ein Knab ein Röslein stehn*. In the selection for his own collection of folksongs (which later bore the title *Stimmen der Völker in Liedern* (*Voices of the Nations in Song*)) he was to claim the same liberty by placing on one and the same plane something that had originated as an 'art-song' with a folksong from the past. All this, from the *Edda* and Skaldic poetry in the broadest sense, to medieval ballads, the old Lutheran Hymn, Shakespeare and contemporary poetry (in the style of the folksong), i.e. even Gleim's ballads, and Ewald von Kleist's and Goethe's verse, was 'folksong' in Herder's eyes. The standard was provided by the original sensuality, in word and tone (and dance), which distinguished such poems from all artificiality and abstraction. Here too Herder took up again a position of absolute opposition to 'bourgeois' Classicism and Rationality. The folksong was in no way a phenomenon of importance for him as another example of antiquarian greatness to be held against classical antiquity, but as an instance of human genius, which Herder saw as stemming, like the poems of wild, savage peoples, from 'the immediate present, from the direct inspiration of the senses and the imagination'.

His picture of Shakespeare, which was to help testify to the concept of originality as already presented in the *Ossian* essay, was in the same vein. Except that, as already indicated, the semi- or total anonymity of the creative genius, as was the case with the songs of the people, could now give way to the glorification of the individual historical artist as the 'second creator' (in Shaftesbury's sense) and the secularised *creator spiritus* of Christianity. In fact, Herder was at least as concerned with the poet's greatness as a 'dramatic God' and with his promethean originality as with the work itself, however penetratingly, indeed powerfully, this was interpreted and characterised. Since Shakespeare was more easily understood than the nebulous figure of Ossian, he became the representative of artistic originality in general – moreover, right from the start, in apocalyptic, larger-than-life dimensions:

> Wenn bei einem Manne mir jenes ungeheuere Bild einfällt: hoch auf einem Felsengipfel sitzend! zu seinen Füßen Sturm, Ungewitter und Brausen des Meers, aber sein Haupt in den Strahlen des Himmels! so ist's bei Shakespeare! – Nur freilich auch mit dem Zusatz, wie unten am tiefsten Fuße seines Felsenthrones Haufen murmeln, die ihn – erklären, retten, verdammen, entschuldigen, anbeten, verleumden, übersetzen und lästern! – und die Er alle nicht höret![7]

This was the standard of greatness the 'Storm and Stress' applied to the artist, a supernatural, mythical dimension. Corresponding to this was the annihilation of the 'gaggle' of defamers, commentators, but also the apologists and uncritical admirers. The 'Storm and Stress' furnished a similar example in Lenz's grotesque comedy *Pandaemonium Germanicum*, but with Goethe in place of Shakespeare on the throne of genius. Shakespeare's 'defenders' also included Johann Elias Schlegel, Lessing and Gerstenberg. They had already transformed the timorous *apologia* for a Shakespeare who at least did not vanish completely in the face of classical antiquity, into an assertion that he was of a different species altogether; now fields of characterisation and realism were allotted the 'modern' poet over against the idealising Greeks. If we recall all this, we become aware of the total, vehement passion manifested in this antithesis between greatness and insignificance. That antithesis remained the dominant theme.

It was, in fact, given support through a masterly application of the empathic and comparing historical sense. Naturally Shakespeare had to be compared with the Greeks and measured against them. And everything that Herder in his philosophy of language and history, in biblical exegesis and revaluation of the

[7] If ever one man appears to me in a mental image sitting high up on a rocky pinacle, at his feet the storm and tempest and raging of the sea, his head however high in the radiant firmament, then that is Shakespeare. Except, of course, with this addition, that down below at the very bottom step of his rocky throne there are crowds murmuring, who set out to explain him, save him, curse him, excuse him, idolise him, deny him, translate and slander him – and all of whom HE does not hear!

concept of education, had so far achieved in versatility of com-
parisons and wealth of suggestive ideas, he resolutely staked on
this favourite theme of his. Here, in accordance with the basic
principle, the individuality of the Greeks must be preserved just
as much as that of Shakespeare:

> In Griechenland entstand das Drama, wie es in Norden nicht
> entstehen konnte . . . In Norden ist's also nicht und darf nicht
> sein, was es in Griechenland gewesen.[8]

The whole Aristotelian doctrine of the three Unities was hereby historically relativised and robbed of its timelessness. By the
same token, however, the possibility of making its non-observ-
ance by Shakespeare an argument for his non-conformity to rules,
as classicistic poetics made out, lost its validity. But on the other
hand, what French Classicism itself represented and achieved,
Herder argued, became anachronistic and also unhistorical and
led to the destruction of originality. Herder accordingly called
French Classicism 'the puppet of the Greek Theatre'. That held
good in his eyes right from Corneille to Voltaire. Their art was
but second- or third-hand:

> Spanisch-senecasche Helden! galante Helden, abenteuerlich-
> tapfere, großmütige, verliebte, grausame Helden, also drama-
> tische Fiktionen, die außer dem Theater Narren heißen wür-
> den . . .[9]

But what was its counterpart? The answer lay in self-invented
drama, which for the author of the *Reisejournal* could be based
only on its own historical reality. The direct consequence was
the call for the one genius who 'would produce from his material
a dramatic creation as natural, great and original as the Greeks
did from theirs'. That person was Shakespeare, who had to be
understood, of course, in the light of his own historicity. But
this historicity was no longer that of the Greeks in their simplicity,
but of the Modern writers in their complexity; in drama, for
example, it was no longer the epoch of the Greek chorus, but of
historical plays and puppet plays. And from these, his own times

[8] In Greece drama rose as it could not arise in the North . . . In the
North, therefore, it is not and cannot be, what it has been in Greece.
[9] Spanish-Seneca-type heroes; gallant heroes, adventurous, brave, magnanimous, amorous, cruel heroes and for that very reason dramatic inven-
tions whom one would call fools outside of the theatre.

he moulded 'social classes and individuals, peoples and modes of speech, king and fools, fools and king into one glorious Whole'. The form it took was that of joint experience of what was encountered. The creative genius became the 'interpreter of nature in all its tongues':

> Mir ist, wenn ich ihn lese, Theater, Akteur, Kulisse verschwunden! Lauter einzelne im Sturm der Zeiten wehende Blätter aus dem Buch der Begebenheiten, der Vorsehung der Welt! – einzelne Gepräge der Völker, Stände, Seelen! [10]

It is unmistakable how Herder the subjectivist placed everything on the Individual and his Rights. Individuality demanded, if one wished to experience it, total identification. For Herder *Ossian* had already found its inimitable scene of comparability: 'on the foundering ship' and the stormy sea at night. And likewise now with Shakespeare there was the matter of identification of poet, landscape and work. And whether it was the fate of Lear or Othello and Macbeth, there was always the sense of involvement in the play, which was made up into 'a living Whole comprised of father-and-children-king-and-fools-and-beggar-and-misery', involvement in the drama which 'transports one's heart, all one's emotions, one's whole soul from beginning to end'. It was not Goethe nor Schelling, but Herder who repeatedly used the word *Weltseele* ('universal spirit') long before them as a symbol of this 'totality' in Shakespeare. And it was also no accident that the philosophical godfather of the 'Storm and Stress', 'that giant God of Spinoza: Pan! Universum!' was likewise invoked as the God of Shakespeare's world. This hallmarked the creative writing of the modern dramatic genius. The limitations of Time and Place disappeared. The dream that could transcend everything, ruled supreme. The concluding note was the sad reflection that 'even this great creator of history and the universal spirit was more and more receding into the past'. It was the inevitable consequence of Herder's way of proceeding by which the timelessness was transformed into something belonging to a point in history. But he tore himself away from the temptation to be melancholy by appeal-

[10] Whenever I read him, the theatre, actors and scenery vanish from my mind's eye. Just individual leaves blowing about in the storm of the times, leaves from the Book of Events, of World Providence – individual impressions of peoples, conditions, souls!

ing to Goethe's drama which had just been completed, namely *Götz von Berlichingen*, in which he felt he saw the guarantee of a renewal of Shakespearian original genius and creative style. This consolation, however, was not tenable, strictly logically speaking. It was empirical. Shakespeare is – even today – topical. The 'rhapsodist' – even today – has proved his Right. But it was a Right taken directly from Life itself, wholly in accord with the 'Storm and Stress' meaning.

3 The Göttingen Grove

About the same time that a group was forming around Herder and Goethe in Central and Southern Germany, an even closer cultural circle was coming into being in Lower Germany at Göttingen. The focal point was the university. Here too there were students with whom an older man, namely Gottfried August Bürger, benevolently associated himself, just as Herder had done in the South. For the most part they originated from North or Central Germany, a fact which was easily recognisable in the peculiar make-up of the circle. It too was a product of Enlightenment sensibility and of the influence of Pietism, but the opposition to Enlightenment as such did not emerge so absolutely as in the 'Storm and Stress' movement that stretched from Strassburg to Frankfurt and Darmstadt. And so the subjectivism here scarcely grew to 'titanic' proportions, nor did it lead to creative works of art like Goethe's Odes or *Werther*, not even in the case of Bürger. But there was a high degree of youthful sentimentality and a heightened sensitivity involved. This found expression primarily in lyric verse. The drama, which predominated in the 'Storm and Stress' south of the river Main, was represented here only by Leisewitz. The Göttingen Grove did not remain without contact with Herder and Goethe, but it derived more in actual fact from Klopstock, and, to be precise, from the Klopstock of the bardic period. Last but not least, the rather mild northern character of the Göttingen landscape, wooded mountains of medium height and water meadows close by (despite the Klopstockian and Goethean myth about the Harz) struck a chord in the enthusiasm for nature that was displayed here. True, there was also revolutionary pathos in the tyrant-theme, in verse particularly with Bürger. In the case of the Stolbergs and Voss, however, this was subdued by the tone and rhythm appropriate to the ode.

Where the real 'Grove' was situated in the rural surrounds of Göttingen has not even been determined. It was really more a question of the genus, which from the outset bore a literary accent borrowed from Klopstock's bardic language. In his ode *Der Hügel und der Hain* Klopstock dealt with the contrast between classical antiquity and the early Nordic times, between Parnassus and the Grove of the Bards, between grace and 'soulful nature'. And that was the theme-song of this student group chosen at their founding ceremony; they produced first of all in 1770 the *Göttinger Musenalmanach* and in 1772 established the formal association under the name 'The Grove'. (The term *Hainbund* was in fact later coined by Voss.)

Heinrich Christian Boie (1774–1806) from Schleswig-Holstein started it all. The later *Landvogt* and Finance Councillor came to Göttingen in 1769 to continue his law studies, and that same year he was joined by Johann Heinrich Voss (1751–1826) from Mecklenburg, who though of a very humble peasant background had worked his way up despite great hardships, rising to the position of private tutor. Boie became the founder and first editor of the *Göttinger Musenalmanach*, Voss the first Elder of the Grove. Both too were excellent organisers. Boie immediately succeeded in getting not only Klopstock and Bürger, but also Goethe to contribute to this influential and thoroughly German imitation of the Parisian *Almanac des Muses*. The Göttingen group quickly developed an identity of their own, as a result of which Bürger could write to the old man Gleim: 'In Göttingen a quite new Parnassus is sprouting forth and growing as quickly as the willows fringing the brook.' The 'new Parnassus', however, grew into a collection of youthful enthusiasts conscious of the *Geniebewegung*, which admittedly only in the case of Bürger assumed those somewhat obstreperous and foolish forms in which Lenz and Klinger, for example, took delight in south Germany. From being close friends Voss and Boie became brothers-in-law. Voss acquired in Ernestine Boie the wife who corresponded to his own nature. In his later stations in life as rector in Otterndorf and Eutin it was she who ran the hospitable household from which the classical idyll *Luise* would result, as also the Homer translation (1781) which became the standard version for generations.

Ludwig Heinrich Christoph Hölty joined these Göttingen friends as the third member. Hölty (1748–76) was the son of a

Hannoverian parson, and a theologian himself. He had a delicate constitution and succumbed early to consumption. He was the really ethereal member of the Circle. Talent and illness perhaps interacted upon him to conjure forth a lyricism which forms a direct part of the background to Novalis and Hölderlin in literary history. Other north Germans who were accepted into the Circle included Karl Friedrich Cramer (1752–1807), the son of the *Bremer Beiträge* contributor and friend of Klopstock (in Göttingen 1772–74), later classical scholar in Kiel, and Johann Anton Leisewitz (1752–1806), a lawyer, and finally as a significant addition, the Stolberg brothers, Friedrich Leopold (1750–1819) and Christian (1748–1821), both likewise lawyers, whose subsequent diplomatic and Court posts one would hardly have prophesied at that time, despite their background. The two Counts established together the personal connections with the 'Storm and Stress' Circle around Goethe; together with Goethe on their Swiss journey of 1775 they had shocked Bodmer in his old age in Zürich through their boisterousness. On the other hand Johann Martin Miller (1750–1814) came from Swabia; he was in Göttingen from 1770 on, later becoming Dean in his home town of Ulm. His sentimental novel of the post-Göttingen period *Siegwart, eine Klostergeschichte* made him more famous than had his Göttingen lyrics. And then along with others who joined the group were Friedrich Wilhelm Gotter (1746–97), a Thuringian, and Johann Friedrich Hahn (1753–79) from Hesse. Several times, in fact, Gotter crossed Goethe's path in Wetzlar and later in Gotha, which was close to Weimar. Yet beside Boie and Voss, Hölty and the Stolbergs, Leisewitz and even Miller too, all the others were only peripheral figures, so that essentially the Grove remained dominated by north German elements.

There is an exact description of the founding ceremony of the Grove on 12 September 1772 in one of Voss's letters:

Ach, den 12. September, mein liebster Freund, da hätten Sie hier sein sollen. Die beiden Millers, Hahn, Hölty, Wehrs und ich gingen noch des Abends nach einem entlegenen Dorfe. Der Abend war außerordentlich heiter und der Mond voll. Wir überließen uns ganz den Empfindungen der Natur. Wir aßen in einer Bauernhütte eine Milch und begaben uns darauf ins freie Feld. Hier fanden wir einen kleinen Eichengrund, und zugleich fiel uns allen ein, den Bund der Freundschaft unter diesen heiligen Bäumen zu schwören. Wir umkränzten die Hüte mit Eichenlaub, legten sie unter den Baum, faßten uns alle bei den Händen, tanzten so um den eingeschlossenen Stamm herum – riefen den Mond und die Sterne zum Zeugen unseres Bundes an und versprachen uns eine ewige Freundschaft. Dann verbündeten wir uns, die größte Aufrichtigkeit in unsern Urteilen gegeneinander zu beobachten und zu diesem Endzwecke die schon gewöhnliche Versammlung noch genauer und feierlicher zu halten. Ich ward durch Los zum Ältesten erwählt. Jeder soll Gedichte auf diesen Abend machen und ihn jährlich begehen.[1]

This then was the style: a feeling for the beauty of nature with a rustic and Rousseauistic touch, oak-wreaths, dancing, enthusiastic oaths of friendship. Whether the immediately established rites of constitution entirely coincided with the basic feeling that prevailed, need not be discussed. From his standpoint as the sarcastic intellectual, Lichtenberg had some grounds for pouring forth his scorn upon the subjectivity and sentimentality of the *Hainbündler*, who did not even understand 'what it was they hummed to the listening circle with lips pale and trembling, and arms moving as if reaping corn in time to the droning bagpipe sounds of ecstasy'. The form of their sentimentality corresponded to the Bardic and Ossianic motif. Each had his bardic name: Voss was called Sangrich, Boie Werdomar, Hölty Haining. Then there were names like Minnehold, Teuthard, and Raimund. This practise was not basically part of the new idea of subjectivism,

---

[1] Oh, my dear friend, you should have been here on the 12th September. The two Millers, Hahn, Hölty, Wehrs and I went whilst it was still evening to an outlying village. The evening was extraordinarily serene and the moon full. We abandoned ourselves completely to the sensations of nature. We drank some milk in a small farmhouse and then went into the open. Here we found a dell of oak-trees and it occurred to us all simultaneously that we should swear a bond of friendship under those sacred trees. We garlanded our hats with oak leaves, laid them under the tree, all clasped hands together and danced around the sequestered tree-trunk – we summoned the moon and the stars as witnesses of our bond, and pledged eternal friendship. Then we promised to observe the utmost sincerity in our judgment of one another, and to this end to hold a regular gathering with even greater detail and solemnity. I was chosen by lot to be the Elder. Each person was to compose poems to this evening and celebrate it annually.

but rather of the old heritage, namely of the Baroque *Sprach-gesellschaften*.[2] And the constitution had much in common with this too. There was the Society Elder, the Journal, the weekly gatherings at which one's own and others' poetry was recited and discussed. It was a custom that continued in Germany well into the nineteenth century (e.g. the Berlin *Tunnel*). Anniversaries and farewell parties were highspots in the history of the 'Grove'. The celebration of Klopstock's birthday on 2nd July 1773 was, next to the actual founding of the 'Grove', its most important and historic day. Klopstock himself was in fact not even present. His garlanded works had to take his place. As with the southern 'Storm and Stress' movement, Wieland represented for them the counter-trend, and a work of his was symbolically torn up and stamped upon. However in the September of 1774 Klopstock did participate on just one occasion as an official member. It was natural that the tears flowed liberally when departure celebrations were held.

The guiding principle of the Circle stemmed from Voss's *Bundesgesang* (1772), namely a strong patriotism in the spirit of Klopstock's *Hermannsschlacht*. In marked contrast to the frivolous passion for fame and glory of the French was his own

> . . . rauhe[s] Lied,
> (Ach! kein Mädchen und kein witziger Höfling liebt's)
> Das, in holpernden Tönen, Gott
> Dieses Märchen! und ha! Freiheit und Vaterland
> Und altväterische Tugend singt! — [3]

Clearly this patriotism could also be seen as a kind of anti-Rationalism. Hölty's ode *Der Bund* was far more sentimental and impassioned than Voss's *Bundesgesang*. The poet himself 'glows with joyous rapture'. The 'soul of German song pours forth with burning fire'. In the Klopstockian style Haining's sworn bond includes his friends in one embrace. Both poems are rhymeless and in classical form, that of Hölty is expressly an ode. This points to the kind of poetry whose history, of all the genres, owes most to the Göttingen Grove. Moreover it has its historical significance

[2] *Vide* Glossary.
[3] . . . rough song (Oh, no maiden nor witty courtier loves it), which in unpolished tones, sings of God – that fairytale character – and with gusto of freedom and fatherland and ancestral virtue!

as far as song is concerned, an importance still further strength-
ened by Abraham Peter Schultz's compositions. It was with
Bürger's *Lenore*, first published in the *Göttinger Musenalmanach*,
that the ballad, in line with Herder's suggestion, took a further
step forward along its victorious path from Göttingen. So the
Grove's compass reached from the classical form treated in a
specifically German manner, but with a technique that revealed
uncanny understanding, to the old Nordic and old English ballad
verse. The central position was held by the *Lied* – still with
clearly traceable anacreontic elements, yet at its best, like the
other forms, pulsating with a new feeling for life.

Like Voss's *Bundesgesang*, his ode *An Goethe* (1773) was a
programmatic poem in the literary sense:

> Der du edel entbranntst, wo hochgelahrte
> Diener Justinians Banditen zogen,
> Die in Roms Labyrinthen
> Würgen das Recht der Vernunft;
> Freier Goethe, du darfst die goldne Fessel,
> Aus des Griechen Gesang geschmiedet, höhnen!
> Shakespeare durft' es und Klopstock,
> Söhne, gleich ihm, der Natur!
>
> . . .
>
> Deutsch und eisern wie Götz, sprich Hohn den Schurken –
> Mit der Fessel im Arm! Des Sumpfes Schreier,
> Schmäht der Leu zu zerstampfen,
> Wandelt durch Wälder und herrscht! [4]

This is nothing less than an identification with the 'Storm and
Stress' Goethe, yet at the same time too with Herder's position
as literary critic: namely, *contra* the rules of classical antiquity,
pro the freedom of a Shakespeare or Klopstock, the Germanic
ideal of Götz (no longer the *Teutschheit* of Hermann). At the
same time it is a panegyric to dominating and unfettered promethean genius. Friedrich Leopold von Stolberg's ode *Genius* had

[4] You who were so nobly enflamed, when Justinian's learned servants bred
but bandits who choke the Right of Reason in Rome's labyrinths, you,
Goethe, free as air, you may sneer at the golden chains forged from
Grecian song! Shakespeare was able to, and Klopstock, both sons of
nature! . . . German and iron-hard like Götz, pour scorn on the rogues – in
chains! The lion is above stamping underfoot these bawlers from the
morass, he roams the woods and rules supreme!

no less promethean an effect. As the lion symbolised sovereign genius with Voss, so the eagle did here, the eagle 'full of primal energy'. Corresponding to the thirst for the sun was the 'wing of lofty inspiration', which bears genius that here appears in the first-person form:

> Mir gabst du Feuer! Durst nach Unsterblichkeit!
> Dies Toben in der Brust! Dies Staunen,
> Welches durch jegliche Nerve zittert.[5]

This verse is constructed in accordance with the regular alcaic form. The theme, however, follows the new feeling of self-confidence of freely creative genius.

Compared with such highly gifted utterances from the young Voss and the younger Stolberg, Hölty's verse has a much more gentle and lyrical quality, even in the ode. Here he provided in the favoured second asclepiadaic, the alcaic and sapphic strophe some of the finest examples in the German tradition, such as *Mainacht*, *An die Grille* or *Sehnsucht*. He favoured the ode to friends, Love and Nature, the last with a strongly idyllic ring. Of his real idylls, *Das Feuer im Walde* (1774) has become a classic of its kind. Just as *Die künftige Geliebte* with its theme common to Klopstock (and Rilke) sounded somewhat muted as against Klopstock's elegy, so too did his ballads suffer in comparison with those of Bürger. A political song such as *Der befreite Sklave* with its theme of freedom from tyranny sticks out like a sore thumb in his total output that was predominantly purely lyric. The sounds of enchantment and bliss had their truest ring in his love poems. The vitality of the drinking-songs, on the other hand, appeared still rather conventional in the anacreontic sense. The same could be said of the nature poems, although (as in Stolberg's famous *An die Natur*) a new note of intimacy could occasionally break across the anacreontic scheme of things in Hölty, as seen in *Mailied*. In the whole of this circle of friends, however, he probably remained the member with the least sense of revolutionary awareness.

This self-assertion was perhaps most succinctly expressed in Leopold Stolberg's inspired prose rhapsody *Über die Fülle des Herzens* (1777). Here the 'gutless century' and its 'silken little men' and

[5] You gave me fire! A thirst for immortality! This raging in my breast! This awe that vibrates through every nerve.

'short-sighted petty rationalists' are attacked, those who analyse everything and hence lose all touch with Nature. The prayer which the poet would say for his first child stands in contrast:

> Gib ihm die menschlichste aller Gaben, die eine göttliche Gabe, gib ihm die Fülle des Herzens![6]

This finds expression firstly in the ability to love, celebrated in words which could have been inspired by Goethe: 'How it fires him, how it courses through him . . .' After love, it bestows an immediate awareness of nature:

> Aus deiner Fülle möcht' ich nun schöpfen, o du, die ich als Mutter ehre, die ich liebe als Braut, Natur! an deren Brüsten ich allein ungestörte reine Wollust atmen kann![7]

Experience must go hand in hand with this passionate feeling for Nature: 'The heart grows sick in the town.' From all this springs the self-assertion of the 'fiery, highly sensitive' genius, who is master over time: 'His is the past, his the future.' Certainly, when he wrote this, Stolberg was no longer in Göttingen, but was already influenced by his friendship with Goethe. Nevertheless he did express what could at least develop in terms of new self-awareness through contact with the essential spirit of the *Hainbund*.

Besides their larger-than-life vitality together with this 'fullness of heart', Johann Anton Leisewitz's *Julius von Tarent* and one-act plays reveal connections with the 'Storm and Stress' dramas in other respects. Leisewitz embodied the radical element within the Göttingen circle, though he later found his way back into the bourgeois world as a Privy Justice.

By contrast Gottfried August Bürger reflected 'Storm and Stress' confusion and chaos in his whole way of life. He was born in 1747, the son of a parson from the Harz region. His parents were well-to-do, though difficult. After an unregulated early upbringing he first awoke to an awareness of his talent during a visit to the Foundations established by the Pietist Francke. But his education in the grammar-school section of the

[6] Grant him the most human of all gifts, the one divine gift, grant him fulness of heart!

[7] From your fulness should I now like to draw, O nature, you whom I honour as my mother, love as my bride, at whose breast I alone can breathe pure and peaceful bliss!

Foundation was abruptly terminated by his grandfather, so that the seventeen-year-old began his theological studies in Halle without having matriculated. Bürger was never able to compensate for this deficiency which marked his education, particularly since the grandfather made him interrupt his studies again and again later on. So lack of restraint and immoderation characterised Bürger's path from the outset. As early as 1767 he was sent down whilst still a student of theology. But in fact he had already shown a preference for philological studies in Halle (and, to make it worse, under Klotz, a figure of vain and questionable character). The now enforced change of university led him to Göttingen. For a short time (roughly 1770–1771), as a result of his contact with Boie and his circle, through which he became friendly with Gleim in Halberstadt, he seemed to pull himself together. Percy's *Reliques* made a decisive impression upon him at that time and opened up for him a new world besides the classical one of Homer, Lucian, Catullus, with which he nevertheless continued to persevere. And it was now that the arch-poet of ballad and 'folk' poetry emerged (the description under which Schiller was to review him so harshly later on in the *Jenaische Allgemeine Literatur-Zeitung*). Yet the fame that soon came his way did not in the long run contribute to an ordering of his life, any more than did his (rather patronising) relationship with the *Hainbund*. A bungled Civil Service career as district administrator which ended in 1780 with his dismissal, a botched private life through his universally-known bigamous relationship with the sisters Dorette and Auguste (Molly) Leonhart, his passion for drinking and gambling, which completely dissipated his not inconsiderable inheritance, and finally after Dorette's death his marriage to Molly, and following her demise an eccentric third marriage which resulted in an early divorce – all this made him quite impossible in bourgeois eyes, although he was made a don at Göttingen University in 1784. Bürger had to blame himself rather than society, which let him fall by the wayside, for his death in 1794, in misery and debt and following a long illness, when he was only forty-six years of age. Next to Lenz, Bürger was probably the person who, in his whole mode of existence, most strikingly represented the extreme freedom of genius which must accept from society the consequences of an asocial attitude and way of life. As an example of unruliness, he had much in common with the wretched Johann Christian Günther, even in the way that he wrested with a certain desperate defiance a considerable poetic achievement from a life totally wrecked by unbridled passions.

Bürger's contribution owed much to the classical world, interspersed as it was with elements of Catullus and Anacreon (obviously still in the fashion of Hagedorn and Uz). *Die Nachtfeier der Venus* (referring to the pseudo-catullan *Pervigilium Veneris*) was not only influenced by the songs to Joy, and hence by German anacreontic poetry, but also displayed an individualistic form of enraptured mythology (a prelude to Schiller) in fervid rhymes and excited enjambement. The verse on the birth of Venus sounds almost like a paraphrase of Botticelli's famous picture:

> Ahnend, welch ein Wunder werde,
> Welch ein Götterwerk aus Schaum,
> Träumten Himmel, Meer und Erde
> Tief der Wonne süßen Traum.
> Als sie, hold in sich gebogen,
> In der Perlenmuschel stand,
> Wiegten sie entzückte Wogen
> An des Ufers Blumenrand.[8]

This goes beyond Uz and Gleim, and is representative of Bürger's early developed sensuality, harnessed through form. Between *Nachtfeier* and *Lenore*, which established Bürger's fame (1773), there emerged some relatively insignificant poetry of an idyllic/anacreontic type. The ballad then seemed, however, to fulfil what Herder, in his *Ossian* essay, had hoped for, and demanded from German poetry if it accepted the pattern of primitive ballad verse. It is known that a German *Kunstballade* or literary ballad did not exist before Bürger. Gleim's *Romanzen* ('Romances'), with their affinity to the popular song and *Moritat*,[9] composed though they were in somewhat childish fashion, rank here at most as a prelude. Bürger's ballad tone too has occasionally something of the style of the *Moritat*:

[8] Wondering what miracle would take place, what divine creation would emerge from the foam, Heaven, Sea and Earth dreamed a deep sweet dream of rapture. When she, gently arched, stood in the pearl conch, enchanted waves rocked her gently to the flower-fringed shore.

[9] *Vide* Glossary.

Als nun das Heer vorüber war,
Zerraufte sie ihr Rabenhaar,
Und warf sich hin zur Erde
Mit wütiger Gebärde.[10]

Something like this could be found too in the low popular ballad,
yet there it is in *Lenore*, the 'classic' German model of the
literary ballad. The connection exists even in the theme, e.g. the
demonstrated atonement of guilt. Here, however, it was not dis-
advantageous, for the *Lenore* ballad set up no 'artificial literary'
form as a counter to the historically accepted tradition in Germany, but on the contrary was embedded in it in a certain sense:
it demonstrated Bürger's keen sense of the possible. At the same
time the *Lenore* theme was 'Storm and Stress' subject matter *par
excellence*. Not only because it treated a thoroughly contemporary theme, namely a theme from the Seven Years War, which had
raged but a decade earlier. Not only because, as in *Julius von
Tarent*, uncontrollable passion led to blasphemy, that the sensual
was here raised to the status of an absolute; the contemporaneity of the topical and the historical reflected too the spirit of
Herder. For Lenore's desperate mourning for her loved one missing in the Battle of Prague then led, on the wild ride with the
spirit of the fallen man to the common grave as the bridal bed
(the old image from the folk ballad), to a totally realistic and
contemporised *danse macabre*. The theme of expiated blasphemy
can in the end be associated with this. Furthermore, the repeated
Chevy Chase verse relates directly to Percy, the source common to
Herder, and the style with its numerous interjections, its 'leaps
and sallies', becomes almost a realisation of Herder's ideal. If all
this is borne in mind, Bürger's ballad can then be understood as
an event that belongs to the history of the 'Storm and Stress'.
Bürger conceived it as just that, as the correspondence with
Boie on *Lenore* (1773) confirms. From this it is clear that through
Boie he had first become acquainted with Herder's *Blätter* whilst
working on the ballad, so that he himself assessed its completion
as a realisation of Herder's ideal:

O Boie, Boie, welche Wonne! als ich fand, daß ein Mann wie
Herder eben das von der Lyrik des Volks und mithin der Natur

[10] When the army was now past, she tore her raven hair and cast herself to the ground with frenzied gesture.

deutlicher und bestimmter lehrte, was ich dunkel davon schon längst gedacht und empfunden hatte. Ich denke, Leonore soll Herders Lehre einigermaßen entsprechen.[11]

Yet another standard work of the 'Storm and Stress' inspired him to new Lenore verses – Goethe's *Götz*:

Hu, wie wird mich der Unverstand drüber anblöcken! Aber der kann mir—! Frei! frei! Keinem untertan als der Natur! – [12]

The style itself reveals the atmosphere of intense excitement in which the poem came into being. And a stylistic preference for the same intensity lies behind Bürger's type of ballad in general. This aimed at starkly contrasting effects and was based largely on macabre (mythical as well as realistic) themes. It could be grotesque with a measure of black humour as in *Der Raubgraf*, or a moralistic extreme as in *Der wilde Jäger*, the piece most closely related to *Lenore* in its presentation of horror. As in the ballad *Des Pfarrers Tochter von Taubenhain*, with its theme of seduction, it can be linked in a social critical vein to the 'Storm and Stress' theme of infanticide, with tones that anticipate Annette von Droste-Hülshoff. It can also, in a serious or joking manner, be linked to the medieval tradition of song and jest, as in *Der Kaiser und der Abt, Graf Walter, Das Blümchen Wunderhold* or *Volkers Schwanenlied*. Finally, it can be topical material, as in *Lied vom braven Mann*. Almost everywhere Bürger's characteristic style is the decisive factor, a style which he saw, even in theoretical terms, as forming a totally consistent whole, bearing the imprint of ideas akin to Herder's (e.g. *Herzensausguß über Volks-Poesie*). Proceeding from the inescapable fact that the vernacular and the scholarly tongues are two separate entities in Germany, just like imagination and wit, poetry and 'versifying', Bürger establishes in this last-named piece his passion for *Naturpoesie*, a passion with which he 'listens in the evening twilight

[11] O Boie, Boie, what joy when I found that a man like Herder taught more clearly and decisively about the lyric poetry of the people, and consequently nature itself, that which I had thought about and perceived but darkly for a long time. I think *Lenore* shall correspond in some way to Herder's doctrine.

[12] Oh, how those who lack understanding will taunt me! But the hell with it—for I am free, free, subject to none but Nature!

to the magic sound of the ballads and street songs, under the linden trees in the village, in the open air and in the spinning-rooms'. From these ballads he hopes too for the rebirth of a folk-epic. Admittedly this would first entail 'the emergence at long last of a German Percy'. Bürger's whole hatred, however, was reserved for the 'philosophunculis' of the Nicolai type, whose *Feiner kleiner Almanach* (1777), the parody of Herder's enthu-siasm for the folksong, he himself in turn parodied. In the accompanying piece 'On the Popularity of Poetry' he attempted similarly a kind of *Aesthetica in nuce* with the definition of poetry as an imitation of the 'original subject' induced for 'the interior sense'. This imitation, however, is a representation, determined by the power of imagination. But as such it must not be poetry for individual classes and ranks, but simply poetry for the people: 'All poetry shall be popular.' The term 'people', though, has to be comprehended correctly not as the *hoi polloi*, but as that totality for which Homer, Shakespeare and Ossian wrote.

Herein lay the key to Bürger's concept of the *Volksdichter*. He was not conceived in a narrow, limited sense, but in a vast universal literary context. It was all the same whether he com-posed his ballads under the influence of Percy and the 'vulgar ditties' heard at first hand, or whether he vied with Goethe and Stolberg in translating Ossian, with Voss and Stolberg in trans-lating Homer, as in fact was the case. The same applied when as a narrator he compiled the tall stories of Baron Münchhausen and when he thus produced not only a book of funny tales, but also a book for children that has few equals. This too was an epic of 'man's sensitivity', here appealing to man's sense for the comic.

Bürger's poetic work covered a wide range of subject matter, even outside of his ballads. First of all it was a reservoir of 'Storm and Stress' subjects with aesthetic as well as political themes. Then it served at the same time to expose the bourgeois figure as in *Prometheus*, rationalistic conformity as in *Mamsell La Regle* with its deliberately insolent punch-line *à la* Klinger:

> Laßt, Brüderchen, die alte Strunsel gehn!
> Nur Kinder mag also ihr Laufzaum schürzen!
> Was tut's, ob wir mal stolpern oder stürzen?[13]

---

[13] Brothers, let the old hag go! Her apron string can then be a hindrance only to children! What does it matter if we stumble or fall?

Finally, denigration of the 'august tyrant' as in *Der Bauer*. None of this was well-tempered, but rather eccentric, without a mean temperature between boiling- and freezing-point. Thus the well known *Zechlied* too manifests a state of intoxication between extremes, a bacchanalian self-awareness, where the drunken genius can say:

> Sind Homer und Ossian
> Gegen mich nur Stümper.[14]

Bürger was half-seriously, half-jokingly aware that there would be a flood of dissertations on him one day. For he also had at his command a kind of tortured humour. So it is no wonder that it was Bürger of all people who made the formula for the age so expressly his own in verse:

> Wie wird mir so herzlich bange,
> Wie so heiß und wie so kalt,
> Wann in diesem Sturm und Drange
> Keuchend meine Seele wallt.[15]

These words appear in *Elegie*, one of the poems to Molly, in which the most intimate passion struggles for expression. Here too is an echo of the related sounds of Johann Christian Günther, but in a new, unchained vocabulary of passion. 'Shriek out', 'pour out', 'burn', 'grow together as one', 'ferment' – this is the temperature of just the verbal imagery in this poem. In addition to this, and hardly by chance, one could find for probably the first time in Bürger's lyric poetry the term 'feeling for life'.

It is scarcely a contradiction to Bürger's 'panting' style of originality, that he was also one of the first masters of the sonnet since the Baroque age. Indeed from the literary historical point of view it is of the utmost significance. For he practised his skill in this genre together with a pupil who was also very famed in it later: namely with August Wilhelm Schlegel, whose Romantic period had then not yet dawned. If we recall that it was Romanticism, that largely formless movement seeking the infinite, which resurrected the sonnet, a form that was to attract even Goethe, the seeming contradiction in terms of Bürger is then

---

[14] Homer and Ossian are but bungling amateurs beside me.

[15] How my heart is so afraid, will beat so hot and cold, when my soul heaves pantingly in this Storm and Stress.

resolved. The stimulus that forced Goethe's *Mächtiges Über-raschen* into sonnet form, may be ascribed to Bürger's passion for the sonnet.

From the literary sociological point of view, with the specific-ally German social patterns in mind, one can understand the – at first sight, rather curious – fact that from the year of the French Revolution onwards the majority of the companions from the one-time *Göttinger Hain* circle, which also included other 'Storm and Stress' figures and Pietists, assembled at a rural centre, namely at the castle of the Reventlov-Schimmelmann family in Emkendorf (Holstein). Over the years Voss, the Stol-bergs, Claudius, even Klopstock too, met there, but in addition Friedrich Jacobi, the Princess Gallitzin and other exponents of the religious movement that laid emphasis on (religious) feeling. This 'Emkendorf Circle' is a familiar concept in modern literary history. It is historically interesting in that it represented in almost model fashion the rapid change in the mirroring of the French Revolution in German intellectual life. As, for example, in the case of Klopstock and Schiller: at first they displayed enthusiasm stemming from that century's feeling for human rights, soon however an imperious assertion of a conservative abhor-rence of the tyrannical attitude shown by the revolutionaries themselves. Thus, whilst maintaining total intellectual alert-ness, they slipped, culturally-politically speaking, into a reaction-ary attitude, corresponding to the predominantly aristocratic composition of the circle. This circle therefore belongs, more than fifteen years after the youthful exuberance of the Göttingen Grove, to an intervening phase between the 'Storm and Stress' and classical forces bent on maintaining the *status quo*, not dissimilar to the intellectually interested society that dominates Goethe's *Unterhaltungen deutscher Ausgewanderten*.

PART II

The Young Goethe

4 Via Leipzig to Strassburg

The story of Goethe's childhood and youth is common knowledge in so far as he himself related it in *Dichtung und Wahrheit* (*Poetry and Truth*). That *Dichtung und Wahrheit* (just like the later publication of the *Italienische Reise* (*Journey to Italy*)) is an amalgam of the most highly authentic and stylised elements – already evident from the title – is similarly a well-known fact. If we concede to the autobiography not only its factual content but also a 'sheer delight in telling a tale', there is then relatively little which essentially contradicts the various original and tangible bits of evidence that the two Goethe Houses in Frankfurt and Weimar still exhibit today as an impressive testimony to Goethe's biography. Most of the problems presented, of course, have already been minutely examined in a way that is impossible within the scope of this present work. Goethe's family tree stretching back over generations is well-known to us. It shows, along with the connection on the mother's side with the Frankfurt patrician class through the Textors, the more simple Thuringian origins on the father's side: innkeepers, artisans, along with clergymen. Goethe's own opinion of the effect of parental heritage on him in terms of character, is known from the celebrated four lines in which he ascribed to the paternal heritage his 'stature' and manly character, to the maternal his cheerful disposition and imagination. This too is richly stylised as far as his father is concerned. The titular Imperial Counsellor lived on his private means without any real judicial office. He had not exactly prospered on his fund of intellect, and in consequence he tended to rule his house if not tyrannically, then at least somewhat strictly. To recognise this fact, we hardly need the gloomy picture of Johann Kaspar as provided by Thomas Mann in *Lotte in Weimar*. It can be deduced from the autobiographical and biographical evidence.

The inheritance in terms of character was at least problematic in this instance, in contrast to that on the mother's side, where the dictum of the 'cheerful nature' and the 'delight in inventing tales' was to find a much more exact expression. The education of the boy by this father and private tutors chosen by the latter was very much in the spirit of the late baroque dissemination of knowledge, as far as the subject matter was concerned; in terms of aesthetic tastes, the standards observed were those of Gottsched, as the charming scene of the self-betrayed secret reading of Klopstock strikingly shows. It is almost amazing that this extraordinarily talented and alertly inquisitive boy did not turn eccentric under such paternal guidance. No less amazing was the fact that his attempts to break away from the *Aufklärung* middle-class atmosphere of his father's household – beginning with the Gretchen-episode in those last Frankfurt days and intensified to bursting point in the early student days in Leipzig (which commenced in 1765) – had no worse consequences than the crisis induced by the illness which forcibly terminated his Leipzig studies and brought back the prodigal, precocious though markedly subdued son into the parental fold.

This Leipzig period – also thought of in terms of the catch-phrase 'the Rococo Goethe' – signified in reality more than just the adoption of Leipzig dandyism by a young man finally liberated from the pedantry of an all too careful paternal home and becoming aware of his own audacity and talent. It included the first social company of his own choosing in the circle of Käthchen Schönkopf (Annette) and the Oeser family. It also included the first friendships to be more than just associations with pals, friendships like those with Riese and Behrisch. And lastly it signified his first steps in the aesthetic controversy of the time, which enabled Goethe early on to value Lessing's *Laokoon* (which had just appeared) for its range and importance, whilst at the same time making fun of Gottsched. There were the studio conversations with the old Adam Oeser, which introduced the young Goethe into this sphere, roughly the same sphere which had stimulated the first writings of Winckelmann a decade earlier. Oeser instructed Goethe in art and this triggered off the personal problem for the latter whether the eye or the word was to determine his future. The decision was not to be reached till later, but the sociable lyric verse of the Leipzig period as well as the first

reflections on the nature and definition of the arts may already
at that time have determined the tipping of the balance in favour
of literature. One thing is certain: *Das Buch Annette* (1767) or
the *Oden an meinen Freund Behrisch* (1767) had already driven
the poetic impulse far beyond the confines of the idyllic and
Rococo-anacreontic verse; 'Storm and Stress' sounds and themes
were already manifest in them, which had nothing as yet to do
with Hamann or Herder, but which stemmed rather from his own
existential and turbulent way of life. And here it must be borne
in mind that the odes to his older friend Behrisch preceded the
Göttingen Grove by five whole years. Even if we include Klopstock in the reckoning, the tone remains unmistakably his own.
His own particular kind of word-composition, pointing the way
to the later odes, was already in evidence. The depiction in the
second ode of the marshy, rotting landscape, which his friend
should flee, could rank at least as a quite individual variant of
Pindar's style:

> Tote Sümpfe,
> Dampfende Oktobernebel
> Verweben ihre Ausflüsse . . .[1]

And the marvellous introductory verse of the third ode:

> Sei gefühllos!
> Ein leicht bewegtes Herz
> Ist ein elend Gut
> Auf der wankenden Erde[2]

remarkably anticipates an existential theme of Goethe's. But
even the so-called rococo poetry of the *Neue Lieder* (1770),
of *Das Buch Annette*, scattered anacreontic conventions to the
winds. The erotic theme, for example, was already from the outset a confession of experienced sensuality, where the expression
of feeling (perhaps still boyishly excessive) at all events abandoned the 'moderation' of the Enlightenment and the tenderness
of the rococo idyll: 'His heart coursing with hot blood', 'with
every kiss a new fire engulfs him', 'a storm bursts from his lips',
'O God, how a shaft of joy shot through my heart!' Admittedly
such phrases are partly also the eroticised language of Pietism.

---

[1] Dead marshes, vaporous October mists weave their effluence . . .
[2] Be unfeeling! An easily moved heart is a wretched possession on this
shifting earth.

On the other hand, it is no accident that later on Naturalism should make specific reference to the sensually realistic elements as seen in *Die Nacht* or *Hochzeitslied* or *An den Mond*. These three erotica in fact fall outside the anacreontic scheme of things with their feeling for nuance, for the twilight zone, for fusion, exuberant rapture, and the corresponding skills in rhyme and vocabulary. Examples like:

> Es blinkt mit mystisch heil'gem Schimmer
> Vor ihm der Flammen blasses Gold
> (*Hochzeitslied*)[3]

or the wonderful illustrative conclusion to the strophe:

> Deines leisen Fußes Lauf
> Weckt aus tagverschloßnen Höhlen
> Traurig abgeschiedne Seelen,
> Mich und nächt'ge Vögel auf
> (*An den Mond*)[4]

are Goethe's own and point the way to the intimacy of the Strassburg Friederike-poems, even though a trace of youthful affectation may still cling to them. For the rest the young Goethe sought with total awareness the feeling of the 'joys of changing desire', as in *Unbeständigkeit*, the first of those poems of personal experience that are shaped like a rushing torrent. These are the 'joys' which must not be 'analysed', which produce their effect mysteriously intensified even by the distant loved one:

> Ew'ge Kräfte, Zeit und Ferne,
> Heimlich wie die Kraft der Sterne,
> Wiegen dieses Blut zur Ruh
> (*Das Glück der Liebe*)[5]

To be sure, such articulations are at that time only achieved in climaxes and determine the standard, rarely sustained, of these youthful poems. But they nevertheless provided a remarkably early hint of the potential of this eighteen-year-old for breaking through the style of the day.

[3] The flames' pale gold sparkles before him with a mystic sacred glow.
[4] Your light foot's step awakens sadly departed souls from caverns excluded from the light of day, me and the night birds.
[5] Eternal forces. Time and distance, secretly like the starry might, cradle this blood to rest.

But this was really true only of the lyric poetry. Both his alex-andrine comedies *Die Laune des Verliebten* (1768) and *Die Mitschuldigen* (1769) were, despite Albert Köster's efforts to upgrade them by relating them to Goethe's love-affairs in Leipzig, no foray in the new style, as was a portion of the Leipzig verse, but an expression of the Rococo comedy after the manner of Gellert; they were in fact averagely viable and stageworthy examples of this genre. Originally both were one-act plays, but later – with the final version completed in Weimar – *Die Mit-schuldigen* was extended to three acts for reasons of psycho-logical balance and unity. The theme of jealousy in *Die Laune des Verliebten* was pure convention. In the theme of complicity, however, may be sensed a preview of the later discussion between Goethe and Schiller on the question of veniality. If the landlord, his daughter Sophie, his guest Alcestes and his son-in-law Söller are all compromised, whatever the degree of (more or less) delicacy or coarseness involved, not one of them is compromised in an irreparable way. That could well be taken as an early indication of Goethe's tolerant attitude towards indulgence. Nevertheless this play really belongs to Goethe's Rococo period in Leipzig, even though it did receive a more polished form later.

After the hemorrhages in the August of 1768 at the end of an all too intensely led life in Leipzig, there followed eighteen months of illness and convalescence in the family home. In the creative sense, it was to be seen essentially as an incubation period. The sick man was compelled to take a grip on himself, to take stock of the past and the future. In this situation he be-came receptive to the remarkable sensitive introversion with which he had come into contact through association with Susanne von Klettenberg, his mother's pietistic friend. Susanne von Kletten-berg (1723–74) had built up for herself an existence of the 'Silent in the land' that was identical neither with that of the Herrnhut Brotherhood[6] nor with the missionary pietism of the Halle group.[7] We know about it from her own notes and letters;

---

[6] Fleeing from persecution, a colony of Moravians settled in 1722 at his invitation on Count Zinzendorf's Saxony estate at Herrnhut, which became the principal seat for the so-called 'Herrnhuter'. (*Translator's note*)

[7] Founded by August Hermann Francke (1663–1727) and noted for mis-sionary zeal in its expression of Pietism. (*Translator's note*)

from these and from personal impressions, the classical Goethe developed the sixth book of *Wilhelm Meister*, the *Bekenntnisse einer schönen Seele* (*Confessions of a Beautiful Soul*). As an inner picture of his mother's friend of brief standing, the *Bekenntnisse* – despite the classical link with the aesthetic problems of Shaftesbury and Schiller – hit upon the essential being of this indubitably significant woman through the very medium of poetic divination. The traces of this stimulus provided by Fräulein von Klettenberg, kept alive and developed further by Goethe, can be clearly perceived in the excerpts and memoranda under the title *Ephemerides*, which linked the last phase of the Frankfurt convalescence with Strassburg, whither Goethe moved with his father's consent in the April of 1770 for the completion of his law studies. He did in fact then get his doctorate there. If one examines the line his reading took, as revealed in the *Ephemerides*, the *Faust*-theme can already be detected. It probably went back to the alchemy experiments which Susanne von Klettenberg conducted like so many Pietists out of a certain curiosity about magic. At all events, the *Ephemerides* prove the reading of Paracelsus, Giordano Bruno and Tauler, of Agrippa of Nettesheim, of Thomas à Kempis and of the extract 'de Abraxis' from Mosheim's History of the Church, and thus reveal a distinct interest directed towards the mystic-speculative, at times too the natural-philosophical. A pointer can be seen here to the exorcism scene in *Urfaust* with the call to Nostradamus. But something else too was made manifest: readings of Shakespeare, books on Skaldic literature, the title of a piece of writing on Ancient Scottish Poems, pointers to the reading of chronicles (first indications of *Götz*). The latter showed that in the meantime the decisive meeting with Herder had taken place, which furnished Goethe with all those impulses and provided a new positive direction to his productivity. At all events this meeting signified a strict schooling throughout, since Herder, aggressive and sarcastic as he was, made no allowances for the development of the younger man, a development that was far behind his own. It was therefore no ecstatic friendship in the manner of the members of the Göttingen Grove, but above all an educational and stimulating association in a mutually obligating way that developed between pupil and teacher, both of them in fact similarly gifted. The enthusiasm for what Herder here had to contribute was displayed on Goethe's side. For his part Herder above all sensed Goethe's productive talent, ideally matched to the handling of great subject matter. It did not prevent him from castigating his adept pupil's 'sparrow-like' nature pitilessly and splenetically according to whim.

Besides the meeting with Herder and the contact with the great themes of Shakespeare, Ossian and the folksong, the last of which made Goethe into a folksong-collector on his rides through Alsace, he experienced his love for Friederike Brion, the daughter of the vicar at Sesenheim. It was a love that quickly developed and soon terminated. Passion formed the basis, but this idyll in the charming rural setting fundamentally corresponded to the worlds revealed to him by Herder: it was, so to speak, a presentation of the human aspect through the 'daughter of the people'. That Goethe awakened hopes in the girl, which his departure then dashed, could scarcely in the bourgeois sense be simply dismissed as inconstancy or faithlessness. Time and again he felt himself attracted to women by his very nature, in a precipitous blaze of passion or in a passion that but gradually developed out of respect and a mutual spirituality. He could be reproached for going always only to the brink of total involvement in these relationships, but never to actual self-sacrifice, as indeed Thomas Mann did in his picture of Goethe. The question remains, however, whether this must be seen simply in terms of egoism, when the law of life as determined and experienced in such a person was transformed into 'fragments of one great confession', that is into creative writing. Who knows whether here on both sides sacrifice and happiness were not intrinsically balanced? At all events from the time of the Friederike experience on, love as a form of self-sacrifice and as a being-sacrificed was inseparably linked with Goethe's creative output. Movement and shape gained thereby substance and reality and thus assumed their really magical force. Even a figure so questionable in real life as Christiane Vulpius played a part in these creative metamorphoses, an imperishable record of which was provided by the old Goethe himself in the symbolic poem Selige Sehnsucht from West-östlicher Divan. And what human variations he subjected to this law of metamorphosis in the course of the years: from Friederike to Lili, from Frau von Stein to Marianne von Willemer and Ulrike von Levetzov!

The lyrics of the Strassburg period that are associated with

c

Friederike Brion marked the opening, in the true sense, of this memorable relationship of Goethe's work and its expanding wordliness to the most intimate realm of personal love experiences. Traces of the Leipzig poems can still be detected in the Friederike lyrics too. But even in these predominantly sportive pieces one can come across a strophe like:

> Denn mich ängsten tiefe Schmerzen,
> Wenn mein Mädchen mir entflieht,
> Und der wahre Gram im Herzen
> Geht nicht über in mein Lied.[8]

Evidently one can not yet speak of the 'egoistic' transformation of love into a poetic confession. Poetry and passion as such have not yet overlapped. The little *rondeau*[9] *Ob ich dich liebe, weiß ich nicht*, a momentary fulfilment at the sight of the loved one, with the reservation contained in the title verse, is on the same plane. Even a poem so seemingly anacreontic as *Kleine Blumen, kleine Blätter*, the folksong quality of which Gottfried Keller was later to bring out impressively in *Sinngedicht*, went consciously beyond the thematic image provided in Klopstock's 'I found her in the spring shade / and I bound her with chains of roses' (*Das Rosenband*). It just did not want to be anacreontic any more: 'And the bond that unites us / be no weak chain of roses'. The three pieces of this group that are rhythmically the finest are *Erwache, Friederike, Mailied* and *Es schlug mein Herz, geschwind zu Pferde!* The first is an intimate *Tagelied*,[10] truly of a realistic intimacy that goes beyond the traditional form. The second, 'How splendidly nature glows for me!', anticipates Werther in May: intoxicated involvement in the moment of fulfilment, but in a naïve, not sentimental manner; nature and love in one, an exclamation rather than a presentation:

> Und Freud und Wonne
> Aus jeder Brust.
> O Erd', o Sonne!
> O Glück, o Lust!

[8] For deep pains make me anxious, when my girl runs away from me, and the true sorrow in my heart does not pass into my song.
[9] *Vide* Glossary.
[10] *Vide* Glossary.

O Lieb', o Liebe!
So golden schön
Wie Morgenwolken
Auf jenen Höhn! [11]

This, taken together with the charming skipping enjambment at
the close of the poem, shows an immediacy and guilelessness which
cannot even be found in the rhythmically similar poem from the
first Swiss journey, 'and fresh nourishment, new blood' (*Auf
dem See*). *Es schlug mein Herz*, the third of these poems,
blended in a similar way the other theme of a heroic-mythical
nature with the bitter-sweet demands of parting after the
moment of bliss. Not for nothing did the poem, borne along on
stirring, excited iambics, which control an eight-line strophe with
its rising rhythm, start on the note of the racing heartbeat and
the frenzied departure to battle. Hence, since it was referring to
the climactic moment of love, the line at the end of the second
strophe: 'In my veins what fire! in my heart what a glow!' This
surge of passionate feeling on the part of the lover is wrested
from a mythically experienced stormy night, when darkness has
a 'hundred black eyes' and the oak tree stands there like a
'towering giant', the wind howls forebodingly: *nox portentis
gravida*. The second half, Kairos and the morning departure,
patently outruns the temptation to become anacreontic (third
strophe): 'In your kisses what joy / In your eye what pain!' It is
the elemental immediacy expressed in Hamann's and Herder's
picture of man in the first person form, it is, if you like, a ballad
of subjectivity.

From here it was but a short step *via* the folksongs collected
in Alsace and the poem *Sah ein Knab*, recognised by Herder in
his *Ossian* essay as a folksong, to the Lili lyrics stemming from
his time spent in the notary's office after Strassburg and to the
purest 'Storm and Stress' genre for Goethe, namely the odes, the
model for which – Pindar – had likewise been revealed to him
by Herder. Ossian translations, which were then incorporated in
Werther, were in the same mould. And there unfolded an exu-

---

[11] And joy and pleasure from every breast, O earth, O sun, O happiness,
O delight!
O love, O love, so golden and beautiful like morning clouds on the
mountains up there.

berant feeling for life – even in the enjoyment of melancholy – in fact an excessive sense of conscious genius, which corresponded most closely to the feelings of his fellow *Stürmer und Dränger*, Klinger (also from Frankfurt) and the Livonian Lenz. It will never be fully possible to determine how far an attraction to Spinoza – an attraction initially still vague, and probably also one inspired by Herder – exerted an influence on this 'titanic' self-assertion, which was the result of his Strassburg experiences. It has been rather overemphasised in Histories of Literature hitherto. Yet it might well stand as a subjective interpretation of the Spinoza formula *deus sive natura*, from the self-assertion of the odes to Werther's feeling for nature: not then as an exact 'influence', but rather as a kind of self-confirmation within the Ganymede and Prometheus context.

Again, however, this is unthinkable without the self-assurance of original genius such as emerged from both the pieces that bear the stamp of Herder's spirit: namely the small discourse in draft form entitled *Zum Shäkspears Tag* (*On Shakespeare*) (1771) and the prose dithyramb *Von deutscher Baukunst*, (*On German Architecture*), which represented an immediate impression of the Strassburg Minster published in Herder's *Blätter*, (1773). Both these products from Strassburg are also quite close stylistically to Herder. Both emphasise the same half sacral, half promethean picture of genius. As for Herder, so too for Goethe did Shakespeare stand head and shoulders above all else: 'full of presentiment and perception, regardless of the cost'. The experience of Shakespeare's works miraculously opened new channels: 'To the very depths of my being I felt my existence enlarged by an infinity.' Shakespeare maintains, Goethe continues, total freedom with regard to rules and any set plan, and for that very reason he is universal theatre 'in which the characteristic quality of our Self . . . collides with the necessary course of the Whole'. Out of the mouth of this genius nature herself utters her prophecies. His creations are of 'colossal greatness' like those fashioned by Prometheus, the moulder of man.

The allusion to the figure of the Titan, made familiar to the German 'Storm and Stress' by Shaftesbury as a mythological symbol of the artist, as an aesthetic analogy to the Creation of the Universe, is found too – and not by chance – at the close of the writing on the Strassburg Minster: 'And more than Prometheus may he guide the happiness of the gods to earth'. The address had validity for the budding artist, the 'boy', who had been granted every fulfilment of experienced reality, and total perfection and truth of the idea of beauty. Also common to both writings was the superciliously free and easy annihilation of the century with its philosophy of Enlightenment and its *bon goût*. Rules fall as chaff before the freedom of Shakespearian genius, just as the 'powdered and rouged doll-painters' of the Rococo age vanish into thin air before the masculinity of Albrecht Dürer. And the legendary figure of Erwin à Steinbach, the builder of the Minster, does not fit any historical purpose at all, but serves exclusively as a prototype of originality: 'He will not be borne aloft and carried away on alien wings, even if they were Aurora's.' The piece is primarily devoted to the purpose of rapturous enthusiasm for this 'godlike genius', only secondarily to the widely acclaimed revaluation of the Gothic style for so long scorned, the 'malformed bristly monster'. And even this revaluation of the Gothic style, of original genius as unity and character, served but to illustrate the greatness of those who knew how to give form to what was so vast and enormous, to whom it was granted to 'beget a tumultuous thought in their soul, complete, great and necessarily beautiful right down to the smallest detail, like God's trees'. Shakespeare and the Minster architect are seen as being one and the same in terms of original genius, the very contrast to the 'weak-kneed pretender to taste'. They are even the same as Nature. It is not by chance that the same image which relates to spring in the ode *Ganymed* is here used with reference to the naturalness of the Minster spire: 'How freshly it shone towards me in the glow of fragrant morning.'

These must have been years full not only of inner adventures but also of a blissful exposure of all the senses and faculties. This can be detected in the youthful feeling of vigour in every form of expression. The fact that the biographical part of the Werther experience occurred at this time – that remarkable *ménage à trois* which developed in those few short months when Goethe was active (or indeed inactive) at the Supreme Court in Wetzlar from May to September 1772 – is really no contradiction of the strength of his feeling for life at the time. Goethe had been basically pampered throughout his life up to that point – Friederike Brion had fallen for and to him without resistance.

The conditions were of a more complicated nature in the case of his Wetzlar experience with Charlotte Buff, who was the fiancée of Goethe's newly acquired friend Kestner. Not only did friendship and love become entangled in an ambivalent relationship here, but there was also the clash of sensual genius on Goethe's side and the amalgam (that was perhaps only possible in Germany) of sentimentality and bourgeois morality on the part of the fiancée. Goethe could not be himself here as he had been in Sesenheim. He had to adopt the dual role of friend and lover. The problem therefore was not even that of the unequivocal contrast of bourgeois and non-bourgeois codes of behaviour. This way of living made existential demands upon him, of the same kind as the later love for, and period of betrothal to Lili Schönemann, the Frankfurt patrician's daughter. Friederike, simple and straightforward in her country-like ways and inexperience of life; Charlotte Buff, of middle-class background, yet already sublimated by sensitivity; Lili, *femme du monde* full of grace and charm, and also manners and upbringing – all this compressed into the short period between Strassburg and Weimar. Self-assured genius alone would have been hard put to it to assimilate all this.

5 The Odes and Poems for Lili

The most important odes had their genesis in this second Frankfurt period. They were an expression not only of Shaftesbury's
sense of creative self-assurance, of ἕν καὶ πᾶν in the sense of the
first summary contact with Spinoza, but also of the twice overcome passion for Lotte and Lili. The form used – again the
guiding hand of Herder is evident – derived from his enthusiasm
for Pindar, whose fifth Olympian ode Goethe translated after his
Wetzlar sojourn. But the original hymnic poems from *Wanderers
Sturmlied* to *Ganymed* and *An Schwager Kronos* are of decisive
significance. It is better to take this period as a whole since the
chronological sequence of such central pieces as *Prometheus*
and *Ganymed* is not undisputed.

The free rhythm of this period, in which style Goethe established the genre that corresponded most strongly to the self-
assurance of the 'Storm and Stress', was already the hallmark of
Wanderers Sturmlied. This form of expression with all its qualities was firmly established in this poem (almost simultaneously
with *Der Wanderer*, early 1772). In *Dichtung und Wahrheit* the
old Goethe termed these verses 'half nonsense', as in fact he had
refused publication altogether, for example, of the *Prometheus*
poem or *An Schwager Kronos* until after the Italian journey. It
was only after its premature publication in Jacobi's *Spinoza-
Büchlein* that Goethe allowed the *Prometheus* poem, the key
piece of the 'titanic' period, to appear.

Wanderers Sturmlied is, in fact, a programmatic piece in
Pindaric form on the awareness of genius, expressly set after the
fashion of Pindar, as the final strophe shows:

> Wie von Gebürg herab sich
> Kieselwetter ins Tal wälzt

Glühte deine Seel Gefahren Pindar
Mut Pindar – Glühte –
Armes Herz – [1]

These words emerge in a kind of stammer from an inner glow, from a roused heart. This corresponds entirely to the four initial strophes to Genius, wherein the quivering heart is induced to sing, to fly with the 'wings of fire', where the heart is open to an inner warmth, to (repeatedly) 'godlike' wandering and soaring. But almost exactly in the middle of the poem come the lines:

Weh! Weh! Innre Wärme,
Seelenwärme,
Mittelpunkt,
Glüh entgegen
Phöb Apollen,[2]

in which *kairos* appears as passion too, lines which are characteristic of the possibility of an instantaneous shift in one's existence when at the vortex of feeling to passion in its dual sense. Corresponding to this concept is the vocabulary of soaring, gushing, flowing, flying, as well as the thematic idea of putting aside Anacreon and Theocritus in favour of Pindar, seen as Castalian 'brooks' so inferior to the stormy godhead of Jupiter Pluvius, from which the poem has taken its title. And finally, the first half of the combination 'Storm and Stress' is contained in it. But what thrusts its way to the surface in terms of immediacy in *Wanderers Sturmlied*, is achieved quasi-idyllically in *Der Wanderer*. Through the dialogue form itself everything assumes a more measured, more disciplined tone. Admittedly this poem is not an 'idyll' in the Rococo sense of the term: not Theocritus nor Anacreon is the ruling spirit, but Homer, taken in a patriarchal sense, such as determined Goethe's interpretation even in *Werther*, and up to the *Italienische Reise*. If *Wanderers Sturmlied*, *Prometheus* and *An Schwager Kronos* represent basically an anti-bourgeois rebellion, there is no trace whatsoever of that here. The eternally and most intimately human element, the young mother

[1] As showers of stones fall from the mountains down into the valley, your soul glowed in the face of dangers, Pindar, Courage, Pindar – Glowed – Poor heart –

[2] Alas! Alas! Inner warmth, warmth of the soul, central point, rush to meet in your glowing Phoebus Apollo . . .

with her child at her breast – an image of the natural order of
things – appears to be the heritage of creative Classical Antiquity.
Her cottage is erected on the ruins of a temple to Venus. The
creative spirit of Classical Antiquity reveals itself to the wanderer
from out of these very ruins in polarity as it were to such tranquil
and constant humanity: 'Glowingly you move over your grave /
Genius!' The young woman who holds out the child to him becomes the symbol of eternal maturity and fruitfulness, the boy
(as heir) appears predestined to enjoy every day in 'divine self-
assurance'. The wanderer speaks as an enthusiastic reveller in
nature, the mother of all feeling for life, the great transformer of
even the transitory: 'Nature, everlastingly germinating nature, /
you create everyone for the enjoyment of life.' Past and Present
become one in this way, as do the remains of the temple (as the
creation of the highest genius) and the cottage (which will rise
time and again on these ruins), the symbol of the simple life,
which nature guarantees.

During the months spent in Wetzlar there originated the three
connected pieces to the three Darmstadt sentimentalists: *Elysium*
to Urania, the lady-in-waiting von Roussillon, *Pilgers Morgenlied*
to Lila, her friend Luise von Ziegler, and *Fels-Weihegesang* to
Psyche, the third of this circle, Caroline Flachsland, Herder's
fiancée. Darmstadt and its ambience shared in the sensitivity of the
Rhine and Main areas, a sensitivity that intensified to the level of
the 'Storm and Stress'. Darmstadt was included in the tourist travel
routes – not only by Goethe and Herder – and even Karl August
von Weimar finally fetched his bride, the Princess Luise, from
there, for that problem marriage which later neither Goethe
nor Herder managed to keep intact in the true sense. These three
poems too drew on the concentrated moment and sought expression of it: 'Omnipresent Love! / you ardently course through
me' (*Pilgers Morgenlied*), or 'Bliss, bliss / the feeling of a
kiss!' (*Elysium*). The compelling immediacy leads to compounds
like 'Myrtenhainsdämmerung', 'Muttergegenwart', 'Sommer-
abendrot', 'Hügelgebüsch'.[3] The dynamism of the verbal language
moves on a subjectivised Klopstockian plane, to which belong
also the darkening grove and the ever repeated word 'heilig'
(sacred). The feeling for love and for nature meet, as later in
Werther:

[3] Myrrh-grove-dusk; mother presence; summer-evening-glow; hill-bushes.

Wo meine Brust hier ruht,
An das Moos mit innigem
Liebesgefühl sich
Atmend drängt.
(*Fels-Weihegesang*)[4]

The unity of the inner emotion and the free rhythm can here be felt. And perhaps too there can distantly be sensed a faint suggestion of a link with Pindar or Klopstock: the subjectivity of feeling and the originality of form are all important.

The feeling of omnipresent love as a being-at-one with Nature was also already detectable in these poems to the 'Darmstadt Community of the Saintly Ladies'. It was earlier customary to categorise this – perhaps all too dogmatically – as the effect of Spinoza on the young Goethe. This pantheistic feeling is featured far more strongly in *Mahomets Gesang*, *Prometheus*, *Ganymed* and *An Schwager Kronos*. Certainly the earliest of this group, *Mahomets Gesang*, was originally – like *Der Wanderer* – a poem in dialogue form from the dramatic fragment *Mahomet*; it conceives the movement of the river sweeping all along with it, right from the source to the mouth, as a kind of mythical pan-union. The movement of the water appears irresistible: a flowing and a feeling of being swept along, a steady increase in volume and momentum, a transforming of the 'brother springs', until the mighty current bears itself and them all 'to the awaiting begetter / with a joyous roaring sound'. This one growing and continuous movement from the moment of creation back into the arms of the awaiting Father governs the entire poem.

The *Prometheu*s poem (a copy of which Friedrich Jacobi later used to provoke Lessing's acknowledgement in his old age of Spinoza, whose ἕν καὶ πᾶν he was supposed to have rediscovered in it) seems outwardly to follow another course, at least in part. The question of the authenticity of the Spinoza-conversation is strictly irrelevant. The ode *Prometheus* was at one time seen as a monologue cut out of the dramatic fragment, but should be interpreted as something which developed of its own volition. The dramatic fragment contained an interpretation of death in its Pandora-theme, which in fact can be regarded as more pan-

---

[4] Where my breast rests here, it presses on the moss breathing heartfelt feelings of love.

theistic than in the poetic draft. The annihilation of the gods by creative genius, here represented by the Titan, was the poem's first concern: 'Have you not accomplished everything yourself / holy glowing heart?' It is the holy glowing heart of the artist-god, the moulder of man (according to one version of the myth, initially late-classical, then again made known through Humanism), which is here apostrophised. The central theme of the Prometheus myth, Prometheus the bringer of light, and hence culture, whom the gods punished for his disloyalty by torturing him in the Caucasus Mountains, is disregarded. Prometheus is the creator of man actuated by artistic genius. The gods, including Zeus, play the role of jealous and malevolent usurpers of reverence and power. The kernel is the holy glowing heart, the Ego, which recognises only the masters common to the gods and itself: 'Almighty Time / Everlasting Destiny'. It is at this point that a divergence from Spinoza is most marked, since Fate can hardly be equated with Spinoza's concept of Nature. At all events, even this genius who scorns the gods retains an awareness of limitation, and with it a remnant of reverence. Yet the powerful self-assertion of the final strophe appears to come closer again to Spinoza:

> Hier sitz ich, forme Menschen
> Nach meinem Bilde,
> Ein Geschlecht, das mir gleich sei,
> Zu leiden, weinen,
> Genießen und zu freuen sich,
> Und dein nicht zu achten,
> Wie ich.[5]

The creature in *Prometheus* is Man as propounded by Herder and Hamann, whose profoundness is based on intense sensuality. Except that, and contrary to the Hamannian idea in any case, the thought of any mediation on the part of the gods is completely rejected in the final lines. Creative genius produces a direct link with God and with nature, provided it has the courage to trust itself. In a certain sense then, *Prometheus* can be seen as a counterpiece to *Mahomets Gesang*. But if *Natura naturans* is the controlling force in the latter, it is *Natura naturata* in *Prometheus*,

[5] Here I sit, make men in my image, a race which shall be like me, to suffer, to weep, to enjoy and be glad, and to ignore you, as I do!

but with the substitution of God by the godlike artist. Here he assumes the position of *Natura naturans*, a symbol of 'Storm and Stress' genius that can hardly be surpassed.

If, as has been explained, *Prometheus* kept within the limits of the classical myth, though these were made absolute in the 'Storm and Stress' sense, the position is completely reversed in the case of *Ganymed*. The beautiful boy, according to the tradition, was forcibly abducted by Zeus's eagle to Olympus to become there the cup-bearer of the gods. Goethe left only the passionate youthfulness of the boy as it was (a lad, incidentally, after Herder's heart). In contrast to the defiant masculinity of Prometheus, however, he equipped Ganymede with a powerful feeling for pantheistic union, that was entirely directed towards Nature, even though the *topoi* of flowers and the nightingale may contain already the hint of human love. The lover addressed, however, is Spring, the symbol of that which 'presses to my heart / with a thousandfold joy of love', Spring: that meant the morning glow at sunrise, sanctified warmth of life, beauty. At the same time, however, it signified a call beyond itself, beyond the earthly and finite to what is infinite love. The movement initiated by the gods and to which Ganymede inclines, cannot therefore be seen as abduction, as rape, but rather as a continuation of the winged flight of the boy's own longing to final union with the Absolute:

> Aufwärts,
> Umfangend umfangen!
> Aufwärts
> An deinen Busen,
> Alliebender Vater![6]

This movement is just as all-embracing as in *Mahomets Gesang*. There it formed a gradual sinking back into the arms of the begetter. Here, however, it strives upwards beyond an earthly moment filled to bursting point to union with the Absolute. The resistance present in the Greek myth becomes in Goethe's poem the striving from earthly to heavenly *kairos*. It is neither the 'masterful stride' of the Mahomet-river nor the manly energy of Prometheus, which has yet to overcome the enmity of the

[6] Upwards! Embracing, embraced! Upwards to Thy bosom, all-loving Father.

gods. It is still a foreboding, a sense of amazement, a love which dedicates itself unreflectingly to love that comes to meet it half-way, from the very first impression:

> Wie im Morgenrot
> Du rings mich anglühst,
> Frühling, Geliebter! [7]

up to the turning-point in the action:

> Ich komme! Ich komme!
> Wohin? Ach, wohin? [8]

Neither Mahomet nor Prometheus could have asked that question. They followed their own dynamic course. In the case of Gany-mede, however, everything is youthful frankness, an indetermin-ate drive, presentiment, longing, trust. Oneness and union are reflected here too, but minimally. It is 'Storm and Stress' in the image of youth, in which Nature still finds its own expression as uninterrupted feeling and direct energy.

What *An Schwager Kronos* – a poem on life and death com-posed 'in a post-chaise on 10 October, 1774' after Klopstock's visit – still had to add to this world expressed in the odes, is the elation of the death theme, which is incorporated into the frenzy of a life filled to overflowing. The other odes do not actually deal with the concept of time in the sense of transitoriness. They express rather the timeless quality of the river, the moment of artistic fulfilment, the dedication of the moment of youth. The postillion, who assumes symbolically mythical traits of the Greek Chronos (Time, not Kronos, the father of Zeus), here leads the way to death, which Goethe did not consider elsewhere in the odes. He included it only in the *Prometheus*-fragment. In the poem, how-ever, as similarly in the dramatic fragment, death is transformed into the supreme moment of life, and indeed not as an illusion, as happened to Faust in the enjoyment of his final moment. The experience of death is rather reality, as was earlier the panoramic view from above 'into life' and the intoxication of love in the stanza in which the traveller halts on his journey. In both life culminates in enjoyment and self-reliance. A logical consequence

---

[7] Beloved, Spring, how you glow at me in the morning light!
[8] I am coming, I am coming! Where to, oh, where?

would be the idea of growing old, but it is eliminated here being conceived of as impossible. The youth snatched from life seeks death at and in the very midst of life, before the sun sinks: 'before old age / seizes me in the morass of misty vapours'. At this moment 'Schwager Kronos' becomes the conductor of souls to the place of the dead, though in a grotesque and boisterous guise. But the decisive factor is that the passenger through life casts himself as if intoxicated into the death-experience, but in the full power and awareness of his senses:

> Trunknen vom letzten Strahl
> Reiß mich, ein Feuermeer
> Mir im schäumenden Aug',
> Mich Geblendeten, Taumelnden
> In der Hölle nächtliches Tor! [9]

This is no self-outpouring back into the arms of the Father as in *Mahomet*, no dedicated upward flight as in *Ganymed*. The downward movement becomes a headlong fall. The height before and the depth now correspond. It is a matter of striving in each direction towards that totality in which feeling for life and for death are one and the same.

What is dithyrambically concentrated in the odes in terms of vitality, breadth and intimacy of outward and personal experience, left its mark too on those lyric poems which originated from the time of the engagement to Lili up to the break-up and separation. The Friederike-poems had given no hint at all of separation. Now, however, the experience had deepened and Goethe felt even during the first Swiss journey of 1775, indeed even up to the beginning of the Weimer period, the sufferer and the victim. In fact, we encounter here the whole scale of tones and semi-tones ranging from *Neue Liebe, neues Leben* up to *Wonne der Wehmut*. Those of the Lili-period are less clear-cut than the Friederike poems, but the richer for it, in part more sublime and with a greater degree of nuance. Rhyme predominates. But the three rhymeless pieces *Bleibe, bleibe bei mir*, *Fetter grüne, du Laub* and *Wonne der Wehmut* are amongst the finest of the group. The first is a passionate declaration of love, the feeling of rebirth: 'Ah, how I experience, how I experience / this

---

[9] Intoxicated as I am from the sun's last rays, a sea of fire foaming in my eye, hurl me, bedazzled and reeling, into hell's nightly portal.

life for the first time!' The second (in the autumn of 1775) concerns autumnal ripening and fructification in the last warmth from the sun and under the cool eye of the moon, in the pregnant end-of-season air. The whole, however, is the attempt by means of the symbol to come inwardly to terms with the law of nature, which harvests even human love as something transitory, like the fruit. In this experience of parting, life and suffering go hand in hand:

> Und euch betauen, ach,
> Aus diesen Augen
> Der ewig belebenden Liebe
> Voll schwellende Tränen.[10]

It is the law of man. This analogy to the ripening fruit stands out clearly. But the human heart is thereby already open to the 'joy of sorrow'. The earliest (Herder's) copy of *Wonne der Wehmut* knew nothing at all of the more sentimental later version, the last words of which were 'unhappy love'. The tears, which should not be dried, because the world would be desolate and dead without them, were originally 'tears of sacred love' and, at the end, of 'eternal love' – identical with the 'eternally life-giving love' in *Fetter grüne, du Laub*. It was a question then not of the private aspect of 'unhappy love', but of something elemental, omnipotent and universal, where both suffering and pain of the individual have permeated and been sublimated.

On the other hand, the rhymed poems of the Lili-period do indeed reveal something of the charm of the girl rendered as Rococo gracefulness, and not only in the long piece *Lilis Park*, in which the young lady – in the style somewhat of the contemporary farces – gathers her admirers around her like a menagerie and the poet himself plays the role of the clumsy bear. Even the rhythmically fascinating *An Belinden* has something of this quality. A more significant factor in these poems, however, is the reflection of enchantment which proceeded from the singular amalgam of nature and sociability in Lili. This sustains the poems *Neue Liebe, neues Leben, An Belinden* and *Auf dem See*. The reflection in the soul of the lover, however, effects a change of heart:

[10] And, alas, tears full of eternal life-giving love, welling from these eyes, bedew you.

Herz, mein Herz, was soll das geben,
Was bedränget dich so sehr?
Welch ein fremdes neues Leben – [11]

This is the tone, trochaic as in *An Belinden*, in the relevant lines referring to Lili here in *Auf dem See*, and in the single verse *Vom Berge* ('If I, dear Lili, did not love you'). The falling beat, the ponderous start with the main stress, where words like 'Herz', 'bleibe', 'fesselt' fit so well, echoes the burden of distress borne by the full heart more than the rising beat of the iambic, which is sounded in only one of the emotionally charged poems, *Sehnsucht*, though, admittedly, it is in evidence too in the light measures of *Lilis Park* and the blissfully drunken movement in the last stanza on nature in *Auf dem See*. As against the Friederike lyrics, there is clearly an increasing note of fervour, which befitted his 'strange new life'. The tension between wanting and not wanting, being enraptured and straining away, the tensions involved in the feeling of rebirth and the question 'am I still myself?', of the tears of love as pain and as joy – this is what marked the new experience since Strassburg, which then in turn inevitably led to another kind of directness of expression.

Its nevertheless existing affinity to the world of the odes is shown most clearly in the two poems from the diary covering the Swiss journey. What appeared in *Ganymed* as a merging with nature in terms of a myth, is presented in the poem *Auf dem See* in its original version *Aufm Zürichersee* as personal experience, as impression, not expression. The diary version ('I suck now nourishment from the world / through my umbilical cord') may be less beautiful than the later one ('And fresh nourishment, new blood'), less deliberate, but the originally intended image of the mother and child in closest unity for the unity of the loving Self with Nature is contained in its completeness in the first version. The phrase (later changed to 'how gracious and generous is Nature') 'And Nature round about is magnificent' preserves something of the intoxicating enthusiasm of the view from the mountains contained in *An Schwager Kronos* ('Far, high, magnificent the view'), the only place where the youthfully ecstatic word 'magnificent' (*herrlich*) is found in the otherwise very emphatic

[11] Heart, my heart, what does this mean? What is it that oppresses you so much? What strange new life –

language of the odes. We also find, however, the upward movement and the reaching-down-from-on-high expressed in *Ganymed*
in the following lines of blissful merging conveyed in the rocking
rhythm of the oars dipped in the waves and the 'mountains rising
up to meet our course'. Then comes the significant change from
iambic to trochaic metre, whereby the poem gains the curious
sense of agitation, the element of unsteadiness, the idea of being
transported back and forth, ambiguity in movement and form,
which constituted the characteristic feature of the Lili-poems,
their maturity, so to speak. Here is the powerfully rejected thought
of what until a short time before had still been for him 'new love,
new life':

> Aug', mein Aug', was sinkst du nieder?
> Goldne Träume, kommt ihr wieder?
> Weg, du Traum, so gold du bist:
> Hier auch Lieb' und Leben ist.[12]

Again his gaze is riveted back to the lake in which lights, reflections and the veiled view into the distance are now observed.
Unity with the landscape is re-established afresh. But the poem
retains a falling beat: it is a unity *refound*, no longer the natural
one of the child in the opening lines, where the rhythm was rising.

---

[12] Eye, my eye, why are you drooping? Golden dreams, are you return-
ing? Away, O dream, golden as you are, here is also love and life.

6 From Götz to Clavigo

Herder's arousing of Goethe's enthusiasm for everything connected with 'Volk' in the original unadulterated, pre-nationalistic sense of the word, produced one immediate result: namely *Götz*. The genesis of this theme cannot just be equated with his interest in studying old chronicles (*Ephemerides*) nor simply with his interest in Götz's autobiography. Similarly it will not merely suffice to refer to the allied spirit of the folk ballads collected in Alsace. All that was but the raw material, not the theme as yet. Goethe must really have shaped the theme in the fruitful moment of contact with Herder's concept of 'Volk' and the image of man derived therefrom. And this image of man in the ideal 'Storm and Stress' sense had to have features belonging to the earliest times, the aspired characteristics of a lost dynamism and unity, the aspired characteristics too of genius that had been atrophied through abstraction and philosophising. This genius could appear in the shape of Faust, Prometheus or Götz. Götz and his world represented individuality and genius seen as a natural expression of a unity of the people in terms of character. Faust and Prometheus stand out in contrast. Götz, on the other hand, represents a totality which is still so fundamental and unbroken, that the great personality, seen as a character, can represent it, without losing his individuality. Character was to signify much more than the mere probity displayed in the olden times. It meant the full preservation of manliness in absolute and unequivocal terms; candour; faithfulness to oneself and others; the strength to stand up on their behalf; a manly breadth of vision too; and an awareness of responsibility towards both family and emperor. The same absolute trust in one's fellow man, which was a part of his simple integrity and could even go to the point of self-sacrifice, also appertained to this strength of character. The relationship between

the historically real Götz and Goethe's figure recalls the writing
on the Strassburg Minster and its builder-architect. Here, as there,
the historical background – the Middle Ages, the period of the
last Knights and the dawning of the Reformation – was used only
as a framework and served as the means of conveying to the senses
the idea of 'Storm and Stress' individuality as an anthropological
motif, which was really its sole concern. Genius was understood
and represented here not in terms of the creative element, but
as a natural ethic. The immediate and quite astonishing effect of
Götz can only be explained by the fact that the drama in its form
and the direction it took was a genuine expression of the times,
just as the hero, as a character, was an expression of the people
of those times. Frederick the Great's scorn for the play testified
to its thoroughly accurate atmosphere. For he saw himself and
his intellectual world of Enlightenment compromised almost
irreparably in the play. Amongst the intellectuals of the older
generation it needed the openmindedness and tolerance of a
Lessing to do more than simply understand it. The fact that
Hamann saw in *Götz* the dawning of a new era of German literature, came as no real surprise.

   Götz von Berlichingen mit der eisernen Hand (*Götz von Berlichingen with the Iron Hand*), as it appeared in 1773, was not
the first version. It was preceded by the *Geschichte Gottfriedens
von Berlichingen mit der eisernen Hand dramatisiert* under an anti-
tyrant motto (later erased) from Haller's *Staatsroman*[1] *Usong*:
'the heart of the people has been trodden into the mire'. This first
draft, that was linked directly with his stay in Strassburg, already
contained all the decisive elements, even the provocative Shakespearian changes of scene in time and place, which were to arouse
the audience and stimulate its imagination to an understanding
of the inner logic involved. The 'marauding soldiers' scenes in
wood and inn; Jagsthausen, the castle of the Berlichingens, in
times of peace and war; the setting of the Imperial Knights'
struggles with Sickingen as Götz's representative; the powerful
opposition circle at the Bamberg Court; and above them all the
Imperial Court itself; the Peasants' War with its leaders and
problems: this already provided a sufficient kaleidoscope of excitement, a tumult of action and a vividness of scene, although
there was more besides.

[1] *Vide* Glossary.

The drama begins quite logically – in both versions, though with variations – from the midst of the people as encountered in the shape of peasants and soldiers in the inn with their uncouth artlessness. Natural simplicity governs the atmosphere and the language is simple, realistic too in the abundance of dialect in the careless forms of speech and the candid vocabulary. The language is differentiated, incidentally, by Goethe according to social class. The educated and courtly stratum of society speaks an outmoded language (at Jagsthausen too). Götz and Brother Martin (Luther) stand somewhere in the centre, in tone common, but not vulgar. The contrast between Götz's circle and that of the Court as representing the contrast between healthy and decadent mankind – the dominating factor in the play – must therefore first be illustrated in the language too. The refined, exaggerated diction of Weislingen indeed anticipates his actions, just as does Adelheid's tongue of intrigue or the unrestrained language of Franz. The scenes in which the relationship of language, status and character are consciously considered, are those involving Götz's small son, in whose pedantic zeal for learning and schoolboy mind the knight does not recognise his own image. The fact that the boy with such a disposition seems well enough suited for the monastery, but not for the world at large and for grand knightly feats, is given expression only too clearly in a scene later cut. This secondary action, which nevertheless touches upon the core of the Götz action, was to a certain extent something preconceived and philosophical, i.e. typically eighteenth century. The figure of the boy has to suffer, so to speak, for the 'Storm and Stress' hatred of book-learning. In the opening monologue in *Faust* we again find the same shift in time.

It is against this background that we must view the well-known action: Götz with his faithful servants like Lerse and Georg and friends like Sickingen against the intrigues of the courtly world with Adelheid and the Bishop of Bamberg as its representatives – the basic contrast between the image of ethical man and that of immorality. In 'Storm and Stress' fashion human greatness is represented only in Götz. For the other side there is only the cynicism of the Bamberg Court with its higher and lower ethical code, as represented by the poisoning of Weislingen and its expiation exacted by the Vehmic Court. Here nothing of this nature is really impossible, just as conversely on Götz's side in the hopeless struggle against his Age almost every aspect of human greatness is possible. The conclusion – common to both versions – testifies to this distinction. Not only the fact that Götz dies with the words 'Freedom, freedom!' on his lips (which meant freedom from princely tyranny), but also the three carefully balanced parting lines of Elisabeth, Marie and Lerse (*Elisabeth*: 'Only there above, there on high with you. The world is a prison'; *Marie*: 'Noble, old man. Woe to the century that rejected you'; *Lerse*: 'Woe to posterity if it misjudges you') indicate that here the question was not just one of a contemporary political conflict, but rather of a universal, timeless conflict with which man is confronted again and again.

The Weislingen-Marie action develops between these extremes. Weislingen is weak, not evil. He can betray Götz, his friend since youth (this too in the absolute 'Storm and Stress' sense), more than once. He does this out of weakness, enfeebled by his courtly upbringing, not because he has lived like Adelheid in the orbit of evil. Weislingen's unreliability consists in the fact that he is nowhere himself. He represents the counterpart of Götz's original genius, indeed even of Adelheid, to whom he lets himself be married, whilst she constantly moves within the sphere of evil. Hence Weislingen, as Götz's prisoner, can become engaged to Marie and immediately be unfaithful to her again as soon as he breathes the corrupt air of the Court once more. Hence he is an example of wretched fickleness and finally becomes its victim. Marie, the unsuspecting pious woman, twice betrayed through disappointment in love, is on the other hand a pure, innocent victim of her very existence between these extremes. She is guilty in her innocence only in the sense that she lacks the strength and instinctiveness of Götz and his wife Elisabeth. She is noble, but strong only in the sense of *passio*, medieval religious piety. Not in vain does she educate Karl to reject the ideal of Knightly valour. She could be seen as heralding the 'Beautiful Soul'. She is no more a 'Storm and Stress' figure than Weislingen.

Thus language, construction, action and characterisation form a convincing totality, whose sense of immediacy can still transport the audience of today into the closed 'Storm and Stress' world which it represented.

Historically *Faust*, like *Götz*, originated from the times of Dürer. But Faust had other characteristics than those of the simple

morality and unequivocal humanity of Götz. To be sure, the hero
of the *Urfaust* is not yet the well thought out figure of the world
theatre, as he appears in *Faust I* and more so in Part II, the product of Goethe's old age. Yet at the same time he does not match
the straightforward character of Götz. Already Faust is here a
man propelled this way and that between the sensual and the intellectual, hungry for the world and for life, a man who is ready
to sell his soul to the devil for the fulfilment of this desire, not
merely for the endowment of a magic power bordering upon hocus-
pocus. This was the subject matter of the puppet play (with which
Goethe was familiar from an early age) and the tradition of the
chap-books. Goethe now translated the mercurial unrest of the
'Storm and Stress', its longing for vitality, its hatred of the 'ink-
slinging age' into this theme.

We should not have known the initial stage of *Faust* at all, since
the manuscript was lost, if a lucky accident had not later allowed
a copy to come to light (1886), which had been produced in the
early Weimar period by the hand of Fräulein von Göchhausen, a
lady-in-waiting of the Dowager Duchess. In it we have the reflection of the inner preparation dating back to the Strassburg
period, and of the later preliminary drafts of 1774 up to this first
attempt at synthesis, from which Goethe read aloud to friends in
Weimar and which was also shown to Frau Aja, his mother,
in Frankfurt. It contained the 'Night' scene (with the invocation
of spirits and Wagner), the scholar-scene (with Mephisto) and the
Gretchen tragedy starting with the first meeting ('Street') up to
the madness-scene ('Prison'); the whole was written in *Knittelvers*[2] with two passages in prose ('Auerbach's cellar', and the
concluding scenes from Faust's words 'in misery! in despair!'
onwards). The prose used in Auerbach's cellar is *Götz*-like;
staccato, realistic 'Storm and Stress' prose is what is found in
the concluding parts, already almost anticipating the young Schiller. The doggerel as the popular verse of the sixteenth century
produced the form appropriate for the historical setting of the
play and for the problems of its characters. If the balance were
shifted, as the proportion of the text demanded, from the seducer
to the seduced, it would then be quite legitimate to take the
Urfaust as one of the several dramas and poems of that time
dealing with the theme of infanticide (from L. Wagner and Bürger

[2] *Vide* Glossary.

to Schiller) and hence to understand it as a piece of 'Storm and Stress' social criticism. From this point of view then it formed one of the indictments of an offending social order which so often condemned the innocent to death. Goethe's aim, therefore, was to integrate the Faust theme with the literary topicality of the Gretchen theme, which had in fact a personally experienced basis (the trial and execution of a woman who had killed her child in Frankfurt in 1772). The Faust theme originated from quite different recollections and earlier years, from his passion for puppet-plays as a child, the interest in mystical experience before and during the Strassburg period, the whole fascination there with Gothic as an original and educational experience (under Herder's influence), the development of the idea of genius. Goethe should hardly be acclaimed for seemingly having achieved this fusion already in *Urfaust*. For in fact it came about only after Italy. The whole with its loose impressionistic sequence of scenes and the slapdash change from doggerel to prose looked too much like the bold, experimental draft for that in the first place. However this cannot be regarded simply as a disorganised *potpourri*, in which Faust is solely the seducer with the result that his individuality is totally subordinated by Gretchen's tragic fate. From the outset Faust appears as a man of significance. His own, equally important dramatic fate, therefore, is how – even in this first fragment – after the 'Prison' scene with the vision of Gretchen overcome by Shakespearian madness, he survives with the entire burden of his personal guilt.

The real meaning of Faust is established once and for all through the first scene 'Night'. Established, that is, in the sense of Herder's image of man, of Spinoza's ἕν καὶ πᾶν according to its 'Storm and Stress' interpretation, established also according to the arrogantly excessive self-assurance of the *Geniezeit*. This is already expressed in the first lines:

> Zwar bin ich gescheuter als alle die Laffen,
> Doktors, Professors, Schreiber und Pfaffen,
> Mich plagen keine Skrupel noch Zweifel,
> Fürcht mich weder vor Höll noch Teufel.[3]

---

[3] I have, I grant, more sense than all those fools, doctors, masters, clerks and priests, I'm not plagued at all by doubts and scruples, and have no fear of devil or of hell.

His 'Storm and Stress' friends Klinger and Lenz could have said those words. Due recognition is given Herder in the next section, which at the same time does full justice to the nature speculations arising from Goethe's pietistic experiences as a young man. Faust's quest for knowledge of the innermost secrets of the world, for instruction through Nature herself following so much textbook erudition and academic pedantry is concentrated, as the motive for the invocation of the Earth Spirit, in the passionate cry: 'Where shall I grasp you, infinite Nature! / your breasts, where! you springs of all life . . .' This same language is seen too in such words as 'effective force', 'spiritual energy', 'Life's motion', 'inner raging', 'superman', above all in compounds with 'spirit', 'soul', 'Nature', 'energy', 'heart', and on the other hand in the verbal vocabulary either as simple or compound forms: 'create', 'effect', 'weave', 'roam', 'boil', 'rage'. This mode of expression appears mysteriously ambivalent, dynamic and, if you like, mystical in the sense of the Greek ἄρρητον, the unutterable. It runs parallel to Hamann's 'cabbalistic' prose and to the sensual obscurity and dark whisperings of Ossian and the old ballads. But as there is a Weislingen for Götz, so there is for Faust the representative of Hell, Mephisto. With Mephisto, however, Voltairean ambivalance, gallic irony, pettifogging logic, the cynical nuance enter into the *Faust*-language. The *famulus* Wagner alone would not suffice to express the contrast of these worlds. He speaks only in a dry and flat manner. On the other hand in the student-scene as in Auerbach's cellar and the Gretchen-action, Mephisto handles the language in all its potential variations and nuances as a means for his evil intent the whole time in a well-balanced amalgam of the fine and the coarse, unanswerable quip and sparkling allusion. The Götz-like language used by the companions in Auerbach's cellar, Gretchen or her brother Valentin, adds a third dimension of expression. We have to bear all this in mind in order to realise what poetic synthesis has in fact been achieved already even in the first draft of *Faust*, and how one-sided, indeed impoverished the monotonous wildness and hyperbole in the dramas of a Lenz, Wagner and Klinger must appear in comparison.

The dramatic fragment *Prometheus* – although it is on a quite different linguistic plane – appears not unrelated to the Faust problem in many respects. The defiance of binding conventions, the challenge of renouncing God (the gods), or the pathetic nature of

sensuality in the human character, is common to both Faust and
Prometheus. Admittedly in *Prometheus* there is the very myth
of creation, so to speak, behind which Faust in his quest for knowledge is only beginning to probe. It is identical with rebellious
determination, which is at the same time the unwavering, exuberant creative will of the artist.

> Ich will nicht, sag es ihnen,
> Und kurz und gut, ich will nicht
> Ihr Wille! Gegen meinen! [4]

the fragment begins. In the scorning of the gods and their miserable egoism the voice of the 'Storm and Stress' creative spirit
speaks out in its awareness of genius against the bourgeois figure.
The words of Prometheus to Mercury, the messenger of the gods
('Can you stretch me / expand me to one world?') testify to this
impulse of the times. But Prometheus finds this extension to an
entire world when looking at his creations, his sculptures, which
seem to lack the very breath of life: 'O could I but give you feeling of what you are.' Only here, where he is an artist, can he
fully be himself: 'Here I experience feeling.' It is scarcely acci-
dental that the two male mediators, Mercury and his own brother
Epimetheus, fail in their mission and that it is the female inter-
cessor Minerva who comes to Prometheus's aid and breathes life
into these sculptures in human form. Then also in Act II it is
Pandora, the finest of the human creations, and hence the female
figure, who is to represent the zenith of human education for
Prometheus. The supermanliness of the central figure seems to
demand the female complement. After Prometheus has set aright
the sensual self-interests of men, it is Pandora who next has to
experience and have interpreted for her the allotted limit of
human existence, namely death. In Prometheus's interpretation
death is the death from *An Schwager Kronos*: the supreme experience of the senses, secretly and unconsciously desired, intoxicating universal feeling, the dissolution of all desires 'in the storm of
delight'. Thus it is not seen as a reducing factor or limitation, but
rather as a heightened experience of this second Creation, such as
is denied the gods in their monotonously lasting existence. And so
we see that in a completed form of the *Prometheus* drama the

[4] I will not, tell them, short and sweet, I will not tolerate their will against
mine.

absolute self-assurance of the artist should have interwoven with the other theme of the meaning and essence of a mankind that had become independent and had come to its senses as a result of superior education wholly within Herder's meaning of the term.

The theme of seduction is found in *Clavigo*, now carried over into the bourgeois world and hence coming close to the sphere of sentimentality. The subject matter was borrowed from Beaumarchais (*Fragment de mon voyage d'Espagne*, 1774), whose sister had experienced something similar. Goethe's drama was written in one short concentrated effort in the spring of 1774, with no drafts, a complete five-act play like *Götz*. Yet Clavigo is not Weislingen, any more than Marie Beaumarchais is Marie Berlichingen, any more than the characters in Goethe's drama are identical with the figures in the novelistic-historical report of Beaumarchais.

The titular hero of the play is the most interesting character; the beloved betrayed by him is the most clear-cut in her feelings. The whole play is enveloped in an atmosphere of exaggerated sentimentality, an atmosphere that was well-suited to the sentimental age and to Spanish passion. Only in this way was the theme at all able to arouse the clearly impulsive interest of the Goethe of the *Geniezeit*. For him the type of the cold seducer (as one finds portrayed first in the Romantics – Tieck, Jean Paul) was quite impossible. Here we find ourselves more in the tradition of Lessing's *Miß Sara Sampson*. Richardson's Lovelace has certainly acted as a model. What Goethe invented in the figure of Clavigo could be regarded as an amalgam on the one hand of calculated egoism, and on the other of self-deception of a not wholly imaginary feeling; and it was on this amalgam that he based the character of his hero. Clavigo juggles not merely with the 'voice of my heart', with the 'inner kinship of our souls', with the lament over 'our passions with which we live in everlasting strife'. He also believes in it (like Weislingen), in moments of subjective honesty. The stirrings of old love on meeting again ('In the first ecstatic moment my heart flew to her') he quickly interprets as mere compassion to his more mature friend Carlos. He is a 'Storm and Stress' character specifically through the vacillation and confusion of his human nature. This is most clearly seen before his death. When Marie has succumbed to love doomed to disappointment, Clavigo's conscience (and his feelings) drives him not to flight but rather to the dagger of her brother Beaumarchais, who has been roused to frenzied rage. The latter speaks here rather like a character from one of Schiller's youthful dramas:

> Mußtest du's wiederholen, Verräter! Das Donnerwort wieder-holen, das mir alles Mark aus den Gebeinen schlägt.[5]

The fact that the unfaithful lover is emotionally overwhelmed by Marie's death 'with all the terror of the night', indeed the fact that he is transfixed ('My heart dissolves in terror'), constitutes the pathos of this confused state, which incidentally is expressed by yet another, the avenger Beaumarchais. Even he appears over-whelmed after the deed by this feeling to the point of paradox, when he alludes to the blood of the stabbed Clavigo as the roses on the bridal bed of Marie and celebrates the consecration of her place of rest with the outburst 'Beautiful! Magnificent!' But Beaumarchais himself unequivocally lived an existence that had feeling as its centre. It was someone else's guilt, not his own, that brought him to the stage of mental confusion. There was nothing calculating in his case. Cold and imperturbable superiority on the other hand is represented by Carlos, Clavigo's friend, who entices Clavigo by his logic to give up Marie, marriage and a prosperous, successful career. But even Carlos is no Marinelli. He does not act in this way from an evil will or delight in intrigue, but rather from an exaggerated knowledge of human nature, which Goethe admittedly took to absurd lengths at the end of the play in the example of the figure of Clavigo, who is supposedly calculable and transparent down to the last detail. Here too it is consistent 'Storm and Stress' being expressed. We could say that it is 'Storm and Stress' at a relatively mature stage. For we can hardly fail to recognise a certain similarity in the Carlos-Clavigo relationship to the later Antonio-Tasso one. In Carlos, calculating reason is conceived in the 'Storm and Stress' sense as a destructive agent (perhaps even as a Mephistophelian cause of all suffering), but it is also, like Mephistopheles in *Faust*, taken seriously as a part, as a principle which belongs to the whole reality of life.

Something similar applies to the drama *Stella*. It originated in the turbulent time of his passion for Lili and appeared at the start of 1776; in 1806 it underwent a reworking of the conclusion, which then turned it into the tragedy. We feel ourselves transported

---

[5] Did you have to repeat it, traitor? Repeat the terrifying word that drives the very strength from my limbs.

into the atmosphere of Gellert's novels or even those of Friedrich
Jacobi. An ageing man, Fernando, vacillates unsteadily between
his wife Cäcilie and his younger beloved Stella and is incapable
of decision, even though he clearly favours the younger lady, incapable accordingly of renouncing either wife or mistress. In
accordance with the 1776 conclusion, Fernando should, through
the magnanimity of Cäcilie, have belonged to both women after
behaving sufficiently as a deranged sentimentalist beforehand.
It proved a heavy-going theme, dripping with magnanimity and
heartache, basically unpsychological and undramatic, a product of
his transitional phase; the Classical Goethe certainly saw this himself, when in 1806 he replaced without further ado the all-per-
missive scene of magnanimity by the death of Fernando and
Stella. This alteration hardly arose simply as a result of its temporal
proximity to *Die Wahlverwandtschaften* (*Elective Affinities*), but
was more the consequence of a now accomplished classical feeling
for style, which had to demand death as a suitable atonement for
the joys and sorrows that reached this level. But even so, *Stella*
could never become a work of significance.

7 Literary Programmatics

If the tragic dramas and fragments of the post-Strassburg years were an out and out expression of this new feeling for the world, which emerged in Goethe as a result of his individual development and his contact with friends, they nevertheless did not represent in any way the complete Goethe of this period. There were also testimonies of a bold, youthful self-awareness in directions other than in the purely dramatic field. Already some poems of the first half of the 1770s (*Künstlers Morgenlied, Der neue Amadis, Kenner und Künstler*) were highly topical expressions of the 'Storm and Stress' concept of art, referring to the times in almost insolent fashion, as much criticism as enthusiasm. The opponent in this context was kept more firmly in the sights. We must recall that the young Frankfurt lawyer was currently practising in the most concrete of all media, namely critical reviewing. The publication to which Goethe had been contributing since 1772 was the *Frankfurter Gelehrte Anzeigen*. Here he reviewed Gessner, Lavater and Sulzer's *Aesthetik*, among others, entirely in a style of his own, though also one somewhat reminiscent of Herder. It was an amalgam of criticism and empathic perception rooted in his own basic feeling.

The real expression, however, of his self-orientation at this time and of his resultant position towards friend and foe came out in the farces. A transition from his poems on the artist to the latter is formed by the playlets *Des Künstlers Erdewallen* and *Des Künstlers Vergötterung*, both of which owed their inception to the high-spirited, emotionally-charged atmosphere surrounding the Rhine trip in 1774, which Goethe as the 'child of the world in the centre' undertook with his newly won friend Lavater and the then most modern pedagogue Basedow. At least Lavater, the Zürich pietist, with the broadest-based education and untiring

initiative, with whom Goethe collaborated on the former's famous
Physiognomische Fragmente, could well have exerted a certain
pressure on Goethe to become aware of his own poetic position in
a form that corresponded to the enjoyment of life experienced
on this trip. This form was not pure *Knittelvers*, but a loose,
free-rhythmic one (provided with the old German freedom in the
falling beat) of rhyming couplets with stylistic elements from
the farce. The substantial dramatic piece *Des Künstlers Erdewallen* is concerned with presenting the relationship between
realism and idealism and the contrast between the portrait of
the ugly woman and the picture of Venus Urania, who is
curiously equated with the 'fountainhead of nature' in an
obvious connection with Faust and Prometheus: 'Drowned
in you / I feel blissfully drunk in all my senses.' But the feeling
of exultation is disturbed by the crass realism that breaks in with
the daily needs of the artist's family and with the vulgar, bourgeois employer. Even the arrival of the Muse, which closes the
scenes, acts as a kind of conscious antidote to pathos. She gives
the artist prudent, realistic guidance and blunt and resolute advice
to make his peace with the needs of this earth. *Des Künstlers
Vergötterung* admittedly accommodates the innocent enthusiasm
of the art-student, but without compromising itself, in the words
of the master: 'Hail to your feeling, youth, I initiate you / before
this sacred picture! You will become master'. Yet even here the
pithy comment is included, that even the divine painter of Venus
Urania was restricted in his life to what is apportioned to the
whole of mankind. There is no mistaking too the realistic touch
in the picture of the artist. It does not correspond to the powerful self-assertion of Prometheus, but rather to his solid, down-
to-earth education of his creations, namely men. Here already
the link between idealism and realism has been forged.

This realistic side now came to light as a direct, indeed
self-satisfied expression of youthful insolence in a whole series
of humorously satirical secondary works in dramatic form.
Whether Goethe called them 'masquerades' as he did the *Jahrmarktsfest zu Plundersweilern* or *Ein Fastnachtspiel vom Pater
Brey*, or farces like *Götter, Helden und Wieland*, or whether it was
an open harlequinade as in *Hans Wursts Hochzeit* – all these
frolicsome satirical plays, which originated from the spring of
1773 to the spring of 1775, were linked formalistically (with the

exception of the grotesque piece on Wieland) with the tradition of Hans Sachs, the plain, honest contemporary of Götz and the manly Dürer. They assumed all the licenses of the *Fastnachtspiel*[1] tradition, not only linguistically, but also in the factual and particularly the personal polemic issues involved.

The *Jahrmarktsfest zu Plundersweilern*, which indeed alluded to the special Nuremberg tradition of the masquerade, started proceedings. Later in Weimar in 1778 Goethe produced a courtly entertainment from it, whereby the piece was extended and became almost an operetta. The original sprightly version of the spring of 1773 is simply an exuberant, almost breath-taking presentation of the hustle and bustle of the market, where the different classes deliberately mix: mountebanks, quacks, singers, gipsies, rhymsters, Hans Wurst and the performers of the interlude play based on the Old Testament book of Esther on the one hand, servants, young ladies, governesses, magistrates and clergy – as spectators – on the other. The kernel is formed by the people in the whole kaleidoscopic splendour of their real and phantasy world, momentary pictures which flip by like the magic lantern shows of the time, but truly living and bouncing with reality, whatever the tempo. There were critical reflections of the day and of society (some of which are today hardly intelligible) which seasoned the whole, the spice deriving partly from the cunning of the fair people, partly from the implication of the gracious spectators from the upper classes compromising themselves. The types of character were drawn with wonderful accuracy.

But the real personal satire is to be found in *Satyros oder der vergötterte Waldteufel* and in *Pater Brey*, satires aimed at acquaintances or friends such as Herder or Merck, even if their characteristics are jumbled together a bit. We can hardly say, therefore, with absolute certainty that Herder is the target in *Satyros*, though his characteristics are clearly in question: his enthusiasm for nature, his persuasive oratory, his concept of the magic of song, but also his somewhat volatile character. But we should not forget either the element of self-irony involved in respect of his own Ganymede and Werther ambience, which Goethe incorporated in the figure of the hermit. The latter is indeed a man of feeling ('Everything bubbling over with creative power'); but at the same

---

[1] *Vide* Glossary.

time too he is a realist, a down-to-earth man who himself lives in accordance with the course of nature, in which a fresh bud is eaten by the maggot, the maggot in turn by the lark: 'And because I too am here to eat, / I shall consume the little lark.' He also then calmly and soberly tends the wounded leg of Satyros, who thanks him with shameless impudence. Satyros is the creature of wild and fertile nature, and is, as befits his status, the ram on the erotic plane too. Through his magic song he seduces Psyche, who overlooks his offensive nakedness and abandons herself totally: 'With what strong radiance he looks around!' Satyros fulfils this expectation in words too, when he embraces her forthwith at the well: 'I have all the fortune of the world in my arms, / such warmth of love – heaven – bliss'. He is a veritable Pied Piper of Hamelin in classical nudity, who will readily take advantage, even in the temple, of Endora, the high priest's wife. In between, however, are the odd scenes where he entices the whole populace to worship Nature, with all the features of Herder's primeval age, which through the mouth of the satyr the satirist now refers to as heading for libertinage. Nevertheless this is done with the promethean touch: 'Blessed is he who can feel / what it is to be God, Man!' The result is that the whole community runs after Nature's acclaimed fare: 'Raw chestnuts! The world is ours.' At the end there is the announcement of the new religion, a successful parody of the popular mystical jargon from Jakob Böhme to Pietism. All this would perhaps still better fit Hamann, whom Goethe did not know personally, whilst it applies to Herder really only in a qualified and distinctly exaggerated way, just as the second attempt at seduction (in the temple), which finally reveals to the people the new divinity for what he really is, would also be a disproportionate revenge on the bilious caprices and causticity which Herder, admittedly a demanding teacher, had vented on his younger friend. We can more readily see Caroline (Flachsland) with her easily yielding emotional susceptibility reflected in the figure of Psyche.

Pater Brey is really a duplicate of *Satyros*, admittedly varied for the lesser subject of the rather questionable and insignificant figure of Michael Leuchsenring. Leuchsenring had managed to insinuate himself into the Darmstadt circle for a time, and had taken the opportunity to do Herder some mischief with regard to Caroline Flachsland, the latter's fiancée. Psyche had shown herself to be vulnerable in this instance too! Pater Brey appears as a kind of pietistic faun, who exchanges spiritual conversations with Leonora, the daughter of a pious bourgeois wife, for only too obvious reasons. However Leonora's bridegroom, Captain Balandrino, a man with a simple peasant nature, has been warned of the danger. The Captain has a sense of humour: 'Let's cure the fellow once and for all and rub his face properly in the mud.' This then happens forthwith. Balandrino disguises himself as a rich nobleman, whose property, which had been neglected as far as the people and the animals there were concerned, is to be set in order again by the parson. The parson volunteers to cure the 'sodomite people' in the very jargon of the travelling pietistic apostle:

> Hab ich doch mit Geistesworten
> Auf meinen Reisen allerorten
> Aus rohen ungewaschnen Leuten,
> Die lebten wie Juden, Türken und Heiden,
> Zusammengebracht eine Gemein,
> Die lieben wie Maienlämmelein
> Sich und die Geistesbrüderlein.[2]

The community, which the parson has to free from the evil spirit, is however the herd of swine. The Captain's love for Leonora triumphs and the culminating point is the imperious dismissal of the parson at the end. It is the Captain, the realistic man of reason, who is responsible for this dismissal. He it is who is supreme, not only as lover, but also as a representative of honest common sense and down-to-earth realism.

Undoubtedly the wittiest piece of this productive period is *Götter, Helden und Wieland*, and at the same time it is the most impersonal-factual testimony of a literary political kind, a clear partisan satire, especially since Wieland was not even personally known to Goethe at that time. Certainly this persiflage thoroughly distorted Wieland's character, but it offered too a sufficiently eye-catching admixture of truth with regard to the notorious weaknesses of the Weimar Prince's private tutor, with whom

[2] Yet with spiritual words on my journeys to all parts I have brought together one community from rough unwashed peoples who lived like the Jews and Turks and Heathens. Like little lambs in May they love one another and their spiritual brothers.

D

Goethe (though he did not suspect it at the time) was soon to be in such close personal contact. The main target was Wieland's personal and literary vanity, as well as his religious hypocrisy, his limited standpoint, above all his frenchified mishandling of the Ancients. For a literary satire it proved to be a brilliant idea to confront the living Wieland, a Rococo pedant from top to toe, with Greek heroes, gods and poets dramatically in the underworld. Wieland is carried off there in a dream (complete with night-cap) in order to meet in person not only the author of *Alcestis*, Euripides, in whose footsteps he had followed with his recently produced musical comedy *Alceste*, but also the shades of all his characters, Admetus, Alcestis, Hercules. The shades themselves, however, are gigantic as against the miserable man from the eighteenth century (whose coolly insolent self-assurance they can nevertheless not shake, incidentally). They are Greeks in accordance with the standard of original genius, Wieland's opera figures on the other hand are 'hackneyed, affected, scraggy, pallid, sorrowfully croaking little puppets'. When Wieland sees the true Alcestis, he is astonished enough: 'You, Alcestis? With a figure like that! Pardon! I don't know what I'm saying.' But the compromising of Wieland and the century of Enlightenment, the gibes not only at his *Alceste*, but also at the vain self-opinionated comments in his lucrative journal, the *Teutscher Merkur*, must all be taken as of less importance as against the 'Storm and Stress' image of the Greeks illuminated here. Their greatness is measured here in terms of Herder's and Hamann's prototype. It is not based on stoicism – and hence it is aimed indirectly against Winckelmann too – but rather, in Lessing's sense of the term, on the greatness of feeling, even in the treatment of death, which Alcestis and Euripides shatteringly (and certainly not in Prometheus' sense) interpret in its total enormity. Hence Wieland's hypocritical moral philosophy is also thrown overboard: 'For virtue! How does the motto run? Have you seen virtue, Wieland?' asks Hercules, who thereupon degenerates into truly Götz-like bluntness when he contrasts the 'good fellow' with the mediocrity of the hero of virtue:

Hatte einer Überfluß an Kräften, so prügelte er die andern aus . . . Hatte einer denn Überfluß an Säften, machte er den Weibern so viel Kinder, als sie begehrten, auch wohl ungebeten.

Wie ich denn selbst in einer Nacht fünfzig Buben ausgearbeitet habe.[3]

That is Homeric coarseness, with the 'Storm and Stress' ideal of 'Kerl', just as Goethe's contribution to Lavater's *Physiognomik* on Homer bore the same stamp. We could say that a consciously powerful, naturalistic Greek image is here erected as a counterpart to the idealistically moralising one, of which 'your whole foolish age of *literati* is capable'. This amounted to an anti-morality attitude and hence meant too the devaluation of the Christian religion to the 'level of slavery'. The reality of an exuberant abundance of energy is offered in its place:

> Denn jetzt hängen dir noch immer die scheelen Ideale an, kannst nicht verdauen, daß ein Halbgott sich betrinkt und ein Flegel ist seiner Gottheit ohnbeschadet.[4]

These are the last words of wisdom which Hercules bestows on the dreaming little Rococo man in the night-cap. It marked the opening literary blow in the opposition to Wieland as a representative of a spineless rationality, and this was attested almost simultaneously, and without any connection with Goethe, by the *Göttinger Hain's* symbolic trampling underfoot of Wieland's works.

[3] If someone had an excess of strength, then he would soundly cudgel the others; if someone had an excess of juices, he would provide women with as many children as they desired, even if unasked. As I myself have procreated fifty children in one night.

[4] For now the cock-eyed ideals cling to you still, you can not digest the fact that a demi-god gets drunk and is a lout without prejudicing his divinity.

8 Werther

The work of Goethe's which, next to *Götz*, made the strongest impression on the age was the novel *Die Leiden des jungen Werthers* (*The Sorrows of young Werther*) (1774). Goethe's image was virtually established on the basis of these two works. The 'Werther costume' became the dress of the young people for a time. Even Napoleon at the time of that well-known conversation in Erfurt identified the poet Goethe and his work by and large with his concept of the author of *Werther*. The autobiographical facts that underlie the novel are well known. 'The easily stirred heart' of the poet ensnared him in the short time he spent in Wetzlar in 1772 into the already depicted ambivalent situation of a sudden consuming passion for Charlotte Buff. But she was already formally engaged, indeed to the lawyer Johann Christian Kestner with whom Goethe was also friends. Goethe hardly had the intention later parodistically imputed by Nicolai (*Die Freuden des jungen Werthers*, 1775) of deceiving his friend and taking his place. In this relationship the problem was not one of estrangement for the purpose of changing their respective roles in any bourgeois sense. The personal analogy can be seen more easily in the context of *Fels-Weihegesang, an Psyche* (Caroline Flachsland), where Herder, the fiancé in this case, must also have felt not too well-disposed. We must also take into account that the Goethe of these years simply yielded to the inflammatory nature of his heart, without reflecting on the consequences. Such was the case in Wetzlar. The emotionally charged tension that was apparent for a time in his relationship with Lotte and Kestner could easily have brought disaster for them all; this was probably only properly considered in the subsequent treatment in the novel of what had in fact been experienced. By that time, admittedly, Goethe had linked his own case with the fate of a young colleague in the

Supreme Court, the son of Abbott Jerusalem of Brunswick. The Legation secretary Karl Wilhelm Jerusalem had not been able to overcome the consequences of a social provocation and a love doomed to failure and had therefore committed suicide, for which purpose he had obtained the weapon from a friend (as Werther did in the novel). In this instance the friend was Kestner. After a most personal inner conflict that was finally overcome in his resolve to make a poetic confession out of that experience, Goethe now used a figure who met with a tragic end and with whom he himself could not be identified, despite all the biographical elements. Thus a blending process resulted, in which the end by suicide due to an overstrained susceptibility (or sensitivity) matched the Jerusalem affair, with which Goethe unhesitatingly amalgamated his own exalted feelings stemming from his relationship with Charlotte Buff and her fiancé.

What emerged was a 'sentimental character' that later served Schiller as a prime example:

> Es ist interessant zu sehen, mit welchem glücklichen Instinkt alles, was dem sentimentalischen Charakter Nahrung gibt, im *Werther* zusammengedrängt ist: schwärmerische unglückliche Liebe, Empfindsamkeit für Natur, Religionsgefühle, philosophischer Kontemplationsgeist, endlich, um nichts zu vergessen, die düstre, gestaltlose schwermütige ossianische Welt.[1]

The same is expressed in Goethe's own interpretation of *Werther*, according to which he

> mit einer tiefen, reinen Empfindung und wahrer Penetration begabt, sich in schwärmerischen Träumen verliert, sich durch Spekulation untergräbt, bis er zuletzt durch dazutretende unglückliche Leidenschaften, besonders eine endlose Liebe zerrüttet, sich eine Kugel vor den Kopf schießt.[2]

[1] It is interesting to see with what happy instinct everything that provides nourishment for the sentimental character, is condensed in *Werther*: ecstatic unhappy love, sensitivity to nature, religious feeling, a philosophic contemplative spirit, and last but not least, the dark ill-defined and melancholic Ossianic world.

[2] Endowed with a deep, pure sensibility and true penetration, [he] loses himself in ecstatic dreams, undermines himself through speculation, until finally deranged by further unhappy passions, especially a hopeless love, he blows his brains out.

The negative aspect could scarcely be more clearly demonstrated, especially to the youthful reader in that highly sensitive age. For him the depth of emotion which he felt in sympathy with Werther was the paramount factor, and the fate of Werther had to indicate certain tragic possibilities within his own subjective nature. And then there was the matter of the form as well: the epistolary novel (with occasional interpolated epic commentary of the narrator as editor). This was indeed the fashionable form of literary confession, derived in Germany principally from pietistic usages and only secondarily from Rousseau's example. This was a form that lent itself to the presentation of innermost thoughts as directly and candidly as was possible. The latter was, so to speak, a document of a specific moment of experience. But it is precisely this that provides the fictional aspect in the case of a character of Werther's genius, since for him too nothing changes so quickly and abruptly as the moment itself. Karl Philipp Moritz, with whom Goethe discussed aesthetics in Rome, well interpreted (*Über ein Gemälde von Goethe*, 1792) *Werther* from the point of view of style, in particular the sentence rhythm, as an inner movement of language, and emphasised the concepts of outline and completion and also the changes of 'rising' and 'falling'. Thus Werther's very essence is characterised in terms of language, in its switching from mood to mood, from exalted joy to exalted sorrow, the juxtaposing of the states of sublime joy and deathly depression, which also preconditions his downfall and his derangement. Since the heart has the final say, the will loses its autonomy. But the 'heart is weak'. And the hypertrophy of feeling signifies not only the setting-aside of the will, but also with it, the conscience. So long as the Ego determines his feeling for Nature, his artistic awareness, his attitude towards society and his passion for Lotte, Werther's reflections and actions remain consistently outside the realm of responsibility. He feels none towards Albert, his fellow men, work, and and none whatsoever towards Nature. It is this which exposes an existence based on pure feeling and mood as inevitably sterile. It is seen even in his passion for Lotte, which loses the dynamism of genuine passion, which should have aimed at supplanting Albert, instead of terminating in the most wretched confusion of the lovers and in endless self-torture. Even the ecstasy of death is here the ruination and resignation of the indecisive enthusiast, who finds himself disappointed again and again, since he continually makes exorbitant demands on life in the absoluteness of his feeling. Hence *Werther* is the complete opposite to an *Entwicklungs-roman*[3]. A development cannot take place in a situation where the hero gives way again and again. Thus the inner motive for suicide is implicit from the outset, as reality will not finally accommodate subjective claims and needs. It is a necessity, but it is certainly not fate. For his fate lies in his being Werther, and is not due to any other force. Lessing quite rightly saw, in a letter to Eschenburg (26 October 1774), the really counter-classical essence of the novel in this motive:

> Glauben Sie wohl, daß je ein römischer oder griechischer Jüngling sich *so* und *darum* das Leben genommen? Gewiß nicht.[4]

The proof for this state of affairs is easily provided. Wherever Werther makes a move, he acts emphatically, but without per-severance. The feeling of energy that dares to compete with the elemental forces (corresponding to the titanism of the odes) yields to the desperate knowledge: 'I am being manipulated like a puppet.' The inclination towards the simple human existence of the peasant and of the child interchanges with scorn for mankind. And even the oft-cited merging with Nature in its partly literal complementation of *Ganymed* remains subject to the transitori-ness of the moment. In the final event it is a misunderstanding of his own Self, for Werther can and will not give up his Self at all, or let it merge with Nature. He seeks only to confirm and in-tensify it again and again in new transmuted forms. So this rela-tionship with Nature is also sentimental, there is no sense of being transported as in the case of Ganymede, but is rather a forc-ing of the self into a condition of rapture (which in pietistic terms one might almost call the 'spiritual awakening') without possess-ing the requisite simplicity of the naïve person. (Klopstock and Ossian must be seen in this light too.)

If we look at the text, we have no difficulty from an analysis of the first letter (4 May, 1771) in ascertaining the cause, the insep-arable confusion of feeling and self-reflection. Werther begins

---

[3] *Vide* Glossary.
[4] Do you think that a Roman or a Greek youth ever could have taken his life in such a way and for such a reason? Certainly not.

there with the recollection of (Friederike-) Leonore in self-tor-
menting fashion and concludes this topic with the words: 'I *will*
enjoy the present, and the past *shall* be put behind me' [the
author's italics]. That is a programmatic note – but not a naïve
plan of campaign; it is the attempt at a fresh start, which is
basically however only a confirmation of Self, and is clearly forced.
And even the genuineness of his feeling for Nature cannot be
trusted in the artificial idyll which Werther had created for himself in the Count's garden, whilst shedding sentimental tears for
the 'feeling heart' of the designer. The well-known letter of 10
May and the complementary ones of 21 June and 18 August do
not contradict this. The 'marvellous serenity' which fills Werther's
whole soul in the May letter and which is really a prose counterpart to *Ganymed* in its identification of Werther with the 'breath
of the all loving God, who bears and sustains us suspended in everlasting joy', in fact signifies a mirroring of the godhead, yet at
the same time reflects the exorbitant demands of the Self:

> Aber ich gehe darüber zugrunde, ich erliege unter der Gewalt
> der Herrlichkeit dieser Erscheinungen.[5]

The letter of 21 June expresses then the disappointment which
follows the moment of blissful rapture at the view from the mountain:

> Ich eilte hin! und kehrte zurück, und hatte nicht gefunden, was
> ich hoffte. Es ist mit der Ferne wie mit der Zukunft! Ein großes
> dämmerndes Ganze ruht vor unserer Seele, unsere Empfindung
> verschwimmt sich darinne, wie unser Auge, und wir sehnen
> uns, ach! unser ganzes Wesen hinzugeben, uns mit all der Wonne
> eines einzigen großen herrlichen Gefühls ausfüllen zu lassen. –
> Und ach, wenn wir hinzueilen, wenn das Dort nun Hier wird, ist
> alles vor wie nach, und wir stehen in unserer Armut, in unserer
> Eingeschränktheit, und unsere Seele lechzt nach entschlüpftem
> Labsale.[6]

[5] But I am ruined because of it, I succumb to the powerful splendour of
these phenomena.

[6] I hurried there, and turned back, and had not found what I hoped. It is
the same with distance as with the future! A great radiant whole reposes
before our soul, our sensibility dissolves there, as does our eye, and we long,
alas, to give our whole being, to let ourselves be filled with all the joy of
one single great splendid feeling – and oh, when we hurry there, when the

On 18 August the comparison between the Then and Now is already drawn – in the past historic tense, even though, still in the *Ganymed* style, it embraces the 'inner glowing sacred life of Nature':

> Wie umfaßt' ich das all mit warmen Herzen, verlor mich in der unendlichen Fülle, und die herrlichen Gestalten der unendlichen Welt bewegten sich allebend in meiner Seele.[7]

It is, however, an 'Ah then!' feeling, for the present has changed the full and warm feeling of the heart into unbearable pain and suffering. Here Werther's universal feeling becomes total nihilism:

> Und so taumele ich beängstet! Himmel und Erde und all die webenden Kräfte um mich her! Ich sehe nichts als ein ewig verschlingendes, ewig wiederkäuendes Ungeheuer.[8]

That is Romanticism anticipated in every aspect: Jean Paul, Tieck, Wackenroder, the transformation of love fulfilled to *ennui*. It is the throwback to the enthusiastic intoxication of the odes that were filled with explosive feeling. Otherwise there is no thematic link with Werther's form of existence. The exclusively aesthetic enjoyment, be it of nature, or of love, entails the law of transitoriness. Since this highest enjoyment was unobtainable, it had to revert to melancholy. Or in line with Kierkegaard, it had to become 'an illness unto death', such as Werther in fact exemplified. Werther's passion, his fluctuating from one extreme to another, representing not merely a type current at that time, but also a mode of human existence within him based on feeling, is what gives the novel its standing even today. Seen in this light, the greatest epic prose work of the 'Storm and Stress' was signing its own death-sentence at the same time.

There becomes Here, everything is as usual and we stand in our poverty, in our restricted state, and our soul thirsts for refreshing liquid that has seeped away.

[7] How I embraced all that with warm heart, lost myself in the unending abundance, and the splendid figures of the infinite world moved all alive in my soul.

[8] And so I reel, disquieted! Heaven and Earth and all the creative forces around me! I see nothing but an eternally devouring, eternally ruminating monster.

PART III

New Subjectivity

9 Man as a Subject of Education and as a Religious Being

The 'Storm and Stress' had inherited from the Enlightenment the interest in the developmental potential and evolution of Man from childhood onwards. Even the young Herder adhered to this tradition. For it was from it that he took over the central position of the concept of education, even though, following 'Storm and Stress' ideas, he set up a new realistic pedagogical method and realistic pedagogical aims in direct opposition to the dominant philosophy of the century. And the same held true for Matthias Claudius and Johann Heinrich Pestalozzi. We could hardly think of them without Rousseau, but through the addition at that moment of religious elements there arose a new realistic kind of concern for the spiritual, for the natural as well as the differentiated intellectual side of Man. The *Erziehungs* – and *Entwicklungsroman*[1] and the autobiographical novel, unfolding, all of them, under pietistic influences, drew their central themes from this combination of factors. The child and the childlike person (and not just from the simple rural classes) embodied not only nature, but at the same time, as children of God, also spirit, the awakening, the observation and the controlling of which was seen as a concern both of practical pedagogy and of literature. The uncomprehended co-existence of nature and spirit in the world of children and young people created the complications and inner tensions which so often formed the subject-matter of the *Entwicklungs* – and *Erziehungsroman*. It appears, however, that this particular subject did not necessarily have to be treated in novels. With Claudius it was not treated in this way and Pestalozzi's

[1] *Vide* Glossary.

Lienhard und Gertrud did not maintain the novel form in the later volumes. The epic element nevertheless did predominate.

Matthias Claudius (1740–1815) came from an old Schleswig-Holstein clergyman's family, and received a solid humanistic education at the Grammar School in Plön. In 1758 he began theological studies at Jena, but changed to law since he did not feel the Church was his vocation. But he never completed his law studies either. In Jena he felt an antipathy towards the philosophy practised by the followers of Christian Wolff. Yet he had utilised his student days well enough, even if characteristically without material purpose as far as a job and livelihood were concerned. (He never possessed this sense of purpose. The later brief interlude in an official post as Senior Provincial Commissioner in Darmstadt in 1776 proved only a source of embarrassment, from which he hastened back to Wandsbeck as soon as possible.) He comprehensively assimilated classical and modern languages and literatures. Later he had cause to regret his sins of omission in the context of everyday life. Yet it was characteristic of him that he maintained a superior cheerfulness of spirit whilst constantly being in every kind of material plight, even later, when his large family was growing up. His home might have been in want of much, but this never led to a life of depression. He remained a modest, happy child of God, just as he became a friend of all the world with this very individuality of his. Nor was it his way to fall out with anyone. The estrangement of his friends Goethe and Voss was of their making. All this was characteristic of the figure of the 'Wandsbeck Messenger', of 'Asmus omnia sua secum portans'. A kindly Fortune took him first (following a temporary return to the family home) to Copenhagen and there into the circle of Klopstock, with whom he became close friends. All the same, the capital kept him but a short time before his rural homeland enticed him back again. Even Hamburg, where he commenced his journalistic work – the Hamburg of Lessing, Reimarus and Basedow – did not attract him as a metropolis. *Der Wandsbecker Bote* (*The Wandsbeck Messenger*), published by his and Lessing's friend Bode, and the editorship of which he himself took over in 1770, attached Claudius to this small outlying place, which combined proximity to the metropolis with rural seclusion. Here he set up house with the daughter of the Wandsbeck joiner in a life-long marriage spent in natural tranquillity and simplicity, a real idyll of family life at its happiest. And this was one of the prerequisites for the 'Wandsbeck Messenger' and formed an integral part of his life's work, simple in the best sense of the word, as seen in the serene, intimate poems to his wife and children or in the letters to his son John (which are somewhat reminiscent of Luther's letters to his children). Indeed, this man, perhaps the most affectionate of the many experts in friendship in that century, was probably the least sentimental of them. His realism was determined by the very naturalness of his family life.

This existence also forced him to collect his thoughts. It was the lack of subsidies which compelled him to be personally responsible for the publication of the *Sämtliche Werke des Wandsbecker Boten* from 1775 on, since his journalistic activities were not prospering. Bode's paper would scarcely have spread his fame beyond Hamburg itself. The edition of the complete works, however, although enjoying only a modest success in material terms, did just that and made him a name. Besides, it made him and the fictional 'Wandsbeck Messenger' independent of Bode, from whom he separated in the same year. Claudius, however, was to continue the *Wandsbecker Bote* until 1812 (eight parts in all); this constituted his life's work. His old age coincided with the confusion of the Napoleonic War, in which the family became entangled through the patriotic activities of the son-in-law, Friedrich Perthes. In 1813 Claudius had to flee from Wandsbeck and live almost a year as an emigré. That wore him out and brought about a speedy death.

Only the few quite outstanding minds of the 'Storm and Stress' had the good fortune to exert such a comprehensive effect both as persons and through their works far beyond the age which had conditioned their being. It was just this totality that constituted the new element when compared with the moralist weekly publications of the first half of the century, though, purely in terms of form, they also were an amalgam of prose and verse, a picture of morals, popular philosophy, aesthetics and pedagogy. But all this remained subordinate to the didactic aim of the Enlightenment (Pietism had its own religious weeklies). Now, in the *Wandsbecker Bote*, the educational and the religious elements are no longer separate. The most important thing, however, seemed to be that the New Man was proclaimed therein, the Man whom Hamann and Herder had in their mind's eye. There was no appeal here to understanding, not even in such absolute terms to ethical will, but rather to a Man of the people; a man conceived as a natural sensual being, still unspoilt, not yet broken by any idea of consciousness; a man then, who was still approachable in a natural sensual way and whose faith was not yet shattered. Hence it was possible to speak to him as a friend and father, as a spiritual adviser, and yet with humour at the same time. It was also possible to expect of him a concept of death as the goal of life – indeed it was a fundamental part of the whole idea from the very dedication of the first part of the *Wandsbecker Bote* to 'Freund Hein' (Death). This was something which, as for Hamann and Herder, signified absolutely no sacrifice of realism. On the contrary, the warmth and fervour through which Claudius was able to work on the reader in various guises becomes so impressive just through this very incorporation of the death theme. In addition, the unity of the changing forms was artistically guaranteed by the conception of a life that was quite naturally geared for death. It was a conception that contained not the slightest hint of any threat. For a comparison we must think back to the image of death in the baroque age. There it was the thought of transience, the very thought of annihilation, often represented hyperbolically. The world appeared to be delivered up to the skeleton and to putrefaction; the picture of life correspondingly appeared as fleeting, something not to be taken seriously by the metaphysicist. On the other hand we can observe the wonderfully fervent abbreviated form of the old *danse macabre* theme in Claudius's *Der Tod und das Mädchen* (*Death and the Maiden*): in the first strophe the almost wild resisting of the creature 'Pass, o pass by, wild skeleton' and the imploring cry to consider the lovable young life he wants to destroy, and in addition, in the following final strophe, the tender cautious care shown by Death, who addresses his victim thus: 'You beautiful, tender creature'; the bearer of a love that lies beyond the human, a love which takes the maiden in its arms to rock her to gentle sleep with intimate kindness, not cruelly, in the tradition of the *danse macabre*, not grotesquely, not even majestically, but fraternally. He is already an early brother of Hofmannsthal's figure of death in *Der Tor und der Tod*.

If we transfer this theme of death now to the 'Dedication' to Death, the 'patron saint and household god', we notice the same thing in a different, urbane form. Asmus says:

Und doch will ich glauben, daß Sie 'n guter Mann sind, wenn man Sie genug kennt; und doch ist's mir, als hätt' ich eine Art Heimweh und Mut zu dir, du alter Ruprecht Pförtner! [2]

Not the slightest romantic enjoyment of death vibrates in these sentences, nor is the baroque horror of death felt any longer. It is a fully realistic timid kind of acceptance, for which there is need of 'courage', 'nostalgia', and, at all events, trust. For Death is also the 'door-keeper' to Eternity, and he bears the familiar name of 'Alter Ruprecht'. In contrast, however, to the Baroque commemoration of death of, say, Gryphius, which grew out of a turbulent will to overcome the transient and earthly, Death is accepted as a companion in life, as similarly later in Hans Christian Andersen; and not for nothing does there appear again and again in the *Wandbecker Bote* the tranquil, organic image of seed and harvest, of germination and withering in the poems on death. The conflict with himself and the struggle for God, who nevertheless still exposes one's dear ones to death, (the theme that still determined Haller's Mariane-poems) is in the case of Claudius himself no longer essential in the poems on the death of his father or of the children. Death appears as one admitted to the ranks of house- and family-spirits. And that is the root of Claudius's humour. This never went, incidentally, so far as the Anacreontic poets' dallyings with the theme and figure of Death. Claudius's humour did not need to overstep the canons of taste, since in his case it was not a question of harmless witticism, but rather of the comprehensibility of a matter of the utmost gravity. This could find expression in various forms: in Klopstock's manner, as, for instance, in the ode-like poem on the death of his sister, *Der Säemann säet den Samen* with its Old Testament imagery and the Klopstockian symbol of the eagle who turns back to the sun. Or in the rhyming poems such as *Nach der Krankheit*, which deals with himself and his conversation with Death, who smiles, yet restores him to the joys of life. It could be the single strophe, in which the departed think back lovingly on those on earth; for death and love do have for Claudius a polar significance (*Der Tod*,

[2] And yet I want to believe that you are a good man, when one gets to know you sufficiently well; and yet it seems to me as if I had a kind of nostalgic feeling for you, and a sort of courage, Ruprecht, you old door-keeper.

Die Liebe). That is the basis for the thoughts on immortality conveyed in the seven letters Über die Unsterblichkeit der Seele in the fifth part of his work. Immortality is the principal thought occupying his attention too in the epitaphs which are linked in poetic form to the Wandsbecker Bote. The final strophe of the poem Bei ihrem Grabe makes a statement that is valid for all of Claudius's poems on death:

> Alle Mängel abgetan,
> Wird sie denn in bessern Kränzen
> Still einhergehn und fortan
> Unverweslich sein und glänzen.[3]

That suicide is self-deception is plainly self-explanatory (Auf einen Selbstmörder). So too is Claudius's reserved view of Werther.

The comfortable way in which life, limited as it was by death, found expression, corresponded absolutely to the idea of human existence itself being founded on death. The keynote in relation to life is not the pathetic 'joy' of Hagedorn or Uz, but a serene cheerfulness full of humour. This is more, too, than the positive note of the Anacreontics in their affirmation of life, which is presented as something worthy. The certainty of not being 'lost' at the advent of death worked as a kind of home-comfort in life, which could be enjoyed as a divine gift. Certainly that dionysian pathos which characterised the theme of joy from the Anacreontics up to Schiller was lacking in Claudius's treatment of that theme. Characteristically in his case it was confined to contentment and cheerfulness. But it had all the more reality for that, which resulted in the creation of a whole group of poems that became party-songs such as Bauernlied, Kartoffellied, Rheinweinlied or Urians Reise um die Welt. They all bear witness to a bourgeois existence which was based firmly on station, family and friendship. A warm human atmosphere raises them above the level of the Anacreontics, just as the style, too, rarely descends to the level of childish triviality. Certainly Claudius, the clergyman's son, was not a son of the people in the true sense. But seen in the light of Herder's Reisejournal he still had the essence of reality, possessed it more perhaps than the members of the Göttinger Hain, with whom he made friends. His close friend Voss could write the classical idyll

[3] All defects removed, she will then quietly move along in better circles and henceforth be incorruptible and shine forth.

Luise; Claudius, however, was not a writer of idylls in this sense. He was not concerned with transfiguring the rural atmosphere as such, but rather with the purpose of seeking out simplicity where it was still in existence. Therefore, even in the *Übungen im Stil*, the style of the man of letters, the piquant or brilliant, had not shown Claudius at his most successful; rather did he fare best with the 'child-like' style. We know that he had enjoyed considerable success with children's songs. Here he was even able to compose the charming lines of *Anselmuccio* to the longed for, but as yet unborn son. And the splendid song *Der Mond ist aufgegangen* represents the theme of childlike simplicity as the earthly goal: 'Let us become simple / and before you here on earth / be pious and cheerful like children!' – a clear antithesis to the Enlightenment pride in reason. It is on the same plane as the language of *Götz* – as the epistolary style of the *Wandsbecker Bote* also testified.

Claudius's credo of the simplicity of the people and the child must be seen on the basis of his view of nature and art. His aversion to textbook philosophy was no less than Herder's. He parodied it thoroughly time and again. It belonged to the artificialities of existence as much as did the new-fangled rationalistic doctrines on which he made repeated assaults. His childlike faith assessed art exactly in the same way. Humorously in *Serenata, im Walde zu singen*, the wood, allowed to grow free and natural, is contrasted favourably with the artificiality of the park, which does not sustain 'the great full heart / of motherly-loving nature'. *Ein Lied vom Reifen* expresses something similar in positive terms:

> Einfältiger Natur Genuß
> Ohn' Alfanz drum und dran
> Ist lieblich wie ein Liebeskuß
> Von einem frommen Mann.[4]

Here the true feeling for nature in flatly reserved for the simple people, the peasant folk. For the townsfolk on the other hand there is but 'art'. Amongst the *Kleine Geschichten* Claudius relates the anecdote of the European and the savage at the Niagara. The European opened

---

[4] Enjoyment of simple nature without much palaver about this and that is charming like a loving kiss from a virtuous man.

große Augen und untersuchte, und der Wilde legte sich, so lang
er war, auf sein Angesicht nieder . . . Was soll man daraus
lernen? Antwort: den Unterschied zwischen Natur und Kunst.[5]

Claudius's answer here is also theological to a certain degree:
the worshipping savage reacts in a natural fashion, the investigat-
ing European represents the 'artificial' Enlightenment.

If we finally reduce the numerous literary criticisms contained
in the *Wandsbecker Bote* to a single common denominator, an
almost startling uniformity is similarly revealed. Claudius scarcely
concerned himself at all with works of secondary importance.
What he brought to his readers in varying forms, consciously breaking or ignoring the terms of scholarly reviewing, were the really
important figures of the time: Lessing, Klopstock, Lavater, Wieland, Herder, Goethe, and from the Enlightenment Nicolai, too,
with his riposte to *Werther*. There is no question but that Klopstock and his odes, Lessing's *Minna von Barnhelm* and *Emilia
Galotti*, and Goethe's *Götz* were given a good reception. A feeling
for class was one of Claudius's qualities. But he likewise possessed
an originality of opinion. Herder, although he was a friend, indeed
the vital sponsor in the matter of Claudius's briefly held position
as Provincial Commissioner at Darmstadt, was treated with a
certain reserve on the subject of his theory of the human origin of
language. Claudius – like Hamann – preferred to believe in the
divine origin of language. Lavater's *Physiognomische Fragmente*
were in fact plainly parodied:

Soviel ich verstanden habe, sieht Herr Lavater den Kopf eines
Menschen und sonderlich das Gesicht als eine Tafel an, darauf
die Natur in ihrer Sprache geschrieben hat: 'allhier logieret in
dubio ein hochtrabender Geselle! ein Pinsel! ein unruhiger
Gast! ein Poet; 'n Wilddieb! 'n Rezensent! ein großer mutiger
Mann! eine kleine freundliche Seele! etc. etc. – Es wäre sehr naiv
von der Natur, wenn sie so jedwedem Menschen seine Kund-
schaft an die Nase gehängt hätte.[6]

[5] his eyes in surprise and explored, and the savage lay down face to the
ground, full length . . . What is the lesson to be learned from that? Answer:
the distinction between Nature and Art.
[6] So far as I have undestood, Mr Lavater looks at the head of a human
and sees in particular the face as a board, on which Nature has written in
her own language: 'Here dwells *in dubio* a bombastic fellow, a simpleton,

Just as uncompromising as his attitude towards everything over-
enthusiastic was his awareness of the dangers inherent in going
to the opposite extreme, as, for instance, in the case of Wieland,
whose *Neuer Amadis* was felt by Claudius to be pure cynicism,
the deadly enemy of the simplicity that he himself represented:

> Ich bin vom Dorfe und kenne die Welt nicht; Mode mag das
> sein, das will ich gar nicht streiten . . . Es hat mir neulich
> jemand sagen wollen, daß in Schriften dieser Art die Tugend
> gelehrt werde. Hm! Tugend gelehrt! . . . Das hieße wohl den
> Bock zum Gärtner gesetzt.[7]

Even *Werther* was praised, in fact, for its naturalness, because
it 'knows how to draw the very tears right from one's eyes'. However for Claudius, given his attitude towards suicide, the work
could only appear as a testimony of human weakness, which he
countered with Man's similarly innate virtue. That then naturally
led to Claudius giving a fairly positive appraisal of Nicolai's
Freuden des jungen Werthers:

> Muß sagen, daß 's Büchel, ob Albert gleich größer und Wer-
> ther kleiner darin gemacht sind, doch 'n feines Büchel sei, und
> viel bon sens, wie die Gelehrten sagen, enthalte.[8]

This finally resulted in a break with Goethe. On the whole, con-
forming to the uncontentious constructive style of this poet and
popular educationalist, the literary criticisms contained in the
Wandsbecker Bote were also uncontentious, though the religious
viewpoint of the writer was never abandoned. Yet Claudius
advocated a religion of tolerance, as the fifth of the letters to
Andres in the fourth part programmatically expressed in connection with the Jews: 'Let us not condemn, Andres!' Since his
whole nature was averse to every blunt 'either – or', this position

---

a restless chap, a poet, a poacher, a reviewer, a great stout-hearted man,
a tiny friendly soul, etc. etc.'—It would be very naïve of Nature if she had
pinned such information concerning everyone on each respective nose.

[7] I come from village life and do not know the world. Fashionable that
may be, I will not dispute it . . . Someone tried to tell me recently that in
writings of this kind virtue is taught. Hm! virtue taught! . . . That really
means 'setting the fox to keep the geese'.

[8] I must say that this little book, even though Albert is made greater
and Werther less important in it, is still a fine book and contains much
bon sens, as the scholars say.

was fully compatible with his aversion to autonomous reason. Its application to the human sphere found expression in his praise of friendship:

> Aber eigentliche Freundschaft kann nicht sein ohne *Einigung*; und wo die ist, da macht sie sich gern und von selbst.[9]

Claudius's aversion to the French Revolution, therefore, was not so much a politically conservative decision as a basic condemnation of war as a crime:

> 's ist leider Krieg – und ich begehre,
> Nicht schuld daran zu sein![10]

It was quite logical, therefore, that he did not condemn the dancers around the scaffold in *Klage* (1793), but pitied them and had the chorus accompany their action with 'Have mercy upon them'.

All this would seem to remove Claudius from the 'Storm and Stress' and its attitude to every revolution. But we must not forget that, as was to be seen in the case of Pestalozzi, Claudius's pacific temperament, tolerance and anti-revolutionary attitude similarly aimed in positive fashion at a different picture of Man from that of Hagedorn, Gleim, the Anacreontics, indeed even Lessing's *Nathan*. It was neither as idyllic nor as intellectual. It was realistic in the sense of Herder's *Reisejournal* and Goethe's *Götz*, even though it was based more narrowly on devout simplicity than on simplicity *per se*. But by virtue of this the type of the 'scholar', the rationalist, was exposed here by Claudius no less than in the militant 'Storm and Stress'.

Beside the impact which stemmed above all from the first parts of the *Wandsbecker Bote*, we have to set the forceful effect of the Swiss Pestalozzi's *Erziehungsroman, Lienhard und Gertrud* (1781–87), or, to be more exact, that of its first part. The two works are related in spirit and in historical setting, between the Enlightenment and the 'Storm and Stress'. Johann Heinrich Pestalozzi (1746–1827) was not a writer in the primary sense as was Claudius. The priority for him lay in the practice of education and also in its theory, but above all in education as a practical

---

[9] But real friendship cannot be without *accord*; and where this occurs, it happens easily and of its own volition.

[10] Unfortunately it is war – and I don't wish to bear the blame for it.

science. This citizen of Zürich, who had suffered many reversals of material fortune and whose progressive educational institutions were not financially supported by the public, lived to a considerable age. His famous attempts to mould orphans and paupers within the spirit of family upbringing into able human beings – and to do so although it involved the highest personal sacrifices – belong to the history of humanity as much as to the history of pedagogy. That Goethe cold-shouldered him when Pestalozzi turned to him in one of his crises, was very much out of character. For Pestalozzi had in fact originally started from Rousseau, however had progressed to Kant and was close in his view of man and culture not only to Claudius and the social ideas of the 'Storm and Stress', but also to the spirit of Weimar. The pedagogic aspect in *Wilhelm Meister* would be hardly conceivable without the ideas which the author of *Lienhard und Gertrud* had disseminated in practical and literary form. As already mentioned, the literary aspect was really not an end in itself for Pestalozzi. His early hymnic-rhythmic attempt *Die Abendstunde eines Einsiedlers* (1780) proved this only too clearly. If the first, the real novelistic part of *Lienhard und Gertrud* achieved a world-wide reputation in its day, this was not due to any intentional artistic form. Karl Philipp Moritz's psychological novel *Anton Reiser*, which had appeared simultaneously with the conclusion of the third volume of *Lienhard und Gertrud*, was a far more artistic piece of work and one aiming at an aesthetic effect, than Pestalozzi's 'Volksbuch'. A similar situation befell him as later occurred to Gotthelf: the epic values transcended the spiritual-educational conception, which was itself not aesthetic.

Here, too, as with Claudius, the realistic element already constituted a programme:

> Ich suchte sowohl das gegenwärtige Historische als das folgende Belehrende auf die möglichst sorgfältige Nachahmung der Natur und auf einfache Darlegung dessen, was allenthalben schon da ist, zu gründen. (*Vorrede*).[11]

And Claudius could just as easily have used the ensuing examples

---

[11] I sought to base both the contemporary historical and the subsequent didactic element on the most careful imitation of nature possible and on the simple exposition of what was already to be found everywhere. (*Preface*)

from Luther and the rabbi's tale as proof of his view of history, with their realistic and spirited message. We may find it remarkable that, quite differently from the intentionally varied and loose form of the *Wandsbecker Bote*, a compact epic pattern is woven here, which is organised into paragraphs, in fact a hundred in all. That points to a strict plan, almost comparable to the form of a law. (Lessing's *Erziehung des Menschengeschlechts* (*On the Education of the Human Race*) also consists of exactly one hundred paragraphs.) Moreover the paragraphed chapters have epic titles, which relate back in terms of form not only to the didactic and entertaining epic of the Reformation period, but have also their own dramatic character, since the recapitulatory element takes second place to the note of inference, so that after the reading of the book the appositeness of what has been related should stick in one's memory. Certainly this exact structuring is linked with the type of work that Pestalozzi intended, namely 'a book for the people', for nothing could be exact and perceptible enough for the people. However a story was incorporated in these hundred paragraphs. In the first place it unfolds as a story of family-, and then village-life, but all the events are imbedded in a sense of civic order, whose incorruptible representative is the good district governor Arner. It deals with the fortune of the family of Lienhard and Gertrud and their children. Lienhard is a poor mason, honest and 'kindhearted', but all too prone to visiting the inn. The real prop of the family is the mother Gertrud, who is primarily responsible for the children's upbringing and education. She is a splendid figure who proves herself in every situation in life. Lienhard's antagonist is mine host of the village inn and deputy governor Hummel, who has a dark criminal nature, an intriguer, the village bloodsucker. And between them ranges a crowd of peasants and minor village people, all of them delineated with highly individual characteristics: devout people, labile characters, obstinate or penitent sinners. The whole is magnificently controlled, the characters are clearly drawn. Alongside the governor stands the priest, the representative as it were of the eternal order, which Pestalozzi however wishes to identify with the civic order. At the end, he also does this in an impressive symbolic manner. The theme of the novel is the struggle for the spiritual wholesomeness of a family preserved intact, for the parental ideal, on which the well-being of the children depends, and against the depravity of the world represented by the landlord Hummel and his band of dependent cronies. All the threads of intrigue are picked up in the figure of Hummel: the tempting of the village peasantry to drunkenness, and of the dependants to perjury and every kind of wrong-doing, which is intended to destroy Lienhard. The reader looks into a thoroughly realistic abyss of village life, in which nothing is idealised, as occurs so frequently in later village stories. That state of affairs goes on until the deputy governor finally hoists himself with his own petard, when in the night he plans to remove a boundary-stone in the mountain forest on the Squire's estate and believes himself to be caught in the act by the Devil. And yet this realistic view of avarice, vindictiveness and superstition is in fact only a foil for what is to shine forth all the brighter as integrity, kindness, love, temporal and eternal order.

This is the world of the three ideal figures: Gertrude, Squire Arner and the parson. In accordance with Pestalozzi's intention, it is they who have strength on their side in the end, because it is an inner strength, a superiority of the heart over all the intrigues of the age. It finds expression in what Gertrud teaches her children:

> Ich bin gern selber mit euch fröhlich, ihr Lieben! Aber wenn man in Freude und Leid ungestüm und heftig ist, so verliert man die stille Gleichmütigkeit und Ruhe seines Herzens.[12]

At the same time the contrast of good and evil corresponds psychologically speaking to the contrast between peace and unrest or anxiety. Here we find not only the prototype of the ideal family and the basis of all educational upbringing, but also the element of purity in the midst of a world assailed by poverty and vice. The similarity to the attitude of the 'Silent in the Land', the affinity to pietism, is unmistakable. And so this characteristic of Pestalozzi must be seen as springing from the same source, without which the 'Storm and Stress' is entirely inconceivable despite its revolutionary air. This is as true for Pestalozzi as for Claudius. The pietistic impact on literature is also discernible in the interesting theme of § 89, which is contained in the wise verdict of Arner on Hummel:

> Hierauf sollst du in das Dorfgefängnis hier in Bonnal geführt werden; daselbst wird dein Herr Pfarrer ganzer vierzehn Tage

---

[12] I like to share your happiness, my dears! But if one is impetuous and passionate in joy and sorrow, then one's tranquil equanimity and peace of mind are lost.

deinen Lebenslauf von dir abfordern, damit man deutlich und klar finden könne, woher eigentlich diese große Ruchlosigkeit und diese Härte deines Herzens entsprungen sind.[13]

This evidence the parson has then to impart to the parish from the pulpit, but this unfortunately does not happen until the second volume, which had already gone beyond the limits of the original conception. (The sermon on his past life would have been a much more impressive conclusion to the novel with its own built-in tension, than that presented in the final § 100.)

A remarkably fascinating atmosphere permeates this novel, so representative of the end of the 'Storm and Stress' period. It is not pervaded by the temperateness of the Enlightenment; the determining factor is the love and humanity of simple piety. And indeed, again as with Claudius, it is a piety that lives not only in the confines of the church, but which also extends its influence outside it. The 'world' – in this case the village – is encompassed by it. It is an expression of Pestalozzi's realistic fulfilment of Rousseau: his view of the 'spoilt' condition of nature. In this sense Pestalozzi is a greater realist than Claudius, who with the same 'fulness of heart' remains to a greater degree an idyllicist in contrast to the Swiss. Yet this is no longer true of Pestalozzi's second 'Volksbuch' *Christoph und Else* (1782), in which the moral tone dominates the epic quality.

A characteristic type of novel, which derived its initial impetus from Pietism, can be seen in this work of Pestalozzi, as already shown in the life story of the criminal that is incorporated in the judgment passed on him. What here appears as a reckoning before the earthly judge is really at root a man's autobiography as a confession and a self-reckoning before God. But as a result of this development, in the course of which pietism became in diverse ways involved with literature, that type of 'diary of an observer of himself' (Lavater) with all the psychological elements which it contains is aestheticised and thus assumes a more or less intended novel form. This development could be described as a secularisation of the pietistic autobiography or diary with a confessional character. Just as pietism in Lavater's *magnum opus*, the *Physiogno-*

---

[13] You are hereupon to be led to the village prison here in Bonnal. In that place your priest will demand from you within fourteen days the facts of your life, so that we can find out clearly and unequivocally whence this great profligacy and this hardheartedness really derive.

mische Fragmente (1775–78), was directly transformed into aesthetic psychology, so too in the cases of Jung-Stilling, Theodor von Hippel and Karl Philipp Moritz there developed distinct epic forms characterised by both the sobriety and factuality of pietistic self-reckoning, as well as its psychological accuracy penetrating to the very heart of the matter. There is no doubt that even *Werther* belongs historically to these types of secularisation as an epistolary confession. Jacobi's novels too, indeed Friedrich Schlegel's *Lucinde*, can be counted amongst them.

Of all these the most precise piece in the biographical sense is probably *Heinrich Stillings Jugend* by Johann Heinrich Jung (1740–1817), which Goethe published in 1777. In Jung-Stilling's life story (*Heinrich Stillings häusliches Leben*, 1789), Goethe's intervention is described as one of God's many acts of providence, especially as Goethe's letter with the honorarium reached Jung in a moment of extreme need. The later parts, one of which under the heading of Stilling's *Lehrjahre* is in imitation of Goethe, give an account of this, but they have nothing like the charm that exists in the story of his youth and childhood, which is what really concerned Goethe. When Jung, the later eye specialist, Heidelberg professor, and Honorary Privy Councillor, produced the subsequent parts of his life-story for publication, he had gradually become so set in the routine of his own style, that here, as with *Lienhard und Gertrud*, it was really only the first version which had any true value. To be sure, this is a gem of a faithful, realistic and honest appraisal of his own past. With a heartfelt intensity that reminds one of Claudius, and insight into the psyche of the child and youth, reminiscent of Pestalozzi too, he presents the life of poverty as an inner richness. The charm of the whole lies in the combination of epic realism and subjectivity. The first lapidary sentence immediately provides a hint of this realism:

> In Westfalen liegt ein Kirchensprengel in einem sehr bergigten Landstriche, auf dessen Höhen man viele kleine Grafschaften und Fürstentümer übersehen kann.[14]

The end of the tale of youth deals on the other hand with the profound experience of the sight of his grandfather's grave, over

[14] In Westphalia there lies a parish in a very hilly district, from whose heights one can survey many small shires and principalities.

which the doves fly in spring and on which grass and flowers flourish 'from Father Stilling's mouldering remains'. To be sure, this subjectivity is not free from sentimentality, yet we do not find here the sentimentality that is an end in itself, as illustrated in Miller's novel *Siegwart* or Sophie von La Roche's *Geschichte des Fräulein von Sternheim*, but rather a warmth and enjoyment of life which reflects the spirit of the period to some considerable extent; piety, sensibility and imagination of that kind could be found among petit-bourgeois folk living within small communities in the eighteenth century. For the closest knit circle is (in the sense of Gotthelf and Raabe) here full of matters of world-wide significance. Not only the experience of convincing individual figures ranging from the grandfather, middle-aged clergymen and rural schoolteachers, or the experience with individual children in the village teaching-posts, Heinrich's employers during the training period, amongst them the mysteriously benevolent figure of Herr Spanier, but also the whole formative world of mystical pietism, very much alive amongst artisan classes (Gottfried Arnold, Jacob Böhme, Paracelsus), crystallise in Heinrich's educational journey. And not only those. The story of his youth is further interwoven with songs, popular ballads, chap books, which Heinrich relates and which the girls sing, without one becoming aware of their interpolation. Not only is one's imagination accordingly aroused, but a characteristic feature of the later Romantic novel as well as *Wilhelm Meister* is anticipated. What occurs in the *Wandsbecker Bote* as a variety of autonomous individual forms, appears here within the binding epic structure in an integrated form, which later was by no means always achieved by the Romantic novel.

A further link between Pestalozzi and Jung-Stilling is the concern with teaching. Jung-Stilling experienced its problems and tested his ideas on it in numerous teaching posts, and in the course of his experiments some ideas occurred to him which strike us as quite modern. Here too the autobiography is a true expression of the time with its educational needs, its educational experiments.

The fact however that education starts from the home, that the forming of the soul takes place by means of the earliest experiences of contact with others and its development occurs in the confrontation between childhood and the impact of the world –

this is what links Jung-Stilling's autobiographical novel with Pestalozzi's pedagogical one, and in the final analysis with the *Wandsbecker Bote* as well. Never again did Jung-Stilling achieve the sense of realism attained in the autobiography, either in the *Geschichte des Herrn von Morgenthau* (1779) or in the *Geschichte Florentins von Fahlendorn* (1781–83).

At the same time as the publication of the first parts of the *Wandsbecker Bote* there appeared the *Lebensläufe nach aufsteigender Linie* (1778–81) of Theodor Gottlieb von Hippel (1741–96). Hippel was one of the odd products of Baltic pietistic circles. He was a bachelor, originally a theologian, then a lawyer, and as such he succeeded in becoming Mayor of Königsberg, acquired, despite all his pietism, considerable wealth, and was raised to the nobility. His conduct matched his eccentricity, as, for example, in the erection of an imitation cemetery in his garden, something his financial means permitted him to do. All in all, he was a remarkable amalgam of worldly wisdom and economic realism on the one hand and religious sentimentality on the other. It was no wonder that a later epic work *Kreuz- und Querzüge des Ritters A bis Z* (1793 f.) was modelled thoroughly on the style of Sterne. It is a mixture of grotesque humour and irony towards the nobility and freemasonry, from whose unnatural ranks and classes the hero, the knight von Rosenthal, finally emerges into the natural state of matrimony. Here everything is quite different from what we find in Pestalozzi or Jung-Stilling: humour is employed as persiflage, not with candid seriousness. The intention of his main work, the *Lebensläufe*, was a kind of chronicle of a family or at least a generation, in which besides his own life that of his immediate forebears, his father and grandfather, were to be presented. In fact only the account of his own life was given (nevertheless it filled four volumes!), but in no way was it so historically clear and so devoid of intentional novelistic traits as in the case of Jung-Stilling. The literary intention, the Sterne-like mannerisms were already manifest in a detailed introduction addressed to the reviewers:

Ich – Halt! – Ein Schlagbaum – Gut – wohl – recht wohl – Ein wachhabender Offizier! – Wieder einer mit einem Achselbande zu Pferde – zu Fuß – von der Leibgarde! – von der Garde der gelehrten Republik – ich ehre ihre Uniform, meine Herren – und damit ich Sie der Mühe überhebe, mir die üblichen Frage-

stücke vorzulegen, mögen Sie wissen, daß ich – wie der Paß
und Taufschein es ausweist – ein Schriftsteller in aufsteigender
Linie bin.[15]

That shows the step into the aesthetic realm, which the genre of
the autobiographical novel had taken. No longer was self-reckoning or even religious confession proffered, but a deliberate
artistic form (which derived its style from Sterne and Swift as
well as from his countryman Hamann). The conscious address to
an imagined literary public is clear. From the literary-sociological
point of view, too, the times had changed. Yet there still remained
in common with Jung-Stilling the recognisable precision of presentation, despite Hippel's tendency (similar to Herder's) towards
anonymity. Hippel insisted even on writing 'not a novel, but
a factual account', on presenting the 'common life'. Actually, the
reservation became null and void through a dialectic trick.
Hippel indeed wanted to present not a novel but a factual account,
but he found at the same time that 'everything in the world is a
novel'. And so the distinction between 'a factual account' and
'novel' obviously disappears. It demonstrates clearly how much
Hippel's work differs in type from Jung-Stilling's life-story, and
the difference is confirmed by the fact that there is an autobiography of Hippel existing separately, from which, by means of
retrospective comparison, the autobiographical elements in the
Lebensläufe can be partially ascertained. On the other hand, what
distinguishes the Lebensläufe from the Kreuz- und Querzüge is
the predominance of humour over the later satire. Above all in
the depiction of childhood of the Baltic pastor's son, the work
excels in a naturalness which recalls the story of youth in Wilhelm
Meister. The Hercules-saga, which the father found especially suitable pedagogically speaking, is presented with fascinating grace:

Die Geschichte von Antaeus, dem Riesen, war mir ein Brand
im Busen; mein Vater goß Öl dazu und maß mir seine Länge
vor: ich stieg auf den Tisch, um sie recht zu sehen, und so wie

---

[15] I – wait a moment – a turnpike – now – very well – an officer on duty –
and one with a shoulder sash on horseback – on foot – from the body-
guard – from the guard of the learned republic – I honour your uniform, sirs
– and that I may spare you the trouble of putting the usual questions to
me, you might like to know that I – as my papers and birth certificate
prove – am a writer with a rising star.

ich mich über die Art des Antaeus freute, sich einen Löwen zum Braten zu fangen, so gratulierte ich dem Herkules, daß er diesen Löwenjäger totzudrücken die Ehre gehabt.[16]

Not only the child, as it absorbs these tales, but also the father as an educator, in the spirit of the period, stands out impressively akin to Herder, when the son can say of this educational experience, 'I learned nature'. In fact this happens in a Rousseauistic manner, namely through the experience that one becomes wise through misfortune. Indeed, the father adds his own doctrine of genius:

Wenn ein Genie allein auf dem Lande geht . . . bleibt es nicht lange allein, die Natur geht ihm an die Hand, und es versteht die Blume, wenn sie sich neigt . . .[17]

As in *Lienhard und Gertrud* and in Jung-Stilling, family life is the starting-point and the link with the later world at the same time. And from this basis the story of childhood proceeds to the story of youth, which includes too the no less charming first love for Minchen, the companion of his youth, all of which is richly conveyed in the sense of the Age of Feeling, yet in a credible psychological manner. His youthful love is driven to her death by a seducer from the nobility. The story-teller leaves the university and becomes a Russian soldier. At Pyrmont, while his wounds heal, he gets to know another girl, whom he marries after a bewildering series of misfortunes. Here the story becomes so sentimental that it almost reminds one of Gellert's *Schwedische Gräfin* (*Life of the Swedish Countess of G.*). The figures of the two loved ones merge into one in the mind of the lover. This is literature and no longer nature, just as other themes in the later parts are overemphasised, for example the infatuation of the pious Count with pictorial death symbolism, which is an almost self-gratifying interpolation. In this book too, as in those of Pestalozzi and Jung-

---

[16] The story of Antaeus, the giant, was for me a burning flame in my breast. My father poured oil on it and in my presence measured its length. I climbed on the table, in order to see it properly, and as I found pleasure in the way in which Antaeus caught a lion for roasting, so I likewise congratulated Hercules on having the honour of killing this lion-hunter.

[17] If a genius wanders alone in the country . . . he does not stay alone for very long, nature takes him by the hand and he understands the flower when it bends its head . . .

Stilling, the parts dealing with childhood and youth are the most convincing. The Enlightenment and 'Storm and Stress' unite here in their passion for education and the spiritual problem of childhood and youth, for the development of individuality and its prerequisites. The analogy to Herder's historical awareness is only too clear.

10 Man as an Aesthetic Being

Autobiography became still more definitely a work of art with Karl Philipp Moritz (1757–1793). Moritz came from sectarian petit-bourgeois circles, from a similar social background to Jung-Stilling's, with whose career his own had certain affinities. There was a difference in that the Hamelin family house and his apprenticeship as a hatmaker in miserable conditions produced a form of religion that was passionate, indeed on occasions fanatical rather than tranquil. Here penitential pietism was linked with the quietistic teachings of Madame de Guyon, as the autobiographical novel was to depict with considerable accuracy. He was the impoverished scholar dependent on clerical and secular patrons, the theologian in Wittemberg supported by the *universitas pauperum*, who slipped into the world of the theatre and was for a short time a teacher at Basedow's Philanthropinum in Dessau. He finally obtained Grammar School teaching-posts at the Potsdam Orphanage and at the 'Graues Kloster' in Berlin. By 1786 however he had had enough. He left his job in order to go to Italy. The reason was that he wanted to catch up on the cosmopolitan culture hitherto denied him. And the breadth of his formulation of aesthetic questions in the *Versuch einer deutschen Prosodie* (1786), in the *Götterlehre oder Mythologische Dichtungen der Alten* (1791) and in the already mentioned *Werther* interpretation of 1792 justified this pretension. He probably experienced the high point of his life as an acquaintance and protégé of Goethe, who in Rome was everything to him for a time. A few years only were granted him after his return to a new post at the Academy of Arts in Berlin. Then consumption brought his life to an end.

The literary work which was to ensure the recording of Moritz's

E

name in the history of literature is *Anton Reiser, ein psychologi-scher Roman* (*Anton Reiser, a psychological novel*) (Parts I–III 1785–86, Part IV 1790). The later novel *Andreas Hartknopf* (1786) is scarcely more than a shadow of its predecessor and even the story of the artist *Die neue Cäcilie* (1794) is devoid of literary merit so far as can be seen from the residual fragment. Not for nothing did *Anton Reiser*, a *nomen odiosum*, have the sub-title 'a psychological novel' a full century before the advent of Naturalism. In it Moritz evaluated the empiricism of pietistic self-observation and the Enlightenment doctrine of sensation in his own highly individual manner and translated it into an 'experimental psychic doctrine' or, as he called it in a magazine published during the decade before his death, 'applied psychology'. In this magazine he collected utterances of self-observation, which he found, for example, in the related works of Jung-Stilling.

The sub-title of *Anton Reiser* is therefore a valid one. Moritz has presented important experiences of his own youth, above all the religious milieu in which he grew up, obviously recorded with faithful accuracy over long stretches. The milieu is determined by Quietists, who have founded a sect in Pyrmont under the leadership of a Herr von Fleischbein, isolated from the world. The members of this 'small republic' are 'persons whose efforts were directed, or seemed to be directed, solely towards a return to their "nothingness" (as Madame de Guyon called it), towards "eliminat-ing" all passions and extirpating all "idiosyncrasies" '. The open-ing of the novel is full of mystical terms of this kind, expressly abstracted as quotes ('inner language', 'departing from one's own self', 'blessed quiescence'). Since Anton Reiser's father is an adherent of this sect, the figure of its leader stands as a constant threat of doom over all decisions which are reached in respect of the life of the boy Anton. The quintessential feature is constantly the presumed success or failure of the child according to the standards of the sect. Whether the boy, who is desperately keen to gain knowledge, is helped in his desire to study or not, depends on his religious 'progress', even later on, when the cleric, Pastor Marquard, becomes his patron (and judge). The real psychological problem consists in the acceptance of this given situation by the boy, who measures himself by the same standards. And so there results an often precipitous interchange of humble submission and opposition, feelings of sin and ecstasy. With intense conviction it is shown how visionary imagination, genuine self-perception and a moving assimilation of education are juxtaposed time and again with sudden reactions and depressions, an urge for reality and a tendency towards illusion. This process of inner confusion is induced, last but not least, by the coolness and lack of esteem with which the social world in which he finds himself treats this child and youth who is so in need of affection. Time and again there are situations of humiliation or hostility reaching the very limits of what is humanly tolerable; there are repeated raptures of the soul in prayer and good intentions, and the mockery and scorn of his fellow men. The constant temptation to fall into a state of complete demoralisation is not overcome by the Christian weapons of the conventicle. It is rather education that affords this true child of the century the weapons of thought and imagination, with whose aid he somehow picks himself up again and again. But at what price? Anton Reiser builds within himself a religious-aesthetic world of imagination, in which the heritage of the conventicle mixes with the effects of literature and of philosophy, in which he passionately immerses himself at different times. Here the lad, growing up, constructs for himself a bulwark which, the stronger it becomes, contrasts all the more with the miserable realities of daily life. Anton Reiser's problem in life is that of overcoming this conflict. Here his inner exaltations and his external frustrations are decided. Here too is to be found the superior artistry through which Moritz demonstrates his abilities as a creative writer. The success or failure of his novelistic hero is never presented other than as being psychologically motivated and carefully conceived down to the finest nuance.

In Moritz's novel the religious comfort dissolves increasingly in the face of reality. Education is a soothing means of stilling his pain, yet it is no real protection, but rather a source of new vexations. The solution of Claudius and Stilling, just like Pestalozzi's confidence in the ability of the world to improve itself, accordingly fails in Moritz's case. The author of *Anton Reiser* is more desperate. And so the melancholy of his hero reaches deeper than the sentimental sadness of the age. It can turn into a self-hatred that is already almost Kierkegaardian:

Daß er einen Tag wie alle Tage mit sich aufstehen, mit sich schlafen gehen – bei jedem Schritte sein verhaßtes Selbst mit sich fortschleppen mußte . . . Daß er nun unabänderlich er selbst sein mußte und kein anderer sein konnte; daß er in sich selbst eingeengt und eingebannt war – das brachte ihn nach und nach zu einem Grade der Verzweiflung, der ihn an das Ufer des Flusses führte.[1]

He therefore entertains thoughts of suicide from self-disgust. But why this intensification which is not in fact motivated in the Wertherian manner? Moritz has carefully let the feeling of 'rejection' mature in his hero with the fullness and increasing excitability of his imagination. The above-mentioned, so Kierkegaardian rejection of himself as being no longer 'acceptable' is really the expression of aesthetic melancholy and not of unfulfilled passion as in Werther. For again the high points of rapture match the low points:

Er las Macbeth, Hamlet, Lear und fühlte seinen Geist unwiderstehlich mit emporgerissen.[2]

Here too is the catch-word for the world into which Anton Reiser finally was to break out: the theatre. These sections too are partly autobiographical, being taken from Karl Philipp Moritz's own temporary life with a travelling troupe of actors. By a remarkable coincidence they date from the same period as Goethe's 'Urmeister', the Theatralische Sendung, which Goethe, when he got to know Moritz in Rome, in fact still kept as a fragment amongst his papers, so that neither can have known of the existence of the other's creation. Shakespeare, even if no longer the Herder version in fact, is the linchpin here too. Moreover Anton Reiser's renunciation of the bourgeois life in favour of the theatre is as temporary as it was for Wilhelm Meister. The wanderings of the hero, beginning in Part III, end in Part IV with the bankruptcy of the troupe, whose deceitful chief actor had sought the wide open spaces with the proceeds from the theatre wardrobe. 'The Speich company

---

[1] The fact that day after day he had to rise with himself, go to sleep with himself, had to drag his hated Self with himself at every step . . . that he now had to be himself irrevocably and could be no other, that he was enclosed and restricted in himself – all that brought him gradually to a degree of despair, which led him to the river bank.

[2] He read Macbeth, Hamlet, Lear and felt his spirit irresistibly transported.

was therefore now a scattered herd.' So runs the final sentence of
the concluding Part. A solution to the theme of wandering and
fantasy *ad infinitum*? Moritz himself in 1790 said of this last part
of his large-scale novel:

> Er enthält eine getreue Darstellung von den mancherlei Arten
> von Selbsttäuschungen, wozu ein mißverstandener Trieb zur
> Poesie und Schauspielkunst den Unerfahrenen verleitet hat . . .
> Eigentlich kämpften in ihm so wie in tausend Seelen die
> Wahrheit mit dem Blendwerk, der Traum mit der Wirklichkeit.[3]

Moritz did not provide the solution to the conflict, yet he did
not point to its insolubility either. He had given a hint at the
end of the preface to Part IV as to *how* the differences might be
resolved. In the end he himself was too much Anton Reiser to have
wanted to expose his own later fate as a solution in the novel. So
it rested with the presentation of youthful development with its
errings and follies, which fascinates in its form that is an end
in itself. Here the two decisive problems of the 'Storm and Stress'
decade have taken on a timeless air: the development and education of man, and the function of the theatre in that process.
Moritz, who presents both these problems, accordingly stands here
as a genuine partner of Goethe.

With the novels of Friedrich Heinrich Jacobi (1743–1819) we
return to the time of Goethe prior to his Italian journey. Jacobi
also has his place in the history of philosophy, not only through
his *Briefe über die Philosophie des Spinoza* (*Spinoza-Büchlein*)
(*Letters concerning Spinoza's Philosophy*), which has already been
the subject of discussion, but also through his confrontations with
Kant, Fichte and Schelling. The 'philosopher of feeling' remained
during his lifetime fundamentally an opponent not only of rationalistic logic, but also of every kind of logic, in so far as the
'systematic belief' in it developed into opposition to the real
philosophy of faith. What Friedrich Schlegel maliciously formulated in the concluding sentence of his famous review of Jacobi's
second novel *Woldemar* is valid in other respects too for this
philosopher of feeling:

[3] It contains a true picture of various kinds of self-deception, to which a
misconceived drive towards poetry and the theatre has spurred the in-
experienced man . . . In fact within him as in a thousand souls truth fought
with delusion, dream with reality.

Und das *theologische Kunstwerk* endigt, wie alle moralischen Debauchen endigen, mit einem Salto mortale in den Abgrund der göttlichen Barmherzigkeit.[4]

From the theological angle, that is no tribute, yet it does strikingly characterise Jacobi's philosophy as a philosophy of faith. It allies him, for example, closely to Hamann, even if it does not do justice to the latter's dialectics. As a writer Jacobi belongs to the historical development of the German novel in its phase of introspective realism. Through an enormous number of friendly contacts, which found expression in correspondence, Jacobi (like Claudius) was very much part of the contemporary literary scene.

The son of a Rhineland merchant, he had to take over the family business, but four years of apprenticeship in Geneva furthered above all his inner development in the spirit – and the circle – of Rousseau. There impressions crowded upon him, which were to remain with him throughout his life. Until 1772 he acted the merchant figure in accordance with the role determined for him, and without, incidentally, jeopardising the family business. Then he abandoned this first of all for the Civil Service and afterwards withdrew to private life in the grand style. His house at Pempelfort became a meeting-point during the 'Storm and Stress' and the subsequent period too, just as Gleim's house in Halberstadt had been for the Anacreontics. Goethe even stopped there as a guest for some weeks. For over twenty years Jacobi extended the most open hospitality, and it says much for his character that in 1794 he resolutely gave everything up, when the French revolutionary armies were at hand. He withdrew to North Germany, to Claudius, to Eutin and Emkendorf. He spent his old age in Munich, where in 1804 he became President of the Academy. Schelling's attacks marred his enjoyment of this position, yet he did not return to his native Rhineland.

Both his novels bear the mark of his friendship formed in 1774 with the author of *Werther*. In Goethe he experienced the power of genius as a reality and this he sought to capture in *Eduard Allwills Papiere* (*Eduard Allwill's Papers*) (1775–76, revised 1781, final version 1792) and *Woldemar* (1779, expanded 1794),

---

[4] And the *theological work of art* ends, as all moral debaucheries end, with a *salto mortale* into the abyss of divine compassion.

which was expressly dedicated to Goethe. As is mostly the case, the first attempt is the most original: *Eduard Allwills Papiere* antici- pates most of *Woldemar* in its presentation of man and the prob- lems of life. As so often too at that time, *Allwill* pretends to be an imaginary correspondence with a fictitious friend as editor. In the introduction the work is expressly described as 'not a novel', in order to intensify that illusion. Sylli comes from a patrician family, she loses her mother early on; her father, 'tor- tured by an insuperable passion to the very point of madness', enters a monastery. It is *eo ipso* an emotionally 'confused situa- tion' right from the beginning. She then marries her childhood friend August Clerdon, a Swiss. Yet the marriage becomes prob- lematic, especially as Sylli lives in stronger spiritual harmony with her husband's brother Heinrich. This friendship finally works up to the 'purest angelic chorus'. After they have been married three years Sylli's husband dies, leaving her in confused and muddled circumstances. In the years after his death she writes the letters from a spiritual state which can be comprehended 'only through sympathetic insight'. In addition to the persons named, others appearing in the correspondence of the spiritual friend Heinrich are Frau Amalia, two cousins of Sylli, her brother Clemens von Wallberg and the key figure of Eduard Allwill together with his earlier love Luzia.

What friendship can be in the sentimental and directly pre- Romantic sense as a form of, and substitute for marriage, appears almost provocatively in this fictitious epistolary exchange between men and women. It is characteristic that the atmosphere is heightened and expressed not as with Werther, through literature (Homer, Ossian, Klopstock), but quite predominantly through the feelings, to which one's own fate and experience react. The psychology of friendship and love, meditations on human fate and existence, an extreme feeling for nature – all interact. The direct affinity to Early Romanticism before the latter had come into being is remarkable from several viewpoints. Perfect synaesthesia in the Tieckian sense characterises, for example, Clerdon's feelings for nature:

Wer an einer Musik für das Auge zweifelt, der hätte diese Mor- genröte sehen sollen. Ein solcher Engelsgesang schwebte mir nie

auf Tönen in die Seele. Doch was weiß ich, mit welchen
Sinnen ich empfand? Ich war außer mir![5]

The fact that this ecstasy passes directly into the 'releasing tremor'
of the enjoyment of death shows the truly pre-Romantic emotional
tension. Sylli's approaching nihilistic crisis over the idea of fate
is no different. As in Wackenroder's *Herzensergießungen* (*Outpourings from the Heart of an Art-Loving Friar*) the naked holy
man goes mad over the thought of being delivered to the horribly
monotonous movement of the wheel of time, on whose spokes he
knows himself to be bound, so with Jacobi the uselessness 'of all
human activity and being' is likewise clad in a mechanistic
symbol:

> *Den Gang im Kranen* mit zugeschlossenem Auge rennt jeder
> vorwärts in seinem Rade, freut sich der zurückgelegten Bahn;
> weiß so viel Torheiten, so viel Jammer hinter sich und merkt
> nicht, daß nah an seinem Rücken alles das wieder empor-
> steigt ...[6]

This Romantic consistency both in ecstasy and in terror forms too
the basis for the psychology of the sensual egoist Allwill; he anticipates the William Lovell type of person, but without the latter's
degeneration into criminality. In Allwill, as revealed first indirectly
and then in his own letters, we find an elemental man of moods,
an egoist, an example of the defiant and self-confident 'Storm and
Stress' genius with Rousseauistic traits. His nature is already
established in the story of his childhood as told by Clerdon:

> Wie er bei seiner heftigen Begierde nach sinnlicher Lust, bei
> seiner Unbesonnenheit im Handeln doch immer grübelte und
> mit ganzer Seele an unsichtbaren Gegenständen hing; wie er
> hierüber zu Ansichten gekommen, deren Größe sein ganzes
> Wesen zerrüttete, ihn bis zur Ohnmacht drückte; so, daß er, um
> den Anwandlungen davon zu entrinnen, sich oft die Hände
> blutig biß oder gar sich die Treppe hinunter in den Keller

[5] He who doubts in a music for the eye, should have seen this dawn. Such
angelic song never wafted on notes into my soul. Yet what do I know, with
what senses I perceived? I was beside myself!

[6] Everyone runs forward on his treadmill wheel with eyes closed and is
glad at the distance that appears to have been now covered. He believes
that so many follies, so much distress, are left behind him and does not
realise all that is again mounting up behind his back.

wälzte; wie er endlich im vierzehnten Jahr ein Pietist geworden . . .[7]

All this is a product of originality and genius, i.e. it is uncontrolled and unbridled in every direction. And Jacobi at once establishes explicitly that these qualities remain true of him as youth and man. What emerges is a man well versed in the art of love, a connoisseur of women, a *bon viveur* with extravagantly lofty as well as base feelings. Small wonder then that he invades the peace of the letter-writing family, referring everything to himself in the unconcerned fashion of the genius, naturally appealing to Rousseau:

> Holde Mutter Natur! o wie laut sagt mein klopfendes Herz mir da wiederum, daß doch allein auf deinem Pfade wahres Heil zu suchen ist![8]

Since it suits him best, he defines virtues as 'immediate natural impulses'. Besides which the whole argument of men of genius, possessed of untamed energy, versus worldly wisdom, morals and fine sentiments is given full treatment. And so in consequence Allwill shows himself to be an earthy and sensual realist, a man of will working for his own ends. Reason is thus driven from this picture of the world:

> Es ist die hohlste Idee von der Welt, daß die bloße Vernunft die Basis unserer Handlungen sein könne . . . Am Ende ist es doch allein die Empfindung, das Herz, was uns bewegt, uns bestimmt, Leben gibt und Tat, Richtung und Kraft.[9]

Whenever Allwill confesses to this 'faith in my heart', then in every instance the affinity in terms of behaviour and self-observa-

[7] How, in his violent desire for sensual pleasure, in his rashness in action, he would constantly brood and cling with his whole soul to invisible objects; how he would reach views on all this, views whose magnitude unhinged his whole being and drove him out of his mind, so that, in order to break free of these fits, he often bit his hands till the blood came or even rolled down the steps into the cellar; how at last in his fourteenth year he had become a pietist.

[8] Sweet mother Nature, O how loudly my beating heart tells me anew that on your path alone true salvation is to be sought.

[9] It is the most hollow idea in the world that reason alone can be the basis of our actions. In the end it is only feeling, the heart that moves us, determines us, gives life and action, direction and energy.

tion to the type of person such as Werther appears extremely great. The question how far Goethe's friend – always easily influenced – repeats Goethe here or whether one must look upon Allwill as a riposte, indicating that he had grown beyond the Werther type with the help of his devout acceptance of a philosophy of feeling, is at all events resolved in the later versions which make it clear that Werther is rejected. But even the first version of 1775–76 in fact ends with the condemnation of Allwill by Luzia, whom he wanted to teach to live 'this unending life'. Here the genius is unmasked, unsparingly because she loves him, exposed in all his egocentricism, which can sacrifice man, through his self-indulgence in utter extremes:

Tigers-Sinn und Lammes-Herz; allgegenwärtig – und nirgendwo; alles – und nie etwas – verdammter zwiefacher Mensch! Unschuldiges, himmelaufsteigendes Blut Abels, und mörderischer, flüchtiger Kain! Ja! – [10]

That seems clear enough already. Yet there is a continuing difference between the first version and the later modification, namely a certain self-fascination through such original genius, a secret moment of grief at its corruptness in the face of so much triumphal strength and indomitable self-assurance. A negation and a compromising of Allwill's character are inevitable, but his presentation is visibly in part enjoyment still, the self-enjoyment of the 'Storm and Stress'.

As is so often the case in this genre, Jacobi's second novel *Woldemar* is, particularly from the anthropological angle, to a large extent a repetition of the *Allwill*-theme. The human and temporal problems of this had clearly not been solved for the author in the slim and loose collection of letters of the first novel. The first version of *Woldemar*, too, later – at the time of the Early Romantics – underwent revision and remodelling, to which Friedrich Schlegel (for it was something bound to concern the author of *Lucinde* intimately) devoted a profound discourse. The novel opens with an enthusiastic dedication to Goethe. On the other hand the preface ends with Herder. The basic form on this occasion is the epic, even though letters are interspersed. The

[10] Tiger mind and lamb's heart – omnipresent and nowhere – everything and nothing – accursed twofold man! Innocent blood of Abel ascending to heaven, and murderous, fugitive Cain! Indeed!

action takes place within bourgeois circles, revolving around the three daughters of a rich merchant, their marriages and friendships. The most significant of the daughters belonging to the self-assertive merchant Hornich is Henriette. Between her and Woldemar, her brother-in-law's brother, there develops the decisive relationship *à deux* (and then *à trois*). Woldemar, once again the man of feeling *par excellence*, is attracted by her, but at the same time resists her spiritual qualities and marries her friend Alwine, as it were in protest against the inner spiritual attraction which Henriette expects of him. Woldemar's conflicting position between the two women – he would like, so to speak, to come again on bended knee to Henriette; she for her part, as a true friend, supports Alwine in her position as Woldemar's wife – forms the real psychological motivation in the novel. In it Woldemar's human nature develops in all its complexity and not just in the relatively simple trait of mental confusion. As regards the technique of the novel, Woldemar's character is again revealed indirectly; it is presented in the form of a letter received by the Hornich family right at the beginning of the novel: he is a man of immediate sensitivity, close to tears and fainting, whenever emotion overcomes him. This situation can be induced by nature as well as by man, even by the mere reading of a letter from his brother. Man appears to him to be posited between heavenly purity and instability:

> Er vermag überall zuviel und zuwenig: darum nichts *Ganzes*, nichts *durchaus Bleibendes* . . .[11]

Here we come to the heart of the matter as far as the figure of Woldemar is concerned, the kernel, so to speak, which is encapsulated by merely a husk of man-of-the-world superiority and adroitness of manner. It separates him from bourgeois life and its society, in which he finds himself placed within the Hornich family circle. In this he resembles Werther more than Allwill, though when it really matters, he seems more controlled than the latter. If Woldemar, socially speaking, asserts his point of view, a standpoint of '*Simplicity! More and ever more simplicity and truth!*' (in another context it is termed 'individuality'), then 'free nature', which he absolutely refuses to see shackled even in horticulture, spells the doom of his own personality. Yet the conflicts of his dual love for

[11] Wherever he turns he can do too much or too little, and so there is nothing total, nothing thoroughly permanent.

Henriette and Alwine are not those of the artist of seduction and self-deception as in the case of Allwill, but really the necessary inner experiences of a 'free naturalist'. However, they appear as it were incorporated into the basic conflict of the 'Storm and Stress', namely that between nature or elemental force in general and 'art' in the sense of the unnatural or artificialisation. The fact that the confusion of emotions, although a consequence of the intensity of feeling, does not end in Werther's fate, but in reconciliation with both the women of his affection, is not so much the consequence of their sentimental noble-mindedness as rather of Woldemar's ability to cultivate 'humility', which certainly was not part of Werther's nature. If Friedrich Schlegel calls this conclusion a 'moral debauch', one can refute this with the fact that Jacobi had indeed envisaged from the outset the possibility of the *'salto mortale* into the abyss of divine mercy' as a quintessential aspect of Woldemar's character. To this extent this novel is an anti-Werther piece of writing even more than *Allwill*. In its general bent it is no more a 'theological work of art', as Schlegel ironic-ally termed it, than *Lienhard und Gertrud* or *Anton Reiser*. Except that Jacobi has at his command neither the realism of presenta-tion as found in Pestalozzi nor that of Moritz's psychology. His novels therefore, especially the later one, are really border-line cases: attempts to give epic form to what in the final analysis is a philosophical picture of man, to give contemporary expression to the *Geniezeit*. Yet already at the same time they constitute no longer a glorification, but a tragic limitation of genius.

Numbered amongst Jacobi's house-guests was Johann Jakob Wilhelm Heinse (Heintze) (1746–1803), a Thuringian by birth, but scarcely less an Italophile than Winckelmann and Goethe. A protégé not only of Gleim, but also of Wieland, he already be-longed to the early period of German Classicism in terms of the subject matter of his work with his passion for Italy and Greece, though in terms of form he belonged to the 'Storm and Stress' movement. If we like, we can say that he was at times the very embodiment of the Woldemar figure, which in itself sufficiently explains Jacobi's affection for him. Like *Woldemar*, Heinse's novels *Ardinghello und die glückseligen Inseln* (*Ardinghello and the Islands of Bliss*) (1787) and *Hildegard von Hohenthal* (1796) represent to a certain degree a bridge between 'Storm and Stress' and Romanticism. Heinse's activity as a translator of Tasso and

Ariosto and also previously of Petronius, which provides a significant indication of his early taste, bears testimony to the direct impact of Italy, where he spent almost four years. It is almost surprising that his life and work as a practical exponent and theoretician of the 'Storm and Stress' did not 'run into the sands', but that he completed his career with a scholarly position at the court of the Elector of Mainz. His decision to convert to Roman Catholicism provides a remarkable analogy to the Romantics.

Ardinghello, to which Heinse really owed his literary fame, signifies historically a kind of culmination and high-water mark of the 'Storm and Stress' novel as a whole. It was a high-water mark, because here in a certain sense the basic *Geniezeit* themes crystallize on a universal plane: a culmination, because at the same time hints of a classical viewpoint emerge everywhere.

There may well remain reservations as to how far *Ardinghello* is a *Künstlerroman*,[12] as it is mostly claimed to be. Certainly the hero Ardinghello-Frescobaldi is a painter. Yet there can be but little doubt that he is more a man of action, for whom life and activity are ends in themselves, and that the deed as his means of achieving a utopian vision of life, weighs more heavily than his artistry. It is stated so several times in the novel itself. Perhaps *Ardinghello* belongs then rather to the type of Utopia as projected in Hölderlin's *Hyperion*, with which it has much in common. Furthermore the utopian character is not limited to the idea of freedom established in the city-state on the Cyclades, to which the action moves, but embraces even the preceding situations facing the hero Ardinghello, which are, in a manner of speaking, already utopias of free love and constantly successful deeds. Certainly Ardinghello is a person of the type of Allwill and Woldemar. But Heinse was far from even having in mind – perhaps out of affection for his friend Jacobi – a devaluation or ruination of that particular type. On the contrary: sensuality and aesthetic enjoyment of the world in general, which are shown as present in the heroes of Jacobi's novels and at the same time refuted on moral-theological grounds, are presented by Heinse in an extreme form and made to appear fully justified. One after the other, all women whom he desires fall to the handsome, shrewd, felinely adroit Florentine nobleman and painter bursting with energy. The fact that at the end he gathers them almost all around him like a harem on

[12] *Vide* Glossary.

the islands of bless is certainly not meant to be ironic, even if it unintentionally produces that side-effect. Fullness of the heart has become fullness of the senses. The bacchanalian orgy in Rome, in which the artists and their Phrynes abandon themselves to the intoxication of nudity, is only one of the phenomena of the en-flamed senses and exuberant vitality, which are here pronounced the highest ideals. The aesthetic existence in a state of perfect freedom – freedom understood as self-realisation in the feeling of vital strength – appears synonymous with life and nature. Such a matter-of-course manifestation of vital energy is already right at the outset the saving of the young Venetian from the flood waters. The taking of Cecilie and her release from her unloved husband by a well-directed thrust of Ardinghello's dagger on the wedding day follows just as naturally. Similarly in Genoa, Ardinghello appears like a young god who must succeed in everything, in order to snatch Fulvia and Lucia from the pirates and thus be victorious even over them. Magnanimity towards the bravest of the captured corsairs gains him his new friend for life, Diagoras, who is later to procure for him his 'islands of bliss' from the Sultan. He then appears victorious in his native Florence and no less so in Rome, where he experiences the crowning of his intoxication with life. He has always been involved in intrigues. Now too there is murder and manslaughter surrounding Fiordimona, the Pope's niece and great courtesan of Rome. All these adventures terminate in Arding-hello freely joining forces with the Turkish corsairs of Diagoras and finally, although it is merely hinted, in the founding of a utopian state on the Greek islands.

In terms of the problematical issues involved and motivation, Heinse's *Ardinghello* proves itself clearly related to the products of Jacobi's pen and also typologically close to Haller's *Staatsro-mane*. With regard to the form, this kinship is detectable in the amalgam of epic presentation and epistolary novel. Not only a fantasy of love is here developed, but also one of beauty and the State. And the latter aspect in no way unfolds solely from Arding-hello's inner being. The lengthy conversations with his Roman friend Dimitri, a Greek by birth, revolve primarily around inter-pretations of Plato and Aristotle and a whole host of writers of classical antiquity. In Ardinghello's letters to his Venetian friend, which form the basis of the course of action, the discussion is equally as specific. Here in a mixture of reflection and feeling is provided almost a kind of 'Storm and Stress' Baedeker guide to the art-centres of Italy, just as the discussions on Titian, Veronese, Michelangelo and Raphael form an essential part of the novel. In this respect then, the work is not a true *Künstlerroman* with regard to Ardinghello's life – for it does not concern itself with the conflicts or happiness of his (secondary) existence as a painter – yet it is a novel dealing with the aesthetic subject of art. These conversations on art and criticisms of artists, plus the enthusiasm that is paramount everywhere, link *Ardinghello* almost directly with that type of novel which Tieck's *Sternbald* was to inaugurate. Even the theme of *ars amandi* is not really naturalistically treated, but remains closely connected with the aesthetic problems of form. The feeling for nature plays an important role, indeed both as an intoxicated viewing of, and identification with the elements, (significantly with the wild, stormy and unending sea in particular), as well as one of the most profound forms of the feeling of existence and strength, in which, as in love and art, man in communion with nature experiences himself.

Indeed, 'nature' stands at the centre in every respect and counts as essential even for art, in which the mere artisans and experienced practitioners play a wretched role as against the 'true, genuine persons' with their 'vibrant heart'. The aesthetics of the 'Storm and Stress' rule supreme in *Ardinghello* in particular, where the 'solemn gothic cathedral with its massive open space' makes possible veritable storms, indeed 'hurricanes' of pious feeling, while the mere imitation of the Greeks, 'be it after the style of the prettiest temple to Venus by an Athenian of the very best taste, has no effect at all upon a man with an unperverted mind'. The decisive factor is the 'unperverted mind', that is: nature. This finds expression in man as fire, as passion. 'Accents of nature' is what Heinse terms the lyrical intoxication of Ardinghello's speeches and songs:

> Es war bezaubernd, dem jungen Schwärmer zuzuhören, und wie in lächelnder Kühnheit das Feuer aus ihm wehte.[13]

Indeed, it is a kind of intoxication of friendship and love, which is here experienced. Thus the views on education contain, fully in keeping with Rousseau, the demand for self-education: 'All nature,

---

[13] It was enthralling to listen to the young visionary, and how the fire wafted from within him in smiling audacity.

if it is to be great and splendid, must freely enjoy the air.' The originality of the child must first grow, 'otherwise a parrot emerges'.

As far as originality is concerned, the people in the novel leave nothing to be desired. Here too there is not the Wertherian mental confusion, but rather unity with oneself in the intoxicated stirring of the senses and the excess of passion.

> Liebe und Geist ist eins und dasselbe unter verschiedenen Namen, nur daß man Überfluß von Geist Liebe nennt.[14]

Pain and sorrow accordingly belong together with happiness, through which strength prevails against all resistance. This strength is the basic feeling that overcomes all abysses. Hence the joy derived in a stormy sea or the very transformation of Pan's hour into a menadic dynamism:

> Unten schien der See zu kochen und eine ungeheure Feuerpfanne von geschmolznem Silber; Eidechsen, Käfer, Mücken und un- zählbare Insekten hielten in der Glut ein allgemeines Fest und die Grillen betäubten mit ihrem Gezirp wie ein Meerbrausen die Ohren.[15]

We notice the difference to Werther's letter of 10 May, how in Heinse everything is far less idyllic, and we note the difference to Jacobi, whose occasional sentimental frenzy remains dull by contrast. Despite the similarity of many subjects touched upon in *Ardinghello* and of educational topics in *Woldemar*, genuine emotion rules supreme in Heinse, where there is only reflection in Jacobi; observation and with it a measure of feeling of strength, where in Jacobi there appear but pale thoughts and self-assurance broken by sentiment. And for this reason Heinse's novel must have its utopian conclusion. A failure on the part of the hero or his refutation would have contradicted the basic concept, which, whilst anticipating individual classical problematical situations, probably embodied the 'Storm and Stress' spirit and self-assurance in its purest form.

[14] Love and spirit are one and the same under different names, save that one calls an excess of spirit love.

[15] Below the lake there seemed to boil a monstrous censer of molten silver; lizards, beetles, gnats and innumerable insects were holding a communal feast in the glowing fire, and the crickets with their chirping deafened one's ears, like the roaring of the sea.

PART IV

Varieties of Inventive Genius

11 Goethe's Friends of Genius and their Prototypes

In 1776, the year following his move to Weimar, Goethe had to ward off – not without some effort on his part – a kind of invasion, when an attempt was made by those protagonists of the belief in genius, who stressed primeval energy as the chief ingredient of genius, to capture for the 'Storm and Stress' the Weimar court of the muses, where the Duke at that time was still only too inclined toward extravagant pranks. At that time Goethe's friends from his youthful days at Strassburg and Frankfurt, Klinger and Lenz, came to Weimar and they were joined by the Swiss 'apostle of energy' Christoph Kaufmann. To Goethe these shades of his own immediate past were extremely embarrassing. For Lenz and Klinger immediately did their utmost to compromise themselves and hence indirectly Goethe too, whose position in Weimar had attracted them thither. Basically this was the moment of truth for the *Geniebewegung*, although it was only then that it acquired the name by which it was to be known in the History of Literature, namely 'Storm and Stress'. At Kaufmann's instigation this was substituted as the title for the drama with which Klinger made his debut in Weimar. The drama was really called *Wirrwarr*. This original title quite clearly did not fit in with Goethe's new position of responsibility in Weimar. When both were asked to leave (how far this was due to Goethe's initiative is questionable), his inner separation from the friends of his youth was only too manifest. The abstruse plan of conquering a princely court for the 'Storm and Stress' with its revolutionary or at least distinctly anti-monarchical tendencies was nipped in the bud. The unhappy Lenz, already at that time mentally disturbed, and Klinger with his confused self-consciousness were quite naturally the victims. We must remember, however, that in that same year of 1776 Goethe invited Herder to Weimar as Church Superintendent in the principality, if we wish to take cognisance of Goethe's change of attitude in this situation. Herder too had been spokesman of the 'Storm and Stress', yet never an 'original genius'. In Herder, Goethe summoned the really creative mind behind the 'Storm and Stress' to its rightful place. On the other hand in the case of Lenz and Klinger he freed himself from the dubious side of his youthful excesses in terms of human qualities and, to some degree, actual behaviour.

Jakob Michael Reinhold Lenz (1751–92), son of a clergyman of German origin and later Superintendent General of Livonia, had studied theology in Könisberg but had not completed his studies. A post as private tutor, begun in 1771, led him, together with the Kleists, his pupils, to Strassburg where his and Goethe's paths crossed. There in Salzmann's circle he took over from Goethe the role of *spiritus rector*. Unfortunately he also similarly assumed the role of Friederike Brion's paramour and became the author of poems which bear such affinity to Goethe's Sesenheim lyrics that the authorship of some pieces remained disputed for a long time. Dating from this period, too, were Lenz's *Lustspiele nach dem Plautus* and his first social drama *Der Hofmeister* (*The Tutor*), which Bert Brecht considered important enough to adapt. Even in his Shakespeare interpretations Lenz followed closely in Goethe's footsteps with his *Anmerkungen über das Theater nebst angehängtem übersetzten Stück Shakespeares* (*Remarks on the Theatre*) (1774). The highpoint of their relationship was probably the spring and summer of 1775, when Goethe visited Strassburg again on his Swiss trip. Lenz had meantime made himself independent of the Kleists and intensified his awe of Goethe to the point of fanaticism. His literary farce *Pandaemonium Germanicum* gives a composite picture of his opinion of Goethe and the priorities in the literature of the day. Yet his relations to the World and Man remained unhappy, of secondary importance so to speak. Just as at first he was impassioned over Friederike Brion, so he now became inflamed with a grotesque passion for Henriette von Waldner, whom he did not even know personally but only from her letters. Her engagement to another man brought to light his latent melancholy. Yet even in this situation he still retained his creative powers. His second social drama *Die Soldaten* (*The*

Soldiers) (1776) originated in this period of personal entanglement, as did too his novelistic fragment *Der Waldbruder* (1776) and the comedy *Die Freunde machen den Philosophen* (1776). In that same year he left Strassburg to set off for that sojourn in Weimar which has already been mentioned. 'Between ourselves, Lenz is like a sick child' was Goethe's initial comment to Merck on this subject. But sympathy declined when Lenz became a lampooner, not even sparing Goethe's relationship with Charlotte von Stein. And so it led to Lenz's expulsion, which more or less meant the beginning of the end for him. He was still socially in evidence at the Emmendingen home of Schlosser, Goethe's brother-in-law, and in Basle and Zürich he still made an appearance in the related circles of Lavater and Pfeffel. But Lenz was already destitute and facing a crisis of despair. In Winterthur at the house of Christoph Kaufmann his mental illness became acute, an illness which could no longer be alleviated even with treatment in the house of the pastor Oberlin in Alsace (1778). Georg Büchner was later to analyse this period in his *Lenz*. Finally his family brought him home to Livonia but this in fact offered him no respite. He did not become completely apathetic, but was still able to teach in Russia. He died in Moscow on the open street.

Alongside the dramas with their social themes, the lyric poems constitute Lenz's real significance. There is expressed in them both a deeply subjective relationship to his fellow men reflected in friendship and love as well as his own particular form of feeling for life and nature. A poem like *Nachtschwärmerei*, though still influenced by Klopstock, fully expresses in concrete terms the vibrancy of genius: it contains childhood reminiscences of the times of unhindered oneness with 'Mother Nature', sacrifice and feeling of the 'whole heart' as an 'enflamed youth', longing for the infinite, a breaking out from the 'too restricting atmosphere', culminating in stuttering verses to Goethe and his Beloved. It is noteworthy how frequently here the word 'heart' and the image of burning and the flame are used. Yet this feeling for life is also to be found in compact form in a poem like *Lied zum deutschen Tanz*:

> O Angst! tausendfach Leben!
> O Mut, den Busen geschwellt,

Zu taumeln, zu wirbeln, zu schweben,
Als ging's so fort aus der Welt!
Kürzer die Brust
Atmet in Lust,
Alles verschwunden,
Was uns gebunden,
Frei wie der Wind,
Götter wir sind![1]

Here feeling for life (as awareness of genius), feeling of absolute
freedom, systole and diastole, rhythm and rhyme truly have become utterly one. But this goal was not often granted to Lenz,
since, however heartwrenchingly done, he mostly linked his own
experiences of life to others. In *Nachtschwärmerei* or in *Lottes
Klagen um Werthers Tod* Goethe's image is supreme. But Jacobi's
Allwill too incites him to expression of his own feeling for life:

Nein, ich schreie – Vater, Retter,
Dieses Herz will ausgefüllt,
Will gesättigt sein; zerschmetter
Lieber sonst dein Ebenbild![2]

Lenz himself is speaking here to be sure, but he is expressing
himself with clear reference to the literary stimulus of Jacobi,
whose figure he sees engaged in struggle for happiness in life like
Jacob and the angel. Lenz bears the 'mortal wound deep in [his]
breast', but his extreme subjectivity is mostly mixed with such a
stimulus. The muse of the poet Lenz is never completely his
own:

O Homer, o Ossian, o Shakespeare,
O Dante, o Ariosto, o Petrarca.
O Sophokles, o Milton, o ihr untern Geister . . .
Gebt mir tausend Zungen für die tausend Namen.[3]

[1] O anxiety, life a thousandfold, O courage, the bosom bursting to reel,
to whirl, to hover as if it were departing this world. The breast heaves more
rapidly in passionate desire, everything vanishes that bound us, free as the
wind, gods are we!

[2] No, I cry – father, saviour, this heart wants to be filled, wants to be
satiated; or else shatter your image!

[3] O Homer, O Ossian, O Shakespeare, O Dante, O Ariosto, O Petrarch, O
Sophocles, O Milton, O you spirits below, give me a thousand tongues for
the thousand names.

The style too of exclamations and anacolutha, interspersed with dashes, manifests the same sense of stimulus both in such poems of rapture conditioned by already existing forms and in the totally subjective *Ausfluß des Herzens* (*Eine esoterische Ode*). Here the same unfortunate tendency is at work in literary terms, which does not distinguish even in love between imitation (or are we to call it contrafacture?) and the real thing. The two poems addressed by name to Friederike, 'Where are you now, my unforgettable maiden' and 'Ah, you are gone', are really very close to Goethe. Yet it remains something of an open question as to how much it is Goethean in feeling and a repetition of the latter's situation. Possibly rural pastoral topics simply find their way in. In the poem *Freundin aus der Wolke* the subject is an imaginary speech by Friederike to Goethe, it deals with gentle entreaty and tender comfort. The closeness in tone to *An mein Herz* is also surprising:

> Kleines Ding, mit Müh und Leiden
> Hier in dieser Brust gepflegt,
> Herz! wenn sich dein Sturm nicht legt,
> Herz! wo sind dann deine Freuden?[4]

Bliss and the abysses of passion merge with the thoughts on death into one vibrant expression. The further Lenz removes himself from this style and thus the more he is true to himself, that is, in other words, the more he gives rein to his fantasy, so correspondingly the more his love lyrics take on a subjective and original air.

To be sure, not merely as a lyric poet was Lenz 'carried away by grief and ecstasy'. His novella *Zerbin oder Die neuere Philosophie* (1776) and his supplement to *Werther*, the novelistic fragment *Der Waldbruder*, bear testimony to this as well. Of these at least the novella is sustained and completed; it is a compact account of the fate of a young Berlin merchant's son 'with a bold and burning power of imagination and a heart which promises to achieve everything'. But Zerbin's desire for the Absolute and Truth, his 'uprightness of heart', developed through study under Gellert, fail when faced with the perils of the slippery path of life down which he slides more and more as a private tutor to a Danish Count. From the ambivalent position of the seducer he creates a libertine philosophy of instinct which is based on the

---

[4] Little thing, fostered here in this breast with care and sorrow. Heart, if your storm does not subside, heart, where then are your joys?

sentence: 'The impulse is common to all men; it is a natural law.' Yet it leads finally to nothing else but a sacrificing of the seduced innocent girl as an infanticide and to the suicide of the utterly depressed Zerbin. Basically this novella offers again no especially imaginative theme, but still presents a mirror both of Lenz's social problems (tutorship and infanticide themes) and also his consciousness of the fallibility of the unbridled heart. The novelistic draft is even more dubious as a transparent mirroring of Lenz's fantastic affair with Henriette von Waldner, the woman whom he did not even know personally. Just as the title *Der Waldbruder* is a play on her name, so too the aesthetic fugitive from the world, who at the end comes close to madness, is called Herz. This follower of Rousseau chooses a theatrically picturesque landscape for his mossy hut: 'Mountains grotesquely piling on top of one another, which seem to firmly ward off the oppressive skies with their black bushes', a contrast to a 'poor but happy' little village in the valley and just the right place for the 'melancholic sensual pleasure' of post-Wertherian escapism. The friend and the female gossips comment *e contrario* on these effusions from the point of view of the town and society. However we learn scarcely as much from this source as we do from Werther's imaginary epistolary correspondent. For here it is not even a case of misunderstood genius, but only the insubstantial victim of the sentimentality of the age: 'a frightful fool's paradise of ideas run wild', as the friend puts it, is unfolded. But these ideas are not so much ideas run wild, but above all an expression of life at second hand once again: thoughts *à la* Goethe, *à la* Wieland, *à la* Rousseau. It is not genius, but imaginary genius, of which the whole world then makes fun and rightly so, that is revealed in these pages. Despite all the assurances of passion, eternal joy, intoxication and rage there is no Werther present but only immoderation in the shape of empty form. The well-intentioned intrigue which enticed the 'Waldbruder' back into the town to the object of his illusory love, can lead but to madness, as the conclusion indicates.

But Lenz's real domain next to the poem was not the epic but drama. Here he was able most of all to free himself from the temptation of interpolating unadulterated autobiographical elements into the literary. In the drama we see his clearest attempt to avoid the Self in favour of the objective element. It is first characterised through his adaptation of the *Lustspiele nach dem*

Plautus fürs deutsche Theater (1774), that is, the translating of five pieces by Plautus into a contemporary context, of which *Die Buhlschwester* (*Truculentus*) and then *Die Entführungen* (*Miles gloriosus*) are the most stageworthy. Lenz's original dramatic *oeuvre* commenced with *Der Hofmeister oder Die Vorteile der Privaterziehung* (1774), in the genre of socio-critical drama which particularly suited him. A piece of like importance, *Die Soldaten* (1776), also belongs to this genre. Both are moralistic satires on prevalent social conditions, an expression of 'Storm and Stress' revolt against unnaturalness in the interrelationship of the classes, above all in the arrogance of the nobility and the conventional attitudes towards sex. If the tutor seduces his aristocratic pupil, then in reverse the bourgeois daughter in *Die Soldaten* falls into the hands of an unscrupulous officers' clique. In both cases the natural consequences follow. In both cases, however, Lenz avoided a tragic solution, in contrast to Goethe's Gretchen-tragedy and Wagner's *Kindermörderin*. Corresponding to his theory of comedy, he even chose the genre designation of comedy. This theory he had advocated not only in the year of the appearance of *Der Hofmeister* in his *Anmerkungen über das Theater*, but had also pursued it in an *apologia* in the *Frankfurter Gelehrte Anzeigen*. It has a partly aesthetic, partly sociological basis. Aesthetically he stipulated characters for tragedy, action for comedy; sociologically he determined tragedy for the 'more serious sections of the public, comedy on the other hand for everyone'. What is interesting is the linking of both genres whereby 'the comic writer creates a public for the tragic writer'. And so comedy becomes as it were the bedrock of drama. But it was not the comedy of the Classical writers that Lenz had in mind here, but rather a piece in the looser sense of the bourgeois eighteenth century which invented the *Comédie larmoyante*: 'a portrait of human society, and if that society becomes a serious matter, its picture cannot assume the mask of comedy'.

But not only as a social critic with a revolutionary stance did Lenz add his voice in these his most significant 'comedies' to the fashionable themes of the 'Storm and Stress', which in his case became even genuine dramatic presentations, he also anticipated Schiller at least in the family theme of *Die Räuber*, in his play *Die beiden Alten* (1776). This showed the murderous design on his own father by a son intent on the inheritance and the rescue from the cellar of the old man believed dead. However Lenz treated it in the final analysis as a didactic play without the other topical 'Storm and Stress' theme of rivalry between brothers that was incorporated by Schiller. And finally, Lenz then has his own place too in the programmatic literary satire of the 'Storm and Stress'. His supreme achievement here remained unprinted because it was not really stageable – the farce *Pandaemonium Germanicum*, which Lenz termed a 'sketch'. It has the language and the hustle and bustle found in *Götz*, a consciously playful confusion of the three Unities, a similarly rapid *denouement* as in the last part of *Der Waldbruder* with the third act of half a page. This is symptomatic not only of the incomplete nature of Lenz's character, but it is also, with its frenetic opening and the rapid trailing off and the sudden termination, typical of his creative manner. The *Pandaemonium Germanicum* depicts the whole literary Parnassus according to its roll bearers, in which, besides Goethe and Lenz himself, their counterparts, the unimportant onlookers, pedants, philistines and journalists together with La Fontaine, Molière, Rabelais and Rousseau, Hagedorn, Wieland, Johann Georg Jacobi, Lessing, Herder and Klopstock and, naturally enough, Shakespeare too appear. The object of attack along with the gaggle of philistines and minor *literati* is once again primarily the French-orientated Wieland, whom Goethe finally pulls about the stage by his hair. The praise of Goethe above all makes the position quite clear and marks the resolute self-exaltation of the author as his fellow genius and friend. The impersonal touch is provided by the contrast of originality and imitation. Despite all the mannerisms of an artificial, childish, even dialectal tone, which is supposed to sound natural, the literary farce is still today a mine of amusing antitheses and a pyrotechnic display of wit for the historical observer of the age and its style. At the same time it is perhaps the clearest expression of that remarkable amalgam of dependence upon Goethe and consciousness of his own originality, which enabled this 'Storm and Stress' figure to attain but rarely a true expression of his creative potential and which made him in addition an unhappy man.

Lenz coming from the Baltic had crossed Goethe's path at an important stage in his life and had sought to link the latter's with his own talent, already morbid from an early stage. Friedrich Maximilian Klinger (1752–1831), the other significant dramatist of the *Geniebewegung* within the Goethean circle, stood even closer to Goethe as a fellow citizen of Frankfurt. He came from the most modest of circumstances and was supported by the labours of his mother who was a laundress and by patrons (amongst them Goethe) as he worked his way through his study of law. His students days of 1774 coincided with his 'Storm and Stress' phase, which lasted up to about 1778. He did not pursue his studies right to the end, although this consciously original genius did have at his disposal the very qualities that Lenz lacked, namely energy, solid strength and indestructible health. After his plans of establishing himself in Weimar in 1776 had gone awry and following a final flickering of his desire for adventure through his connection with the Seyler troupe, he found in Lenz's homeland of Russia the profession that corresponded to his practical energy – military service. As did Goethe, he in his service attained the title of 'His Excellency'. Finally as Curator of the University of Dorpat he proved his energy again in the intellectual field. The fact that he, like Goethe, worked his way through to 'manhood' after confused and wasted years seems all the more remarkable when we take cognisance of his literary participation in the *Geniebewegung*. He indeed manifested a natural vitality, but in a phase of inner 'confusion' which was in no way second to Lenz's disorderliness. The difference between them lies not in this facet, but rather in Klinger's self-confidence and unshakeable nerves in contrast to the deep insecurity experienced by Lenz.

The most significant and at the same time most topical original works produced by this mind, that was totally absorbed during that period by dramatic productions, appeared within a very limited space of time, namely the years 1774–6. The form of the works shows the influence of Shakespeare and of Goethe, the spirit of the pieces that of Rousseau, the style in the narrower sense is related to Goethe and to Lenz and points to that of the young Schiller. What marks his own originality, which goes beyond the 'Storm and Stress' naturalism, is his desire for immediacy and at the same time a condensation of language which in places sounds directly pre-expressionist.

The tragic *Ritterspiel Otto* (1775), Klinger's opening work, displays this stylistic intent already in a fully accomplished manner. After the fashion of *Götz* (and its interpretation of Shakespeare, in this case King Lear), this initial play still revealed more epigonal traits than a style of its own. Klinger's own original bent lies in this instance in the disregard of the 'historical element', which is treated with far less concern than in *Götz* and represents the trappings rather than the essence. But then he expressed his true self in *Das leidende Weib* (1775), which was conceived very much under the direct influence of Lenz's *Hofmeister*, so that even the figure of the fraudulent Läuffer was taken over by name and given a similar characterisation. At the same time we are tempted in this piece to think ahead to the young Schiller, above all on account of the contrasting of the honest family of the privy councillor with the corrupt world of the prince's court and its people, something which is not found in Lenz. Caricaturing aimed at the *beaux esprits* of the bourgeois world in the spirit of pre-Schillerian attacks on an 'ink-slinging century', can be seen in the figures of Läuffer's comrades. An analogous seduction scene is performed in these two spheres of the courtly and of the bourgeois. Yet the analogy is part and parcel of the picture of the age. The main action of the plot concerns the seduction of the ambassador's wife by the passionate Herr von Brand and the love – a love that links both classes – of her brother Franz for the harp player Julie, a sentimental, but also tender passion in which the male partner might be thought to bear a partial resemblance to Klinger. Klinger lets the finally convicted ambassador's wife perish with her lover, and the love of Franz and Julie be betrayed by Läuffer. Courtly intrigue enters into everything, intrigue which at the close of the last act excludes from society the circle of the honest people who are left. We perceive how everything is incorporated that smacks of social criticism, right from *Emilia Galotti* to *Der Hofmeister* and *Kabale und Liebe*. But not only this. Klinger's originality is expressed above all in the extremism of his figures and his language.

Franz is the most convincing of the characters in the 'Storm and Stress' sense; unequivocally upright like Götz, also hostile to the court like Götz. Unswerving and single-minded likewise in his passion for Julie, as whose victim he finally remains alone. 'Down, ardour! See, it rages in me' – this is self-assertion in true Klinger fashion. Corresponding to this immediacy too is the inclusion of the world of the children belonging to the ambassador's wife, with whom Franz, like Werther, finds affinity in line with Rousseauistic belief in what is natural. The 'Storm and Stress' figure in the courtly circle is the seducer von Brand, with traits less of Lovelace than of his descendant Mellefont in *Miß Sara Sampson*: he too is passion through and through, striving after his great love, clearly separated from the hostile world of intriguers and *beaux esprits* (as the representatives of bourgeois anti-Rousseauistic artificiality).

Passion and turbulent emotion for their own sakes, less sentimental, but all the more intransigent therefore in the tragic sense, characterise Klinger's most epoch-making work, namely *Die Zwillinge* (*The Twins*) (1776). The brothers-theme that is here taken up is not to be understood in an original sense but directly as a characteristic theme of the *Geniebewegung* ('brother' was the favoured epistolary address!), hence it should be seen dialectically. If Lenz, Goethe and Lavater addressed one another as 'brother', it only expressed a specific stage of friendship, which to some degree consciously contrasted with the erotic vocabulary of friendship in the anacreontic phase. At the same time alongside the more masculine tone stretching beyond Pietism there echoes the immediacy of Christian brotherliness within the 'Storm and Stress' movement. The North German 'Storm and Stress' of the *Göttinger Hain* represented historically a kind of bridge between Klopstockian-anacreontic pathos of friendship and the new brotherliness of geniuses. Dialectically, however, the theme of friendship is seen as a fraternal one in the 'Storm and Stress', because it forms at the same time the opposite pole to promethean subjectivity. In the *alter ego* of the friend as 'brother' the original genius finds his highest and most intense counterpart, he finds the equally sensitive and similarly striving 'Thou'. For here it is not a question of Self-limiting, but rather of the duplicating or multiplying of the Self in changing human reflections. At the same time (in the 'Storm and Stress' drama predominantly in the narrowest sense of kith and kin) 'brother' is also the confirmation of individuality through the theme of dissimilarity, of antithesis, indeed of the split between Man and Man, particularly between brothers. And here the brothers-theme becomes the dramatic means of expression of the human tragedy, especially in its accentuation towards the favoured theme of fratricide. The tragic element lies in the conception of the 'Storm and Stress' writers that procreative nature itself divides human qualities, divides brothers of whom each possesses unequivocally what nature has denied the other of the same flesh and blood. Anthropologically this theme is perfectly sound. For therein is revealed an existential suffering from the very limitation of the vigorous Self, which affirms its originality through the absolute nature of its qualities. If the qualities of Klinger's twins were apportioned to *one* person, he would be the perfect vigorous individual and would not be delivered up to tragic destruction.

In the most important aspects of the play Klinger had his predecessors and his rivals. There was Gerstenberg with his *Ugolino* (1768), and Leisewitz, the sole dramatist of the *Göttinger Hain*, with his *Julius von Tarent* (1776), which had been unsuccessfully submitted for the same drama competition organised by Schröder's Theatre Troupe as Klinger's *Die Zwillinge*. Heinrich Wilhelm von Gerstenberg (1737–1823), the inaugurator of the Skaldic poetry and the editor of the *Schleswigsche Literaturbriefe*, once again proved with his dramatic theme taken from Dante's *Divine Comedy* his vigour and instinct for what was new. To begin with, the courage for such a venture was remarkable, since it aimed to present on the stage events that were seemingly no longer possible since the Enlightenment, yet made use of the very psychology of the Enlightenment. The death by starvation of the Count with his three sons in the tower at Pisa, into which the vengeance of the tyrant had cast them, is, indeed, the only event which is actually presented. But this was nerve-shattering enough and did not shrink from naturalistic consequences. The whole piece is one long torment, which is protracted all the more horrifically when child, boy, youth and man have to suffer this fate together. Destruction in the form of Shakespearian madness is the conclusion. The peculiar relationship of the 'Storm and Stress' to death can already be traced here: death is no longer heroic-rhetorical, rather is it as realistic as possible. At the same time, however, this death can be seen as an entelechy of the Self, in which the final reality, original genius, lies hidden, the essence of existence, which can even become a form of enjoyment of Self and of the world, as in Goethe's *Prometheus* and *An Schwager Kronos*. In Gerstenberg the approach is all the more impressive, as the realism of death in *Ugolino* is dramatically effective in the three stages of childhood, and doubly so in the case of the awareness of the man and father.

Among the members of the *Göttinger Hainbund* Leisewitz had specialised, so to speak, in the theme of *in tyrannos*. Both his short contributions to the *Göttinger Musenalmanach* of 1775, *Die Pfandung* and *Der Besuch um Mitternacht*, are not one-acters but one-scene plays and already leave nothing more to be desired as far as clarity is concerned. If the first shows the greater inner superiority of the peasant couple over the Prince who drains the land mercilessly, then the night scene of the second play has a comparably more crass effect: before the Prince, who is expecting his mistress, there appears – in Shakespearian fashion – instead of her the ghost of Arminius, to hold up to the weakling the image of a prince: 'That you are the tyrant of slaves and slave of a whore!' Hermann prophesies the beginning of freedom to the fainting man.

Leisewitz then submitted the tragedy *Julius von Tarent* in that competition which Friedrich Ludwig Schröder had advertised in 1775 for his famous group of actors, and it was a remarkable case of plurality that there should have been submitted at that time no fewer than three pieces with the theme of fratricide. Unlike the treatment of the theme of infanticide by Leopold Wagner and by Goethe in *Urfaust*, in this case none of the authors knew anything of the others' works. Leisewitz certainly did not know Klinger's *Die Zwillinge*. As in the latter's play, so here too in *Julius von Tarent* it is the individuality of the brothers that leads to the tragic conflict. Of the two the titular hero is the representative of passion. His language is also a guide to his temperament. He defines himself to his friend Aspermonte already at the start of the play:

> Nennen Sie mir eine Empfindung, ich habe sie gehabt. Immer ward ich von einem Ende der menschlichen Natur zum andern gewirbelt, oft durch einen Sprung von entgegengesetzter Empfindung zu entgegengesetzter, oft durch alle, die zwischen ihnen liegen, geschleift.[5]

The dynamic verbs 'whirl' and 'drag' go stylistically beyond Leisewitz's model Lessing. We could find them too in Klinger. They express the same idea that the action too presents: the scorn of the

---

[5] Name me a feeling, I have experienced it. I was always whirled from one end of the spectrum of human nature to the other, often dragged along in one go from one emotional scale to another, often through all the intermediate emotions.

sensual man for reason and philosophy, which are replaced by imagination, dream and passion that knows no bounds. The words 'how shall I still my hunger for sensations' constitute Julius's character. Yet he remains open to his adviser Aspermonte, just as he retains a certain measure of self-control.

This however is not the case with his brother Guido. Obsessed with thoughts of honour, which he intersperses with those of love, he pursues everything to the point of senseless madness. He is the man of action, the enemy of sensitivity and speculation. 'Speculation kills courage.' Guido himself defines his position as that of a beast of prey which wants at least to bite into the bars of his cage, a Prometheus in the form of the 'Storm and Stress' *Kerl*, more than a match for fate even through his own decisions. In contrast to him stands Julius himself, the dreamer from childhood on, in the image of the prince, the father. In reality however the two brothers are not counterparts, but merely two different stages of the same vigorous man of action.

Hence the outcome is determined from the start. Since both direct all their passion towards the same girl Blanca, the more deliberate energy of Julius can lead in fact to the carefully conceived plan of escape with Blanca, but which must fail before the incalculable sudden anger and self-assertion of his brother. And so Julius is then stabbed by Guido in the ambush, and for the unfortunate father there only remains the duty of letting the eternal law take its course with the second son, the immoderate one, who then – in voluntary expiation – dies at the hand of the supreme judge and father. It becomes evident how in 'Storm and Stress' dramas of this variety in which anti-bourgeois and anti-Enlightenment paths are followed there is a return to classical *hubris*, to the classical idea of fate and, in consequence, to classical tragedy. With good reason then the theme of *Julius von Tarent* and *Die Zwillinge* could be taken up again by Schiller at the height of the Classical period in *Die Braut von Messina*. We have to take into account of course that for the 'Storm and Stress' writer the theme of *hubris* in his dramatic heroes has scarcely anything to do with God or gods. The idea of judgement (in both cases) is patriarchal. It is the ultimately unavoidable formal principle which averts chaos. The love of the 'Storm and Stress' authors however is directed towards the vital genius of the transgressors, the extraordinary nature of their humanity, the self-assurance that proves their greatness. Their real antithesis they see in the tedium of Wieland's philosophy of moderation.

Klinger's image of man and the language in his dramas mirror such associations perhaps even more clearly than those that can be found in Lenz or in fact in Leisewitz. This point is illustrated in the very comparison of *Die Zwillinge* with its rival piece *Julius von Tarent*, where we need only change the list of *dramatis personae* to arrive at Klinger's plot. In Klinger's piece the sons are called Guelfo and Ferdinando, the girl desired by both of them Camilla, the friend and mentor of the unrestrainedly passionate Guelfo is Grimani. Between them and the father, the old Guelfo, almost the same course of action is played out as in *Julius von Tarent*. All the more characteristic then are the differences and shifts of emphasis. In Klinger's play alongside the feeble old knight there stands the figure of the mother, whose role as mediator makes clear the powerlessness of compromise in the face of a man of action. The young Guelfo's 'brother' and pernicious mentor Grimani possesses no Antonio-traits like Aspermonte in Leisewitz's play, but is a man of sombre Ossianic thoughts and a melancholic delight in death, though at the same time he has features of the intriguer. Camilla is not the passionate Blanca, but at one with herself and her engagement. In the case of the twin brothers it is not absolute honour and equally absolute love that are in contention, but two completely contrasting temperaments. Ferdinando, the heir and Camilla's fiancé, is quiet and thoughtful, a man of order, of self-control and averse to conflict. Guelfo however appears as if obsessed by a demon spirit, a solipsistic genius, who recognises no other standards than his own will, which is unbridled and borders on madness. Basically this figure is almost a harking-back to the tyrant of the courtly baroque novel and drama, who also foams and vents his spleen and who is here merely re-identified with the emotional tempest of the young hero and his psychological motivation now possible for the first time. For here it is a question of emotion for its own sake, and nothing else, as is manifest above all in the difference compared with the fraternal conflict in Leisewitz's work. There the brothers' antagonism can be traced back to their respective passion for Blanca. In Klinger however the antagonism is based, apart from the clash of temperaments, namely moderation and immoderation, not on the relationship

F

with Camilla, but on the feeling of being slighted on the part of the more assertive of the two brothers. He simply covets his brother's possessions, the entire inheritance: bride, the property, the finest horses, and he emits torrents of rage, hatred and scorn against the wicked world which cannot grant him all this by the very natural order of things. It is from this basic feeling that Guelfo's contempt for the world becomes condensed into personal hatred of Ferdinando, because he is the more favoured one, and of his parents because they obey the laws of equity and primogeniture. Perhaps in no other instance in a theatrical piece which is to be taken seriously – and the later *Sturm und Drang* can hardly be claimed as such – is the linguistic expression of dynamic originality so manifest. Here there is a howling, a roaring, a rattling, a bubbling and raging; people choke, are convulsed, cringe, hurl, bite, reel, gasp and quiver. The preference for vulgar language as a supposed expression of immediacy is striking. The use of adjectives is on the same plane – wild, monstrous, rough, hot, glowing, gloomy and confused. We come across self-descriptions of the hero like 'I have courage, fire, spirit, strength' or 'I want to clasp these clouds of fire, summon up storm and tempest and plunge shattered into the abyss'. As long as he himself is the lion, the others are for him merely skeletons or puppets. This manic Ego expectorates in a language which frequently borders on the blasphemous and goes beyond the mere expression of boundless self-confidence. The intention to *épater le bourgeois* may be seen as fully achieved. Inversions, anacolutha, interjections like 'Ha' and 'Hihi' must have been designed for a witches' 'field-day' of feelings, designed for a theatrical effect of dynamism as an end in itself. It is already far removed from Shakespeare and *Götz* or even *Clavigo* despite the many still obvious points of contact, and despite the fact that the inherited dramatic structure of the five-act play with its *peripeteia* in the fourth and the catastrophe in the final act is not actually disturbed.

The fact that the passionate South provides the setting for *Ugolino, Julius von Tarent* to *Die Zwillinge* and Klinger's subsequent drama *Simsone Grisaldo* (1776), in which again the figure of the man of action and absolute dynamism forms the focal point, is scarcely an accident. Italy or Spain (this latter for *Simsone Grisaldo* and *Clavigo*) seem to fit this sphere of the 'Storm and Stress' drama, since the problems presented revolve around passion, self-realisation and the resultant tragic downfall, not around social criticism as with Lenz. In a form which can create the impression of self-parody, but is no way intended as such, this seething and challenging emotionality of the 'Kerl' is shown in the piece that he brought with him in 1776 to Weimar, a piece about contemporary family revenge set in America. Klinger pertinently wanted to call this piece *Wirrwarr*, but in Weimar it was re-named *Sturm und Drang*. Here appear three men of action with the symbolic names of Wild, La Feu and Blasius, united through close brotherliness in the above defined sense. Wild, the most unruly, is the man of action after Klinger's heart. La Feu is the optimistic sentimental poet easily aroused. Blasius is not unrelated to Grimaldi in *Die Zwillinge*, highly imaginative, egotistic, rather phlegmatic despite his funereal romanticism and longing for solitude. Both of them are taken off by Wild from Europe to America for the sake of adventure. The action is correspondingly fantastic. Wild seeks through the whole wide world – this is the motive, not the cause of his restlessness – for the lost love from his youth, a gentle English lady, who, together with father and sentimental aunt, then promptly lodges in the same American inn as the three men. The decisive theme this time is not fraternal conflict but family revenge. On the one hand there is the Berkley family, the kith and kin of his Beloved. On the other, the Bushy family, hated and persecuted senselessly by father and son Berkley. Naturally Wild is really Lord Bushy – his name is just an assumed one. Without any resort to psychological motivation everything is satisfactorily sorted out in the end after constant misunderstandings and confusions, in which the roughest man of action in the drama, a ship's captain, plays a considerable role. This latter figure is Berkley's son, believed dead, a kind of Guelfo transformed to still more brutal proportions. Old Lord Bushy, Wild's father, who was cast adrift on the ocean by the young Berkley, appears like a *deus ex machina* and brings about the reconciliation of the divided families, against which only the captain holds out to the end in almost insane defiance. One is forced to say that the drama here has become, without any regard to form or sense of the genre, a mere means of expressing a picture of Man that has become almost an *idée fixe*: it is onesidedness for its own sake. 'Mad heart! you should thank me! Ha! rage and then relax, revive yourself in chaos!' This is the all determining motive of the introductory words of Wild, which are amplified at the end of the same scene: 'Look, I am bursting with strength and health and cannot sit idly by'. The presentation of this theme of vigorous subjective genius, in reality a self-presentation of the 'Storm and Stress' as of value in itself, constitutes the essence of the whole drama. By way of comparison the action may be seen as *kitsch*-adventure, as proved in fact to be the case.

At the end of the seventies Klinger – partly from reasons of profitability – turned from the drama to the novel. To all outward appearances his 'Storm and Stress' phase was now over. Indeed, his novelistic satire *Plimplamplasko, der hohe Geist* (1780) reads like a complete satire not only on the vital genius of the Christoph Kaufmann type, but also on his own past. This does not alter the fact that much of the poet of the 'Storm and Stress' phase has still been incorporated even into his conception of the Faust figure. Klinger's version of the Faust-theme, *Fausts Leben, Thaten und Höllenfahrt* (1791), was a prose epic too, but moralistic in tone and had little in common with Goethe and Maler Müller, the other two poets treating the Faust theme, in terms of the breadth of invention. The rejection of a connection between this comprehensive work and 'everything that had been composed and written about Faust hitherto' cannot be regarded as credible in view of the characterisation of Faust:

Strebende, stolze Kraft des Geistes, hohes feuriges Gefühl des Herzens und eine glühende Einbildungskraft . . . , die das Gegenwärtige nie befriedigte, die das Leere, Unzulängliche des Erhaschten, in dem Augenblicke des Genusses aufspürte . . . Früh fand er die Grenzen der Menschheit zu enge und stieß mit wilder Kraft dagegen an, um sie über die Würklichkeit hinüberzurücken.[6]

If we accept what Klinger says about Faust's thirst for truth, which finds no satisfaction in individual sciences, we are presented

[6] Aspiring, proud strength of spirit, a lofty, fiery feeling of the heart and a glowing power of imagination . . . which the present never satisfied, which traced out in the very moment of its enjoyment the void, the insufficiency of that which was grasped . . . Quickly he found the limits of Man too narrow and struggled against them with savage energy to extend them beyond reality.

after all with the entire concept as found in Goethe. Yet with Klinger the narrative expands rather than tending to penetrate to any depth. Klinger's sympathy sides basically still with the emotional and intellectual vitality of Faust, which he unfolds in the five parts that make up the novel. But the viewpoint – in the absence of parodistic tendencies – is like that of *Plimplamplasko* in the final analysis. Klinger's Faust is not an example of intellectually excited and excitable Man, but (*circa* 1790) rather of the moralist to whom Faust's life and deeds appear as a misunderstanding of Self and as an erroneous course. The 'Storm and Stress' figure was no more.

Heinrich Leopold Wagner (1749–79) was born in Alsace. He studied law with Goethe in Strassburg, continued to keep in touch with Goethe and also became a lawyer in Frankfurt, though admittedly only after Goethe's departure to Weimar. They had in fact met in the Salzmann circle at Strassburg, and if *Dichtung und Wahrheit* is a precise and accurate record, Goethe had already told him at that time about his plans for *Faust* at the stage of the central Gretchen tragedy. From this resulted Wagner's sole theatrically effective drama *Die Kindermörderin* (*The Infanticide*) (1776), which was however indebted not only to Goethe, but also to Lenz. It is a drama with the theme of seduction in keeping with the times, in no way as extreme as Klinger's, yet quite unequivocally a bourgeois drama of social criticism and hence capable of exercising the same kind of effect as Lenz's social dramas. And it is a bourgeois tragedy in the line of development that leads to Hebbel's *Maria Magdalene*, at all events certainly in its first version prior to the revision with its subsequent happy ending. Naturally there are frequent changes of scene in the drama (even if it is vaguely set 'in Strassburg'), the action stretches over the nine months from the time of the seduction to the birth of the child. Inevitably the seducer von Gröningseck is a lieutenant, just as the father of the seduced Eva Humbrecht is an honourable and solid citizen through and through. The affinity of the theme to Lenz's *Die Soldaten* springs to mind, except that here the girl's mother out of stupidity and vanity assumes a role of a procuress. She plays the role of the really guilty one too in the first act (which has been cut out almost entirely in productions because of its setting in the brothel and the raping of Eva that takes place there, almost in the presence of the mother, who has been made drunk). The seducer himself hardly appears in so bad a light as she does and even the girl is anything but frivolous. Hence the possibility of a final reconciliation has already been basically provided, although the mother has in the end to atone for her role with her death and the girl has to survive all the sufferings of utter distress, including the killing of her child in final desperation. The real monster in this drama, however, is Gröningseck's cunning comrade, who makes his friend appear as a cynical libertine by means of forged letters and hence drives the girl to her act of desperation. It is against him that the linguistically most powerful lines are directed after his unmasking:

> *Gröningseck:* Ha! wie will ich mir wohltun, mit welcher Herzenswonne will ich mich in seinem Blute herumwälzen![7]

Otherwise Wagner's mode of expression is sentimental and delicate rather than the product of original genius. Linguistically he shows himself to better effect as a 'Storm and Stress' author in satirical writings, for example in the farce *Prometheus, Deukalion und seine Rezensenten* (1775), of which, it is true, he did not publicly admit authorship. It is really a satirical *Werther-apologia*, in which Goethe represents Prometheus, Deukalion is Werther, and wherein Goethe's critics like Nicolai and Matthias Claudius appear in disguise. The form is somewhat reminiscent of Goethe's *Jahrmarktsfest zu Plundersweilern* and modelled on Hans Sachs. The critical viewpoint appears unequivocal, just as in the later dramatic satire *Voltaire am Abend seiner Apotheose* (1778), the literary clique is depicted coarsely, yet at the same time wittily and ingeniously. The idea of giving this vain representative of the Rule Book a glimpse on the evening of his death of the verdict of a future encyclopedia on him and letting him die of it, is excellent.

---

[7] *Gröningseck:* Ha! how shall I enjoy myself, with what heartfelt desire shall I wallow in his blood!

12 The Stamp of Realism

It was no accident that the real initiator of the *Frankfurter Gelehrte Anzeigen* was Johann Heinrich Merck (1741–91). He came from Darmstadt and was firmly attached to his home town, spending but few periods elsewhere. He later served as Army Paymaster and 'Kriegsrat' there. He acted as *spiritus rector* to the Darmstadt 'Community of the Saintly Ladies', that is, to those three ladies of sentiment, to whom Goethe has dedicated three odes. Merckian traits have gone into Goethe's *Satyros*, but above all in the figure of Mephisto in *Faust*. This too characterises the man. The productive poetic vein was not dominant in him. He was more a critic of surpassing ability, witty and discursive, not with totally nihilistic tendencies like Mephistopheles, but nevertheless a critic in the existential sense. When the 'Storm and Stress' and with it the *Frankfurter Gelehrte Anzeigen* had had their day, he placed his talents at the disposal of Wieland's *Teutscher Merkur* with contributions which in no way denied his origins as a critic within the 'Storm and Stress' movement. Indeed he underwent a development which corresponded roughly to that of Klinger and was roughly contemporaneous with it. Yet it scarcely led to recantation or to self-parody like Klinger's *Plimplamplasko*. His contributions to Wieland's *Merkur* are not only original in their epistolary, dialogue and essay form, but also interesting in the breadth of viewpoints and form with their stimulating subject matter (*Von dem Ritterwesen, Für das Andenken Albrecht Dürers*) a bridge to Romanticism. He displayed a sense of form and culture that was remarkably wide-ranging for Goethe's circle (with the exception of Goethe himself and Herder). He was as familiar with the pictorial arts as with literature, and with individual interpretations as much as aesthetic theory. He excelled Wagner in standards, and Lenz and Klinger in clarity and integrity of thought. And so he formed a kind of link between the Franconian–Hessian 'Storm and Stress' ambience and Weimar, whose claims he recognised without giving up the idea of strength and greatness which he had advocated with Goethe of the *Werther*-period.

With express reference to Goethe, Merck clearly adjusts his picture of the landscape-painter to Werther's image of the world:

> Fürs erste gehört wohl eigentlich das große poetische Gefühl dazu, alles, was unter der Sonne liegt, merkwürdig zu finden und das Geringste, was uns umgibt, zu einem Epos zu bilden . . . Wenn der Jüngling nicht in ewigen Träumen von Helldunkel gewiegt wird, wenn er nicht stundenlang an einem Bache ruhen oder von Wollust trunken das hohe Gewölbe des Waldes mit allen Gespenstererscheinungen von Streiflichtern und Schlagschatten anstaunen kann; wenn er nicht, von Spähsucht befallen, die dunklen Gewölbe der Brücken und Kreuzgänge durchwandelt oder nach der Dämmerung läuft, die so alles, was von Licht und Schatten zerstreuet war, in einem Bündel bindet – so ist er wohl zu seinem Beruf verstümmelt, und weg mit ihm zu einer anderer Beschäftigung![1]

Here the aestheticism of the 'Storm and Stress' is expressed, which Merck was to surmount with a certain sagacity in his later contributions to the *Teutscher Merkur*. It should not be forgotten, however, that essays like *Für das Andenken Albrecht Dürers* or the communication of the Roman letters in the *Tischbein* essay with their picture of Raphael, form a direct link with Wackenroder's *Herzensergießungen*, nor that they are not at all 'mephistophelian' in the sense of the picture of Merck as presented in *Dichtung und Wahrheit*, but show him to be occupied with values and with an already occasionally vibrant tone of early Romantic

[1] In the first instance the great poetic feeling is really required to find everything under the sun remarkable and to make the slightest thing that surrounds us into an epic . . . If the youth is not gently rocked in eternal dreams of *chiaroscuro*, if he cannot rest for hours at a brook or cannot gaze in a state of drunken bliss at the sylvan vaulting with all its spectral apparitions of shafts of lights and deep shadows; if, overcome by inquisitiveness, he does not wander across the dark vaults of bridges and archways or run after the dusk which binds together everything that was diffused by light and shade . . . then he is probably crippled and unfit for his profession, and off with him to another occupation!

fervour. The influence on Wackenroder seems to stand out immediately. We should view Merck, therefore, not only as the stimulus behind the *Frankfurter Gelehrte Anzeigen* with an emphasis on causticity and irony, but also as a productive critic, which was in fact what he later became, of those men of genius 'without straightforward human understanding'.

Like Merck, the remarkable double talent of Friedrich Müller of Kreuznach, 'Maler Müller' as he called himself, (1749–1825), had its effect upon a new age and at the same time beyond the limits of literature. In common with the Swiss Gessner and Füssli (and even Goethe himself), he not only possessed like Merck a mind that critically embraced both literature and painting, but was also productive as painter and poet. In the Palatinate he initially pursued his art as a courtly craft; it was an artistic development which he, as the son of an innkeeper, attained only with great difficulty. He started first in Zweibrücken and soon proceeded to Mannheim, the Mannheim of the famous Hall of Antiquities, about which Schiller later wrote, and the home of the Dalberg theatre. This stay (1774–78) coincided with the height of the 'Storm and Stress' movement. Eight years before Goethe, his exact contemporary, he went to Italy, which was to be his final chosen home. Moreover like Winckelmann he became a convert prior to this change of country. The close connection with Goethe that he had enjoyed from his Mannheim period later stood him in good stead in Rome, where Müller lived not so much from his artistic labours as from his activities as a guide for art-connoisseurs.

When he went to Rome, his reputation was firmly established in Germany above all as a writer of idylls. This indeed makes us recall that other painter-poet, Gessner, rather than think of any attachment to the 'Storm and Stress'. But this closeness to Gessner relates merely to linguistic form, not to Gessner's genre. This is evident to begin with in Müller's renunciation of Gessner's sentimentality, but still more in the 'naturalness' (ascribed to him by Heinrich Leopold Wagner in the *Frankfurter Gelehrte Anzeigen* in 1776) amounting practically to dialect use, which might have occurred much more naturally to Gessner.

Between the two of them, however, lay the clear contrast of idealism and naturalism. And this naturalism was the real dowry brought by the 'Storm and Stress' into a genre that still was pre-occupied with sentimental topics.

Müller's reputation as a writer of idylls was indeed based on a development which started with a subject from the Bible under the stimulus of Gessner's writings on biblical themes: *Der erschlagene Abel* (1775). But by *Adams erstes Erwachen und erste seelige Nächte* (1778) Müller had largely freed himself from his model. The landscape description before the gates of Paradise *à la* Theocritus ('sheep-pens and meadows and springs and lowing cattle with their herdsmen') still follows Gessner's lines to some extent. Not so, however, the 'Storm and Stress' feeling which fills it to bursting point: 'Arouse such noble, strong, true feelings of the first God-created man in me.' The vocabulary smacks more of Klopstock than of Gessner. We can hear echoes of Shaftesbury's hymn to nature and pietistic spiritual warmth. But 'Storm and Stress' stammering – indeed, of the type of Klinger and Lavater – is manifest over extensive stretches and in many places in the syntax with its inversions, anacolutha, and abundance of inter-jections and neologisms. The patriarchal Adam becomes in the process a sensitive peasant who, however, experiences inklings of a Pandora-moment in which he will blissfully 'fade away into death'. The youngest daughter of the first human couple, Tirza, however, incorporates almost every conceivable emotional expres-sion in the 'Storm and Stress' vocabulary: 'The lofty, fiery soul', the 'urge for sensations', which the 'stuttering tongue' cannot follow, the 'intoxication of sacred devotion' and 'spiritual strife'. Certainly it is still a tale of patriarchism in prose, yet it is also fanciful and more than just sentimental. Adam's tale of awaken-ing in Paradise works up to the hymn to nature on the linguistic plane of the young Goethe:

> Ich sprang Hügel, Auen, Felsen an – überall mir entgegen-strömendes Wunder, neues auf mich einstürzendes Entzücken, durch alle meine Sinnen, alle meine Adern – da strömte Gefühl auf Gefühl, Schauer auf Schauer, Wonne auf Wonne in mein Herz – Ihr blühende Wiesen, fallende Bäche, steigende Wälder, alles! Licht auf Licht! Kraft auf Kraft! – Schlag auf Schlag! [2]

[2] I leapt on hills, meadows, rocks – miracles streaming towards me from every direction, new raptures befalling me through all my senses, all my

We can understand how the earlier 'sketch' *Der erschlagene Abel*, begun merely as an idyll, could blossom into a Klingerian dramatic scene of fratricide.

As with Gessner, so too with Müller the course adopted led to the classical idyll in the *Satyr Mopsus* (1775). But it is realistically contrived antiquity, transposed to northern latitudes, reminiscent of Dutch paintings such as van Ostade's. When Molon, the faun, bemoans the death of his wife, he does so like a small farmer in the style of the 'Storm and Stress' social drama:

> Was soll ich mit meinen Kleinen anfangen? Wie die Würmchen ernähren, wenn sie ihre Mäulcher aufsperren, lallen und für Durst am Däumchen nullen? Oh! – du lieber Gott![3]

With this last exclamation we can already question why the classical fiction is maintained here at all. The fact that the discrepancy clearly strikes the poet himself is shown in that he immediately changes it into classical terms with 'May Pan have pity on me!' Maler Müller then took the final step to the Middle Ages and the Present in the 'Pfalz Idylls', *Die Schaaf-Schur* (1775) and *Das Nußkernen* (1776). The *laudatio* of his home town, *Kreuznach*, (1778) belongs here too. Here his realism is furthest removed from Gessner's vague sentimentality. Sometimes we think we see before us dramatic scenes in the Lenz fashion, limited merely in their practicality. Not only is this achieved by the use of the vernacular which comes close to dialect, but also other formal elements correspond to the 'Storm and Stress', as, for example, the narrations inserted in the form of medieval tales or the crass tale of the infanticide in *Das Nußkernen*. An echo of the 'Storm and Stress' and at the same time a prelude of Romantic form is further to be found in the insertion of folk-songs and party-songs and occasionally also ballads and even the hymnic prose epic tale of Michel Mort in *Kreuznach*. Linguistically this is of the greatest interest as showing how far Müller's style had advanced.

veins – there streamed feeling upon feeling, thrill upon thrill, joy upon joy into my heart – You meadows in bloom, cascading brooks, ascending forests, everything, light upon light, strength upon strength – impact upon impact!

[3] What am I to do with my little ones? How shall they feed, the poor mites, when they open their tiny mouths, stammer and quench their thirst by sucking their thumb? Oh – dear God!

Schließ auf, Grotte der Vorzeit, Heldengesang hervor, geharnischt im Stahl, daß männlich ertöne meine Seele im Lobe des Starken.[4]

This is Ossianic in style. The tale itself seeks the proof of its immediacy in Herderesque leaps and bounds, compressed, often verbless sentence structures which recall the later Expressionistic style (partly too Schiller's style at the time of the *Anthologie*).

Und nun Reiter auf Reiter gewaltig zusammen! Männer zu Fuß im braunen Staubwirbel aufeinander los! Speer und Schwertgeklirre hoch! Säbelhiebe pfeifen durch gespaltene Luft, abrasselnd auf Panzer und Tartsche! Geknirsch Getroffener, Niedergehauener, dem Tode Entgegenwälzender, Pferdezertretener![5]

Here the other side of Maler Müller's style becomes clear; language is presented as something taut and expressive, just as the language of the people and of the child in the Idylls seeks a different realistic expression of 'Storm and Stress' nature.

This language, which characterises *Kreuznach*, is also that of Müller the dramatist, who like Goethe and Klinger obstinately struggled with the Faust-theme, even though he did not successfully realise it. Besides he was captivated by it in another aspect. His Faust was to be a kind of amalgam of Goethe's Prometheus and Klinger's 'Kraftkerl'. This at least was what was proposed in the dedication of *Fausts Leben dramatisiert* (*Faust's Life, dramatised*) (Part I, 1778):

Das Emporschwingen so hoch als möglich ist – ganz zu sein, was man fühlt, daß man sein könnte – es liegt doch so ganz in der Natur . . . Es gibt Momente im Leben, wer erfährt das nicht, hat's nicht schon tausendmal erfahren, wo das Herz sich selbst überspringt, wo der herrlichste beste Kerl, trotz Gerechtig-

[4] Open up, grotto of primeval times, forth epic poetry harnessed in steel, that boldly my soul may resound in the praise of the strong.

[5] And now rider on rider powerfully together! Men on foot in clouds of brown dust let loose on one another! Spear and the ring of swords on high! Sabre-cuts whistle through the cleft air, rattling on coats of mail and shield! The grinding sound of those struck, those hewn down, those wallowing towards death, those trampled underfoot by the horses!

keit und Gesetze, absolut über sich selbst hinausbegehrt. Von dieser Seite griff ich meinen Faust.[6]

In the first published fragment, the *Situation aus Fausts Leben* (1776), where Mephistopheles in the stuttering language of Klinger contrasts the genius of Faust with the mob, we find something similar:

> Gibst du keinen Unterschied Seelen und Seelen, jenen königlichen Seelen, Gebild, ausgeschmückt als Lieblinge dessen, der uns niedertyrannisiert? – Senk ein Gebirg' ins Meer – was drauf sitzt und lebt – eine Welt Pöbelseelen wiegt so eine einzige nicht auf, geschaffen, aus Myriaden ausgewählt, Seraph oder Teufel zu werden – [7]

But the first part of *Fausts Leben* does not present the insatiable spirit like Goethe's *Urfaust* already does, as one thirsting after knowledge, but above all rather as the sorcerer who, because of a life gambled away in pleasure, is finally driven into the arms of the devil. Moral debauchery, but not the urge for truth, grotesquely supported by an almost self-motivated underworld of devils, from which the compressed terseness and lucidity of the Devil's scenes from Lessing's *Faust* fragment are almost totally lacking. The five-part dramatic cycle which was planned would have been monstrous.

Golo und Genoveva (begun in 1775 and completed 1781), the play originally dedicated to Goethe and brought to fruition in Italy, is on the other hand stageworthy. It was not based on the impossible, like *Faust*. The medieval world with its knightly subject matter was more familiar to Müller than to the Goethe of *Götz*. That is demonstrated in the very presentation. The language is Shakespearian in its flights of fancy and in the element of the

---

[6] Soaring as high as possible – to be fully what one feels one could be – it is so completely a part of nature . . . There are moments in life, who indeed does not experience this, has not already experienced it a thousand times, when the heart bursts, when the finest and most splendid fellow, despite justice and laws, craves for something absolute beyond himself. From this aspect I conceived my Faust.

[7] Don't you make any distinction between souls, those regal souls, creatures, decked out as darlings of him who tyrannises us? – sink a mountain into the sea – and what sits and lives on it – a whole world of rabble souls does not make up for one such single soul, created, chosen from myriads to be a seraph or a devil –

gruesome, but it also has the idyllic-romantic aspect through its closeness to dialect and its colourfulness, which occurs both in the changes of scene and in the insertions of song. It is no wonder that it was Tieck who first of all published parts of the manuscript in 1811. Not only did the dramatised legend appeal to the Romantics, but so too did its pre-Romantic form.

The same can well be said too of the really lyrical part of Müller's poetry, above all the love poems like *Verlangen und Sehnsucht* or *Du grünbewachsenes Tal*. They must have been easily acceptable to the Romantics, as also the poem *Heute scheid ich, heute wandr' ich*, which became a *Volkslied*. The programmatic 'Storm and Stress' poems to Klopstock, Shakespeare, Ossian are, on the other hand, expressions very much in the mood and taste of the day. Maler Müller's individual significance lies really in his affinity to the 'Storm and Stress' and Romanticism, which did not require the classical transition.

The Swiss 'Storm and Stress'

It is not surprising that the most fervent relationship with the German 'Storm and Stress' should develop in the country which first advocated the validity of imagination in poetry and hence the right of 'the miraculous', counter to Gottsched's view, and where a new historical consciousness was awakened in the same Zürich circle through the intensive propagation of medieval literature. The express appreciation of the elderly Bodmer for originality had already contributed towards it. Zürich became the goal not only of Klopstock and the young, still 'seraphic' Wieland, but also of Goethe and the Stolbergs. Lavater and his disciple Christoph Kaufmann for their part travelled through Germany. And so there resulted numerous bosom friendships both sides of the border. And as Lavater influenced Germany, so too did Herder's theology and philosophy of history have a lasting effect on Switzerland. Nor must we forget that Switzerland was also Rousseau's land of origin. And it was Barbara Schulthess, Goethe's Zürich friend, who preserved for us the 'Urmeister', *Wilhelm Meisters theatralische Sendung* (*Wilhelm Meister's Theatrical Mission*). Lavater's correspondence not only with Goethe, but also with many other significant Germans of the day testify to these relations. Finally, his *Physiognomische Fragmente* were the result of co-productive efforts with the German 'Storm and Stress', whose interest in the natural history of the human soul they expressed, as it were, vicariously.

Johann Kasper Lavater (1741–1801), as a child already destined for the Church, was really intellectually awakened for the first time at the Zürich Grammar School by Bodmer and Breitinger's influence. He displayed great vivacity and flexibility, always committing himself wholeheartedly, yet he was easily overcome by his gift of oratory and the ease with which he put pen to paper. He offered in his day the picture of a temperament that was engaged universally and impelled by a strong sense of mission. This was so marked that frequently the choice of the means at his disposal was not duly considered. The result of this was that ambivalence, that appearance of ambiguity which later caused Goethe to break with him quite deliberately despite the intimate communion of an entire decade. The reproach of insincerity, indeed of slander, not merely that of doubtful practices was often loudly raised against him amongst his contemporaries. This is something that must be correctly interpreted. The sincerity of Lavater's views and objectives can hardly be questioned, even where it borders on the scurrilous. It is characteristic of the whole man that his career began with an act of justice and public spirit and that his life ended with a patriotic outburst regardless of the consequences for his own person. Both indicate the unswerving nature of his sense of right and wrong. It was unheard of in Switzerland that a twenty-two-year-old man, a quite young priest, together with a friend of note, (Johann Heinrich Füssli) should publicly accuse the all-powerful Governor Grebel, son-in-law of the ruling mayor, of illegal self-aggrandisement whilst in office and should compel the courts to sentence him. His patriotic stand in 1798, when the French marched in, similarly marks Lavater's steadfastness of character. Imprisonment in Basle and the gunshot which hit him whilst bringing succour to wounded soldiers in Zürich and which proved fatal, can be attributed to this steadfastness.

All this should make it evident that Lavater's problem was less a problem of character, as the polemics of the classical writers directed against him might lead one to suspect, than a question of temperament and the ambivalence of his devout pietism in general. Dogmatic and believing in miracles on the one hand, tolerant and open-minded on the other, to the point of intellectual curiosity, loyal in human relations, but also gossipy and occasionally prone to intrigue, Lavater does fit a certain type that was developed through Pietism at that time. Amongst the prominent visionaries he was not the only one who could fall for such dubious characters as Cagliostro, who saw operative in his life and that of his friends the hand of God in the literal sense or who wanted to remove mountains through the power of prayer, in his case the 'Albis ob Zürich'. If prayers and other miracles did not succeed, that did not upset him in any way. A born dilettante in many respects, he could not be affected deep down by disappointment. Herein lay an affinity with his friend Friedrich Heinrich Jacobi; he was an impressionistic theologian just as Jacobi was the impressionistic philosopher. A perspicacious superior mind like Herder could write to him in 1773: 'Restrict yourself, so that you dig more deeply.' But this was just what Lavater could not do. Yet at the same time the form of his genius was determined by this very fact. Had he not been incapable of limiting himself, his ability to draw everything that stirred the age into the orbit of his own life and piety would have been unthinkable. Herein lies the secret of his influence that was felt far beyond the confines of Switzerland. Goethe, who commented at the time of their discord that Lavater was deceiving himself and others, provided in the just wisdom of his old age in *Dichtung und Wahrheit* the key to Lavater's influence on other men:

> Keineswegs imstande, etwas methodisch anzufassen, griff er das einzelne einzeln sicher auf, und so stellte er auch kühn nebeneinander.[1]

The well tempered picture in *Dichtung und Wahrheit* exactly estimates his weakness and strength and concludes with a fine characterisation of Lavater's works:

> sie stets eine leidenschaftlich-heftige Darstellung seines Denkens und Wollens enthielten und das, was sie im ganzen nicht leisteten, durch die herzlichsten, geistreichsten Einzelheiten jederzeit ersetzten.[2]

Previously, at the time of their deepest alienation, Goethe expressed very different views of course, for example in the epigrams on Lavater, in which the amalgam of visionary and rogue provides the key theme. Or again in the transformation of Lavater into the crane in *Faust*: 'I like fishing in the clear waters, and also in the muddy.'

Of Lavater's works the *Physiognomische Fragmente zur Beför-*

[1] In no way capable of tackling something methodically, he seized upon the individual items in turn with a sure hand and thus boldly juxtaposed them.

[2] They constantly contained a passionately violent presentation of his thinking and wishes and invariably replaced what they did not achieve *in toto* with the most delightful and most ingenious individual points.

derung der Menschenkenntnis und Menschenliebe (Physiognomical Studies) (1775–78), although thoroughly couched in the spirit of Herder's sensualism, did not have such an undisputed effect on the 'Storm and Stress' period. Certainly they aroused the greatest amount of attention. But the dilettantish coarsening effect of the interpretation of the human character from facial features, an interpretation that was pietistically inquisitive and at the same time a materialisation of Leibniz's psychophysical parallelism, soon evoked a certain scepticism amongst his friends, and mockery amongst his enemies (e.g. Lichtenberg's fragment Von Schwänzen). The impact of the Aussichten in die Ewigkeit (1768–78), in letters to Johann Georg Zimmermann, and the Geheimes Tagebuch von einem Beobachter seiner selbst (1772–73) was more unequivocal. Both these works were in existence when Lavater and Goethe met. Although the Aussichten in die Ewigkeit like the later Physiognomische Fragmente combine the intellectual and the sensual, in that they endow the life of the Blessed after death with sublimated traces of earthly existence, thus rendering them theologically questionable, they nevertheless do strike a chord precisely because of this sensual note as far as the understanding of the age is concerned. It is the same basis from which Pietism addressed the age. In Moravia too and similar places the heavenly city and the soul in the bridal bed of Christ were painted in all the sensual colours available.

The Geheimes Tagebuch von einem Beobachter seiner selbst fitted of course into that selfsame pietistic tradition and had to comply with the 'Storm and Stress' demand for absolute sincerity as proof of character over and above the theological province of accountability. A later publication of the eighties, entitled Pontius Pilatus oder der Mensch in allen Gestalten . . . oder ein Universal Ecce Homo oder Alles in Einem (1782–85) was of a markedly visionary, missionary nature. It is nothing less than a Christian anthropology, yet unmistakably in Lavater's style:

> lesbar für Christen, Nichtchristen, Unchristen, Antichristen, für kaltblütige und warmblütige, schwärmerische und weltweise, dichterische und undichterische Menschen.[3]

---

[3] . . . readable for Christians, non-Christians, Unchristians, anti-Christians, for cold-blooded, warm-blooded, visionary and worldly-wise, poetic and unpoetic people.

In keeping with the vastness of the goal which he sets himself is the breadth of the terrestrial distance covered, be it real or merely imaginary. It is not possible here to name the entire corpus of edifying writings by Lavater. They have their place in the history of theology. He was quick, often all too quick to formulate. He tended to be over-influenced by the impact of initial feelings. He was moreover driven by his missionary zeal and extended the flow of his thoughts untiringly to include quite intimate, partly handwritten exhortations to his friends. His useful activity as a citizen of this world, as a participant in state and society and as a patriot is also founded on exactly this feeling of responsibility. To be sure, he was not so very successful as the poet of the *Schweizer Lieder* (1767) and of the *Zwey Hundert christliche Lieder*, for he lacked both aesthetic culture and also taste for poetry in strict metre. What emerged was something that was formalistic or simply naïve. But his prose, as impressively exemplified by something like *Ein Wort eines freien Schweizers an die große Nation* (1798), could even become a piece of classic rhetoric. Generally speaking, in the history of German prose Lavater signified above all an element of vigour and immediacy, of emotive expression, and, as a true representative of the 'Storm and Stress', a break with syntactical regularity and a vocabulary that had ossified into formulae. Certainly the stirring-up of his imagination stemmed not from aesthetic, but from religious pietistic grounds. Consequently his interest in people was intense to the point of being passionate, his engagement in all contemporary spheres of activity always total. This very fact made him a partner in the German *Geniebewegung*.

Lavater's inclination to friendship of every social shade made him the centre of a circle which included both disciples and apostles of his missionary idea of the need for a spiritual awakening. This circle, important when considered in the historical context, comprised his colleague Konrad Pfenninger and the rather dubious figure of the 'apostle of strength' Christoph Kaufmann, who finally settled in German Moravia as a doctor, and both have their rightful place in this group just as much as the more significant figures of old Johann Georg Zimmermann and his contemporary Füssli.

Johann Heinrich Füssli (1742–1825) was originally destined to be a theologian like his school-friend Lavater and, involving himself with the latter without regard to his own personal career in the Grebel affair, threw theology overboard in a moment of true self-assessment and followed the call of painting. In 1764 the English Ambassador in Berlin, where Füssli had commenced his artistic training, took him to London. This, and the eight-year stay in Rome in the seventies, was a decisive factor in Füssli's development as a painter. The style which he developed was influenced by Michelangelo rather than Raphael, and in England this made him seem to have an affinity to William Blake. But his aesthetic talent was twofold. He also has his place in the history of literature as a writer and poet. Indeed his historical significance as an artist cannot be separated from his poetic enthusiasm. Easily impressionable like his friend Lavater, though due to his predominantly aesthetic talent, endowed with a pronounced sense of style, he implanted his easily aroused enthusiasm for literature, which he had inherited from Bodmer, both into the writing of his own odes and also into the thematic arrangement of many of his pictorial compositions. He was a writer not only as a composer of odes in the 'Storm and Stress' sense, but also as an apologist for Rousseau regarding the latter's affairs in England in 1776. In the same spirit he worked as the depicter of original genius in an abundance of pictorial conceptions (which themselves reflected genius), with appropriate literary subject matter from Dante, Shakespeare, Milton and Ossian. Their artistic style is a Michelangelo-like sentimentality which could well express Ossianic pathos, heroic feelings of strength and mythical symbolism. This is all the more noteworthy as Füssli had to extricate himself from the rococo conformism of the time and hence act counter to his age and origins. Italian mannerism which he took up in Rome offered him this possible line of development as an artist. But without the previous literary bent and cultivation of his taste, his formal experimental desires as a painter would hardly have led to this development.

Füssli's poems date basically from the sixties and seventies. Recently (through Eudo C. Mason) we have had brought to our attention a hitherto unknown group of poems dating from the later period. Fundamentally however they represent no really new stage of development in his old age, but rest still on the style of his early odes, a style determined above all by Klopstock. The more gentle tone of the odes of the *Göttinger Hain* is recalled in but a few places. From the point of view of contemporary history however, and also as a key to Füssli's twofold artistic talent, the poems are nevertheless of the utmost interest. As so often in the 'Storm and Stress', these poems do not aim at clarity, but are directed – crammed to overflowing as they are with historical and allegorical names and mythological references – at the subjective emotions of the reader. A clear indication of his extreme emotional tension is displayed in the odes to Lavater, to whom he also dedicated the early prose work *Klagen*, the last of which is an ode in dialogue form on his friend's death. It records their common work on the *Physiognomische Fragmente* and their congenial past, an *apologia* for his friend reproached for his ambivalence and his egoism, and in all like Goethe's poem to Schiller's cranium, a deep meditation on the reality of life and death. Initially the odes on art still emphasise Winckelmannian standards in respect of Michelangelo and Mannerism:

> Des ist die Stärke, welchem die Arbeit nicht
> Die Nerve spannet oder die Muskel bläht
> Und dem der Adern Labyrinthe
> Nicht an den berstenden Armen starren;
> Und des die Würde, welchem nicht Leidenschaft
> Vom Auge flammet oder den Mund zerreißt.
> Dem stille Majestät und Anmut
> Selbst in dem Zorne das Antlitz krönen.[4]

In a personal extension of Klopstock's style such pieces correspond still to the pre-'Storm and Stress' as far as content is concerned. In the second ode on art dating from Füssli's Roman period, however, he attacks in a thoroughly 'Storm and Stress' sense the 'dregs of the arts' of the present day and age with its disputes over the rules. The crisis of genius, for which Michelangelo's Sistine Chapel stands as it were as a symbol, becomes clear.

> In Sixtus' Tempelhalle, so dünkte mir,
> Stand ich, was Zeit des wankenden Abends Licht

[4] His is the strength, for whom labour does not tauten the nerves or stretch the muscles, and whose labyrinthine veins do not stand out in his tensed arms; and his is the dignity, for whom passion does not flame from his eyes or distort his mouth. For him serene majesty and grace crown his countenance even in anger.

Auf ihrer Bilder Götterscharen
Schauernde Schönheit und Majestät gießt;
Mir däucht', ich sah den Schleier der Ewigkeit
Zerrissen; Zeit und Raum und der Stoff gebar:
Es strömte von der Allmacht Finger
Leben, und Adam sprang auf vom Staube! [5]

This effusive *laudatio* of great original genius with its implicit rejection of the 'dregs of the arts', which the Academies had reared,
finds an echo even in the eighties, in the ode *Adelaïdes Locken*, a
passionate invective against the Parisian fashion similar to the
kind of attack launched by the German 'Storm and Stress' so
frequently. The tragic power and significance of German mythology, the medieval epic, the greatness of Homer, Dante, Shakespeare and Milton represent the other side of the coin. This is
echoed in the odes on the *Nibelungenlied* and to the artists of
Switzerland. Füssli clings in constant gratitude to his teacher
Bodmer, to whom he is indebted for the universal literary themes
of greatness.

Füssli's presentation of Rousseau in 1767 was written in English
and entitled *Remarks on the Writings and Conduct of Jean Jacques
Rousseau*. But the editor Eudo Mason was perfectly right to isolate
the treatise from the dispute between Rousseau and Hume and
to claim the picture of Rousseau in the Foreword and in the seven
chapters as 'one of the most impressive testimonies to the new
feeling for life'. And it can be seen only in this light. The interpretations of *Emile* and *La nouvelle Héloise* undoubtedly form the
highlights. They maintain throughout what appears as the original
motivation for the treatise:

> The motives, which produced the following remarks on the
> writings and conduct of John James Rousseau, are gratitude,
> humanity, indignation. – If to give instruction grace, is the great
> duty of genius, Rousseau has done his –

This attitude is thoroughly anti-bourgeois in the 'Storm and Stress'
sense.

[5] I was standing, it seemed to me, in the Sistine Chapel and the flickering
evening light showered thrilling beauty and majesty on the heavenly hosts
depicted in the Chapel's pictures. I thought I saw the veil of eternity torn
apart; time and space and substance gave birth. Life streamed forth from
the Almighty's finger, and Adam sprang up from the dust!

Not outside, but on the periphery of Lavater's sphere of influence was the remarkable figure of Näbis-Uli, the poor man from the Toggenburg, the shepherd, the soldier in Frederick the Great's army, smallholder and cotton-trader Ulrich Bräker (1735–98). He was a person to whom, sociologically speaking, from the point of view of origin and self-education, Karschin,[6] the 'German Sappho', most closely corresponded at that time. The differences between them, however, are of greater significance. The poetic products of Karschin were not moving, but involuntarily comic. In Berlin Ramler and Gleim had mechanically crammed her with the whole artificiality of the Rationalists' writing of lyrics and odes, so that soon every natural sound had died away. With Bräker however there was a genuine, not an artificial destiny which entangled him against his will in Frederick the Great's battles, until he deserted; a destiny which, following his return to his old village, awakened him with a passionate urge for the light of learning – and this still amidst all the miseries of a life that remained ever impoverished. Fortunately he did not have a patron like Karschin. And so in a really stirring way he represents a kind of borderline possibility of naïvety and self-education such as was probably only conceivable in that century. Stimulated by an abundance of reading material partly picked at random, partly selected according to his needs, aroused by the religious problems of the age, affected (almost unavoidably due to Lavater's proximity!) by the age's passion for self-observation, he became an autobiographer and recorder of his own life-story, which appeared in 1789 in Zürich under the title *Lebensgeschichte und natürliche Ebentheuer des Armen Mannes im Tockenburg* (*The Poor Man from the Toggenburg*). Walter Muschg was scarcely overdoing it when he called these pages 'a gem of veracity and colourful story-telling'. What is impressive in the work is Bräker's struggle with the literary language, whose rules he never mastered. Thus his language could never reach the noble simplicity of Jung-Stilling, even though he comes close to it on occasions, in the note of sincerity. In the lack of syntactical polish one can discern a mixture of genuine educational difficulties and emotional impulses. This is recognisable, for example, in the meditation on the night of the full moon (Diary, 22 August, 1782):

[6] Anna Luise Karsch (1722–91); her *Auserlesene Gedichte* appeared in 1763. (*Translator's note*)

Oh, so eine helle Vollmondsnacht – über mir der gute, freundliche Himmel; unter mir das stille, ruhige Tal – wie ein reiz-
ender Lustwald – mit Bäumen bespickt, von Schimmer und
Schatten meliert – Ha! – welch wonnevolle Nacht – solche
Nächte warens auch, da ich anno 55 zu meiner Anna hinflog –
die letzten Küsse zu verschwenden. – So schien mir der Mond in
Berlin – da ich ratlos unterm Fenster lag – und Vaterland –
Schweizerland, Toggenburg – ach, ach, liebes Toggenburg-Wattweil – mir lauter heilige Wörter – seufzte.[7]

The language proceeds in fits and starts, but, as happens too in
Lavater's letters, rather from compressed feelings, and not in a
deliberate manner as with Klinger and partly, too, Maler Müller.
The vocabulary may be astonishing for a man of the people. Yet
the use that Bräker makes of it on the basis of his own self-
education is not at all unnatural.

The most remarkable testimony, however, which he has left in
his writing is offered in his personal account of a passionate
reading of Shakespeare: *Etwas über William Shakespeares Schau-
spiele* (*On William Shakespeare's Plays*) (1777). Certainly in his
days as a soldier Bräker had travelled beyond the narrow confines
of his homeland. Yet his sphere of experience remained limited
within the simple social stratum from which he stemmed as a
smallholder. He could have had no experience of the great, wide
world which Shakespeare mirrors inwardly and outwardly. The
enthusiasm of the smallholder, inflamed with Shakespeare's
dramas, had to be entirely awakened from within. That this
obsessed and extensive reader should have remained completely
free of contact with the German 'Storm and Stress' interpretation
of Shakespeare, particularly that of Herder, can scarcely be
accepted. But at least he fused these interpretations with his reading at source and his subsequently aroused enthusiasm. This fusion
was a result of Bräker's natural modesty and a dedicated humility

[7] Oh, such a clear night of the full moon – above me the good, friendly
heaven; below me the quiet, peaceful valley – like a charming grove – brist-
ling with trees, blended with light and shade – Ha! – what a blissful night
– they were such nights as these when I hastened to my Anna in the year
of '55 – to lavish the final kisses. And in this way did the moon appear to
me in Berlin – when I lay beneath the window helpless – and sighed –
Fatherland – Switzerland, Toggenburg – O dear Toggenburg-Wattweil – for
me pure sacred words.

towards the work of the genius in the full consciousness of the fact that he was offering a 'childlike praise'. Yet at the same time it was an honest praise which in its judgement retained his own taste for the realistic:

> Aber da sollst du sehen, lieber William, daß ich ein Klotz bin, grad die Personen, die vielleicht am schönsten sind, mag ich am wenigsten – Prospero und seine Miranda sind mir gar zu schön.[8]

As here for *The Tempest*, so, similarly, we read of *A Midsummer Night's Dream*:

> Es freut mich, daß es ein Traum ist – sonst aber wollt ich am liebsten mit Squenz und seinen Gesellen in der grünen Flur zwischen Zaun und Hecken spielen.[9]

How graceful a cadence and how unpretentious! And so is the whole throughout: a homely-unsophisticated dialogue with Greatness on the personal level, full of humour and always within his own limits of understanding and language. Think of his words about *The Winters' Tale* in connection with Antigonus and the child:

> Wie sein Herz blutet und sein Auge tränet! Mein Herz möchte mitbluten ...[10]

or when he writes of *All's Well That Ends Well*:

> Helena, o Helena, du bist der Ball des Schicksals, um deinetwillen muß alles sein, was es ist ...[11]

Thus Bräker penetrates the symbolical element of Shakespeare's female characters as well as Shakespeare's fools, but he fits it to

---

[8] But you shall see, dear William, that I am a blockhead, just the very people who are perhaps finest of all, I like the least – Prospero and his Miranda are far too fine for me.

[9] I am glad that it is a dream – otherwise I would dearly want to play with Quince and his fellows in the green meadow between fence and hedgerow.

[10] How his heart bleeds and his eye weeps! My heart should like to bleed too ...

[11] Helena, O Helena, you are the ball of destiny, wheel of fortune, for your sake everything must be what it is ...

his own life-situation, so that the expression never becomes a
game with artlessness, is never therefore stylised. And this is to
be highly praised above all in respect of the tragedies, where one
cannot assume the same degree of understanding as in the
comedies. In places Bräker's realism rises to criticism of Shakespeare from the position of the Enlightenment. Thus the simple
child of the eighteenth century cannot accept the idea of any
serious intent in Shakespeare's use of the witches-theme in
Macbeth:

> Pfui, fort mit den Hexen und ihrem schmutzigen Geköch.
> Wegen der Geistererscheinungen will ich ein andermal mit dir
> reden. Dein Genie ist in diesem Stück sehr groß. Aber die Hexen
> sind nicht dein Geschöpf.[12]

Then again, the introduction to *Hamlet* seems surprising and
historically of the utmost interest, as linguistically – from the
bottom rung as it were – it leads to similar forms to those used
by the 'educated' 'Storm and Stress' writers working *down* the
ladder:

> Hamlet, Hamlet – ha, dein Grillisieren, Phantasieren über Gegen-
> wart und Zukunft, über Leben und Tod, Schlafen und Träumen
> und all der rätselhaften Dinge – ha, das macht einen so voll
> Gedanken – [13]

In the conclusion he once again defines the standpoint of his
comments, which he disassociates from all arrogant criticism:

> Aber ich leugne es schlechtweg, ich habe keine Kritik gemacht,
> es mag auch dreinsehen, wie es will – [14]

Against that he sets the productive criticism of his method, with
which he wanted to render for his own benefit an account of the
coherence and depth of his impressions.

---

[12] Phui, away with the witches and their filthy brew. I'll talk to you another time about the appearance of the ghosts. Your genius is very great in
this piece. But the witches are not your creation.

[13] Hamlet, Hamlet – ha! your capricious ways, your phantasies about the
Present and the Future, about Life and Death, Sleeping and Dreaming and
all of these mysterious things – ha! it makes one very thoughtful –

[14] I absolutely deny it, I have not made any criticism, even though it might
appear as such.

Herder might well have been satisfied with the rhapsody from the mouth of this childlike man. Only in that linguistic area of Switzerland was that rhapsody possible with its naïvety and stylistic unity, embedded as it was in unintended linguistic blunders and imperfections, and yet genuine in its expressiveness.

14 The Swabian *In Tyrannos*

The part played by Swabia in the 'Storm and Stress' movement had its own peculiar character. It also marked the start of Schiller's career. Duke Karl Eugen, who was extremely headstrong and autocratic, ruled in Württemberg. By comparison the regime of the soldier-king in Prussia could be termed patriarchal. The Württemberg Duke's opinion of himself showed him to be far removed from Frederick the Great's definition of the prince as 'le premier serviteur de l'Etat'. Opposition or even impudence (such as Frederick II expressly granted the Berliners) were not tolerated. A Württemberg man was a subject, not a citizen. The Duke belonged also to those sovereigns who sold their regiments as mercenaries to colonial powers for extra revenue. A song that soon became one of the most popular in Germany, Schubart's *Kaplied*, emanated from Württemberg – and for good reason. In Schubart's as in the young Schiller's fate it becomes clear what an absolute claim Karl Eugen despotically made on his subjects. The fact that in his old age under the soothing influence of the Countess von Hohenheim, his morganatic wife, he maintained his severity but in a somewhat more paternal fashion (as people like to stress today), was a shift of emphasis but hardly a change of system. The interpretation of the relationship of Schiller and the Duke from the point of view of a father complex can hardly therefore seem to be an acceptable premiss.

Schubart's like Schiller's writing mirrors the personal bitter experience of despotic tyranny. This contrasts with the arm-chair anti-tyrannic attitude as cultivated in the Klopstock school, the *Göttinger Hain* and 'Storm and Stress' drama. Here the theme of the day was actually experienced and was not a bardic gesture of freedom and revolution as found in Klopstock and the Stolbergs. This must be borne in mind even if we concede that both Schubart and Schiller had such unruly, very self-conceited and ambitious temperaments that a completely undisciplined development and upbringing would possibly have led to more harm than good. Christian Friedrich Daniel Schubart (1739–91) can be compared in this context of undiscipline, which led to years of dissoluteness, to Christian Günther. In the latter's case also, self-confident genius and unchecked impulses cannot be separated in their effect on a desperately ruined life. From his father, a Kantor and later Deacon, he probably inherited the musical talent, from which in his case (as later with E. T. A. Hoffmann) his twofold endowments as writer and musician developed. Yet we must not confuse Schubart with the later poet-musicians of Romantic phantasy. He did not come to grief on account of his twofold talent, but through his sensual impulses and his role in society. The conventional initial study of theology led him not to the pulpit, but only to the teaching profession. With good reason, for already his demands on life as a student had been somewhat extravagant, and his interest in music and poetry had already dominated his student days. He had married at the age of twenty-three, obviously rashly, and then began his life of misery, in which incidentally his wife proved her worth, while Schubart, living constantly beyond his means, finally and brutally rid himself of his family. This catastrophe was sealed when he was offered a post at court in 1769. This was the position of music director in Ludwigsburg. There he lost all sense of moderation. In his autobiography – admittedly in a somewhat exaggerated way in keeping with his turning to pietism – he sets out the facts of his double-life as artist, hard drinker and libertine in an almost repugnant self-accusation. The whole business ended with the dissolution of his marriage, excommunication, prison and exile. He then lived an absolutely bohemian existence. In Augsburg and then in Ulm he finally gained a foothold with a literary enterprise, in fact, that was for once respectable. This was the *Deutsche Chronik*, a paper paid for entirely by himself and one that was perceptive and original through and through but not destructive in its general outlook. For all that however it became the cause for the famous ten years' imprisonment in Hohenasperg, Karl Eugen's state fortress; it was a sentence that rocked the whole of Germany. The Duke in person supervised the conversion of the prodigal son with utter inflexibility until finally in 1787 the intervention of Frederick the Great led to Schubart's release.

The prisoner in the Hohenasperg had dedicated a rapturous hymn to the king, the effect of which excelled that of the Berlin bards at Frederick's court. But Schubart was a broken man and remained so. Reconciled with his family and the Duke, theatrical and musical director in the capital Stuttgart, materially free from cares, religiously converted and politically subdued, though undisciplined as ever in the conduct of his life, he died four years after his release from captivity.

His significance as a writer lies predominantly in the sphere of the lyric. The editor and author of the *Deutsche Chronik* indeed shared with Schiller, who took over the family-theme in *Die Räuber* from Schubart, an interest in the anecdotal and in the literature of entertainment. Yet Schubart's poems have more individuality than his prose, which is less due to the form than to topicality of theme and subject matter. His poems *Die Fürstengruft* and *Kaplied* acquired a popularity – admittedly of a political nature – which was in no way inferior to the unpolitical popularity of Bürger's *Lenore*.

Schubart himself published (1785–87) that collection of his poems which made him a success, whilst he was in captivity and with the Duke's permission, after a tendentious selection *Gedichte aus dem Kerker* had appeared in Zürich in 1785. He introduced it in the style of his autobiography:

Hier ist diejenige Sammlung von Gedichten, die ich teils im Gefängnisse, teils in der Freiheit verfertigte. Erstere weint' ich in der Nacht des Jammers nieder; diese macht' ich meist im Taumel der Welt, im Glutgefühl der Jugend und heiligen Freiheit.[1]

The poet makes fitting use *ad lectorem* of the theme of the dungeon, 'out of which the voice of the wretched man cries forth', of the origins of the majority of his poems, which he 'wrote down more often in blood than in ink'. Actually, parts of the *Zaubereyen* (1766) and the *Todesgesänge* (1767) are also incorporated in the collection. The *Todesgesänge* dating from his period as a teacher are most clearly allied in terms of content to the religious poems of his time in captivity. He believed he needed some sort

---

[1] Here is that collection of poems which I prepared partly in prison, partly in freedom. The former I wrote down tearfully in the nights of misery; the latter I composed mostly in wordly ecstasy, in the fiery feelings of youth and blessed freedom.

of explanation for the late-anacreontic style of the *Zaubereyen*. He took further poetic material from the *Deutsche Chronik*. However already the preface to the *Zaubereyen* parodies the anacreontic idyllic landscape, the contrast of which is his own reality, and seeks comfort in the self-assuredness of genius:

> Doch mitten in dem Kummer braust
> In meiner Brust olympisch Feuer,
> Und stürmend schlägt die kühne Faust
> Die Silbersaiten meiner Leier.[2]

We don't find that in rococo poems; it is already Klopstockian. The pieces from the *Todesgesänge* were conceived as dirges and were accordingly adapted to current sounds and styles. As poetry they do not attain the fervour of Matthias Claudius. On the other hand, and quite rightly so, a number of Schubart's poems were included in Hoffmann von Fallersleben's collection *Unsere volkstümlichen Lieder* (1856), for example *Ich Mädchen bin aus Schwaben* and *Als einst ein Schneider reisen soll*. Schubart knew the style of the wayside inns from his own bohemian days and knew how to capture it, generally more in the simple humorous song than in the imitation of Bürger's popular ballad style (*Fluch des Vatermörders*). Schubart's soldiers' songs are much more genuine too than Gleim's, and indeed for the very fact that they treat more of the reality of suffering and death. This is really true of *Kaplied* (1787), which owes its popularity to the gravity of its theme of departure which corresponded as much to the emotional need of the day ('And tears flow forth'), as it gave expression to the simple vitality of the people.

Schubart did not seek this emotional note in the really political 'Lied'. The poem to Frederick the Great, which procured him his freedom, is really a hymn exaggerated in content and rhythm, rhymeless, not without a certain bardic tone, yet with its own verbal dynamism which streams forth and storms:

> Er stäub' und donner' im Tale
> Meines Hymnus Feuerstrom,
> Daß es hören die Völker umher![3]

[2] Yet in the midst of worries there seethes olympian fire in my breast and like a storm the bold fist strikes the silvery strings of my lyre.

[3] Let it fall as spray and thunder in the valley, my hymn's fiery stream, that the peoples around may hear it.

The famous poem, smuggled out of prison in 1779, *Die Fürsten-gruft*, which brought him seven years further confinement, has its effect, like the *Anthologie* poems of the young Schiller, directly through the rhythmically varied rhyming strophe, which an extravagant vocabulary fills with a visible delight in the macabre. Here and in Schiller's *Anthologie* under the common threat of tyrannic dominance the Swabian portion of the 'Storm and Stress' puts its originality on show. The terrors of putrefaction in the *Todesgesänge* are mild as against the angry political verses of *Die Fürstengruft*:

> Beräuchert das durchlauchtige Gerippe
> Mit Weihrauch, wie zuvor!
> Es steht nicht auf, euch Beifall zuzulächeln,
> Und wiehert keine Zoten mehr,
> Damit geschminkte Zofen ihn befächeln,
> Schamlos und geil, wie er.[4]

Certainly the rhyming ode also acknowledges the existence of 'better sovereigns', but the tendency is unequivocally *in tyrannos*, tyrants who as the scourges of God are the rage and torment of the peoples. The Duke could not possibly misunderstand the prisoner's song. Even the possibility of depicting the Prince in such a revolutionary way was treason.

[4] Go on sprinkling incense on the illustrious skeleton! It does not rise to smile approval at you and no longer bawls obscenities, so that painted ladies-in-waiting may fan him, as shameless and obscene as he is.

15 The Young Schiller

Just in time the young Schiller avoided the autocratic authority which had finally broken Schubart's life. He had foreseen a similar danger and fled his homeland in order to secure for himself eventually a second home abroad. Nevertheless like Hölderlin, Schelling and Hegel later, he remained a character unmistakably bearing the stamp of his origins; he was self-willed, energetic, an absolute idealist and sure of his star of destiny like all these other Swabians too. His birth on 10 November 1759 in his mother's home town of Marbach on the Neckar occurred a decade after Goethe's, which in many respects was a decisive factor in his development. His earliest poetic attempts date from the eighties, when the 'Storm and Stress' had really already outlived itself. At the same time however the French Revolution was already on the horizon when he made his literary debut. Pietism, too, the special Swabian form of which shaped his development, had passed its peak outside the frontiers of Swabia. On the other hand, Kant's three *Critiques* appeared in the same decade, in which ethics, aesthetics and religion were thought out anew and substantiated on the basis of the refined intellectual processes of the Enlightenment. Goethe, a neo-Platonic mystic by predisposition and self-education, on the closest of terms with leading Pietists like Lavater, had, quite justifiably, from his point of view, taken no cognisance of Kant's writings prior to his friendship with Schiller. Besides he had no childhood pietism to work off. This pietism on the other hand dominated Schiller's youth with a paternal absoluteness and with a quasi-military strictness. His father, Johann Kaspar, was loyal and unequivocal, intelligent too, as the autobiographical sketches and prayer drafts in rhythmic prose testify; and he made no claims for himself beyond his orbit, which was the bourgeois world of a military official. He it was who resolutely determined the education of the children. His mother, Elisabeth Kodweiss, daughter of a baker and innkeeper, supported the gravity of the father's influence in her own pietistic devoutness. In Goethe's home it was the other way round. Schiller's childhood was therefore filled quite differently with religious and moral seriousness, discipline and work. The Duke interfered with the resolve that the boy should become a theologian, for he claimed the talented lad for the Hohe Karlsschule which he had founded. And so he entered an institution for the élite of the rising generation of officers and officials and was dressed in a military uniform. From law, in which he soon lost interest, Schiller turned to medicine, which resulted in a professional career as a military surgeon. Yet his educational goal was on a grand scale, so that at the Hohe Karlsschule the basis was also laid for Schiller's philosophical interests, which he owed to his excellent teacher Karl Friedrich Abel, a disciple of the Scottish popular philosophers. In their optimistic sobriety they formed the natural bridge between authoritarian dogmatism which ruled his childhood and Kant who was to dominate his manhood. After he had completed his training Schiller entered upon the preordained career and became regimental medical officer. At the same time however he was a poet and enthusiastic for poetry in an energetically ambitious sense, at an earlier age and on more absolute terms than the young Goethe. His first work *Die Räuber*, begun whilst he was at the Karlsschule and which was stimulated, as already mentioned, by Schubart, bore in addition all the marks of the impact of Goethe and his friends. He had already got to know Shakespeare and Rousseau, Goethe, Wieland and the *Geniebewegung* when he was at the High School and they dominated his early dramatic work too. Not until *Don Carlos* did he succeed with new forms of his own. Now this does not mean of course that the three early dramas were not original. For they are that both in conception and in language, yet they remain within the framework of a highly individual variant of the style of the age.

It is common knowledge how the young Schiller had to struggle for his freedom to be an independent writer; how Karl Eugen angrily reacted to the performance of *Die Räuber* in Mannheim; how he was so enraged that he ordered a complete ban on writing for Schiller, when diplomatic complaints resulted because of the passage about Graubünden being the land of the robbers and highwaymen. Schiller had the choice between his native land and his genius. He decided upon the famous night-flight on 22 September 1782 with Andreas Streicher, whose description has provided an accurate record. The gravity of this decision of his can be measured by the fact that it meant not only rebellion against the Duke, but also separation from his family, in which Schiller was far more deeply rooted than Goethe was in his. For his pious, upright parents it meant too an especially severe blow. This flight was the start of a long period of travel, full of painful deprivations, the material uncertainties of which, together with inner turmoils, laid the basis for the illnesses that were with him constantly throughout his life, illnesses from which he had to wrest his classical works, and to which he succumbed when only forty-six years old. It was indeed the violent fluctuations of fortune which destroyed him, not even real misfortune of the kind that befell Günther or Schubart. For always friends and patrons were found who would help him over the worst crises: Dalberg, the Director of the Mannheim National Theatre, Henriette von Wolzogen with her generous hospitality at Bauerbach in Thuringia; then, following the second failure of the Mannheim Theatre projects, the self-sacrificing friendship of the Körner household in Dresden, the unexpected stipendium from the Duke of Augustenburg, the Chair of History at Jena through Goethe's good offices, finally the secure and ample living in Weimar after his already chronically affected internal organs, above all the lung, had not allowed him to carry on his job any longer. Yet apart from those five years of homelessness, life had not denied Schiller anything as far as basic values were concerned, not even a wife: Charlotte von Lengefeld from Rudolstadt was to order and control the whole decisive Thuringian phase of his life in a genuine partnership of hearts and minds, but also with constant gentle energy. In her Schiller found the hub of his own home life, in which his clever children grew up, just as friendship with Goethe, that was finally achieved in 1794, guaranteed every intellectual comfort. We are therefore confronted with the biography of a happy man, not a melancholy one, in which the indefinite and confused ideals and passions of the early period (above all for the ambivalent Charlotte von Kalb) mean nothing quintessential. Thomas Mann's interpretation of Schiller, which bases the poet's existence on suffering – in contrast to Goethe, the child of good fortune – can therefore be accepted only with reservations, historically speaking. The fact that he was bad at managing his affairs was something Schiller shared with Goethe and that was no tragedy in itself. Even the struggle for the physical strength to achieve the high level of tasks self-imposed was not unique to him. The picture of the bourgeois home however, which Schiller the Classicist drew in *Lied von der Glocke*, came from one who saw it not from the outside, but from within.

When we draw a comparison with Goethe, however, we must take account of the fact that Schiller, in the early period extending from the flight to Mannheim until the two years spent at Dresden with the Körner family, exposed himself more dangerously both in respect of his personal safety and as regards his ideas. Goethe could almost be consumed in his passion for Lotte, Lili, Frau von Stein. Schiller could only be consumed by ideas, which then frequently became poetic themes. How much more temperate is freedom as a motive of human character in Goethe's *Götz* than the idea of freedom from society as portrayed in Schiller's *Die Räuber* and its political accentuation in *Fiesko* and *Luise Millerin*! How much more significant is the role of the philosophical reflective themes in the poems of the *Anthologie auf das Jahr 1782* than those of the *Laura* poems, which so frequently border on the involuntarily comic element! And here too the position is just the reverse in Goethe's case.

The conception of *Die Räuber* (*The Robbers*) (1781) occurred at the time of the Karlsschule period. His recitation of it to his comrades, incidentally, is preserved in a well-known picture. The success of this drama, to which the publisher added the provocative motto *in tyrannos* only in the printed version, was due to several reasons. Firstly, the adoption of character as a central motif is striking, coupled with the theme of family tragedy. What seems new as against the source work, Schubart's anecdote *Zur Geschichte des menschlichen Herzens* (1775), is that from the mere hereditary intrigue there springs the intrigue concerning Amalie, his brother's intended bride, whom Franz Moor, the 'canaille', would like to snatch from his brother Karl together with the father's inheritance. What is further new is that Franz is depicted as an absolute nihilist who must perish and who cannot be converted – in contrast to Schubart's character. There further enters into it the Rousseauistic sylvan romanticism of the robber theme as a symbol of a life in freedom, not only in freedom from the compulsions of bourgeois society, but also from the denial of rights for the poor person in a faulty system of public order. Furthermore, this theme is also an expression of the new feeling for life awakened by the 'Storm and Stress'. Karl Moor's alienation from class and society bears the stamp not only of private revenge, but denotes advocacy of a new social order. Not merely his demise confirms this fact when he intends the price set on his head for the poor man with the many children. It is borne out equally by his leadership – idealistic in the absolute sense – of the robber band, the reality of which (in the shape of Schufterle and Spiegelberg) finally frustrates the hero as avenger and reformer. A further reason for the effect it had is the high tension of feeling. Karl's filial affection, which is never extinguished, but only disappointed by his brother Franz's intrigue, and his passionate love for Amalie stand in carefully calculated contrast to the adventurous and bloody image of the robber-chief. Karl Moor's fate and character are directly determined by this contrast between the absoluteness of his idea of freedom and the restrictions imposed on it by his ties with his nearest and dearest, whom he loves with equal absoluteness.

We have to imagine all this in the language which the young Schiller developed partly by inborn talent, partly through the stimulus provided by the style of the 'Storm and Stress' writers. It is not the language of Berlichingen. It is as if it were crammed to overflowing with images and pointed appeals to our senses. It bubbles but does not drivel on, as can sometimes be the case with Klinger in his striving for an apparently similar end-effect. Indeed, despite the excess that seems to swamp everything, the sense of expression is tenaciously established. Every image, however extreme, has the function of expressing just this very sense. A linguistic analysis, for example, of Act I, Scene 2 must arrive at this conclusion. There the cascades of images tumble together into one pool, in which virtually every programmatic point of the 'Storm and Stress' from its earliest days onwards is reflected. Rousseau's concept of Nature, Herder's educational realism lie behind the very first words of Karl Moor: 'I loathe this age of scribblers, when I read of great men in my Plutarch.' The contrast of rationalism and greatness corresponds naturally at the same time also to the young Goethe, with whose and Herder's Prome-

theus-idea the following sentence is in tune: 'The blazing flame
of Prometheus has burnt out'.

And so it continues to 'shame on the indolent century of
eunuchs' in a pyrotechnic display of radical expressions which
touch upon nearly every crucial tenet of the *Geniebewegung*:
the lack of creative ability and physical strength, of nature and
heart; miseducation by the schools, a 'costly substitute for your
dissipated lineage'. And there is no lack of the passionate invective against convention and law in general, the 'laced bodice'
imposed on genius:

> Das Gesetz hat zum Schneckengang verdorben, was Adlerflug
> geworden wäre. Das Gesetz hat noch keinen großen Mann
> gebildet, aber die Freiheit brütet Kolosse und Extremitäten aus.[1]

And finally there occurs too the missing key-word of the departed
spirit of Hermann the Cheruscan, which opens the way to the
famous tirade:

> Stelle mich vor ein Heer Kerls wie ich, und aus Deutschland soll
> eine Republik werden, gegen die Rom und Sparta Nonnen-
> klöster sein sollen.[2]

One can hardly blame Karl Eugen for reacting to such a contribution to the linguistic and figurative treasury of the most revolutionary 'Storm and Stress' by one of his subjects, with the greatest
degree of anger.

Two years after *Die Räuber* Schiller completed his first historical
drama *Die Verschwörung des Fiesko zu Genua* (*The Conspiracy
of Fiesco*) (1783). It was originally entitled 'A republican tragedy',
an epithet which Dalberg promptly deleted from the Mannheim production. Moreover *Fiesko* was not staged until 1784 after
Dalberg, to whom the poet had fled in the meantime, had initially
rejected it outright. The production got only a cool reception
not comparable with that given to *Die Räuber*. It is not surprising.
The fault lies in the piece itself, which in fact has as its basis the

---

[1] The law has reduced to a snail's pace what would have become the
flight of the eagle. The law has not yet produced one great man, but freedom hatches out colossi and the exceptional.

[2] Put me before an army of fellows like myself, and from Germany there
would emerge a republic against which Rome and Sparta would be mere
nunneries.

political theme of despotism and its counterpart, namely the ideal republic of free citizens, but which then allows this conflict to run out of steam. And the root of this weakness lies in the character of Fiesco himself who, Caesar and Brutus in one, wavers in his decisions now to the one side, now to the other, and hence is *a priori* not fit for leadership of the democratic revolution. But the fault lies too in the character of his antagonists: the old Doria, who is too distinguished to be a real tyrant (possibly Gianettino, his heir, might have become one), and Verrina, the old revolutionary champion, who is however changed in the conclusion of the play from a real Brutus to a resigned tactician of power. When Verrina in fact recognises that Fiesco is striving not for the civic crown in Genoa, which is now freed of tyranny, but for the ducal crown for himself, he removes the usurper from his path in the very moment of his supposed victory by pushing him into the sea. But this happens not because he wants to set up himself a Republic that corresponds to his ideas, but in order to close Act V with a highly effective play on words; in reply to the question 'Where is Fiesco?' he first answers 'Dead through drowning', and then adds 'through being drowned, if that sounds better – I'm going to Andreas'. Here the young Schiller's stylistic striving for effects turns somersault and leads to cynicism. So that through it not only is the essential meaning of the 'tragedy' put in question (which was already the case anyhow), but also the philosophical basis of the exposition becomes unbalanced since the question of the meaning of History is left totally unanswered.

The modern reader would be none the wiser either if he drew parallels between the *Fiesko* ending and Hofmannsthal's *Turm*. The ambivalence of Schiller's ending is not mystical philosophy of history, but a failure of his feeling for the great dramatic conclusion, a feeling that otherwise rarely misled him. Schiller seemed to have been aware of this weakness since he considered it necessary – as if to make amends – to provide his *dramatis personae* with a comment on their characterisation. Even this introduces quite glaring psychological effects in a prejudicial manner. One may well see here a hint on his part concerning the corrupting evil inherent in power because he discredits all three figures who fight for that power, namely Doria, Fiesco and the old partisan fighter Verrina. But in that case the theme (or the poetic imagination) goes beyond the basic premise of the social order and of history.

For the theatre-going public of the day the thought of the corrupting evil inherent in power was after all outside their experience and hence could not set them aflame, despite individual significant passages of mono- and dialogue. Neither the philosophy of the Enlightenment nor the philosophy of Feeling had posed this question in such a radical form. Today it would perhaps be quite a different tale.

Schiller returned to a contemporary subject with *Kabale und Liebe* (*Intrigue and Love*) (1784), as Iffland named the next piece – whilst the author had originally considered the name of the heroine *Luise Millerin* as the title. In other words, it was really the theme of the 'Roman Virginia', which Lessing had already brought up to date in *Emilia Galotti*. But Lessing's Emilia still acts within the stipulations of rank in the court circle, whilst Schiller now consciously presented a 'bourgeois tragedy' after the 'republican' one. The stipulations of rank are here broken and that signifies that the 'Storm and Stress' drama, above all the social plays of Lenz, as well as Lessing's *Emilia* acted as a model for Schiller. The drama, which was completed in 1783, had its première in Mannheim a few months after *Fiesko*. Its success showed that Schiller was better able to treat contemporary pieces at that time than historical dramas, which is quite in contrast to his classical dramas which without exception project ideas and problems against historical backcloths. And there was no need of an index of characters in this instance as in *Fiesko*. What was shown to be a weakness in *Fiesko* – namely the amalgam of positive and negative qualities on both sides – is integrated here into the theme itself in an extremely effective way. Virtues and vices are found both at court and amongst the honest and upright bourgeoisie. The lovers Ferdinand and Luise incorporate the positive side of court society as well as bourgeois integrity. But Ferdinand is the son of the President von Walter, in whom the villainous features of society at the courtly level culminate. And Luise's suitor, the President's secretary, who is really of the same social class as she, is accentuatedly a child of the bourgeoisie and remains so whilst in courtly service. However he acts as the worst intriguer in the service of the court. On the other hand the Prince's mistress, Lady Milford, acts as the representative of humanity of feeling and compassion. She – the most questionable representative of the courtly circle in the bourgeois sense – appears more intact than

Wurm, the bourgeois figure, in the moral and humane sense. Luise Millerin's end is not like Emilia Galotti's at the hand of her father, but at that of her lover and she dies together with him. She is not the victim of Enlightenment virtue, but of passionate feelings, in which her fate is finally fulfilled and not violently cut short as in the case of Emilia. In reality it is just this very feeling that breaks down the divisions of class and rank or at any rate subordinates them to a common human denominator. Middle-class daughter and aristocratic officer are of equal rank as human beings. But the barrier of class prevents their uniting. In this lies the basis for greater sharpness in the treatment of the theme of social criticism in Schiller's play as against Lessing's. Lenz's touch and probably also the Goethean example of *Clavigo* have left their mark. Intrigue and fallibility (e.g. in the case of old Miller over the President's offer of money) are again human and beyond the confines of class. The contrasts between robbers and society, between ducal house and republicans that one encountered in the young Schiller's preceding dramas are here no longer perceptible as partisan conflicts. The tragedy lies in the human element, in the characters, just as the catastrophe, Ferdinand's deed of passion, is the product of his character. The deed is admittedly provoked — and here lies the tragedy in the play — by the impropriety of society, which wants to hold fast obdurately and obstinately to an out-dated law that keeps the social classes separate against a new age that is dawning.

The role of lyric poetry in Schiller's early work is mirrored in the collection *Anthologie auf das Jahr 1782*. Although Schiller contributed most of the pieces from his own hand, he adhered to the character of the Almanac, since the publication was also to represent at the same time a kind of polemical counterpart to Stäudlin's *Musenalmanach auf das Jahr 1782*. This explains both the anonymity and the game with different ciphers in the individual pieces, behind which the editor hid. Schiller in fact included only a good third of his contribution to the *Anthologie* in the later edition of his poetry. The collection is dedicated to the 'high and mighty Tsar of all flesh', Death, with a preface which is literary and polemical in tone, but which at the same time cannot deny affinity with Goethe's *Schwager Kronos*. It is at the same time a transposition of Matthias Claudius's dedication of the *Wandsbecker Bote* to 'Freund Hein' into the grotesque: 'Your digestion is like cast iron; your appetite, insatiable!' Some of the poems, which however are more unpolitical than the lyric poems of the *Göttinger Hain*, are also grotesque like the macabre figure of this patron. The love poems to Laura, the historical model for whom was the steadfast wife of a captain, just as much as those to Charlotte von Kalb are really the product of 'fantasy', not of experience. That does not prevent them from uttering the most ecstatic language of the 'Storm and Stress':

> Meine Laura! Nenne mir den Wirbel
> Der an Körper Körper mächtig reißt.[3]

Or:

> Aus den Schranken schwellen alle Sehnen,
> Seine Ufer überwallt das Blut,
> Körper will in Körper über stürzen,
> Lodern Seelen in vereinter Glut;[4]
>
> (*Phantasie an Laura*)

It is no earthly love as in Goethe's Erotica,[5] but a flight 'beyond this world' up into the ether:

> Leierklang aus Paradieses Fernen,
> Harfenschwung aus angenehmern Sternen
> Ras' ich in mein trunken Ohr zu ziehn . . .[6]
>
> (*Die seeligen Augenblicke, an Laura*)

Not for nothing does the word 'fantasy' appear amongst the most frequently chosen titles or sub-titles of the *Anthologie* poems. Schiller, the young lyric poet not bound here by any exigency imposed when writing for the stage, soars into a world that is chimerical and intoxicated, in which there are word compositions that are unknown in plain, straightforward language.

We find verbs which do not exist either and whose compression is designed to produce an absolute dynamic effect which is also not

[3] My Laura! give me the name of that force which powerfully pulls two bodies together.

[4] All the sinews burst out of their barriers, the blood wells over its banks, body wants to plunge on body, souls aflame in one common fire.

[5] A reference to the *Römische Elegien*. (*Translator's note*)

[6] The sound of the lyre from distant paradise, the plucking of the harp from more pleasant stars, I am frantic to draw these to my intoxicated ear . . .

of this world. Klopstockian plural forms appear in bewildering abundance, abstracts are forcibly welded into the province of sensuality. Here too we find the germ of Schiller's later intellectual lyric poems. That poetry, as represented already in clear cut fashion by poems like *Hymne an den Unendlichen, Zuversicht der Unsterblichkeit* or *Die Größe der Welt*, constitutes, as it were, workshop pieces for the great philosophical poems of the later period. In the final analysis this branch of the ancestral tree, so to speak, goes back to Haller. But Haller is tame as against the pathos of, say, *Hymne an den Unendlichen* or *Gruppe aus dem Tartarus*. Besides, the great natural scientist never ventured into the anatomy of death and putrefaction so naturalistically in his own verse as the young Schiller did in *Leichenphantasie* and *Die Pest*. The ballad-like pieces *Die Kindsmörderin* and *In einer Bataille* (later *Die Schlacht*) also number amongst these macabre fantasies. They revel in contrasts and hyperbole, and the battle poem, as a linguistic venture, is plainly expressionistic. Just as *Die Kindsmörderin* takes up a 'Storm and Stress' theme, so too do other accusatory poems like *Rousseau* or the group of pungent epigrams. Enthusiasm and terror at the same high pitch, intoxication, dream and daring images crowd for expression and storm about in the poems of the *Anthologie*-period. The intention is clear – to transform the abstract into the sensual, to make the language capable of expressing it, as it were, from out of a state of chaos. The young Goethe, on the other hand, possessed the sensual element without seeking for it. Certainly the bare decade which separates his 'Storm and Stress' poetry from that of Schiller can be seen too as a decisive factor historically speaking, quite apart from the distinction between the 'naïve' and the 'sentimental' poet. Schiller's pathos created at an advanced stage of the period is set alight through contact with an attitude and a style of life which others before him had fashioned.

PART V

Early Classicism

16 Pioneers: Winckelmann and Wieland

In the history of art a classicistic current was already in existence in the Baroque Age, which became concentrated in the course of the eighteenth century and finally led by way of the Empire-style to the Classicism of the Schinkel era. Weimar Classicism was also the result of an organic development. Humanism and the Renaissance as a cultural heritage more extensively dominated Baroque than research on Baroque literature generally admits. An unshakeable vision of classical antiquity is just as much to be found in the eighteenth century, which presents its own kind of Classicism in phenomena such as Gottsched. The decisive change which marks the novel profound interpretation of Antiquity occurred shortly after the middle of the century, namely in Winckelmann's early work. With him, Lessing and Wieland we find ourselves already in the hallway of German Classicism. Indeed if we consider the efforts, for example, of the 'Storm and Stress' for a new Homer-image, the role of the Socrates-symbol in Hamann, the annihilation of French Classicism as a false interpretation of a genuine Classical world – something that is to be found in Lessing, Herder and the young Goethe – we cannot deny the part played by even the *Geniebewegung* in the general movement towards a German form of Classicism. Whether with Rationalistic or 'Storm and Stress' emphasis, the preparation for Weimar was everywhere to be observed. The dispute over Laocoön was just a symptom of it. So were the arguments on the theme of 'How the Ancients portrayed Death', on the problem of Shakespeare and the Greeks. The debate on the drama remained essentially an enquiry into the validity of Aristotle and Horace. And this applies with equal force to the fight over the poetic values of the different genres and indeed of the arts themselves.

Certainly 'the' German Classicism with Weimar as its focal point is defined by Goethe's Italian journey and Schiller's *Die Götter Griechenlands*. It is also defined by Herder's *Winckelmann*-torso and his *Plastik*, and even earlier with Wieland's *Agathon* as far as its philosophy of culture is concerned. But inseparable from these early and anticipatory products (which, as mentioned, are not the real roots) lie the preceding and sometimes passionate efforts to create a German National Theatre from Lessing in Hamburg to Dalberg (together with Schiller) in Mannheim. From Möser and Lessing on, it was clear that a German 'Classicism' comparable to the French was only conceivable when supported by one 'Nation' and one capital. The speculations of the young Herder in the *Literatur-Fragmente* already manifested this problem clearly. The series of polemical publications concerned with Frederick the Great's *De la littérature allemande* also revealed it, this time from the historical angle. The fact that then neither Berlin nor Hamburg, nor Mannheim, nor one of the old cultural cities in the Catholic South, not even Vienna, became the dreamed-of abode of Classicism, but rather the small Central German principality, can scarcely be attributed solely to the good fortune of the towering personalities of Karl August and his mother Anna Amalia. Catholic Vienna (including its South German dependencies) was Hapsburg in attitude with its sights on Spain and Italy rather than 'German' in the spiritual sense. The Prussian might in the North was not only in its way petty nationalistic with its gaze directed towards the East, but was moreover so frenchified culturally amongst the highest circles through the person of the king himself, that it consciously ignored the various German literary voices and trends and virtually had nothing but scorn for them. Right up to the death of Frederick – and that occurred at a late point of time in the history of ideas – the thesis of Bouhours and Mauvillon ruled supreme there, namely the idea that a German could not be *un bel esprit*. Hence both these capitals – the natural capitals, as it were – in the German-speaking world forfeited through their folly the chance of becoming capitals too in the sense of an intellectual centre of Classicism. Perhaps also for another reason it was no accident that Central Germany from Frankfurt to Weimar, Jena, Leipzig and Dresden occupied the place that had been left empty through a special set of circumstances – this had already happened once before, namely at the time of Luther. 'High German' had its origins there. After that Central Germany held the literary balance quite naturally in the Baroque era too. It was not only the cradle of the Language Societies (*Sprachgesellschaften*), but also the leader in literature itself through Saxony and Silesia. The function of Leipzig as a focal point through Gottsched and his school continued despite all the feuds until shortly before the advent of Weimar Classicism. All these factors have to be taken into account.

From out of the welter of micrological, polyhistorical, antiquarian and generally theorising dissensions of scholars over the Classical heritage, which had been broken down into a host of individual problems, a genuine form of Classicism could not have arisen, since the guidelines were missing. These guidelines in fact did not appear until Winckelmann, Lessing, later the essential philology of Heyne and Friedrich August Wolf, Wieland and the young Herder. A real history of the style and the thought of classical antiquity was not conceived therefore until the second half of the eighteenth century and only then the essential basis for Weimar Classicism had been created. This period of the genesis of Classical thought from Winckelmann to the Weimar of Goethe prior to his Italian venture will here be referred to as 'Early Classicism'.

The emergence – remarkable for the time in view of both his origin and upbringing – of Johann Joachim Winckelmann (1717–68) laid the foundation. This son of an Altmark shoemaker achieved a grammar-school and university education despite the most pitiful circumstances, though the fact that his most important teachers recognised his precocious talents admittedly worked in his favour. After his grammar-school days in Stendal and Berlin he attended the University of Halle in 1738 for a period of study which had no satisfactory outcome as such, but where he managed to display unheard-of powers of concentration in his favourite subjects, namely the Humanities and *belles lettres*. The first job after that was an Assistant Master's post in the small Altmark town of Seehausen where he suffered for five years (1743–48). But it was just in that very period that the miracle occurred, namely that this child of the lowest social class, in addition to doing a burdensome job which would have fully occupied others, laid the foundations for a universal education in the grand style with an energy both tenacious and unprecedented. We must remember that Winckelmann indefatigably undertook at that time journeys on foot to Hamburg and Berlin in order to procure the necessary books. The inner resolve held firm. The external resolve came with the summons to the post of librarian in Nöthnitz near Dresden with the Count of Bünau, a Saxon Minister notable on account of his *Reichshistorie*. That one change meant a break into an entirely new world: the giant library was at hand, Dresden the metropolis with its art collections close by, there were the intellectually congenial personalities. Present among these personalities at this time were above all Ludwig von Hagedorn, the aesthetician, and Adam Friedrich Oeser, the copper-plate engraver, artist and also theoretician, later Goethe's art teacher in Leipzig. In the conversations in Oeser's studio, Winckelmann's famous early work *Gedanken über die Nachahmung der Griechischen Wercke in der Malerei und Bildhauerkunst* (*Thoughts on the Imitation of Greek Works in Painting and Sculpture*) (1755) had its origin. It was not merely the first project, but also to some extent an outline plan of Winckelmann's total later work. In it was contained the guiding formula for the interpretation of Antiquity, the formula of 'noble simplicity and quiet grandeur', which worked like a revelation for the movement towards Classicism. And then beyond Classicism too it was to remain the determining factor for the idea of beauty from Wackenroder up to Thorvaldsen, Stifter and Mörike.

Winckelmann's conversion to Catholicism also fell in the period of this initial work and the two commentaries which he wrote after it. This step aroused the feelings of many at the time and indeed moved Goethe to analyse it in detail in *Winckelmann und sein Jahrhundert* (*Winckelmann and his Century*), that highly stylised swan-song of Weimar Classicism. Was it the act of a renegade? Was it dishonesty and calculation? Did Winckelmann remain a crypto-Protestant even in Rome where he provenly continued to read the Lutheran hymn-book? Even the correspondence that is available today through Walter Rehm's good offices does not solve this puzzle. The fact is well established that his conversion to Rome was worth a Mass as far as Winckelmann was concerned, The rapid climb, whereby he advanced within a decade *via* the posts with the Cardinals to the curatorship of Roman antiquities, would have been inconceivable without the change of faith. Yet it can hardly be doubted that it was not Rome, but his passion for Greece for which his real sacrifice was made. And that it was indeed a sacrifice, and no light one at that, emerges from comments in correspondence. Winckelmann was not inclined to frivolity. On the other hand we have to take into account the fact that Italy, initially adopted as his spiritual home from free choice, grabbed hold of him – much more firmly than was the case with Goethe – right from the moment when the papal nuntio Archinto, the initiator of his conversion, arranged in 1755 for him to go to Cardinal Albani in Rome, up to his violent death. Lessing and Herder had travelled through Italy a little like nordic phantoms. Goethe and Winckelmann however grew roots there and were really alive in the South. That explains the sensual and sensuous side which is also part of Winckelmann, namely the enjoyment of life and also the joy he found in beautiful persons, a joy which, as similarly later with Platen, was admittedly restricted to people of his own sex. At all events his fine sense of beauty was also sensually inspired, it was not merely the product of scholarly cultivation. But from both causes nevertheless he became the greatest archaeologist of the age. His sole publication on aesthetic education, *Abhandlung von der Fähigkeit der Empfindung des Schönen* (1763), verifies this connection between theory and real life. Besides the descriptive and reference works of the Italian period, the work on the famous collection of glyptographs of Baron Stosch in Florence (1760) and the *Monumenti antichi inediti* (1767), the great work of synthesis that won Winckelmann European stature was *Die Geschichte der Kunst des Alterthums* (*The History of Ancient Art*) (1764–67). What Germany had deprived him of as far as the viewing of originals was concerned (after all, Berlin and Dresden at that time were endowed with only chance acquisitions; and therefore the Greek formula contained in the Dresden writing was drawn up as much from Classical Antiquity in reproduction as from Raphael's *Sistina*), Winckelmann could now enjoy to the full in Italy from Florence to Naples and Pompeii. Without this vantage point – with Rome as the key observation post – the *Geschichte der Kunst des Alterthums* would be inconceivable. And so his great passion for antiquity and the country that was the object of his contemplation, Italy, were fused in Winckelmann to create the very secret of his existence. The end of his life demonstrated that clearly enough. His final journey (after thirteen years in Rome), that was planned with the most honourable of intentions on the basis of invitations to the courts of Vienna and Berlin, turned into a catastrophe for him. He could scarcely bring himself to cross the Alps. In Regensburg he broke his journey like a fugitive. Nevertheless he allowed himself to be persuaded to go to Vienna, where Maria Theresia bestowed imperial honours upon him. He wanted to take flight for home, as if seized by hysteria. The fact that he confided so openly in his murderer Arcangeli in Trieste would seem to fit the pattern of behaviour. On showing the precious gifts of honour from Germany, he was attacked and stabbed by the travelling companion who was really unknown to him, and Winckelmann soon bled to death from his wounds. His death aroused the deepest feelings in the homeland he had left.

Winckelmann's statement about the noble simplicity and quiet grandeur of the Greeks was meant to be obligatory for good taste:

> Der gute Geschmack, welcher sich mehr und mehr durch die Welt ausbreitet, hat sich angefangen, zuerst unter dem griechischen Himmel zu bilden.[1]

This is the basis of the *Gedanken über die Nachahmung*. It is historical substantiation and aesthetic norm at one and the same time:

> Der einzige Weg für uns, groß, ja, wenn es möglich ist, unnachahmlich zu werden . . . ist die Nachahmung der Alten.[2]

This formulation is hardly intended as a word-play or paradox, but signifies the abrogation of the mechanical mimesis-interpretation of Aristotle in German and French Rationalism, above all of Gottsched and his school.

Winckelmann's starting point at that time still lay much more in classical literature than in the plastic arts, namely in Homer, and yet more Homer. Just as Homer is symbolic for the literary skill of the Ancients, so Laocoön acts as a symbol for the plastic arts in Winckelmann's *Nachahmung*:

[1] Good taste, which is spreading more and more through the world, had its origins initially under the Greek skies.
[2] The only way for us to become great – indeed if it be possible, inimitable . . . is by imitating the Ancients.

Laokoon war den Künstlern im alten Rom eben das, was er uns
ist; des Polyklets Regel; eine vollkommene Regel der Kunst.[3]

Just as Homer and Laocoön are seen as standing side by side, so too
Plato, Pindar and Sophocles are related to Phidias and the Vatican
Apollo. But the basic formula for Hellenism was developed in
Laocoön.

The most important and most exciting factor for the age was
Winckelmann's sense of a classical unity and totality. What he
worked out here, Goethe and Schiller were able to assimilate
directly into their 'Classicism'. And for this very reason Winckelmann stands in contrast to the Baroque and Rationalistic study
of Antiquity. He was indeed a historical antiquary and supreme
connoisseur, yet no less an enthusiast as well. Through making
Homer and Plato his literary starting points, he set up a normative Classical concept that was much more cogent than those
fashioned by French Classicism or Gottsched. Experience and a
lively consciousness of quality were the decisive factors with
Winckelmann. What was to be imitated – Antiquity – was not
therefore valid *because* it was ancient, but because it coincided
with every creative act by men of distinction.

Here too we find the connection with Winckelmann's knowledge of Plato and Platonic philosophy. For the roots of Winckelmann's idealistic aestheticism were also Platonic. First of all his
concept of nature can be seen as thus determined. The artist must
not copy the diminished reality of the world comprehended by
the senses. Such reality led to the Dutch naturalism that Winckelmann hated. That concerned only the reality far removed from
divine origins, no longer an ideal reality but a material, fortuitous and impure one. It was much more the duty of true art, such
as the Greeks had conceived it and after them (in Winckelmann's
eyes), in the fullest way possible, Raphael, Michelangelo too in
part and Poussin (though already no longer Leonardo and Dürer!),
to recapture Beauty in a selective and hence also synthetic process
gleaned by means of scattered clues. The great work of art would
thus again manifest original beauty, but only as an 'imitation' of
'beautiful', not 'common' nature. This distinction of beautiful
and common nature is self-evidently aesthetic idealism and as such

[3] Laocoön was for the artist in ancient Rome exactly what he is for us:
Polycletus' principle; a perfect principle of art.

it was subsequently to determine Schiller's doctrine of Beauty and Goethe's Classical distinction between Truth and Reality. This understanding however was not proof against misuse in the hands of classicistic imitators. Winckelmann's overflowing enthusiasm for the eclecticism of a Raphael Mengs revealed his lack of practical safeguards in this direction.

And Winckelmann's idealism is exposed on another front too, similarly revealed in the *Nachahmung*. That book had already tended to recommend a doctrine of allegory that could be taught and learned. Later in Rome Winckelmann completed this train of thought in the *Versuch einer Allegorie, besonders für die Kunst* (1766), without however changing his standpoint. This belief in allegory can likewise be seen as deriving from his Platonism. Already the famous Laocoön-interpretation in the *Nachahmung* just as much as the later one in the *Kunstgeschichte* progresses towards an ideal human image of stoic character, that entails the containment of pain by the mind. And this was the point at which Lessing took offence in his *Laokoon*, because for him this concept was too idealistic and not sensual enough. Winckelmann's doctrine of allegory goes however back to the same idealistic prerequisite of the 'mind'. He explains allegory as a sensualisation of the intellectual world of ideas through art. That the Baroque Age had already known however, yet Winckelmann had emphatically rejected Baroque art (both as Mannerism and as Naturalism). This affinity could not have been clear to him, since he arrived at his concept of allegory in the long run not historically, but philosophically. Winckelmann could not possibly suspect that at the time of 'High Classicism' the dry classicistic painter Hans Asmus Carstens would push allegory to such a point that he even tried to portray pictorially the Kantian categories of space and time. Yet even the Goethe of the *Propyläen*-period was to be more inclined to allegorical art than was in keeping with his nature. The allegorical doctrine as a later classicistic convention – that was the danger!

In all this Winckelmann's own style remained lucid and carefully reasoned but not abstract, nor cool either but sensuous, indeed enthusiastic on occasion. Besides the Laocoön interpretations, other examples of interpretation like that of the so-called torso of Belvedere, which fills a separate masterly thought-out piece of writing, or the enthusiastic description of the Vatican

Apollo in the *Kunstgeschichte* had already been termed poetic dithyrambs in his own day – and rightly so. For there indeed emerges from them both persuasive objectivity and poetic fantasy. The question of archaeological accuracy can really only be of secondary importance in all this.

It is not terribly important if the Belvedere torso is not even interpreted any more today as Hercules, or if Winckelmann's model for classical Hellenism, the Laocoön, is established as a late work, not Classical, but Hellenistic. The importance lies much more in the unprecedented desire for synthesis. Herein lies Winckelmann's significance in the history of ideas, namely in his exemplifying of the ideal of the beautiful and great person in terms of classical art. The task demanded powers of divination together with, and incorporated in an expertise down to the last detail. In the writing on the Hercules torso we read:

> . . . so lernt hier, wie die Hand eines schöpferischen Meisters die Materie geistig zu machen vermögend ist.[4]

He says this about the body, not about the head. The latter Winckelmann poetically invents in the consciousness of the Platonic idea from the inner image of the beautiful man:

> Und indem sich so ein Haupt voll von Majestät und Weisheit vor meinen Augen erhebt, fangen in meinen Gedanken die übrigen mangelhaften Glieder sich an zu bilden: Es sammelt sich ein Ausfluß aus dem Gegenwärtigen und wirkt gleichsam eine plötzliche Ergänzung.[5]

The model too for the projected undertaking – an enormous one for the age – of the *Kunstgeschichte* becomes apparent here. In the final analysis that project amounted to the brilliant divination of a totality from a fragmented world of remains preserved by chance. With the two writings of 1759, *Erinnerung über die Betrachtung der alten Kunst* and *Von der Grazie in Werken der Kunst*, together with the *Abhandlung von der Fähigkeit der*

---

[4] . . . then learn here how the hand of a creative master is capable of making the material spiritual.

[5] And as such a head full of majesty and wisdom rises up before my eyes, the remaining missing limbs begin to take shape in my thoughts: There is a gathering outflow from what is actually there, giving rise as it were to a sudden full complementation.

Empfindung des Schönen in der Kunst, Winckelmann continuously clarified his interpretative procedures as well as his aesthetic principles in a similar style that lies between intellectual reasoning and imaginative writing. He worked too with complete understanding of what constitutes genius:

> Gib Achtung, ob der Meister des Werkes, welches du betrachtest, selbst gedacht oder nur nachgemacht hat . . .[6]

Diligence alone does not make talent, despite the high assessment of everything craftsmanlike that characterised Winckelmann's judgements. On the other hand, for him talent could be manifested without diligence – which is not to be understood as an apology for negligence, but rather as an expression of a deeply rooted aristocratic view of genius.

Winckelmann's doctrine of Grace is on the same plane, a direct precursor of Schiller's *Über Anmut und Würde*: 'It is shaped through education and reflection and can be transformed into Nature . . .' The phrase taken from pietistic language 'It is at work in the simplicity and in the stillness of the soul . . .' is contiguous with the formula in the *Nachahmung* concerning Greek art and finds an echo still in Wackenroder and Stifter. From the point of view of the history of ideas this is of more importance than the definition of Grace as 'that which is rationally pleasing' in the eighteenth-century meaning. As it is both the 'most sensual of all' and teachable, it fits in, too, with Winckelmann's Platonism.

In the *Empfindung des Schönen* Winckelmann again reveals an aristocratic emphasis and is almost classicistic in his aversion to Gothic (with its 'little men in our old cathedrals'); here in this work on aesthetic education he employs as a basis the doctrine of Platonic love. Thus he possesses all the necessary requirements to write the *Geschichte der Kunst des Alterthums*: the enormous knowledge of Antiquity culled from literary sources, already acquired before going to Rome, the breadth of vision, consciously aimed at and systematically made his own in Rome, Florence and Naples, the synthesising gift through which everything was ordered, philosophically too, and given a meaning within its historical setting. Montesquieu's knowledge proved helpful to him in this

---

[6] Pay attention to whether the master of the work you are considering has thought it out himself or only imitated it.

(as it did later to Herder). From the Frenchman he was able to learn what historical genesis was, the insight into the growth of classical culture from specific conditions of the country, climate and the indigenous peoples. Montesquieu's early work *Considéra-tions sur les causes de la grandeur des Romains et de leur décadence* (1743) had already developed, or at any rate hinted at a kind of historical morphology: national history as a process of origin, blooming and withering away analagous, so to speak, to the natural historical process of growth. In Winckelmann's hands the history of art became not merely, as he put it in the Preface, the 'account of chronology and the changes within it', but in fact the first example in the German language of a grand scale stylistic history based on the circumstances of its growth. Herder's *Ideen zur Philosophie der Geschichte der Menschheit* would later ex-pand Montesquieu's and Winckelmann's conception to a history of the evolution of mankind.

The first books on the origins of art and its early stages among the Egyptians, Persians, Phoenicians and Etruscans are magnifi-cent and directly pre-related to Herder. Only then does the book proceed to the Greeks themselves. But it is there, in a decisive passage in Book IV, that the basic aesthetic viewpoint and its philosophical hypothesis is clarified for the first time in any detail. He calls it God within the Beautiful, and at the same time he defines it as the 'highest concept of humanity'. Therefore Winckelmann was already writing history from the point of view of humanitarian philosophy (Humanität). This attitude explains why this founder of the German Classical style is so totally absorbed as a personality by his classical subject matter, and at the same time it elucidates his comprehensive way of viewing everything from a Platonic-idealistic standpoint. On the occasion of the other interpretation of Laocoön (in Book X) this is con-densed to the sentence:

Der Weise findet darinnen zu forschen und der Künstler unauf-hörlich zu lernen, und beide können überzeugt werden, daß in diesem Bilde mehr verborgen liegt, als das Auge entdeckt; und daß der Verstand des Meisters viel höher noch als sein Werk gewesen.[7]

[7] The wise man finds scope for research and the artist scope for unlimited learning, and both can be convinced that more lies hidden in this picture

Small wonder then that the young Herder of the *Literatur-Frag-mente*, long before he founded his *Denkmal* to him in 1778, set himself the task of becoming, along the lines of the Winckelmann in the history of art, a 'Winckelmann in terms of literature', and really throughout his life (up to *Adrastea*) he remained fascinated by this model. In 1805 Goethe then gave the grandest, most com-plete, statuary-stylised picture of Classicism in his contribution *Winckelmann und sein Jahrhundert*. Clear proof of the lasting nature of this fascination.

If Winckelmann was, so to speak, the precursor of Classicism in an aristocratic educational sense, then Wieland is such as the populariser of Greek subject matter, in which he either clothed his own works or which he spread as a translator to broader strata of society. And if Winckelmann offered the intellectual back-ground, Wieland provided its sociology. His activity as a writer helped in considerable part to provide the Classical authors with a public and later, from Weimar, to spread their wealth of ideas and of formal achievements directly or indirectly through the medium of discussion in his journal *Der Teutsche Merkur*. He was constantly capable of assimilating the fashionable modes of the day, tolerant and versatile to the limit of what could justifiably be presented; he was capable of distancing himself, so that he could compare himself with a chameleon, able, resourceful and with a nose for scenting out things. These qualities made him the dis-tinguished catalyser of energies stored in the higher intellectual sphere. Wieland achieved what neither Winckelmann nor Herder nor Goethe could, what Schiller's rhetoric managed only on occasions: this was to address his contemporaries in a compre-hensive fashion even on aesthetic matters, to popularise the Classical thoughts on education. Admittedly this ability was the result of a lengthy, indeed erratic development.

Christoph Martin Wieland (1733–1813), the son of a vicar from the vicinity of the little Swabian town of Biberach, received an excellent, humanistic education there and later in the monastery Berge near Magdeburg. He was one of the precocious youthful prodigies of the age like Haller and Lessing. To the University of Tübingen he brought, together with his knowledge of the Humani-ties, an already extensive knowledge of the Moral Weeklies and

than meets the eye; and that the mind of the master has far excelled his work.

Shaftesbury, probably the most lasting of his models. At that time he was seventeen years old, sensitive and sensual, and experiencing his first youthful love for his older cousin Sophie Gutermann, the later Sophie von La Roche. In Tübingen he began to shape into a man of the world and to develop already an appropriate philosophy for life (*Zwölf moralische Briefe*) (*Twelve Moral Letters*) (1752). He was to establish himself later in this context, also as an academic for a short time in Erfurt, before he was summoned in 1772 to Weimar as tutor to Karl August. It is significant however that Wieland's educational path up to this last stage was not determined by his law-studies which he had chosen, but by his free resolve on *belles lettres*, to which he devoted himself to the utmost. In 1752 Bodmer (following his disappointment with Klopstock) invited him to Zürich. For more than two years Wieland lived at the old man's house and understood how to fit in perfectly with him. He annotated Bodmer's *Noah* and used that model to write the verse epic *Der gepryfte Abraham* (1753). And in his imitation of Bodmer the young Wieland himself proceeded to the composition of hymns and psalms. But that could not last. The man of the Enlightenment, who was already at home with Voltaire's works, had completed in the manner of Lucretius (and Haller) a didactic poem *Über die Natur der Dinge oder Die vollkommenste Welt* (1752), in which he had advocated a kind of deistic Eudemonism, and who had used Ludwig von Bar's elegant fashionable philosophy contained in the *Epitres Diverses* as a model for his own *Moralische Briefe* – and all this when he was seventeen to eighteen years old! – could only assume Bodmer's patriarchal religiosity as a mask. Even the following period (which he spent in Berne, where there occurred a short-lived relationship with Julie von Bondeli, later Rousseau's friend, a relationship which nevertheless went as far as an engagement) had to appear to Bodmer as nothing other than apostasy. And indeed, following his insincere seraphic period, Wieland returned in 1760 full-speed to worldly life. This was again in his hometown of Biberach, close to which the Count Stadion encouraged at his castle a worldly social life in the late Rococo style. The love of his youth, Sophie von La Roche, had arranged the meeting with the Count, whose considerable library became useful too in Wieland's further education. Out of the seraphic poet grew the Rococo poet in classical garb, satirical and graceful. In the sixties came the *Komische Erzählungen* (*Comic Tales*) (1762–65), *Musarion oder die Philosophie der Grazien* (*Musarion or The Philosophy of the Graces*) (1768) and above all *Die Geschichte des Agathon* (*The Story of Agathon*) (1766–67). Altogether, his work at that time was characterised by an amalgam of the classical and the romance worlds. *Der Sieg der Natur über die Schwärmerey oder Die Abentheuer des Don Sylvio von Rosalva* (*The Victory of Nature over Ecstasy or The Adventures of Don Sylvio of Rosalva*) (1764) was a comic novel after the manner of Cervantes, not the classical writers. It is in the first three mentioned works however that Wieland appeared as a pathfinder for Classicism. In terms of content as well as of form they represented, so to speak, a complete contrast to the seraphic Wieland. If he had set himself up during the Zürich period as a judge of morals against the Anacreontics in the *Empfindungen eines Christen* (1757), he would now have had to summon the censors to pass judgement on himself in respect of the suggestiveness of themes in the *Komische Erzählungen*. He presented neither Winckelmann's Antiquity nor ethical grace, but courtly grace along French lines. And so the French fairy tale could also clothe Wieland's desire for grace as well as could the Classical Antiquity of Lucian or even Petronius. Indeed the *Komische Erzählungen* might be understood as a kind of reaction to the Christian pathos of the Swiss period. As in the Spanish-orientated *Don Sylvio*, so too here does a 'victory of Nature over ecstasy' take place.

Yet a 'golden age of morals' is mirrored, an age in which not yet

> gleisnerische Heiligkeit
> das höchste Gut der Sterblichkeit,
> den frohen Sinn, um seine Unschuld brachte.[8]

Wieland's Antiquity was a one-sidedly happy naturalness and contained nothing of an idealistic obligation as with Winckelmann. The guiding light here was not Raphael, but the graceful sensuousness of Watteau and Fragonard. And so Wieland felt no hesitation in capitalising on Antiquity for an operetta in a carefree matter-of-fact manner, both in *Alceste* (1773) and *Pandora* (1779). And this early naturalistic and also courtly classical conception

---

[8] Hypocritical sanctity cause[s] the highest gift of mortal being, a happy disposition, to lose its innocence.

led him later in 1777 in his *Teutscher Merkur* to venture an essay entitled *Auch die Griechen hatten ihre Teniers und Ostades*. Contained in it was an open criticism of Winckelmann, for whom the very formulation of this question would have been an outrage. And indeed, Wieland's attitude to the Ancients was not directed like Winckelmann's at a different nature of the Greeks, and hence at the necessity for Moderns to become different, but rather at an all too intimate familiarity with the Greeks, as Goethe's farce in fact made compromisingly clear. At all events, Wieland's Rococo Antiquity was later to become virulent again, even if on a considerably higher plane, in Goethe's *Maskenzüge* and indeed even in *Faust II*. And the starting point there lay in Wieland's *Komische Erzählungen*. If Wieland dwelt there, to the extent of being suggestively salacious, upon the physical charms displayed by Diana whilst bathing or by Leda when meeting the transformed Jupiter, we must interpret it not merely as a doubtful element, but also as an attempt to bring an all too idealised Antiquity firmly back to earth. Despite so much gloss instead of depth in his picture of the Greeks, we must give Wieland the credit for erecting through his clear and broad-based appeal a dam, so to speak, against the Winckelmannian stylisation, which could easily have become not Classical but classicistic. Moreover in Wieland's work as against the rococo of the Anacreontics with its unmistakable bourgeois tone, there also blows a breath of elegance in the insinuatingly refined language. Yet Winckelmann would rightly have missed the sense of style. If Mercury is addressed by the prince as Mr Hermes in the *Paris* story, or Venus is described as she is there, the effect so achieved is contrary to Winckelmann's intent. Antiquity, in danger with Winckelmann of becoming all too etherealised, is all flesh and blood in every sense with Wieland.

The small verse epic *Musarion*, on a similar formalistic plane as the *Komische Erzählungen*, is again anti-sentimental. Here a rich, handsome, cheerful Greek youth is cured of the whim to consider the world from a different aspect for once, namely from philosophical seclusion, and is won back to the world of love through the appearance of a beautiful coquette. Now that is a theme from the Gottschedian stable of comedy, a Rococo-ised version of the pastoral set-up with all its ingredients. It needs neither invention nor originality at all. Phanias is the young

Athenian, who, when the money gives out, takes leave of the world as a den of vice in company with a cynic. He basically represents the cavalier who after bankruptcy plunges headlong into bigoted piety: 'full of the great truth that all is vanity'. Here too we find antiquity reduced to the level of the fairy tale. For alongside that philosophy should stand the alternative way out: 'enter upon noble adventures / and stain the offensive world with giant's blood.' Musarion appears to Phanias amid such thoughts, in order to test the new way of thinking which 'had poured upon him grief, philosophy and distress'. And all the ploys of a Rococo maiden are here brought into play for this. Thus from the intended philosopher's country seat there emerges a temple of the Graces 'in joys, which the genuine stamp of innocence and nature marks as pure joys'. The key is a hedonistic one. The charming philosophy of love triumphs over philosophical hypocrisy which 'speaks constantly of virtue'. What the acclaimed 'innocence' consists of, remains undisclosed.

In this philosophy of the Graces developed by the Wieland of the pre-Weimarian period and which he also presented in other works, there is much that is at the same time suggestive and unequivocal, above all the wit invested in it. But his work brought classical themes, ideas and allusions to the people, it was particularly bound up with an inexhaustible activity on his part as translator (his Shakespeare translation incidentally was also part and parcel of this and corresponded to Wieland's Protean nature). To meet the reproach of frivolity he was consequently compelled to give to the theme of sensuality the interpretation of a spiritual love and inner beauty (Die Grazien, 1770; Der Neue Amadis, 1771; Der verklagte Amor, 1774). Also to be numbered amongst these self-vindications are Sokrates mainomenos oder Die Dialogen des Diogenes von Sinope (1770) and the confrontation with Rousseau dating from the same year: Beyträge zur Geheimen Geschichte des menschlichen Verstandes und Herzens, aus den Archiven der Natur. The intellectual means of vindication was Shaftesbury's balanced harmony of sensuality and morality. The multifarious effects of this Platonist of English Enlightenment on the German 'Storm and Stress' have already been alluded to. Wieland was the Shaftesbury disciple from the other camp.

So in theory everything looked more temperate, more Platonic. Indeed already prior to the appearance of Musarion, self-reflection

had manifested itself in a significant literary achievement which
had been slowly maturing (from 1761 on) and which began to
appear in 1766. This was the *Bildungsroman, Agathon,* which Lessing called in his *Hamburgische Dramaturgie* the 'first and only
novel for the thinking mind of classical taste'. If Lessing could go
to such lengths as that in his praise, it may be presumed that
this 'classical' novel could satisfy other claims than those of the
Komische Erzählungen and *Musarion.* The story of *Agathon* is a
novel of development in the real sense, hence of its type a direct precursor of *Wilhelm Meister.* The subject matter alone is demanding:
it is a picture of the time of Socrates. Its central figure is a young
man equally open to intellectual and sensuous influences, who is
made to find his way through the world of politics and the sphere
of philosophical intellectualism. Again Wieland pours into the
story of his hero his own educational experiences. We find the
seraphic note *à la* Klopstock and Bodmer represented by the virtuous over-enthusiasm of the young Agathon; the philosophy of the
Graces to the very point of a refined hedonism; finally, the
Platonic, Shaftesbury-like corrective to both in the increasing
world-acceptance by the young Greek. Therein lies the real importance in terms of historical development, supported as it is by the
role of the sophist Hippias, which is socratic in part, though over-
whelmingly Mephistophelian.

We should briefly remind ourselves of the course of events in
the tale. We meet Agathon with his youthful integrity and passionate nature in the region of Delphi, a pure fool of enthusiasm,
so to speak. (It is Wieland up to the end of his Zürich period.)
Pirates sell him as a slave to the sophist Hippias, who sets everything on converting him to his philosophy and experiences. The
ecstasy of the young Agathon is naïve enthusiastic Platonism.
Hippias soon elicits this from the slave:

Die allgemeine Stille, der Mondschein, die rührende Schönheit
der schlummernden Natur, die mit den Ausdünstungen der
Blumen durchwürzte Nachtluft, tausend angenehme Empfindungen, deren liebliche Verwirrung meine Seele trunken machte,
setzten mich in eine Art von Entzückung . . . Dieses brachte
mich auf die Gedanken, wie glücklich der Zustand der Geister
sei, die den groben tierischen Leib abgelegt haben und im
Anschauen des wesentlichen Schönen, des Unvergänglichen,

Ewigen und Göttlichen Jahrtausende durchleben, die ihnen nicht länger scheinen als mir dieser Augenblick.[9]

Against this enthusiastic Platonism Wieland sets the naturalistic ethical code of Hippias, one which was similarly based on the Enlightenment:

> . . . und dieses allgemeine Gesetz, was könnt' es anders sein als die Stimme der Natur, die zu einem jeden spricht: Suche dein eigenes Bestes; oder mit anderen Worten: befriedige deine natürlichen Begierden und genieße so viel Vergnügen, als du kannst.[10]

Nature and epicureanism are here therefore identifiable as the same thing, so to speak. To this 'state of nature' is correlated the 'state of society'. And only the social contract determines the concepts of virtue and vice. They are however relative, differently determined by the profit or loss to every individual nation. Naturally all illusions of absolute and universal moral philosophy thereby become untenable for Agathon. And Hippias makes practice follow theory and forthwith produces the suitable courtesan for Agathon – the beautiful Danaë. Unexpectedly however the two approach each other only on a platonic level, counter to Hippias' intention. Having thereupon been enlightened by Hippias as to the courtesan past of his beautiful partner, Agathon flees in order to meet Danaë again at the end of the story – now on another plane of education and experience. However Agathon first avoids the demands of Hippias to realise his naturalism, by taking flight.

And it is with this that his real story of development begins beyond the private sphere, his experience in the social-political realm. At the court of Dionysus of Syracuse Agathon becomes a

[9] The general calm, the moonlight, the stirring beauty of slumbering nature, the night air scented with the smell of flowers, a thousand pleasant sensations, whose delightful headiness intoxicated my soul, transported me into a kind of rapture . . . this led me to the thoughts of how blessed the condition of spirits was, which have laid aside the rude animal form and live for millennia in contemplation of the essentially beautiful, the immortal, the eternal and divine, millennia which to them do not seem any longer than does this moment to me.

[10] . . . and this general law, what else could it be but the voice of nature that speaks to each and every one: Search for what is best for you. Or in other words: Satisfy your natural desires and enjoy such pleasures as you can.

man of the world, foundering outwardly on his own convictions. Only here does he experience for the first time the limits which reality places on every absolute idealism. He learns to make reductions in his demands on man and thus gets a whiff of worldly ways. Yet he acknowledges only its empiric necessity. He does not adopt Hippias's cynicism of relativity as an ethical code at this stage of life. Hippias has to take cognisance of this when he seeks out Agathon in his misfortune. Thanks to Plato and Shaftesbury, the hero, who has now undergone his experiences, finally finds the solution in conversation with his old mentor and liberator Archytas and in the reunion with Danaë in Tarentum. There is an attitude of understanding wisdom, in which the antithesis of virtue and sensuality is resolved. To attain it, one has to have undergone experiences which protect one against a utopian assessment of man, without leading to the egoism and the scepticism of a Hippias. Man is neither wholly animal nor wholly intellect. It is in fact the golden mean of the Enlightenment.

After the 'satirical novel' *Don Sylvio von Rosalva*, a descendant of Don Quixote (save that the hero is handsome and young, and the object of the satire is not outmoded chivalry, but the fashionable motif of the 'faerie'), came his *Die Abderiten, eine sehr wahrscheinliche Geschichte* (*The Abderites, a very Probable Story*) (1774), a tale this time with a different point to make and a considerably greater impact. This was due to the fact that no longer merely a fashion – that of fanatical enthusiasm – but man as a philistine of the bourgeois age in general was here the subject of attack. The ancient Gothamites' town of Abdera in Thrace is presented as a guise for what is meant to be in reality the typical small provincial town of the eighteenth century. For in many respects this novel is a kind of *Schlüsselroman*:[11] the 'case of the ass's shadow', for example, relates a true episode from Wieland's time as an official in Biberach, while the prudery of his own age finds a reflection in the occasion when the Abderites in fact buy a Venus of Praxiteles, but place it where it can not be seen. The historical Abderite Democritus forms a central figure in the novel. He, the only reasonable person amongst his fellow citizens, is to be declared mad – admittedly unsuccessfully so – by Hippocrates. Satire on the theatre is not lacking either (on the occasion of a

---

[11] *Vide* Glossary.

H

visit by Euripides). It revolves around the exposing of intellectual narrowmindedness in general; in this way it is of universally human interest and on account of its topical flavour was also quite naturally acceptable to an age so accustomed to satire. Wieland has made this reference sufficiently clear in his key to *Die Abderiten*:

> Sie sind allenthalben immer noch die nämlichen Narren, die sie vor 2000 Jahren zu Abdera waren.[12]

To this extent then *Die Abderiten* is indirectly an educational novel, the subject of which is bourgeois society itself.

It can also be seen as based already on experience gained in Weimar society and indeed as a mirror held up to this society. For after the short interlude as Professor of Philosophy at Erfurt from 1769 to 1772 Wieland was summoned to Weimar by the Dowager Duchess Anna Amalia. His pupil was Karl August himself, who at that time was still a minor and of a not easily controllable character. Wieland had recommended himself for such a position not only through his *Agathon*, but also through his recently published pedagogic novel *Der Goldne Spiegel oder Die Könige von Scheschian* (*The Golden Mirror, or the Kings of Scheschian*) (1772) with its special theme of princely responsibility. It represented an admiration garbed in symbolic form for Joseph II, and hence for enlightened absolutism. The location of the kingdom of Scheschian removed this scene again to the Orient, to the fairy-tale ambience. The golden mirror is a symbol of princely self-recognition. For only with that purpose in mind does one see oneself in it and one's own fate as well as that of the people. The motto of the old Tifan, the first of the Scheschian kings, who was the sometime author of the Book of Duties for the Monarch, is that of Frederick the Great and Joseph:

> Diese Gesetze, welche wir beschworen haben, werden unsere Richter sein! . . . und wegen alles Guten, welches wir zu tun unterlassen, wegen alles Bösen, welches wir getan haben, wird dereinst ein unerbittlicher Richter Rechenschaft von unsrer Seele fordern![13]

---

[12] They are everywhere ever the same fools they were two thousand years ago in Abdera.

[13] These laws which we have sworn to uphold shall be our judge. And for every good which we fail to do, and for every evil which we have committed, a pitiless judge will one day demand us to render an account of our soul.

That is moral philosophy, it is an open call for a sense of responsibility and conscience, more specific still than Agathon's political experiences. It must have been this Wieland, not the seraphic one and also not the Wieland of the philosophy òf the Graces, whom the niece of Frederick the Great summoned as tutor to the Crown Prince – a happy choice as it was soon to turn out. Wieland retained the gratitude of the later Duke even after the fulfilment of his task. And in this way he remained in Weimar, well provided for and with all the leisure he required for further development. This development incidentally can be seen in his continuing productivity as a translator of Horace, Cicero and Lucian. These works were in fact more in his line than the twenty-two Shakespeare plays he translated in the sixties. In the very founding too of journals like the *Attisches Museum* (1796–1804; continued to 1809) he became a publicist of the antiquity of his choice. He was even more significant as editor of the *Teutscher Merkur* (1773–89), a leading journal for the whole of Germany, a periodical of great range covering aesthetic, literary and popular philosophical matters. From the profits of this he was able to acquire for himself and his large family the beloved country estate of Ossmannstedt. His literary work revolved increasingly around the court. That was to be seen not only in the aforementioned musical comedies, but was also manifest in his most popular work, the epic poem inspired by Shakespeare, namely *Oberon* (1780), which had even Goethe's unqualified approbation. This verse epic – as imaginative as it is graceful – in free rhythmic stanzas is at all events an 'excursion into the old romantic countryside', as the introductory strophe states; yet besides the thematic source, namely the *chanson de geste, Huon de Bordeaux*, Wieland expressly draws upon Chaucer and Shakespeare as inspiration for the figure of the fairy king. The result is an amalgam of the charming and the grotesque (Huon's herculean tasks at the Sultan's court), in which the adventures of the hero, his love for the Sultan's daughter Rezia and the Oberon-action take place, and in which the note of humour rings stronger than that of the horrific and the gruesome experiences. This really serene verse epic was to have a greater effect on the Romantics than Wieland's diffuse novel of his old age, *Aristipp und seine Zeitgenossen* (dating from the years 1789–1801), though this did employ Friedrich Schlegel's Diotima theme and courtesan theory, was co-determined by the poet's affection in his old age for the prematurely deceased Sophie Brentano, and therefore originated after the beginnings of Romanticism. Yet what Wieland's recent biographer Friedrich Sengle says in a striking formulation concerning this work is true: 'The brightness and clarity of Greece which this work displays, lacks substance.'

When Wieland died in 1813, Goethe paid tribute to his old contemporary in the famous funeral oration, as in fact he had similarly done earlier for Winckelmann. But the testimony that he bore for Wieland is for good reason warmer and more emotional. And this finds expression not only in the title *Zu brüderlichem Andenken Wielands* (*In Fraternal Memory of Wieland*), but also quite unequivocally in the verdict given. In this funeral oration Goethe celebrates the cosmopolitan Wieland, the kindred spirit of the Greeks right down to the very understanding of their Orphism and hetaerism. The classifying of Wieland as a trailblazer of Classicism is clear:

> Er hat sein Zeitalter sich zugebildet, dem Geschmack seiner Jahresgenossen so wie ihrem Urteil eine entschiedene Richtung gegeben.[14]

Goethe sees this gift and these abilities as founded on the perfect harmony between Wieland the man and the writer: 'He wrote as a living man and lived as a writer.' Indeed, without Wieland the stricter and deeper and hence also more aristocratic Classicism of Goethe and Schiller would scarcely have found a sounding-board in society which was so indispensable for Classicism.

---

[14] He has formed his age in his own mould, given a decisive lead to the taste as well as the standards of his contemporaries.

17 Weimar

When Goethe had set out for the first time on his way to Italy, he was intercepted by an equerry of the Duke Karl August, who had just come of age. He arrived in Weimar on 7 November 1775 and found a social circle which distinguished this small Central German court clearly and specifically from others. The determined and decisive leading figure of the Dowager Duchess Anna Amalia of Brunswick had just stepped down from the Regency. Yet she was still young, only thirty-six years old and in no way intending to withdraw from active public life and while away her time in her palace. Between her and the now ruling eighteen-year-old son there was tension. For both of them possessed energy and also self-will. Besides she was obliged to witness a period during which the young prince insisted on getting accustomed to his new position while enjoying himself in youthful fashion. To the Dowager Duchess and her older Ministers and officials such pursuance of exuberant jolly escapades had to appear aimless. But Anna Amalia had already coped with worse things. She had had to bring up alone – she had been left a widow after only two years of marriage – under the eyes of jealous relations her two sons, the refractory Karl August and the shy, inhibited, eccentric Prince Konstantin. She had been Regent for seventeen years and had skilfully conducted affairs of state. And now she was building up, as systematically as ever, her own court circle of literary and artistically inclined people, since she was no longer involved in the affairs of state. The result was an extraordinarily favourable situation, since Karl August – not for nothing the keen pupil of Wieland – strove for the same ends too, though admittedly his taste was quite naturally somewhat different, embracing as it did the exuberance of the 'Storm and Stress'. Wieland's mildness and moderation determined Anna Amalia's circle, vitality that of the Duke, who had surrounded himself in a robust style of living with a group of the youngish landed aristocrats. He had got to know Goethe on his recently completed journey to fetch his bride and had experienced the strong charm and fascinating influence of the personality of the man who was only about eight years his senior. He clearly expected two things from the invitation extended to Goethe and the latter's potential connection with his court: a person who was not going to be a spoilsport in his own youthful wantonness, but at the same time someone who would be a friend and adviser, sure of his own genius and conscious of his own path through life. Both of these things Wieland could no longer be for the Duke.

The young Duke had yet another problem. He had just brought home his bride, the Princess Luise of Darmstadt. The Darmstadt court was associated with Herder, Goethe and Merck through its quietly enthusiastic 'Storm and Stress' variant group,[1] whom Goethe had honoured with his three hymns. From this ambience the eighteen-year-old Princess brought with her something of the sensitive subjectivity which afforded devotion, yet expected guidance. Karl August however was too young to accept both, also too different by nature and too self-determined. Added to this was the prim, sightly reserved and inhibited character of the young Duchess. Being highly sensitive and anti-pathetic towards that which was alien to her made the process of acclimatisation to Weimar the more difficult for her. And so it was obvious early on that a harmonious marriage was out of the question. Karl August's marked sensuality was not satisfied, especially as Luise had neither beauty nor grace to show. His nature sought compensation. The Duchess however withdrew into herself, showed an early disposition to embitterment and also developed her political acumen (as Louis L. Hammerich has recently established). Goethe was therefore soon to find out that he was faced with a dual task as an educator: he had to reconcile the Duke gradually to the duties that were confronting him, at the same time to alleviate as many as possible of the problems of the princely marriage that had been contracted so early. Goethe – and from 1776 on, Herder – faced up to the task for more than a decade with complete success in the

---

[1] An allusion to the three companions of the Princess, i.e. Caroline von Flachsland, Fräulein von Roussillon and Luise von Ziegler. (*Translator's note*)

first instance, though only with moderate success in the second. It was a task which bound them to Weimar as teachers and as men.

For Goethe was kept in Weimar through the direct contact with the Duke, which presently led to companionship amounting to their addressing each other with the familiar *du*, and the Privy Councillorship that was pushed through by the Duke with the influential consent of Anna Amalia. But at the same time his advice to the Duke, matched, on his part, by the same shrewdness, enabled Herder, his old friend and mentor from the Strassburg days, to come to Weimar as Superintendent General. Vacillating as to whether he should exchange his Bückeburg position for the originally aspired Chair at Göttingen or go for the post now offered him of top church official at the new intellectually important court, Herder decided on Weimar, and he too remained there like Wieland, Goethe and later Schiller.

Around the ducal family and the three leading minds who had been attracted to it, there assembled a circle of courtiers and princely officials, which provided for good company and festivals, amateur theatre and public readings in the city residences and hunting lodges of Weimar. Of these Anna Amalia's little palace of Tiefurt with its intimate park in particular, but also the great Weimar gardens on the Ilm with their various hermitages achieved importance. Goethe in fact had taken up residence there too in his summer house, until the Duke's favour provided him, following the journey to Italy, with the house on the Frauenplan that was worthy of his position – the 'Goethe House', which was to attract visitors from the Old and the New World in the first decades of the nineteenth century.

Amongst the courtiers the Chamberlain Karl Ludwig von Knebel, Prince Konstantin's erstwhile tutor, stood out. He was a versatile member of the inner circle, a distinguished expert above all on Roman antiquity, translator of Lucretius and Propertius, and himself a not untalented writer of epigrams. On the whole he was a good-natured, aesthetically inclined person with a touch of melancholy and unworldliness. Knebel was very close to the Duke and to Goethe, but most of all to Herder in fact. Amongst the influential courtiers too was numbered the Baron von Einsiedel, whose character exhibited more eccentric features. The seduction of a lady at court and the secret liaison with Corona Schröter, whereby he cut out Goethe in her favour, were of such a nature as to scandalise the small court. Einsiedel too entered the literary field as an expert on the theatre with his *Grundlinien zu einer Theorie der Schauspielkunst* (1797). A third figure from the personal and literary annals of this period was Karl Sigismund von Seckendorff, translator of Camões' *Lusiade*. The Duke's Keeper of the Purse too, Johann Justin Bertuch, the previous owner of Goethe's summer house, had a cosmopolitan literary outlook, was a poet, translator and editor of foreign dramas, a man with an interest in journalistic enterprises too, active for a time on Wieland's *Merkur*. Of the women in the ducal family circle two persons had a special role to play. One was Luise von Göchhausen, Anna Amalia's lady-in-waiting, to whose zealous interest in intellectual pursuits (incidentally not free from some intriguing) we owe the preservation of the *Urfaust*. Charlotte von Stein however was Goethe's star of destiny. She was wife of the Lord Grand Master of the Horse, a figure of rare human and at the same time intellectual importance, appreciative of the highest that Goethe wrote at the time, and for whom he then too wrote his key works, a woman beautiful in a thoroughly spiritual way, who drove Goethe to a state of utter passion. She sent him her son Fritz to educate in his house, and the flight to Italy in the autumn of 1786, precipitate and secret as it was, was in no way merely the result of the magnetic attraction of Winckelmann's Rome, but was also an expression of the inner helplessness into which this unfulfillable passion had finally plunged Goethe. His letters to her rank amongst the great testimonies of German Classicism. Her own to him were destroyed. She never forgave him for the step he took in living with Christiane Vulpius in common-law marriage following his return from Rome.

What Goethe found in this circle was of extraordinary significance in human terms. The task assigned him there was however no less extraordinary. The sportive revels of the young Duke and his company with hunting whip through villages and woods, at communal May dances, and on secret playful trips amongst the peasants and their womenfolk, enraged the populace and the trusty servants of the Duke's household. Goethe must have felt it, when he finally came to settle down in Weimar. The First Minister back in Anna Amalia's time, the President von Fritsch, threatened to resign when the Duke wanted to include the companion of this frenzied period in the influential governing body. Even Klopstock, who had got to hear the gossip, wrote a letter of entreaty in which he begged Goethe to put an end to the undignified pursuits, which however the latter cordially but frankly rejected. He knew what he wanted. But he proceeded with caution. From the start he was quite aware of the Duke's good points. He was equally in no doubt as to the need for caution, which forced him to let things be for a time. His sending for Herder to help him, again siding with the Duke against Fritsch and his party, was a significant move. The second, even more unequivocal step was the sending on their way of Klinger and Lenz in the same year of 1776. It was only in a third move that he ventured to attempt any direct influence on Karl August. This was naturally not achieved without temporary setbacks, above all when it concerned the relations between Karl August and the Duchess Luise. Yet the tensions never led to a rift in the friendship, and the court elders had to realise eventually that the success was Goethe's. The eighteen-year-old Duke was already a self-confident ruler. Under Goethe's influence however he became a ruler conscious of his responsibilities. This goal could never have been achieved by a moralising guide and mentor. It proved possible however by Goethe setting an example in responsible action. It was just because Karl August came to sense initially that there was still a good bit of high-spiritedness and 'Storm and Stress' originality in the young Goethe which was in accord with his own unrestrained ways, that he now had to understand and respect the renunciation and the self-limitation of the present official servant of his house, had to recognise the act of sacrifice involved. For his part Goethe, by nature a man of individual genius, by profession a simple lawyer, had to turn his hand to the most varied practical and mundane administrative duties: civil engineering and forestry, the levying of recruits and finances, the operation of mines and the University of Jena, to which was later added the management of the theatre. He made himself thoroughly acquainted with everything, one thing after another without regard to the time which was thereby lost for his literary activity. And that does not take into account either the benefit which accrued to the social life of the Court through his intellectual gifts. No one could fail to recognise, least of all the Duke himself, that all these energies were expended at the cost of literary productivity. But an ideal thus emerged, which enthused the young Duke as no sermon could possibly have done. And there are probably hardly more impressive testimonies to the decisive process of education and self-education in those years than the poems *Seefahrt* (1776) and *Ilmenau* (1783). This latter poem cannot be taken independently of the first.

Seefahrt starts with the intoxication of departure into the unknown and steers a course to outwit the adverse winds by tacking to and fro: 'Loyal to the objective even on an uneven course' (there is no more beautiful image for the caution of this first Weimar period), culminating in the 'manly' overcoming of the storm, an experience shared by his friends lamenting on the shore:

> Doch er stehet männlich an dem Steuer.
> Mit dem Schiffe spielen Wind und Wellen,
> Wind und Wellen nicht mit seinem Herzen.
> Herrschend blickt er auf die grimme Tiefe
> Und vertrauet, scheiternd oder landend,
> Seinen Göttern.[2]

Here is the first impulse – perhaps not as yet fully realised – of German Classicism as personal discipline and attitude towards Classicism seen as classical subject matter (even if the 'gods' are present as well). The concept of 'manliness' as it occurs here remained an ethical principle for Goethe from Early to Late Classicism and still determined the figure of Prometheus in the *Pandora* festival play of 1808. It signified self-confidence through self-discipline, positive action, useful works. In the poem the friends remain behind full of emotion, lamenting to no effect. The distancing says almost as much as the new position. If we then turn over the pages of another seven years to the poem for Karl August on his birthday in 1783, set in Ilmenau, the little mining town, the scene of onetime youthful pranks and soon afterwards of serious manly and dedicated work for the silver mines, the gap between the 'I' and the 'Thou' is bridged. The teacher, who first had to discipline himself to manliness, could look back with pride on what had been achieved: 'A peaceful people quietly at work' – the example set by its Prince:

[2] Yet manly he stands at the helm. Wind and waves play with the boat, but wind and waves not with his heart. He looks commandingly at the raging depths and puts his trust in the gods, whether he is shipwrecked or lands safely.

Du kennest lang' die Pflichten deines Standes
Und schränkest nach und nach die freie Seele ein.[3]

Now it could be said openly, for it no longer hurt. It had become part and parcel of the criteria in life for this circle, which now represented Early Classicism, though still unconscious of it. This stage of development was based on the early attainment of maturity within this thoroughly youthful circle, and not yet based on the standards of Winckelmann's Hellenic ideals. When Goethe brought such ideals back with him from Italy, Early Classicism became High Classicism. But another five years had to pass before that could come about.

But Goethe's path to Classicism can be fixed not only in the biographical context, in this instance from the viewpoint of education and self-education; also the odes from the beginning of the eighties, *Grenzen der Menschheit* (1781) and *Das Göttliche* (1783), show in complete contrast to the 'Storm and Stress' hymns the urge for self-limitation. Indeed they go beyond the recognition of the gods as testified in *Seefahrt* to a reverence for the Divine together with the simultaneous strengthening of humanitarian awareness. Actually the two titles do correspond to each other exactly. And in line with that development, the poems also approach classical form rhythmically speaking, and hence clearly remove themselves from the immediacy of the linguistic turbulence found in the earlier hymns. The verses can now be determined in accordance with definite classical measures, even if they certainly did not originate in scanned form. In his pre-Italian days Goethe formed classical rhythms so to speak out of his own head, which corresponded to the latent classical ethos within him. The fact that in those same years the prose versions of *Iphigenie* and *Tasso* originated, also signified a state of half-conscious transition. In both cases the trend was for classical or at least Renaissance material, though they were still formal drafts, which Goethe recast in verse only when he had undertaken his Italian journey. This change to verse, however, could then be achieved over wide stretches of the plays with only minor alterations to the original, because the prose was already extensively iambic in form. Perhaps one may interpret this phenomenon as the clearest form

[3] You have known for a long time the duties attached to your position and gradually you have limited the freedom of your soul.

of Goethe's Early Classicism: he was still without a definite awareness of form, and without a clear artistic programme, but in the
tendency towards self-limitation and in the recognition of human
obligations he was steering a course with an inner inevitability
towards Classicism.

For the classical subject matter alone did not bring it about.
Indeed Goethe was already making use of such material in his
'Storm and Stress' phase. Only at that time it was not yet
Winckelmann's Antiquity. We can perceive this pre-Winckel-
mannian Antiquity as a Goethean theme even at the beginning of
the Weimar period in the one-act play *Proserpina* (1776), which
was inorganically incorporated later into the *Triumph der Emp-
findsamkeit*. Here the hymnic verse form is still predominant,
moreover everything revolves around rebellion, calamity and dark
abysses and has nothing of Winckelmannian composure. At best his
disposition towards compositions by Gluck might be viewed as a
step towards Wieland's classical world. How significant it is that
Goethe should later link *Proserpina*, which was originally not
intended in such a way at all, with that comedy which was meant
as a means of self-education and education for the court, as a
strict parody of sentimentality.

The Goethe of these first Weimar years consistently developed
towards the 'Classical' objective in every expression of his being
(his offices, the guidance of the Duke, the abandonment of Lenz
and Klinger are all part of this). In human terms this appeared
bound up with the obligating relationship with Charlotte von
Stein, which signified more and more for him as friendship quickly
blazed into passion. Only with a great inner effort had he been
able to free himself from the relationship with Lili which had
deeply disturbed him. The fact that this new Weimar friend now
stepped within his range of vision, assuaged his grief. She was entirely different from anyone he had previously loved. It was already
an expression of his new Weimar personality that Goethe should
turn to her without long deliberation and inner struggles, but
with an immediate burning passion, as the letters prove. Neither
Friederike Brion nor Charlotte Buff, nor Lili Schönemann had
possessed that sense of judgement and empathy and that spiritual
and intellectual profundity which Charlotte von Stein possessed.
It is extraordinarily remarkable how she managed to keep her
relationship with Goethe always at the extreme intellectual and

sensual limit. Six years she let him woo her on the closest intellectual and spiritual terms, before she let him know of her reciprocal love. For a further five years she kept their relations in a state of tension resulting from the frank knowledge of their mutual affections, a tension to which she was equal, but from which Goethe finally tore himself away with his sudden departure for Italy. It must have been the significant sum total of her being: lofty mind and curbed sensuality at one and the same time, which exercised this fascination on the younger person who had been so pampered (by women too).

The pains he suffered in human terms were only to be borne through exercising an extreme amount of self-discipline. The *Tasso* theme or the complexity of questions raised by the *Urmeister* are the fragments of this confession, of which he himself expressly speaks already in the first month of the correspondence:

> Liebe Frau, ich werde wieder weggerissen und hab dir so viel zu sagen. Heut hab ich wieder Wieland viel meiner letzten Jahrsgeschicht erzählt, und wenn ihr mich warm haltet, so schreib ich's wohl für euch ganz allein. Denn es ist mehr als Beichte, wenn man auch das bekennt, worüber man nicht Absolution bedarf ...[4]

Quite close in time was the first of the two splendid poems entitled *Wandrers Nachtlied*, dating from the February of 1776 'on the slopes of the Ettersberg', as the copy for Charlotte von Stein indicates. Both Night Songs, 'Der du von dem Himmel bist' ('Thou which art from heaven'), as well as 'Über allen Gipfeln ist Ruh' ('Over all the hill-tops it is still'), which latter was dedicated in the September of 1780 to the wooden hunting lodge above Ilmenau, not only had their origins directly in the world of nature, but were at the same time an expression of longing for peace and tranquillity. In the second poem this becomes an open expectation of death ('Wait! soon you too will be still'), but in the first is a clear expression of the disquiet of life's painful tensions, as revealed in

---

[4] Dear Lady, I am again torn away and have so much to say to you. To-day I have again told Wieland much of the events of the last year, and if you think warmly of me, I would indeed write this for you and no one else. For it is more than a confession if one also confesses that for which absolution is not required ...

'Oh, I am weary of this restlessness!' This wanderer is a different one from that of the 'Storm and Stress' odes. The tone is not ecstatic but resigned, tender – even the rhythms – as nowhere else in the lyric verse of this period. From these poems we learn too that one must founder in this mood, or regain one's existence by dint of work and service. In the same way the first version (1778) of the poem *An den Mond* ('Once more you fill the sweet valley'), which was not yet associated with the unhappy Christiane von Lassberg but with the poet himself, was one of the expressions of shock caused by his own passion. 'So movable you know this burning heart to be' still meant in the draft the poet's own heart. To Goethe in this new situation Werther's shadow appeared doubly demonic.

Apart from the development of the *Iphigenie* and *Tasso* themes as such, Goethe had at that time written other dramatic and lyric works 'approaching classical form' subsequent to the outmoded 'Storm and Stress' style of *Proserpina*. The *Elpenor* fragment, originally intended for the anticipated birth in 1781 of a Weimar Crown Prince, was in fact rather an approximation to Wieland's Classicism as seen in his *Festspiele*, and even linguistically was still a kind of hybrid: rhythmic prose which later in 1806 was easily transposable into verse. The return to the three Unities and the limited number of actors was also part of the conscious process of self-discipline. The subject of *Elpenor* is the superannuated one of fraternal feuding with the resultant exchange of children. Neither of the themes was new in any way, not even from the point of view of the 'Storm and Stress'. Here they appear worked up into a piece of classical intrigue with strong Wielandian French overtones. Only the scenes of radiant boyish joy before the gates of life in constantly heightened expectation which Elpenor experiences, are impressive. We can regard this as already being Winckelmannian Classicism, but the theme of intrigue – which incidentally includes allusions to the historical family feud of the Thuringian House – is not classical, it is still pre-classical. If we disregard the great dramas which were not to develop beyond the draft stage, Goethe's classical attempts in the pre-Italian Weimar decade remained – like the *Elpenor* fragment – occasional pieces of literature, serious *divertimenti* for the ducal family and the court: thus the *Maskenzüge*, for example. *Der Geist der Jugend* (1782) is, formally, a kind of amalgam of rather Wielandian faerie-like and amoresque elements. The *Aufzug der vier Weltalter* of the same year might already be seen as more of an Early Classical allegory of the time, from which one could well draw a line to the centenary festival play *Palaeophron und Neoterpe*. There are occasional poems of specifically craftsmanlike character, for example, park and monument inscriptions, poems enclosed in letters; in short, fashioned conceits in epigrammatic form: these are the pieces dating from those years, which Goethe designated as 'approaching classical form'. These examples of classical craftsmanship sometimes revealed an affinity back in time with the Baroque as well as forwards with the 'Ding-Gedicht' of, say, Mörike. And it is almost moving, too, to observe how Goethe here sharpened the weapons of mythology and how he sometimes succeeded in making transparent something of the quiet serenity of Winckelmann in the peaceful flow of creation. The first grasping after classical form was here manifested. At the centre lay the idea of moderation, so that passion remained under control. Such is the message of epigrams like *Die Geschwister* or the park inscription *Einsamkeit*.

We can regard the fragmentary series of stanzas of *Die Geheimnisse* as a speculative testimony of pre-Italian self-reflection in poetic form. From these Goethe later created as independent poems in their own right *Zueignung* and *Denn was der Mensch in seinen Erdeschranken*. This important fragment owed its origin to a creative burst which began in the middle of 1784 and ebbed in the following spring. In 1783 his relationship with Herder – considerably strained over the years – once again became unreserved, indeed intimate, during the genesis of Herder's key work, the *Ideen*. As was later the case in the correspondence with Schiller, letters and manuscripts also passed to and fro between the friends at this time, even when away on short journeys. The connecting link was once and for all the notion of humanity. The close tie lasted beyond the Italian journey, the most important despatches of which were still sent to Herder. Incidentally it was from the third Weimar partner, namely Wieland, that Goethe took the choice of form of the stanzas. Nevertheless the wealth of ideas contained in this philosophical poem stemmed from the renewed communication with Herder. It was the attempt to set up a kind of universal concept of humanitarian philosophy in the required form of allegory. In *Zueignung* he let the divine appari-

tion declare in clear and well-defined terms his own personal point
of departure, namely the Classical ethos of the manly:

> Kaum bist du sicher vor dem gröbsten Trug,
> Kaum bist du Herr vom ersten Kinderwillen,
> So glaubst du dich schon Übermensch genug,
> Versäumst die Pflicht des Mannes zu erfüllen!
> Wieviel bist du von andern unterschieden?
> Erkenne dich, leb mit der Welt in Frieden![5]

But in the independent version of *Zueignung* the main emphasis
falls on the problems of artistic loneliness. The allegory of the
Geheimnisse would have had to express the human element
embracing this too. Not for nothing is the principal figure called
Bruder Humanus. Yet for all that, the 'ideal Montserrat', which
Goethe lets his wanderer reach, is indeed no classical spot, but a
symbolic Christian-medieval one, rather an early form of the areas
reclaimed for settlement at the end of *Faust* in keeping with
Goethe's self-interpretation of 1816. And the pious society of the
twelve wise masters grouped around Humanus on the Holy Mountain has a somewhat secularised monastic air about it. It is indeed
designated a rosicrucian one, so that it corresponds too with the
secret society in *Wilhelm Meister*. The Christian preacher of
humanitarianism, Herder, is here perceivable. The theme of universality in the fragment could in its way be interpreted as collecting
under one heading all of Goethe's problems at Weimar. The community of the twelve brothers we would see as spanning in
symbolic types the whole compass of experience that accrues
to man from his very existence and destiny. The fate of all people
was somehow to be interwoven with the universal fate of
Humanus, whose growth and development was finally to be interpreted as a symbol of the history of mankind in a form of
allegory determined by Herder. The basic theme was an optimistic
one: the holy spirit of humanitarianism is so to speak pentacostally
at work in all. But it no longer has need of the Church's guidance.
And thus a synthesis emerges derived from Lessing's *Erziehung
des Menschengeschlechts* and Herder's *Ideen* in line with their

---

[5] Scarcely are you safe from the grossest deceit, scarcely are you master of
the first infant will, than you already believe yourself a superman, you fail
to fulfil the duty of man! How very different are you from others? Come,
recognise yourself, live at peace with the world!

conception of evolution. Certainly the symbolism is rosicrucian-mystical and hence far removed from Greece. But that is not the whole story. While the relationship with Herder and Lavater still continued here, and there were also echoes still of his youthful friendship with Susanne von Klettenberg, the *Geheimnisse* symbol-ised too the continuance of Goethe's development towards Classic-ism. The opponent of terrestrial revolutions as well as political ones himself developed organically. Yet the application which Goethe was now making of this formulation of his own personal history no longer corresponded to Pietism, nor to the 'Storm and Stress'. That is impressively manifested in the twenty-fourth stanza of the *Geheimnisse*:

> Denn alle Kraft dringt vorwärts in die Weite,
> Zu leben und zu wirken hier und dort;
> Dagegen engt und hemmt von jeder Seite
> Der Strom der Welt und reißt uns mit sich fort.
> In diesem innern Sturm und äußern Streite
> Vernimmt der Geist ein schwer verstanden Wort:
> Von der Gewalt, die alle Wesen bindet,
> Befreit der Mensch sich, der sich überwindet.[6]

Again here we find the ethos of manliness that is present within the 'Limits of Mankind'.

If one wants to understand all facets of the maturing that can be traced in Goethe's works up to the point where he was ready for the flight to Italy, one must take into account his predilec-tions for the natural sciences which developed at that time. It has been said often enough that Goethe was a writer who created under the impact of what he saw ('Augenmensch'). And it is in this faculty that the capacity for objective observation of nature lies first and foremost. As yet however Goethe had made use of it more for the indulgence of his imagination and for his enjoy-ment. Even so through co-operating with Lavater on the latter's *Physiognomische Fragmente* he already found himself forced to his first practical studies of, for example, the human skull. With

---

[6] For all force presses forward into the distance, to live and to work here and there; the river of the world hems in and checks against this on every side, and seizes us along with it. In this inner turbulence and outer struggle the mind becomes aware of a word difficult to understand: From the power which binds all beings does that man free himself, who overcomes himself.

Weimar came the official duties, and out of the hunt and the forest resulted botanical and zoological observations. In connection with Goethe's favourite administrative task, namely the management of mines, there even arose the need to study mineralogy and also chemistry with precision. Finally, we must not forget that the scientific departments of the provincial university of Jena were soon Goethe's responsibility too. All this made it clear to him that what signified manliness in the ethical sphere was synonymous with responsible exactitude in man's relation to nature. The accord of ethos and science is already revealed in part of a letter to Charlotte von Stein on the journey in the Harz mountains in the December of 1777:

> Der Nutzen aber, den das auf meinen phantastischen Sinn hat, mit lauter Menschen umzugehen, die ein bestimmtes, einfaches, daurendes wichtiges Geschäft haben, ist unsäglich. Es ist wie ein kaltes Bad, das einen aus einer bürgerlich-wollüstigen Abspannung wieder zu einem neuen kräftigen Leben zusammenzieht.[7]

This is an express utterance *against* the kind of life led by the Duke, who was then still taking too much pleasure in 'making what was natural into something of an adventure, instead of letting himself get enjoyment from the adventurous when it became natural'. This is unequivocally realistic, no longer romantic Rousseauism.

We can follow Goethe's new course most clearly in the sphere of geology and mineralogy. Already in the summer of 1776 he investigated the lodes of the silver mines in Ilmenau, which were again to become lucrative for the country. Such an activity by its very nature demands responsible specialised knowledge. And it was from this same Ilmenau that he wrote to Frau von Stein about the eternal truth of self-limitation, which was equally valid for the poet, the artist, the man. So from the outset Goethe's knowledge of natural science was not an expert knowledge in an isolated sense and form, but was *one* expression of properly understood 'Humanität'. Even in the most specialised instance it remained part of a universal concept. We may well take it as symbolical that in

---

[7] The benefit however, which my imaginative powers have derived from associating only with people who have a specific simple, lasting, important job, is tremendous. It is like a cold bath which shakes one out of a bourgeois-lax fatigue into a new vigorous life again.

the diary notes on the Harz journey in 1776, amongst sketches of mineshafts and natural history collections there occurred the passionate Bible quote on the Brocken walk: 'What is man that you should think of him'. The new factual way of observation on the Harz journey is seen again two years later on the second Swiss trip, this time undertaken with the Duke. By design, it was to be a carefully planned educational journey for both the Duke and his companion. The insight into the laws of nature was already now so advanced that the sight of the enormous rock movements which had brought about the formation of the mountains gave a 'lofty feeling of eternal stability'. The thought of the inconceivable length of time during which the mountains were formed, was calmed by the knowledge that 'time too operates in obedience to eternal laws'. Goethe's acceptance of this universal law perceivable in *all* things is almost moving, when from a consideration of roots, mosses and rock plants there follows the reflection:

Man fühlt tief, hier ist nichts Willkürliches, alles ist langsam bewegendes, ewiges Gesetz.[8]

Goethe the natural scientist and Goethe the Early Classical writer form one inseparable unity.

From the fragment *Über die Natur* and the breathtaking treatise *Über den Granit* we can discern step by step Goethe's need to conceive nature in passionate striving for its practical forms, both as law and a universal organum. The first testimony dates from two years after the second trip to Switzerland, that is 1781; the second originated in 1784, two years prior to his departure for Italy. Goethe's part in the fragment *Über die Natur* cannot be firmly established. Goethe provided it for the *Journal von Tiefurt*, the organ of the inner court circle, but stated expressly that though it was closely related to his own thinking it had been penned by someone else. In Charlotte von Stein's Notes mention was made of the author being a young Swiss theologian from the Lavater circle, whom Goethe had got to know on his second Swiss trip. This Georg Christoph Tobler would have been twenty-four years old at the time of the composition of the fragment, and hence of an age when man's ability to re-echo things that he has heard and understood properly, is considerable. Only this can explain why

[8] One deeply feels that here there is nothing arbitrary, everything is a slowly moving eternal law.

forty years later Goethe was again uncertain as to the extent of his authorship. At all events the fragment corresponds to his mind and spirit, even to the point of style. Half poetry, half natural philosophy, it is a testimony to the transitional state in this sphere. Obviously at the root of it lay Goethe's attempt to find common ground beween Spinoza, who had been taken up again in the dialogue with Herder during this period, and the intimations and results of his own urge to investigate nature, a pursuit that now had a proper scientific basis. Hence the fragment is determined philosophically by the rejection of the idea of progress in favour of the idea of an eternal cycle in nature. 'It is an eternal life, with development and movement in nature, and yet nature does not progress further.' 'Everything is new and yet ever the old thing.' Nature, as Goethe saw it at that time – whether through the medium of Tobler or not – does not merely go its course according to unalterable laws, it really delights in the fullness of the meta-morphoses, and one of these is death, seen as 'her device to have an abundance of life'. The sphere of the teleological interpretation of nature is thus abandoned. This interpretation of nature is vitalistic, pure self-presentation: 'Even the most unnatural thing is Nature.' Essentially the fragment ends in Spinozism on the philosophical plane, when the concluding sentence on Nature runs: 'Everything is her fault, everything is her merit.' It is, so to speak, another formulation of the idea of *deus sive natura*. Feeling – and indeed surely Goethe's feeling for life at that time – still unmistak-ably influences logic in this transitional period. The relation of man to this nature is on the one hand familiarity, on the other hand it entails the knowledge that nature, though it produces only what is individual, nevertheless cares nothing for individuals, thus it amounts to a feeling of being lost in the infinite.

A reworking of Spinoza also crops up in the *Philosophische Studie* (1784–85), especially with regard to the proof of our par-ticipation in eternity, despite all the limitations which experience allots to us as individuals. The stronger emphasis on this restriction of the individual results from the experiences that Goethe had meantime gained as a natural scientist. But he zealously guards against the interpretation that this is resignation. This he attributes rather to the too quickly satisfied view of Nature adopted by the Christian faith in all its certainty. On the whole, the fragment and the study betray that recognition of the 'Law', which underlies too the poem dating from the second Swiss trip, namely *Gesang der Geister über den Wassern* (1779). It proclaims recognition of the law, but not the resignative consequences deriving from Man's participation in Eternity; a striving for balance, but not yet uniformity.

The treatise *Über den Granit* also originated in that same year of 1784. It may be viewed as an attempt to treat a natural scientific theme as it were in Winckelmannian manner. It is of importance therefore not only from the point of view of the history of evolution, because indications of Goethe's participation in the great dispute of earth historians in favour of Neptunism as against Vulcanism are therein provided, but also because the connection of Goethe's natural scientific studies with the deepest human and artistic concern with life perhaps finds there its finest expression. In it, after all, he gives an account as it were of his own inner course that led from the human heart and its subjectivity to the sublime peace through seeing natural objects as the objective world. At the same time the ultimately religious background to these observations of nature becomes manifest too:

> Ich fürchte den Vorwurf nicht, daß es ein Geist des Widerspruches sein müsse, der mich von Betrachtung und Schilderung des menschlichen Herzens, des jüngsten, mannigfaltigsten, beweglichsten, veränderlichsten, erschütterlichsten Teiles der Schöpfung, zu der Beobachtung des ältesten, festesten, tiefsten, unerschütterlichsten Sohnes der Natur geführt hat. Denn man wird mir gerne zugeben, daß alle natürlichen Dinge in einem genauen Zusammenhange stehen . . .[9]

So the observer of nature on his bare granite rock feels 'raised to higher considerations of Nature'. He makes the analogy to the religious sacrifice, to the loneliness of the religious seeker after truth in his feeling of the 'first, most secure beginnings of our existence'. This new self-awareness of the natural scientist is still enthusiastic, warm, indeed intoxicated in his survey across time

[9] I am not afraid of the reproach that it must be a spirit of contradiction which has led me from consideration and depiction of the human heart, the youngest, most manifold, most stirring, most fluctuating, most shakeable part of Creation, to the observation of the oldest, most solid, most profound, most unshakeable son of Nature. For one will gladly grant me that all natural objects stand in an exact relationship to each other . . .

and space. The 'sceptical realism', which Goethe reached towards the end of the century and which was to characterise the Notes on the third trip to Switzerland, is still very distant here. The speech on the opening of the Ilmenau mines radiates peace, tranquillity and the measuredness of a man sure of his case, for whom it was no longer possible to maintain a divorce between theory and practice. An entirely logical development has taken place: in ethics and the perception of art, the order of Creation and its natural law. Thus we can and must perceive unity within the first stage of Classicism even in Goethe's minute catalogue of stones, the geognostic analyses of landscapes, the practical efforts in smelting processing in mining (as well as their profitability). Knowledge of Nature, service, voluntary self-limitation – these are the expressions of a single unity of outlook.

18 *Frater Humanus:* Herder

No less versatile, but in the profounder sense potentially more capable of development than Wieland was Herder, the third partner in Weimarian Early Classicism. At least his versatility was not that of a chameleon, but a real receptivity for impressions, which was based on his exceptional empathic capacity. Wieland's changes of interest were a dull affair in comparison to the intensity with which Herder amalgamated 'Storm and Stress' and Pietism, in order then to start on his development towards the concept of *frater humanus*, not in the wake of Goethe, but along his own path, yet in a genuine communication with Goethe. In much, indeed the majority of things Herder had anticipated Goethe. The substance of Herder's ideas had affected Goethe a lot. In Strassburg he had taken the lead, in Weimar he was indeed no longer Goethe's teacher, but nevertheless very much the stimulating force and in addition still the ally in the spiritual guidance of the ducal pair and in the affairs of Anna Amalia's palace. As against Goethe and Wieland he was rather a scintillating writer of fragmentary pieces, constantly crammed full to overflowing with material which was given shape by a superior mind that often improvised. At the same time he was sensitive and difficult to deal with; one moment he would keep his distance, the next he would seek Goethe's company. Not having Wieland's gentleness of approach, which worked superficially against his own nature, he could become uncompromising, mistrustful, even malicious, jealous too, as the later relationship with Schiller showed. The battle in his old age against Kant, which he conducted in the *Kalligone* and in the *Metakritik* pieces, manifested the same characteristic on a purely intellectual plane. Where he remained open-minded, as above all in the periods of close contact with Goethe or in his later relations with Jean Paul, we can observe his whole richness of character. Gregarious by nature and temperament, he suffered from periods of isolation, in part self-induced, to the point of embitterment. Also his clerical office contributed to the fact that in his old age a retrogressive trend towards Enlightenment and its moralistic attitude took effect, which went well with his ecclesiastical role as father of liberalism. The fact that he could be pretty intolerant in the sphere of personal and human relations – as indeed seen in the final break with Goethe that followed from Herder's acrid condemnation of Goethe's common-law marriage with Christiane – reveals Herder's human limitations.

When Herder was summoned to Weimar in 1776, he brought with him his own long prepared advance towards Classicism. He had studied Winckelmann very closely, much earlier than Goethe, for whom this confrontation was really only to begin in Rome. His knowledge of classical literature was far superior to that of Goethe. The period of the *Literatur-Fragmente* and the *Kritische Wälder* had already shown this panoramic vision. Through his enormous powers of receptivity and innate richness of thought and constructive talent, the author of the *Älteste Urkunde des Menschengeschlechts* (1774–76), the *Briefe das Studium der Theologie betreffend* and the collection *Stimmen der Völker in Liedern* was well versed in world literature and receptively aware of the literatures of the East much earlier than could be said for Goethe. In this very receptivity, which facilitated a universally-erudite dialogue with Lessing and Winckelmann, Herder became the real moulder of the Classical humanitarian idea, without which the development of the Goethean ideal in *Iphigenie*, *Tasso* and *Wilhelm Meister* would have been unthinkable. Herder's elaboration of Winckelmann's ideas proceeded from the *Kritische Wälder* on to the ode in Klopstockian style, *Laokoons Haupte* (1770), and the hymn of the same year, *An seinen Landsmann Johann Winckelmann*, reaching its climax in *Denkmal Johann Winckelmanns* (which was an unsuccessfully submitted Kassel prize-essay of 1778), from which a polished essay was abstracted in Wieland's *Merkur* under the title *Winckelmann* (1781). Moreover Winckelmann had already been a key figure for the Herder of the *Literatur-Fragmente*, in which he expressed his ambition to become 'a Winckelmann with reference to literature'. Laocoön was a theme that touched on matters of principle for him as for Lessing too, and his *Kritische Wälder* tried to adopt an intermediary position between the latter and Winckelmann. The confrontation with Winckelmann's History of Art still remained a permanent theme of the Classical Herder. Above all Winckelmann as a person and Laocoön as a symbolic motif represented in Herder's view his own variant of Early Classicism, since they were marked by a Christian humanitarian interpretation that was common to neither Goethe nor Schiller (nor even Lessing). The ode and hymn of 1770 reflect this, where Laocoön becomes the 'messenger of the godhead', to whom – in genuine pietistic form – the highest beauty appears in death, and whom indeed the angels release from his pain. In the hymn however the figure of Winckelmann appears almost as a Christian martyr, carried off to Elysium, where the dwelling of the spirits will turn out in Christian-neo-platonic fashion to be the 'one and only fountain head'. Indeed Winckelmann here becomes the common denominator of an aesthetic Christianity, along a line of thought adumbrated by Plotinus and by Spinoza as well. The prize-essay of 1778 is a testimony of the indelible impression made on Herder by Winckelmann's thought and personality. As regards the thought, Herder states, among other things, that Winckelmann's writings will remain as long as the German language survives; writings that he had read 'like the letter from a fiancée far away'. But just as firmly he testifies to the high moral influence radiating from Winckelmann's own life: 'Young man, when you read these letters, let them fill you with courage, if ever a similar fate should befall you.' Thus in this phase of Herder's Early Classicism Winckelmann as a personality is turned into the ideal example of the very concept of Classical humanitarianism. In his fate are embodied the moral and spiritual energies of that idea of humanity which wants to take the ideal of 'noble simplicity and quiet grandeur' as its guideline. Such a line of thinking can extend so far that in the later *Adrastea* essay on Winckelmann's History of Art *Herculaneum* (1803), Herder developed in further pursuit of Winckelmann's notion of noble simplicity the idea of a 'beautiful domestic simplicity', which was finally to be realised in the Empire style freed from all accessories and decorative embellishments.

Yet this was only the narrower sphere of viewpoints which enabled the leading spirit of the 'Storm and Stress' to develop into the Classical writer, although for Herder particularly among all the Weimar Classicists, the mental image and outward example of Winckelmann obviously remained of the most lasting and ever present importance. If we survey Herder's work from the beginning of the Weimar period up to the year of the completion of what was probably his most Classical work, the *Ideen zur Philosophie der Geschichte der Menschheit* (*Outlines of a Philosophy of the History of Man*) (1784–91), the year which lay midway between Goethe's return from Italy and his alliance with Schiller, we are struck by the richness of material and the range of viewpoints, in which an extraordinary personal realisation of budding Classicism is manifested. The significant continuation of the earlier comparative literary historical interests *Von der Ähnlichkeit der mittleren deutschen und englischen Dichtkunst* (1777) came in this period, also further work on physiological aestheticism of the senses in *Plastik* and *Vom Erkennen und Empfinden der menschlichen Seele* (1778). There further date from the years 1779 to 1781 three writings in which Herder estimated critically the mutual influence of the arts and *belles lettres* on State affairs and public morals. Two of these writings were prize-essays. In his own sphere of theology he produced the major draft of the *Briefe das Studium der Theologie betreffend* (1780–81), and then *Vom Geist der Ebräischen Poesie* (1782–83), in which the liberal spirit that breathed in the Theological Letters is reinforced by aesthetic interpretation of the Scriptures, and finally, in an especially fervent exchange with Goethe, the Spinoza-piece *Gott* (1787), in which he tried to treat the pantheism of the philosopher as not far removed from a panentheistic interpretation of the Christian concept of God. From 1784 on, however, the *Ideen* began to appear, the decisive view of history from the period of Classical thoughts on organic growth. They signified the broadening of the historico-philosophical question postulated a decade earlier in the 'Storm and Stress' period and contained in *Auch eine Philosophie der Geschichte zur Bildung der Menschheit*, which pointed towards the Classical standpoint. In the Preface to the *Ideen* Herder states his new goal and programme:

Was ist Glückseligkeit der Menschen? und wiefern findet sie auf unserer Erde statt? wiefern findet sie bei der großen Verschiedenheit aller Erdwesen und am meisten der Menschen

allenthalben statt, unter jeder Verfassung, in jedem Klima, bei
allen Revolutionen der Umstände, Lebensalter und Zeiten?[1]

Herder seeks the standard by which to measure and then raises the
question of meaning, which is teleological at the same time, namely
whether a 'principal ultimate goal' of Providence could be established, given all the differentiated abundance of phenomena. From
the outset he also establishes the theological background to the
use he is going to make of the term 'Nature':

Gang Gottes in der Natur, die Gedanken, die der Ewige uns in
der Reihe seiner Werke tätlich dargelegt hat.[2]

And later on he states expressly:

Die Natur ist kein selbständiges Wesen; sondern *Gott ist alles
in seinen Werken.*[3]

This comprehensive concept of Revelation also formed the basis
of Herder's liberal (and aesthetic) theology. It determined the
dogmatic candour both of the *Briefe das Studium der Theologie
betreffend* as well as the interpretation of the 'Hebraic poetry'
from aesthetic-psychological standpoints. In the *Briefe* he begins
the young man's apprenticeship by placing him in, and confronting him with Nature. It is the same Nature as that found in the
Ideen, the universal realm of God's Creation. Man is obliged by
the sense of historical consciousness granted to him alone to comprehend this organically in its proper order. Historical and philosophical order is therefore an act revealing one's concern for
humanity, a classically binding one admittedly: 'He who wrote
this was a human being, and you are a human being, you who
read this'. Hence the great venture of the *Ideen* appears as a mutual
assistance extended by man to man.

The course of the great project which extended over eight years
cannot be presented here in detail, but only characterised by
mere hints. Herder's assurance that he had read 'practically every-

---

[1] What is Man's happiness? And in how far is it realised on this earth?
And in how far is it realised in the great diversity of all earthly beings
and most of all amongst human beings everywhere, in every state, in every
climate, in every change of circumstance, age and period?

[2] The path of God in Nature, the thoughts which the Eternal One has
actually demonstrated to us in the course of his works.

[3] Nature is no independent being; but *God is All in His works.*

thing' that the age had produced on the history of Man is certainly no idle boast. At the back of the conception there still persisted the influence of Montesquieu and Winckelmann, supplemented by Goethe's natural-scientific idea of organic growth. Thus the *Ideen*, despite all the questionability of individual historical associations and judgements, became a magnificent evolutionary and educational history of the human mind from its most primitive beginnings, the old favourite theme of the 'Storm and Stress' writer. However for Herder (as also for the Classical Goethe) God and Nature, body and soul were and remained realities of the 'one and the same fountain-head', and *natura naturans* and *natura naturata* could signify nothing to the contemporary Spinoza-interpreter Herder but different *modi* of the one substance. And so it was no sacrifice of intellect for him to see his ideas of the history of the mind and education of Man as identical with Goethe's natural-scientific thoughts on organic growth, and to conceive the conditions for evolution not only in an analogy to, but even in a final union with the natural processes of growth – with the climate, the flora and fauna, with the character of the landscape and the conditions for life governed by it, with the consequences of history, from which morals, education and the arts, the cultures of the peoples uniformly developed step by step. It is not so much a question of the famous criterion contained in Book IV of erect locomotion as the beginning of specifically human existence. It revolves rather around what Caroline Herder accurately pointed to in a letter of 1783 about the first volume of the *Ideen* and its meaning:

> Die wunderbar rührende Verwandtschaft des Menschen mit allem, was ihn umgibt, und doch sein hoher Stand, seine unvergleichliche Organisation . . .[4]

In the final analysis the stress lies on the word 'despite', though in accord with what went before. For shortly before the commencement of work on the *Ideen*, still in the time of the first alienation from Goethe, Herder had already been so fascinated by the idea of evolution, that in a contribution to the *Teutscher Merkur* in 1781 under the title *Drei Gespräche über Seelenwanderung*, he turned this very theme, which Lessing's *Erzie-*

[4] The wonderfully touching relationship of Man with everything that surrounds him, despite his elevated status, his incomparable organisation . . .

hung des Menschengeschlechts had popularised at the time, from
mere metamorphosis into a theme of progress, anticipating the
historical concept of the *Ideen* and laying the basis of a doctrine
of organic immortality. Small wonder that the theme was expressly
taken up in Book VII of the *Ideen*:

> Der ganze Lebenslauf eines Menschen ist Verwandlung; alle
> seine Lebensalter sind Fabeln derselben, und so ist das ganze
> Geschlecht in einer fortgehenden Metamorphose.[5]

But it is clear that this metamorphosis is an earthly historical
one, grounded in nature and necessity, and not a mystically miraculous transformation. In Book XIII in Winckelmann's footsteps a kind
of morphology of Hellenism could be developed from this. And not
by chance there follows on the picture of Graeco-Roman classicism
the central Fifteenth Book with the chapter 'Humanity is the aim
of human nature, and with this purpose God has passed over into
the hands of our race its own fate'. In this book Herder weighs up
the destructive forces of nature against the forces of preservation.
It is allied to the Goethean optimism of that time and is formulated partly in dithyrambs. The destructive element must 'ultimately serve for the creation of the whole', totally reminiscent of
Mephistopheles's function in that layer of the *Faust* drama that
bears the Classical imprint. He made that remark with reference
to Nature, but Herder extends the analogy to Man without any
reservation:

> Wie? und im menschlichen Leben sollte nicht eben dies Gesetz
> walten . . . Kein Zweifel! wir tragen dies Prinzipium in
> uns.[6]

With these words the picture of Man in the *Ideen* (in analogy and
union with Nature) is seen in the light of an optimistic philosophy
which indeed stands rather closer to the Enlightenment than to
the biblical image of man. Not for nothing is the ideal condition
dominated by concepts of 'reason', 'fairness', 'welfare', to which
the organic development of cultures was directed. Not for noth-

---

[5] The whole life-course of a man is metamorphosis; all his ages are illus-
trations of the same, and so the whole human race finds itself in one continuous process of metamorphosis.

[6] What? And should not this very law rule supreme in human life . . . no
doubt at all! We bear this principle within us.

ing is this picture of humanity termed a 'rich design of talents and energies', nor the individual described in Classical terms as possessing the disposition to 'achieve even development of his energies, because in such alone lies the fullest enjoyment of his being'. That too corresponds with Goethe's image of man as does the definition of man's activity: 'Reason, Plan and Intention'. To Goethe that meant being sensible, energetic and creative.

Perhaps it is in the conclusions which Herder drew from all this that one becomes aware of his characteristic divergence from Schiller and his equally characteristic proximity to Goethe. Especially since his assimilation of Kant, Schiller built his picture of man and the world on postulates. He considered as valid all that which should exist according to the moral law. Not for nothing did he awaken in Goethe for a long time the mistrust that he was wronging Nature. Herder and Goethe however proceeded from a final union of the moral and the natural law, Herder at all events in his Classical period. Hence in their case the recognition of what *is* predominates over the dualistically conditioned *what should be*. Goethe's especially close connection with Herder in the very years when the *Ideen* and the Spinoza-piece *Gott* had their origin, was conditioned by this common attitude towards the law of Nature, and did not just rest on Goethe's recognition of Herder as the most competent judge of artistic values in his pre-Italian and Italian works. Thus the central Fifteenth Book of the *Ideen* culminates in one of the most beautifully formulated Classical interpretations of the world:

Ich beuge mich vor diesem hohen Entwurf der allgemeinen Naturweisheit über das Ganze meines Geschlechts, um so williger, da ich sehe, daß er der Plan der gesamten Natur ist. Die Regel, die Weltsysteme erhält, und jeden Kristall, jedes Würmchen, jede Schneeflocke bildet, bildete und erhält auch mein Geschlecht: sie machte seine eigene Natur zum Grunde der Dauer und Fortwirkung desselben, solange Menschen sein werden. Alle Werke Gottes haben ihren Bestand in sich und ihren schönen Zusammenhang mit sich: denn sie beruhen alle in ihren gewissen Schranken auf dem Gleichgewicht widerstrebender Kräfte durch eine innere Macht, die diese zur Ordnung lenkte. Mit diesem Leitfaden durchwandre ich das Labyrinth der Geschichte und sehe allenthalben harmonische göttliche Ordnung: denn was irgend geschehen kann, geschieht: was wirken kann, wirket.[7]

If we consider the fundamental concepts, these are law (here the 'rule'), fine cohesion, balance, order, harmony. They are all Goethean guiding principles too. Together they produce the picture of Classical universality.

However we also find revealed here the inner link with the discussion stimulated once again by Friedrich Heinrich Jacobi's booklet in which he dealt with Spinoza as philosopher of the *deus sive natura* notion. Herder made the statements but at the same time he spoke for Goethe. Indeed the essay *Gott*, which resulted, re-established at the time of Goethe's Italian journey the warmest contact between the two. The essay consists of five conversations, a form very close to Herder's heart. They contain an often enthusiastic *apologia* for Spinoza, and in this way they counteract the bias evident in Jacobi's *Spinoza-Büchlein*. Herder makes reference to the person as well as to the doctrine:

> Ein sonderbarer Mann, dieser Spinoza. Wie auch sein *System* sein möge; es ist etwas Wahrheitssuchendes, Standhaftes und Selbstbeständiges in seinem Charakter und Leben.[8]

And then, after quoting from the *Tractatus de intellectus emendatione*:

> Träume ich oder habe ich gelesen! Ich glaubte, einen frechen Atheisten zu finden, und finde beinahe einen metaphysisch-moralischen Schwärmer.[9]

[7] I bow before this sublime plan of universal natural wisdom governing the whole of my race, all the more willingly as I see that it is the plan of nature in its totality. The rule, which maintains systems of the universe and forms every crystal, every worm, every snowflake, formed and maintains my race too: it made its own nature the basis of permanence and of the continuation of my race as long as there ever will be human beings. All God's works have their inherent permanence and their fine innate cohesion: for they all rest in their certain limits on the balance of conflicting forces through an inner power, which guided them into order. Following this thread I wander through the labyrinth of history and see on all sides harmonious divine order: for whatever can happen, does happen: whatever can function, does function.

[8] A strange man, this Spinoza. Whatever his *System* may be, there is something that searches after the Truth, something steadfast and self-reliant in his character and his way of life.

[9] Am I dreaming or have I been reading! I thought I found an impudent atheist and I find almost a metaphysically moral visionary.

We may find the one as exaggerated as the other. At all events it sets out clearly the standpoint of Herder's interpretation of Spinoza. It becomes tenable only if we take the use of the word 'God' in Spinoza not as a philosophical working term, but in its theological sense. Besides, one must view Spinoza's philosophy as something that is not very far removed from the systems of both Leibniz and of Shaftesbury. Not for nothing is the translation of Shaftesbury's hymn to nature appended. We must further note the colouring of Herder's language with pietistic *topoi*, for example, the frequent use of the word 'fervent', the translating of Spinoza's 'mens' by 'the innermost'. In this sphere a Spinoza emerges on the plane of Herder's *Ideen*, whom we can interpret along the following lines:

> Je mehr Geist und Wahrheit, d.i. je mehr tätige Wirklichkeit, Erkenntnis und Liebe des *Alls zum All* in uns ist, desto mehr haben und genießen wir *Gott*, als wirksame Individuen, unsterblich, unzerteilbar.[10]

Thus the attempt is made to understand the philosopher in a Christian-mystical light, even with the help of Augustine's *frui Deo*, but at the same time in such dynamically active terms, that the world exists primarily as a play of forces, engaged in constant living transformation. There remains from Spinoza the idea that nothing exists outside of God. And this means that here, as before in the *Ideen*, all is Nature, as long as the whole of it is seen in neo-Platonist and panentheistic fashion, not pantheistically in accordance with Spinoza's consistent logic. Thus the essay *Gott* sounds like a self-exposition of the philosophical background to the *Ideen*, a confession at the same time in opposition to Friedrich Heinrich Jacobi's philosophy of faith.

Herder's main literary work of this period was the *Zerstreute Blätter*, which appeared in five collections from 1785 to 1793. He (or rather Caroline) collected in them old and new material both of aesthetic and literary critical content as well as, for the first time, his own poetry, of whose strictly lyrical parts he himself had a low opinion. Indeed, the great empathic figure, for whom rhyming and scansion went easily, was frequently a victim

[10] The more Mind and Truth, that is, the more active reality, knowledge and love of the *universe* for the *universe* is alive within us, the more do we possess and enjoy *God*, as effective individuals, immortally and indivisibly.

of his own all too exact critical knowledge when it concerned his own poems. That did not however prevent genius making itself felt in individual pieces in his own verse collection *Bilder und Träume*. Thus the tone of the theme of transience in *Das Flüchtigste* is wonderfully maintained in its amalgam of intoxication for life and resignation:

> Tadle nicht der Nachtigallen
> Bald verhallend süßes Lied;
> Sieh, wie unter allen, allen
> Lebensfreuden, die entfallen,
> Stets zuerst die schönste flieht.[11]

The same theme is found in *Der Regenbogen*. The tone is nearer to Goethe than to Schiller, despite the occasional affinity in the preponderance of the pensive lyrical strain. A feeling for style, the universal poetic mood and the verbal music create pre-Romantic tones too. Thus we sense the hint of Novalis' tone in *Das Saitenspiel*, and moreover Novalis-like themes:

> Verhall, o Stimm', ich höre
> Der ganzen Schöpfung Lied,
> Das Seelen fest an Seelen,
> Zu Herzen Herzen zieht!
> In Ein Gefühl verschlungen,
> Sind wir ein ewig All,
> In Einem Ton verklungen,
> Der Gottheit Widerhall.[12]

A direct correlation to the *Ideen* is provided by the poem *Die Natur*, a dithyrambic poem totally his own even in the strophic form, in praise of life and creation, blossom and growth, abundance and palingenesis:

> Hast du, hast du nicht gesehn,
> Wie sich alles drängt zum Leben?
> Was nicht Baum kann werden,

[11] Blame not the nightingale's sweet song, soon fading. Behold, how of all, all the joys of life that slip away, the most beautiful always flies away first.

[12] Fade away, O voice, I hear the song of all creation, which draws souls firmly to souls, hearts to hearts! Enveloped in one feeling, we are an eternal totality, lost in one sound, echo of the Divine.

I

Wird doch Blatt;
Was nicht Frucht kann werden,
Wird doch Keim.[13]

The whole is permeated by the thought of organic growth and palingenesis and by the rapture of unity which reigns supreme 'in the world full of divine life'. Spinoza is thus not far away.

The finest thing meanwhile to be found in Herder's lyric verse are the rather muted and soft tones which he uses for the thematic complex of dream, sleep and death, touched by the melancholy of transitoriness, but not marked by uncertainty or doubt. From the early *Abendsegen, Schlaf und Tod, via Das Flüchtigste* and *Das Lied des Lebens* there extends, on this particular theme, a series of poems which attain a high formalistic standard, culminating in perhaps the most mature strophe of a German *Zeitgedicht*, from Herder's old age:

> Ein Traum, ein Traum ist unser Leben
> Auf Erden hier.
> Wie Schatten auf den Wogen schweben
> Und schwinden wir.
> Und messen unsre trägen Tritte
> Nach Raum und Zeit;
> Und sind (und wissen's nicht) in Mitte
> Der Ewigkeit.[14]

Certainly these are high points of his lyric work that was fabulously rich thematically, abundant in material, indebted to many models, and on the whole too fond of rhetoric. Yet they are achievements in the absolute sense and on a par with those of Goethe and of Schiller. The fact that a considerable portion was also stimulated by foreign literature, indeed were translations (from the English, Italian and Spanish as well as the classical and oriental languages), leads to the second important function of the *Zerstreute Blätter*, which impressively highlight that amalgam of Herder's kindredness of spirit and originality; they include the

[13] Have you, have you not seen how everything strives for life? That which cannot become a tree, becomes however a leaf. That which cannot become fruit becomes a bud.

[14] A dream, a dream is what our life is here on earth. As shadows on the waves we hover and vanish. And our sluggish steps we measure according to time and space; and (though unaware) we are in the midst of eternity.

Blumen aus der griechischen Anthologie gesammelt, the *Para-mythien,* the oriental *Blätter der Vorzeit,* in all of which Herder the author has played just as much a part as Herder the editor and translator. Though they are neither really his own poetry nor strictly translation, they are at the same time a form of communication and a Herderesque paraphrasing of the poetry of past times and peoples, the result of strong and lasting impressions which are fused with what he himself had to offer.

19 Schiller's Path to Goethe

Up to *Don Carlos, Infant von Spanien* (*Don Carlos*) (1787), Schiller's youthful dramatic plays had not displayed any Classical features and even *Don Carlos* itself can at best be interpreted as a willing acceptance of the possibility of a drama of ideas as envisaged by Lessing at an early stage of Classical thought, as a sign of a transition from Shakespeare to the philosophical play. This is already reflected in the genesis of the story, which advanced from a 'family portrait in a Princely House' (with an admixture of the old idea of *in tyrannos* contained in *Die Räuber*), *via* intermediary stages in which prose was replaced by five-foot iambics, to a first attempt at a historical play of ideas on Schiller's part. To be sure, it is no longer the message of Karl Moor, of Luise Millerin or Fiesco which the real main character, the Marquis Posa, has to advocate. It is the theme of the century, that of humanity, which required the enlivening breath of free-thought and also a certain freedom of political self-determination. The figure of Posa only gained full significance in gradual stages, in the period of Schiller's sojourn in Saxony, just as the figure of King Philipp attained its tragic depth only in this last stage of work on the drama. Through both developments *Don Carlos* was transposed from the 'family portrait' into the drama of ideas, the utopian flavour of which betrays the fact that it constituted the first youthful attempt by Schiller in this genre. Posa, the reformer, is not required to show consideration for anything, not even his own life, save at most for his weaker friend (an echo of 'Storm and Stress' subjectivity); the ruler of the Spanish Empire has to take everything into consideration and therefore however gladly he would like to show humanity in the moment of being awakened by Posa, he just cannot afford so to do. This tension between the two is what lifts the action above the sphere of the private. In the final analysis the action is something more too than merely historical. The idea of freedom is merely exemplified in the Netherlands' struggle for liberation. Consequently *Don Carlos* in no way becomes a political-historical drama. First and foremost it develops into a play of ideas through the tragic position in life of each of the two protagonists, for the presentation of which the historical plot only acts as the vehicle. The tragedy of concern for humanity on the one side (Posa) and responsibility for established order on the other (Philipp) remains on a thoroughly abstract plane. Don Carlos still lacks 'life and vitality' (to use here Goethe's phrase from Italy), despite the love affair between the Prince and the Queen along with the Eboli intrigue. Even Schiller the historian was not able to offset that in any way through the creation of colour-effects and atmosphere. So a link exists rather with the Early Classicism of *Nathan der Weise* than with that of *Iphigenie* or *Tasso*. In addition there is an echo of the sentimental pathos with which Herder treats the figure of the martyr in the face of the protagonist for freedom, Posa, and similarly in that of the king.

Viewed against Schiller's earlier dramas, the renunciation of the crass and provocative elements in the style here is clear, so too thematically is the manifestation of the idea of freedom as a moral idea, of which sacrifice is a part. By contrast *Die Räuber* is still a confused play. In this context Schiller in his transitional phase stands closer to *Iphigenie* and *Tasso*.

But whatever Schiller's dramas, even in the case of *Don Carlos*, lacked in realism, without which an affinity to Goethe could not develop, Schiller made up for in another sphere: that of narration. From the age of twenty-three he had cultivated that form, compelled as he was by his constant need for money. Only since the advent of the Moral Weeklies had it been possible in Germany to earn money through journalistic ventures. One must realise that Schiller had to try to avail himself of this opportunity. In contrast to Goethe, he enjoyed security neither through parental support nor through an early professional position. He was in no way merely an idealistic poet, but to a considerable degree also a literary entrepeneur from economic reasons (as was Wieland in fact with the *Teutscher Merkur*). *Württembergisches Repertorium, Rheinische Thalia, Neue Thalia, Horen, Musenalmanach* are all stages along Schiller's journalistic path. One may perhaps think of Heinrich von Kleist who, no less an uncompromising poet than

Schiller, involved himself for similar reasons in the *Berliner Abendblätter* and *Phöbus*. And through that activity both became 'gripping' writers right down to the minor epic form of the anecdote. Besides this literary-sociological viewpoint there can indeed also be perceived a personal motive, and the later dramatist and aesthete Schiller is not to be divorced from the early story-teller Schiller (and the same holds good for Kleist too). Here he was stimulated by the abundance of material, here he sharpened the weapons for the art of characterisation and psychological analysis. Here, much more than in drama or verse, lay Schiller's realistic side, his 'naïve' relationship to Life's strange fates, preliminary material of historical interest, to curious legal cases in which the emotions and aberrations of the human soul manifested themselves. That is the deeper meaning of the partly merely planned, partly executed collection of enterprises on the part of Schiller the journalist, for example the *Causes célèbres* of Pitaval, that collection of famous cases, or important memoirs. All this was material for the history of the human soul; reality therefore and wholly consistent with this, Schillerian reality, for here the focal point is Man and Man alone, not Nature surrounding him, as frequently happens with Goethe. For Schiller the reality of the world was anthropological. Neither nature nor 'things' were of significance for him. That finds confirmation later in his High Classical period in such central poems as *Die Glocke* or *Der Spaziergang*. In the one the 'thing', in the other nature is introduced as a framework motif, in both however Man is clearly the cardinal point of reference. And so one need not wonder that Schiller's material-realistic side can be sought in an aesthetic-moral curiosity about the perceptible phenomena of the human psyche. With such a development away from abstraction to the material aspect, Schiller the narrative writer can be seen taking the first steps in the direction of Classicism.

In 1784 Schiller had announced in the *Rheinische Thalia* a story conceived after Diderot with the comment that it would show 'new-found cogs in the incomprehensible clockwork of the soul'. For the *Thalia* two years later he wrote the tale *Der Verbrecher aus verlorener Ehre* (originally '. . . aus Infamie', in the sense of a good reputation destroyed). Stylistic objectifying, tempering of images and making the vocabulary down to earth, avoidance too of risky syntactical experiments characterise the work. The theme is historical, the criminal case of the Swabian innkeeper's son Friedrich Schwan who became a robber. In the nineteenth century Hermann Kurz then refashioned the theme in his best-known story *Der Sonnenwirt*. The inner development of a man into an anarchical figure makes us recall Schiller's first drama and anticipates the theme of Kleist's *Kohlhaas*. Christian Wolf, originally granted only the awkward gifts of ugliness and poverty, becomes the disappointed suitor of a girl from his village and turns poacher. Branded by the law, he lapses still further and becomes a convict; all the result of 'injured pride, deprivation, jealousy, vengefulness and passion'. Expelled from society like a wild animal, he finally shoots the gamekeeper, the rival who had exposed him as a poacher. Strictly speaking unintentionally he then falls in with the robbers. Here he, the bold poacher, is now accorded the honour and respect denied him by the bourgeois community. For a year he lives as the terror of the land. Then once again humanity stirs irresistibly in him:

> Auf dem höchsten Gipfel seiner Verschlimmerung war er dem Guten näher, als er vielleicht vor seinem ersten Fehltritt gewesen war.[1]

So his resolve strengthens to regain his integrity through an honourable death as a soldier. Arrested at the frontier, he makes atonement in another way: through a voluntary confession before the kind old judge:

> Schreiben Sie's Ihrem Fürsten, wie Sie mich fanden und daß ich selbst aus freier Wahl mein Verräter war – .[2]

This finale is not so pathetic as the one whereby Schiller allows Karl Moor to quit ('that man can be helped'). From the standpoint of psychological consistency, freedom of choice here is only possible because honour has been satisfied through the courteous and humane nature of the judge – 'honour', that is, understood as a legitimate part of humanitarianism. In the field of drama Lessing had led his Major von Tellheim through painful experiences to a similar interpretation of honour as a problem of

[1] At the highest point of his depravity he was closer to good than he had perhaps been before his first wayward step.

[2] Write to your Prince, how you found me and that I myself was my betrayer of my own free choice.

humanitarianism. Moreover Schiller's introduction to the story has close affinities to Herder's idea of 'the natural history of the human soul':

> Stünde einmal, wie für die übrigen Reiche der Natur, auch für das Menschengeschlecht ein Linnäus auf, welcher nach Trieben und Neigungen klassifizierte, wie sehr würde man erstaunen, wenn man so manchen, dessen Laster in einer engen bürgerlichen Sphäre und in der schmalen Umzäunung der Gesetze jetzt ersticken muß, mit dem Ungeheuer Borgia in *einer* Ordnung beisammen fände.[3]

Two different things are here expressed which go far beyond the confines of the story: the realism of psychology as a task of the writer and the measure of Greatness attained in it. Both factors however point the way to Classicism, it is no longer reality deduced from the idea, but experience. When Schiller extols psychology 'because it extirpates cruel derision and the haughty assuredness with which untested honest virtue commonly looks down on fallen virtue', then that is antipathetic, contrary to his own inclination towards the ideal antithesis, down-to-earth, realistic, 'naïve'.

One year later, in 1787, Schiller turned to a new epic theme, from which then arose the great torso *Der Geisterseher* (published 1787–89), again a contribution to the secret record of the soul, but this time more powerfully permeated with elements of contemporary social psychology. The curiosity over miracles on the part of the outwardly enlightened century, as it emerged in the esoteric circles of the secret societies and was often linked with the picture which people conjured up of the clandestine activities of the banned Jesuit order, became an interesting literary theme for Schiller at the same time that Goethe was turning his attention to the figure of Cagliostro. In *Der Geisterseher* it is a German prince who falls into the snares of a secret society in Venice. Prophecies, meaningful incidents, rigged apparitions

---

[3] If for the human race too, just as for the other realms of nature, there were a Linnaeus, who classified according to impulses and inclinations, how very astonished we would be if we were to find many a person whose vices must now be stifled in a narrow bourgeois sphere and in the restrictions imposed by the laws, alongside the monster Borgia in one and the same social order.

awaken new qualities in the victim, who is calculatedly turned
into a religious sceptic through the magic hocus-pocus. By these
means the faculties for a worldly life are awakened: a passion
for prodigality and gambling, amorous adventures, the incurring
of debts and the indulging in intrigue. Together they all produce
the psychological preparation for the prince's conversion to
Catholicism and also the provoking of an ambition originally
alien to him, which was to have led in the planned continuation of
the work to the usurpation of his country's throne. Schiller completed the story, however, only up to the total destruction of the
inner as well as the outer situation of the 'hero', that is to the
point of complete spiritual dissolution, which makes him ripe for
the ministrations of the Holy Fathers. However the emphasis of
the story by no means lies in the philosophical, in this case an
anti-Catholic attitude, but once again in the disinterested pleasure
in the 'natural history of the human soul'.

> Ein entlarvter Betrug machte ihm auch die Wahrheit verdäch-
> tig . . . Von diesem Zeitpunkt an regte sich eine Zweifelssucht
> in ihm, die auch die Ehrwürdigste nicht verschonte.[4]

That – and the resultant consequences – constitutes the real theme.
The susceptibility of people at that time for the humbug of
secret rites, for alchemy that was widely practised even in Pietism
and the quest for the Philosopher's stone provides the social-
critical backcloth. Both factors however – specific contemporary
criticism and the fascination of the soul's mysteries – lay too on
Goethe's path to Classicism. Quite apart from the Cagliostro theme
in the *Großkophta*, we find something similar too already in the
'Urmeister'. Yet at the time neither of the two poets had known
of the process of growing spiritual kinship which was manifesting
itself in this area.

Hence one does find more evidence of tentative and early
Classicism in Schiller's narrative works, so far removed from the
world of Antiquity, than in his lyric verse of this period. Partly
this is still philosophical poetry within the framework of the
Enlightenment, partly it aspires to be an approach to the world
of the Ancients, though only qualifiedly so in the early classical

---

[4] An unmasked deception made him suspicious even of the truth . .
From this point on there stirred in him a scepticism that spared not even
the most venerable.

sense. For both aspects the three major pieces of this period
appear to be representative: *Lied an die Freude, Die Götter
Griechenlands* and *Die Künstler*. We cannot fail to recognise
the buoyancy of feeling for life in *Lied an die Freude* (1786),
the thoroughly personal experience and expression of friendship
in the Körner household. This feature is perhaps particularly noticeable when we think back to the poem *Resignation*, which was included in the *Anthologie* and meant to mark the disturbed Mannheim period. Formalistically *Lied an die Freude* bears traces of the
style of such earlier poets who sang of joy as Hagedorn and Uz
and even too a breath of Klopstock's seraphic pathos. But Schiller's
buoyancy in contrast appears intensified to the point of intoxication, and is expressed in images which hover in the clouds of an
elysian pleasure and allow scarcely a vista down to the profane
earth. The original version was perhaps still more exuberant with
its more distinct removal of the chorus from the main strophes.
But Christianity is not yet excluded from this world. The Klopstockian God of Creation characterises the choruses, indeed belief
in the Resurrection is even referred to (in the fifth strophe). The
dramatic tension in the poem reaches still into the transcendental,
therefore, despite the stressed immanence of the *kairos*-theme.
Perhaps the sixth strophe with its introductory theme:

> Göttern kann man nicht vergelten
> Schön ist's, ihnen gleich zu sein.[5]

may appear as a kind of scarcely conscious breakthrough to the
classical utopia of human worth.

Die Götter Griechenlands appeared in the March 1788 edition
of Wieland's *Teutscher Merkur*. It was a poem that aroused a stir
and caused offence; still a decade later Novalis sharply attacked
it in the Fifth Hymn of *Hymnen an die Nacht* from the standpoint
of the Romantic-Christian view of death. Not for nothing was it
Wieland, the *praeceptor Germaniae* in matter of classical antiquity, who had coaxed Schiller into letting him publish it. The
poem signifies, so to speak, a philosophy of history in verse, which
gives sentimental expression to the lament over the beautiful
though departed world of the Greeks, interspersed, indeed over-
laid by a mythology which the poet had made his own in diligent,
unaided studies: Antiquity is the primeval golden age of beautiful

[5] Gods one cannot repay, it is fine to be their equal.

sensuality and 'fullness of life', of serenity and enjoyment; an age in which the secret of the world had still not been unravelled by intellect and consciousness. Mirroring the dialogue between Winckelmann, Lessing and Herder on the theme 'How the Ancients fashioned death', Schiller takes sides vigorously in the classicistic sense:

> Damals trat kein gräßliches Gerippe
> Vor das Bett des Sterbenden. Ein Kuß
> Nahm das letzte Leben von der Lippe,
> Seine Fackel senkt' ein Genius.[6]

In short, Christianity is in every sense responsible for the alienation of man from the world in which he was once at home:

> Alle jene Blüten sind gefallen
> Von des Nordes schauerlichem Wehn,
> *Einen* zu bereichern unter allen,
> Mußte diese Götterwelt vergehn.[7]

The first version (in the *Teutscher Merkur*) is in this respect still more radical, for example in the strophe later deleted on the Christian conception of God:

> Freundlos, ohne Bruder, ohne Gleichen,
> Keiner Göttin, keiner Ird'schen Sohn,
> Herrscht ein Andrer in des Äthers Reichen
> Auf Saturnus' umgestürztem Thron.
> Selig, eh' sich Wesen um ihn freuten,
> Selig im entvölkerten Gefild,
> Sieht er in dem langen Strom der Zeiten
> Ewig nur – sein eignes Bild.[8]

It is a negation of Christianity, to which Goethe did not advance until the discordant tone of the *Venetianische Epigramme*, that is when he was over forty years old. Schiller anticipated this

[6] At that time no horrible skeleton stepped before the bed of the dying man. A kiss took the last drop of life from his lips, a genius lowered the torch in his hand to extinguish it.

[7] All those blossoms have fallen by the North's chilly wind, to enrich *one* amongst them all, this world of the Gods had to perish.

[8] Friendless, brotherless, without peers, son of no goddess nor any mortal, another rules in aether's realms on Saturn's toppled throne. Blessed, before beings rejoiced around him, happy in the deserted fields, he sees in the long river of time forever merely – his own image.

attitude on his path to Weimar at the age of twenty-eight, to no small extent due to his much stronger involvement in Enlightenment thinking. The terrible majesty of the Christian Godhead enjoying itself in isolation appeared to Schiller inhuman. The *Merkur* version pointedly expresses the contrast in a play on words: 'Since the gods were yet more human, / men were more divine.' When the High Classical Schiller came to modify the passage, he toned down this point in the conclusion: 'What is to live immortally in song / must perish in life.' This however was a new, additional theme of Classical aestheticism. The fact that Classicism was identified with paganism was obvious much earlier in Schiller's case – earlier in the sense of age – than in Goethe's. For Goethe this paganism was a consequence of experience. With Schiller it stemmed from the radicalism inherent in the idea and formed part of the very essence of his being.

In the autumn of 1788, following the stir that *Die Götter Griechenlands* had caused, Schiller set to work on a new major allegorical poem for Wieland's journal. In the February of 1789 he found the form for it, to which he provisionally adhered. If *Die Götter Griechenlands* constituted an Early Classical philosophy of history in verse, *Die Künstler* now represented a versified cultural philosophy. In contrast to Herder's Christian humanitarianism as the goal, 'Humanität' is here extolled as having been attained:

> Wie schön, o Mensch, mit deinem Palmenzweige
> Stehst du an des Jahrhunderts Neige
> In edler stolzer Männlichkeit.[9]

Manliness was also the ethical core of Goethe's Classicism (the poem *Seefahrt*: 'and manly he stands at the helm'). But for Schiller it had predominantly the stamp of Enlightenment optimism. The humanitarian consciousness which sustains the poem is Classical in expression. But Enlightenment is reflected in the awareness of progress not limited by resignation, an awareness which would be utopian for the Classical Goethe. How then does art appear here? As a 'naïve' anticipation of morality. Schiller had defined the theme of 'allegory' to Körner as the veiling of truth and morality in beauty, in the poem itself we read: 'Only

[9] How fine you stand, O being, at the close of the century with your palm branch in proud and noble manliness.

through the morning gate of the beautiful / Did you penetrate into the land of knowledge.' Art therefore stands here in
analogy to the pedagogic role of Revelation in Lessing's *Erziehung
des Menschengeschlechts*. But in Lessing's philosophy of history
Revelation renders itself superfluous with the stages of development. Childhood in fact does not remain. This is not what however Schiller means when he speaks of anticipation of morality
and reason by art. Art is a dowry of man for all time, time
future as well as past. If, in the primeval golden age, however,
art anticipates philosophy and morality, then it is difficult
to see why man in his evolution will always be in need of them.
For art indeed is also the anticipation of the Beautiful Soul.
From the outset artists are always morally free, according to
Shaftesbury: 'The heart steers them in gentle bondage /
disdains the servile attendance of duties.' But why then the
necessity of development 'towards the sublime realm of the
spirits'? The sequence is a necessity in Herder's *Ideen*, which
Schiller had valued very much at that time. It has no validity
for Schiller's historico-philosophical approach to art. The happy
time of mankind, a time of universal harmony through symbols –
how is it that it required a crowning through the dignity of ideas?
Why must there be the passage: 'The advanced man bears art /
thankfully aloft on raised wings'? It would have been no dilemma
for Goethe. But for Schiller it was typical. He had to struggle
to attain a balance between the timeless exceptional position
of Antiquity which he fervently adopted at that time, and the
optimism about progress on the part of the Enlightenment, whose
child he was and which then had not yet been muted by any
Kantian criticism. It represents a happy medium between Winckelmann and Wieland. That is exactly what this great poem is, considered in its historical context. In systematic terms Schiller's central
philosophical and aesthetic problem began to clarify itself here, a
problem which was to pursue him to the end of his days. If at the
end he wanted to force a solution to the historico-philosophical
contradiction by urging on the Age of Reason Art and Beauty as
the former initiators and one-time achievers of that path which
first awakened Thought, then tension and contradiction were only
superficially evaded, not eradicated. The tension remained between
the enthusiasm for the human ideal as expressed by Marquis Posa
in the play, and sensuality, concreteness and validity of art in

accordance with the Classically Antique image. No longer could the verses exclaim:

> Zuletzt, am reifen Ziel der Zeiten,
> Noch eine glückliche Begeisterung
> Des jüngsten Menschenalters Dichterschwung,
> Und – in der *Wahrheit* Arme wird er gleiten.[10]

The Early Classical Schiller's theory can only confirm what the poetic work of that period teaches us. Already the Mannheim essay of the twenty-five-year-old *Die Schaubühne als eine moralische Anstalt betrachtet* (*The Stage as a Moral Institution*) (1784) had decidedly steered towards 'Humanität' as the effective goal of the theatre:

> Jeder einzelne genießt die Entzückungen aller . . . und seine Brust gibt jetzt nur noch *einer* Empfindung Raum – es ist diese: ein *Mensch* zu sein.[11]

The *Brief eines reisenden Dänen* originated in the same year: this bore the sub-title *Der Antikensaal in Mannheim* and appeared in the *Rheinische Thalia* at the beginning of 1785. In Book Eleven of *Dichtung und Wahrheit* Goethe touched on this collection of casts made of classical masterpieces when he discussed how valuable they were for the acquisition of knowledge about Antiquity in a country so badly supplied with original pieces. For Schiller, who in contrast to Goethe, Lessing and Herder never got to see Italy, Mannheim meant the all-important viewing of Greek art (apart from copper-plate engravings). Later he could add the Dresden collections to his visual experiences. This was decisive however for his picture of Antiquity, so much more speculative than one based on the language in which the originals were couched. Hence from the start he could only aim at the total concept, at the idea. It was easier still for Schiller as an autodidact to provide himself with the necessary concept than for Lessing who boldly maintained that 'a stay in this hall of antiquity provides the studying artist with several advantages as against making

[10] Finally, at the ripe goal of ages, yet one more blissful ecstasy brought about by the poetic flights of the last age of mankind and – into the arms of *truth* will he glide.

[11] Each individual enjoys the delights of all – and his heart finds room now for but one feeling – and it is this: to be a human being.

a pilgrimage to the originals in Rome'. And Lessing was not of the type that is inspired by visual experiences like Winckelmann or Goethe, he was, like Schiller, a man of ideas. What is still un-classical in Schiller's essay is the social starting point along 'Storm and Stress' lines: the contrast of poverty and wealth which per-mitted only princes and patrons to develop further and enjoy art. But the panegyric praise for the sense of unity in this centre of art – a unity that was undisturbed by any dissonance – is already classical in tone. This hall of art becomes for him, as he elaborates on it, almost an aesthetic utopia:

> Empfangen von dem allmächtigen Wehen des griechischen Genius trittst du in diesen Tempel der Kunst . . . du stehst auf einmal mitten im schönen lachenden Griechenland, wandelst unter Helden und Grazien und betest an, wie sie, vor roman-tischen Göttern.[12]

This is Winckelmannian enthusiasm, just as Schiller's interpreta-tions depend on him. Schiller's criticism on the placing of a Vol-taire bust alongside that of Homer, 'I know of no more biting satire on our age', shows the aesthetic-historico-philosophic dilemma of *Die Künstler*. Man at the close of the century appears ridiculous beside the greatness of Antiquity. However, the notion of evolution contained in *Die Künstler*, equally at variance with the idea of timelessness associated with Antiquity, also comes to the fore:

> Der Mensch brachte hier etwas zustande, das mehr ist, als er selbst war, das an etwas Größeres erinnert als seine Gattung – beweist das vielleicht, daß er weniger ist, als er sein wird?[18]

Yet what does such an eschatological structure achieve, if it rests still on the noble past? There is an echo here of the original version of *Die Götter Griechenlands*:

> Die Griechen malten ihre Götter nur als edlere Menschen und

[12] Welcomed by the almighty breath of Grecian genius, you step into this temple of art . . . suddenly you are standing right in beautiful, laugh-ing Greece, you wander amongst heroes and Graces, and worship, like them, before romantic gods.

[18] Man here accomplished something that is more than he himself was, that recalls something greater than his *genus* – does that show perhaps that he is less than he will be?

näherten ihre Menschen den Göttern. Es waren Kinder *einer* Familie.[14]

We know where the young Schiller had acquired that attitude towards the Enlightenment, which gave life to *Die Künstler* and would have been quite inconceivable in Goethe's development. It was the moral philosophy already engendered in him at the Karlsschule with its origins derived from the Scottish school of Hutcheson and Ferguson. Shaftesbury's well-bred Platonic-aesthetic sense of virtue was supplemented in their case with a 'moral sense' which aimed at universal happiness. From the Scots and their German interpreter Garve, Schiller was able to acquire the evolutionary idea of happiness which bordered on the social utopian, and the inherent concept of the beautiful deed (*Don Carlos*). This historical concept (teleology of happiness) remained a constituent feature of the inner tension underlying the questions posed by Schiller's philosophical writings. For the classical Grecian concept did not entirely match the Enlightenment picture of history. The Classical Schiller was to secure for himself the help of Kantian philosophy to solve the problem that was sorely pressing him. But in the philosophical work of the transitional period, the *Philosophische Briefe* (*Philosophical Letters*) which appeared in the *Thalia* from 1786 on, one may still notice quite plainly how – thrown back on his own resources – he gropes and struggles to define the legitimate scope of reason. This indecision can in fact be historically explained too; uncertainty remains regarding the exact time at which Julius's theosophy arose. In some ways it relates back to the time of the Karlsschule. Furthermore, it is difficult to determine exactly Körner's role. With their aim of presenting a contribution on the developmental history of reason, the *Briefe* lie essentially half way between the interpretation of the Mannheim antiquities and *Die Künstler*. The naturally didactic contribution was to 'show the hidden dangers on which proud reason had already foundered'. The pedagogic means was the horrifying account of the extreme contrasts which dominate the area of nascent reason before it can mellow into 'quiet wisdom'. The *Philosophische Briefe* are governed by one framework theme; two friends correspond: Julius, childlike, sensual, enthusiastic,

---

[14] The Greeks painted their gods merely as more noble humans and made their humans close to the gods. They were children of *one* family.

and Raphael, the older, more manly person, the free thinker who for a long time had been conscious of the responsibility of rational thought. The structure of this piece of writing repeats the relationship between the partners that exists in Lessing's *Ernst und Falk*. And thus it becomes formalistically a dialogue in letter form, not an epistolary novel, despite Jacobi's earlier example. The younger correspondent suffers from the loss of the happy, emotional warmth of childhood:

> Was hast du aus mir gemacht, Raphael? . . . Gefährlicher großer Mensch! daß ich dich niemals gekannt hätte . . .![15]

The unsuspecting Julius, at one with himself and the world, finds himself entangled in a net of inferences and erroneous conclusions. He finds himself irrevocably swept away by the superior, older man who, 'hardened in the strict school of resignation', is sure that he is merely accelerating a crisis within his friend which had to erupt at some point. In this confronting of the extremes of emotion and thought, youth and manhood of the spirit, Schiller wanted nevertheless to show the possibility of synthesis. Basically he succeeded more here than in *Die Künstler*, which took up the idea of synthesis not as the theme of evolution with regard to subjective thinking, but concerning the whole of mankind. Particularly the idea that man's predetermined advance towards reason entails suffering is established more profoundly here, and hence becomes comprehensible as man's fate and as necessity. But the limitations of Raphael's freethinking were also demonstrated. What is Early Classical therefore is the idea of moderation, which is valid both for feeling and for thought. Thereby one can then arrive at a true synthesis. The golden days of Antiquity and progress in *Die Künstler* could only be reconciled by an act of force and not persuasion.

Thus Schiller was inwardly prepared in the best possible way to respond to the Classical Goethe in the general direction of thought when through the latter's good offices his official link with the Duchy of Weimar ensued in the September of 1788. He was called to the Chair of History at Jena. But Schiller was to be able to occupy the chair for only a short time. His almost fatal illness

---

[15] What have you made of me, Raphael? . . . Dangerous, great man, oh that I had never known you . . .

already put an end to his teaching activities in 1791. That coincided in time with his discovery of Kant and interest in philosophical problems which once again took precedence as a result. But the great rhetorical historical works, the *Geschichte des Abfalls der vereinigten Niederlande von der Spanischen Regierung* (1788) (*History of the Defection of the United Netherlands from the Rule of Spain*) and the *Geschichte des dreyßigjährigen Kriegs* (1791–93) (*History of the Thirty Years War*), still lay ahead of him at that time. His inaugural lecture in Jena, which appeared at the end of 1789 under the title *Was heißt und zu welchem Ende studiert man Universalgeschichte?*, was of typical significance for Schiller in his transition to Classicism. What mattered now was not so much the differentiation between science as a pure search for truth on the one hand and the meaningless and slavish pursuit of it for material ends on the other, but the relation of every historical factor to man and likewise of man to it. An awareness of history should mean the realisation of man's resolve to acquire true humanity, the goal being for each and every person 'to educate himself as a true human being'. Schiller had therefore to conceive universal history as a philosophising science whereby man was led back to himself through acquiring knowledge of the 'causal connections between phenomena'. Certainly in the picture of evolution outlined by Schiller and in the other minor universal historical writings too which date from these years and form a mosaic pattern of history there still lurked a strong echo of Enlightenment thinking, above all rationalistic pride in the overthrow of barbarity and superstition. Here too the dilemma of *Die Künstler* manifested itself. But that attitude was at least not far removed from Classicism, namely as an expression of its consciousness of beauty, of its taste. The opposite pole to coarseness and distortion had indeed to be culture and harmony, the didactic sequence of progression was bound to lead 'from the asocial cave-dweller to the witty thinker, to the educated man-of-the-world'. It was a long path, corresponding to the succession of cause and effect. That meant once again Herder and hence indirectly also a stage on Schiller's path to partnership with Goethe in the area of High Classicism.

PART VI

The High Period of Classicism: Foundations

20 Antiquity Experienced: Goethe's Italian Journey

In the autumn of 1786 Goethe went seemingly in flight from Karlsbad on a journey to the land of Classical Antiquity. Only the Duke had cognisance; neither Frau von Stein nor Herder had been informed. Nevertheless he did not depart on the spur of the moment, but was well prepared in every respect, merely adopting complete secrecy as to his plans. His pedagogic task at Weimar, the surreptitious guidance of the Duke, was now complete. Karl August was on the point of entering the Prussian army. For Goethe there could scarcely be any point in working his fingers to the bone still further in the administrative work of the Duchy, to the detriment of his artistic creativity. The confines of Weimar had grown too limiting in every respect. The relationship with Frau von Stein could also not be continued in the same way as hitherto. The tension had become almost unbearable. If we recall these rather negative reasons, his departure for Italy seems a natural outcome, even its abruptness becomes understandable. It is quite clear from what has been said that on the positive side, too, reasons for the departure had been increasing over a long period: Goethe required breadth, experience, discipline for the senses, and he sought all that as a 'regeneration' in the land of classical tradition that was now within his reach, a land to which he, like Winckelmann, had geared his whole existence in advance. The songs from the 'Urmeister' of 1784 and 1785, *Kennst du das Land* and *Nur wer die Sehnsucht kennt, weiß was ich leide*, testify adequately enough to this preparation. The diary of October 1786 programmatically notes at the time:

Auf dieser Reise, hoff ich, will ich mein Gemüt über die schönen Künste beruhigen, ihr heilig Bild mir recht in die Seele prägen und zum stillen Genuß bewahren. Dann aber mich zu den Handwerkern wenden, und wenn ich zurückkomme, Chymie und Mechanik studieren. Denn die Zeit des Schönen ist vorüber, nur die Not und das strenge Bedürfnis erfordern unsere Tage.[1]

These words bring together the aesthetic and ethical principles in complementary fashion. And the educational idea of the whole classical plan followed suit. Despite the concomitant return to the Original, despite the ever recurrent theme of rejuvenation, this could be taken as corresponding to a considerable degree to Schiller's formula of 'aesthetic education'.

The decisive period lasted from September 1786 to Easter 1788. But one must not accept the reports about this journey from the subsequent stylised version of the *Italienische Reise*; for this was above all a bookseller's enterprise, which was neither fully reliable nor even formed into a complete artistic whole. Only the diaries can be counted as unimpeachable sources, though they cover but a part of the period, and the authentic letters to Charlotte, Herder, Karl August and also Knebel. These sources verify even in their very tone the inner liberation, and that too before he ever got to Italy. The words from Regensburg 'and yet nothing that exists is enigmatic to me. Everything speaks to me and reveals itself to me . . . I revel in it' already mirror this new state. In Bolzano Goethe speaks further of the happiness of the sensual impressions and the experiments touching on his powers of observation: 'whether and to what extent my eye is luminous, clear and pure . . . and whether the wrinkles that have entered my spirit and left an imprint on it, can be erased'. Quite clearly, a new, all-embracing vitality here set in, the expression of which was the thought of rejuvenation, not the educative experience of Antiquity. For his joy in the Jesuit Baroque in Bavaria was totally unclassical, and his rapture over the simple life of the people from Malcesine to Venice seemed more Netherlandishly realistic, childlike and a little roguish, more lustily happy than solemn. The oft-cited diary entry from Verona on the first classical places he saw:

[1] On this journey I hope I shall set my mind at rest through the Fine Arts, and stamp their sacred image in my very soul and preserve it for my quiet enjoyment. Then however I hope to turn to the craftsmen and study chemistry and mechanics, when I return. For the period of the 'beautiful' is over, only exigency and strict necessity are what our times demand.

'The wind that blows over from the graves of the Ancients comes with sweet scents as over a hill of roses', is still an expression of such heartfelt feeling, it is not pathos. One has to emphasise this feeling of 'change', this vital rejuvenation, more strongly than the educational basis of the Italian journey. Lessing and Herder went as strict Winckelmann-experts to Italy, which (perhaps for that very reason) did not satisfy their ideal. Goethe on his departure was no more than a rather vague admirer of Winckelmann. Not until Rome did he really study the *Kunstgeschichte*. The basis of the prose version of *Iphigenie*, which he took with him, was admittedly the same in atmosphere as for the young Winckelmann – namely the atmosphere of the studio-conversations in Leipzig with Oeser, who was the instructor for both of them. But that was really only very vague, no more than a prelude which in the case of the Veronese *stelae* could then lead to tears of emotion. If Winckelmann and Oeser influenced Goethe, then they had prepared his feeling, not however his approach to Antiquity by means of understanding. This attitude still found expression even in Vicenza, where the course of duty began with the study of the buildings of Palladio, which Goethe conceived as representative of the effects engendered by the Classical Renaissance. Even at that time he wrote to Charlotte:

> Du weißt, was die Gegenwart der Dinge zu mir spricht, und ich bin den ganzen Tag in einem Gespräch mit den Dingen.[2]

At the same time however he sought to avoid the danger of sheer enthusiasm and to consciously restrict himself to a diet, 'so that the objects find no exalted soul, but rather exalt the soul'. These are the words still of the Early Classicist who incidentally was starting work at the same time on the revision of *Iphigenie*. The important thing however was that Goethe was experiencing his own vitality and rhythm of life as something identical with his need for Hellenism. It was this very thing that already distinguished in Goethe's case the start of the Italian journey from the classicistic world as subject material for Lessing and Wieland, indeed vastly different even from Herder's venture. Goethe could say in Venice that it appeared to him 'not as if I were seeing the things, but as if I were seeing them again'. Thus did he experience

[2] You know what the presence of objects says to me, and I am in conversation with the objects the whole day.

Italy 'inwardly prepared'. Thus could he write from Rome at the beginning of 1787 to Frau von Stein that he 'had recovered to enjoyment of life, history, poetic art and the antiquities'. The sequence is significant: enjoyment of life first, antiquities last. Gundolf's differentiation of 'original experience' and 'educative experience' would be fully applicable to the assimilation of Italy in this sense.

For all that the course of the journey seems determined not only by the moment, but also by the inner picture of Rome as the hereditary capital of Antiquity. Goethe's 'manly' plan went so far that he hastily passed from Venice through Upper and Central Italy, took no notice of Florence, just as little of Franciscan Assisi, where he valued only the insignificant temple to Minerva as a foretaste of the hoped-for greatness of the sights to come. Everything that he skipped on this journey has been more than adequately held against him. But this utterly untouristic and un-historic flight was nothing else than the shortest route to the centre, it was the spirit of 'seriousness', of 'inner solidity' (as Goethe wrote to Herder), in short, the feeling of duty which manifested itself – still in the spirit of Classicism – as a spontaneous feeling of re-juvenation. To which was also added the ethos of Goethe the natural scientist who urgently sought out the evidence of Antiquity as an objective substance for knowledge ('as I treat Nature, so I treat Rome'). In the last resort all this was one and the same thing; for already on 10 September 1786 he could say to Char-lotte von Stein *àpropos* the 'regeneration':

> Daß ich aber so weit in die Schule zurückgehen, daß ich so viel verlernen müßte, dachte ich nicht. Desto lieber ist mir, ich habe mich ganz hingegeben, und es ist nicht allein der Kunst-sinn, es ist auch der moralische, der große Erneuerung leidet.[3]

The force emanating from the situation in which he finds himself therefore calls forth a surrender on his part and at the same time affects his moral substance.

As is well known, Goethe arrived in Rome under a pseudonym. He was too well known not only as a poet but as a Minister too, even if only of a Central German State. Naturally however his

[3] That I would have to go so far back to school, that I should have to un-learn so much, I did not imagine. But I like it the more, I have surrendered myself completely, and it is not only the taste for art, it is also the moral sense which undergoes great rejuvenation.

identity was not concealed from the circle of artists which he entered in Rome. There Goethe's path crossed those of significant figures like Wilhelm Heinrich Tischbein, Angelika Kauffmann, Philipp Hackert, whose editor Goethe later became, the copperplate engravers Lips and Volpato, and besides this guild of artists the Swiss Johann Heinrich Meyer, but above all Karl Philipp Moritz, whose mentor Goethe became and to whose importance for a new classical aestheticsm the *Italienische Reise* bears witness through its inclusion of fragmentary *aesthetica* by that author. Some of these intellectuals came and went, some were replaced by others, some helped Goethe find his feet in Rome and further his studies in drawing and painting. For Goethe's development was, as ever, not an exclusively aesthetic one. The natural scientist revealed himself not only in the diary observations, but also in the fact that the 'idea' of the original plant in Palermo could take precedence over the really Mediterranean poetry of the Italian period, namely the *Nausikaa*. Then too, in his correspondence with the Duke, Goethe envisaged a heightened public service on his part following his return to Weimar on the strength of his rejuvenated vitality and artistic impulse. It was a total blue-print for life that Goethe was here producing

We have to admit that the cultivation of classical taste which Goethe assimilated in Rome and Sicily was in fact not far removed from ideas propounded by Winckelmann which Goethe had only recently made his own through diligent study. In this connection we need only consider the number of casts of classical works with which Goethe was to decorate his new house on the Frauenplan in Weimar. But what he saw above and beyond that in Rome as an example of the classical, was late classical art, like Winckelmann's Laocoön and Apollo of Belvedere, like the Antinous and the Juno Ludovisi or the Zeus Otricoli, not genuine antiquity, in which he saw his inner ideal expressed. From this we may infer that the cultivation of Goethe's classicism was really accomplished 'from within', so that it really proves nothing if his classicism was even founded on not inconsiderable historical errors. The passage in a letter to Karl August of 17 March 1788, shortly prior to his return, proves however, on the contrary, much more:

Lassen Sie mich an Ihrer Seite das ganze Maß meiner Existenz ausfüllen und des Lebens genießen, so wird meine Kraft, wie eine nun geöffnete, gesammelte, gereinigte Quelle von einer Höhe, nach Ihrem Willen leicht dahin oder dorthin zu leiten sein.[4]

This statement occurs immediately after his report to the Duke on how he had found himself again as an artist in the eighteen months he had spent in Italy. 'The full measure of existence' and the palingenesis as artist – quite obviously Goethe himself understood it as one and the same thing.

The drawing of parallels between his viewing of art and of nature that occurs in the documents also forms part and parcel of such universality. Goethe's gaze could be directed just as much to the flora and fauna and the geological conditions as to the study of the volcanic elements at Vesuvius and in Sicily. Furthermore the concept of the original plant, through which he was later to find a point of contact with Schiller, kept pursuing him, especially on the journey to Naples and Sicily. It cropped up in the intimate communication to Frau von Stein of 8 June 1787 directly following his return from there:

Sage Herdern, daß ich dem Geheimnis der Pflanzenzeugung und Organisation ganz nahe bin und daß es das einfachste ist, was nur gedacht werden kann. Unter diesem Himmel kann man die schönsten Beobachtungen machen. Sage ihm, daß ich den Hauptpunkt, wo der Keim stickt, ganz klar und zweifellos entdeckt habe . . . Die Urpflanze wird das wunderlichste Geschöpf von der Welt, über welches mich die Natur selbst beneiden soll. Mit diesem Modell und dem Schlüssel dazu kann man alsdenn noch Pflanzen ins Unendliche erfinden, die konsequent sein müssen, das heißt: die, wenn sie auch nicht existieren, doch existieren könnten . . . Dasselbe Gesetz wird sich auf alles übrige Lebendige anwenden lassen.[5]

[4] If you allow me to fill the full measure of my existence at your side and enjoy life, then my strength, like a now opened, channelled and pure mountain spring, will be yours to direct easily in this way or that according to your will.

[5] Tell Herder that I am quite close to the secret of plant generation and organisation, and that it is the simplest thing one could ever imagine. Under this sky one can make the finest observations. Tell him I have discovered quite clearly and without a shadow of a doubt the main point where the germ is situated. The original plant turns out to be the oddest creation on earth, for which Nature herself shall envy me. With this model and the key

If we take cognisance of this, it is not logically clear how later in the famous conversation with Schiller, Goethe could take exception to the fact that his partner declared the original plant an idea instead of an experience. For this is just what Goethe himself was declaring it to be here. Only he believed he had in fact seen it with his own eyes in Palermo. The 'Urpflanze' like the viewing of art belonged, in accordance with Goethe's consciousness and ethos, to classical realism, which he wanted to develop in Italy and had in fact done. The study of Winckelmann in Rome helped to clinch it, but it was not *the* decisive factor. The ethos was already observable beforehand, for example in his observations on Mantegna and Titian in Upper Italy. Thus in the pictures of Titian he praised 'the energy of their nature, illuminated by the spirit of the Ancients', which led to truth. Mantegna however signified for Goethe an equally 'sharp, sure Present':

> Von dieser ganzen, wahren (nicht scheinbaren, Effekt lügenden, zur Imagination sprechenden), derben, reinen, lichten, ausführlichen, gewissenhaften, zarten, umschriebenen Gegenwart, die zugleich etwas Strenges, Emsiges, Mühsames hatte, gingen die folgenden aus...[6]

The definitive nature of an ethical choice, as this abundance of attributes prescribes it, already contains Winckelmann *in toto*, naturally not as a statement concerning the history of art, but concerning the ethics of art. In Rome Goethe was similarly to conduct himself when he took up his own sketching again, 'painstakingly' and with sweat on his brow. After the youthful fumbling attempts and the already more serious continuation under Oeser in Leipzig, and following an intermediate stage as an artist which corresponded to the poetry and natural science of the Weimar decade (sentimental landscapes of a type reminiscent of his poem to the Moon, landscapes depicted from a geognostic point of view, portrait sketches from his environment), he now sought in Rome to shake off as far as possible the dilettante approach

to it one can invent plants *ad infinitum*, plants which must follow a logical pattern, that is, those which could exist even if they do not exist. The same law can be applied to everything else living.

[6] From this complete true Present (not an apparent Present, deceptively affecting, appealing to the imagination), a blunt, pure, lucid, detailed, conscientious, tender, circumscribed Present, which at the same time had something strict, industrious, painstaking about it, the following emerged ...

by improving on his craftsmanship, his treatment of perspective and of accurate outlines. What Goethe aspired to in Rome at that time was exactly that which, as late as 1811, he was to praise in the work of his artistic companion of the Rome period, the Neapolitan court painter Philipp Hackert: 'competence, accuracy, acuity, energy and perseverance'.

Exactly the same consistency of approach was operative in the literary works that were accomplished in Italy, however fundamentally diverse in form they are. For indeed they ranged from the transposition of the prose *Iphigenie* to the verse version, and experiments with the 'Mediterranean' *Nausikaa* material which remained but fragmentary, and the completion of scenes and parts of *Faust* in Rome, to *Egmont* and *Tasso* and still further to certain poems, quite apart from the aesthetic stock-taking of himself which was pursued above all together with Karl Philipp Moritz.

Amongst all these works we should first focus our attention on the adaptation of the *Iphigenie* manuscript to the new situation created at the very beginning of his changed emotional life. The early form of the drama of 1779 had failed to satisfy Goethe right from the outset. The revision, begun in Malcesine and completed in Rome, was already the fourth version. It was only this last version that produced the drama in a classical form. The 1779 version still belonged amongst Goethe's attempts to become master of his relationship with Frau von Stein. That original draft links the project according to its inner motivation with *Seefahrt*, *Das Göttliche* and *Grenzen der Menschheit*. In the figure of Orestes there exists something still of a bridge constructed between the 'Storm and Stress' and the classical verdict on Tasso. At the same time it is not first and foremost a question of a concept of Hellenism and its 'Humanität'. Extreme demands are made on the three main figures Iphigenie, Orestes and Thoas, but they differ from those in the Greek drama of Euripides. In Euripides relations between the gods and mortals remain completely unpsychological by nature, and correspond to the unequivocal aspect of fate. 'Orestes is dead, consecrated to death by me' – that is the Euripidean theme already anticipated in the opening dream. Iphigenie's position as a Greek in the 'barbarian land' over which Thoas rules is thus also unequivocal. The unequivocal nature of her tragedy lies in the fact that she as a Greek and priestess amongst bar-

barians has to offer even Greeks in sacrifice in accordance with barbarian custom. The position of her antagonist, the barbarian Thoas, is likewise unambiguous. Mistrust, thirst for revenge, and immoderate rage, sudden turn of events through proskynesis when Athene intervenes in person: 'How would I prevail against divine might' – all this is totally unbounded, clearly directed towards the barbaric. The relationships in the triangle Iphigenie – Orestes – Pylades are correspondingly fixed in advance. There is no breath of sentimentality. Orestes is the matricide pursued by the Furies, instructed by the oracle to free himself from the curse by stealing the image. Pylades has the role of Polymetis, and as a kinsman is involved in the affair. The continuing tension lies in the outwitting of Thoas and the question of the rescuing of the fugitives from his revenge. Divine decision is forcibly realised by Athene, who acts *ex machina*.

What then has Goethe changed in the existing Greek subject matter? The ethical claims discernible already in the 1779 text can find no place in the Grecian structure of relationships. In Euripides, Iphigenie does not set herself the task of bringing a healing influence to bear either on Orestes in his madness, or on Thoas in his barbarity. Goethe introduces both aspects, though clearly treading nevertheless Winckelmann's path of noble simplicity and quiet grandeur. The theme of barbarity is thus as good as removed. Thoas has become noble, kind and generous almost beyond the limits of credibility. For her part Iphigenie thereby finds herself in a totally un-Greek moral conflict, a humane post-classical conflict of conscience over Thoas, who now himself becomes the benefactor. Betrayal of the magnanimous friend accordingly signifies being unfaithful to oneself. With the confession of the plan for escape (only conceivable on the basis of the Christian confession that had meantime come into being), integrity is in fact preserved. Thoas however finds himself in a thoroughly modern situation that demands almost the impossible of him. It is ultimately the situation of Winckelmann's Laocoön: extreme self-control in renouncing revenge and self-mastery to the extent of forgiveness. There remains nothing more for Euripides' Athene to do. Gods no longer need to be troubled, the 'quiet grandeur' of human beings has already accomplished everything. On the other hand the splendid *Parzenlied* in the original version provides the clearest classical presentiment. Here the obvious and cruel autocracy of the gods lies outside of the moral standards which govern the actions of the human figures in the drama. So the real plot in Goethe's version consists in the overcoming of the family curse imposed by the gods through the 'Humanität' of those afflicted by the curse. Even the oracle, which in Euripides is an instruction to carry out a straightforward theft for the sake of the gods, has been given a new meaning in Goethe's play, signifying Socratic support for the moral faculty of man. In short, fate is replaced by ethos in the eighteenth-century sense of the term. Goethe would have been no more aware than Winckelmann of the close affinity here to the 'drama of magnanimity' of Baroque origins. And that can be seen expressed too in the linguistic conception of the original *Iphigenie* which was so characteristic of the situation in 1779, that synthesis of naturalistic prose and integrated rhythm, which revealed what Goethe was unable to do as yet at that time, though too what he had no intention of doing. The chopping and changing in the revisions of 1780 and 1781 – first the inclination to verse, then back again to prose – was characteristic. The new, uniform stylistic design was still lacking. It was only to come with the exaltation of Italy, when Goethe also learned to conquer his 'Storm and Stress' aversion to pure idealism. The change was above all a question of style, it did not express itself for example in a stricter motivation governed by the spirit of Antiquity. The magnanimous Thoas, Iphigenie's double educative task, the rendering innocuous of the oracle motif remained as before. It was in Italy that Goethe sought first and foremost the suitable form for this problem child of his transitional period, and he did not wait for Rome, though it was not until then that he completed the transformation 'in proper continuity'.

> Mein Verfahren dabei war ganz einfach: Ich schrieb das Stück ruhig ab und ließ es Zeile vor Zeile, Period vor Period regelmäßig erklingen.[7]

One can believe this procedure in his case; less so the attempt made in the *Italienische Reise* (under the date of 10 January 1787) three decades later to infer the influence of Karl Philipp Moritz's versification on the revised text. In the first place mention

---

[7] My procedure over this was quite simple: I copied out the play in peace and quiet and recited it line by line, period by period following the regular rhythm.

of Moritz does not occur until 1 December and by the turn of the year *Iphigenie* was already complete. Secondly Goethe would have to have completed his rhythmic version based on Moritz's theory already prior to Rome, since no break in style is perceivable. Moritz's theory on the relative values of syllables could have influenced individual decisions on rhythm in the final phase, but no longer the style. Against that we have to reckon with a rather important compensatory influence on Herder's part, who was sent the manuscript with full authorisation to polish or to change it, in particular with regard to the euphony. Yet in the accompanying letter to the *Iphigenie* manuscript Goethe made reference also to Wieland:

> Auch wünscht' ich, daß es Wieland ansähe, der zuerst die schlotternde Prosa in einen gemesseneren Schritt richten wollte und mir die Unvollkommenheit des Werkes nur desto lebendiger fühlen ließ.[8]

We will therefore also have to take into account Wieland's pre-Classicism as a fermenting force. In the final analysis, however, a comparison of the original version of the *Parzenlied* with the Italian version shows that the whole Roman 'regeneration' was involved over and above the question of stylistic influences exerted by friends. *Iphigenie* had become more harmonious, and not just in the sphere of euphony. It was precisely the rather cool reception of the new version by his Weimar friends, who had not similarly experienced Goethe's development away from the sentimental aspect, that confirms the change.

Indeed the decisive lead that Goethe now took over his Weimar circle was to be found in the disciplining of the senses. However his experiences led in the first instance not to independent and completed works, but only – apart from a small flow of poems – to fragments, revisions and elaborations. Under the latter, besides *Iphigenie*, come *Faust, Tasso* and *Egmont*. *Nausikaa* remained fragmentary, almost a torso.

Work on the *Nausikaa*-drama served as a substitute, taking the place of the Iphigenie motif which he had originally planned to

---

[8] I should also like Wieland to see it, since he first wanted to direct the stumbling prose into a more measured rhythm and made me feel all the more acutely the imperfection of the work.

pursue further. The projected 'Iphigenie in Delphi' with the Electra-theme at its core would supposedly have revealed right from the outset the 'transapennine' factor, which had still been withheld from the Taurian Iphigenie in the original version. It was precisely this 'transapennine' element however that was now to characterise the *Nausikaa* drama, since it was confined to mere plans as far as the second Iphigenie was concerned. Already on the journey through the Apennines (under the diary date of 22 October 1786) Goethe came up with a plan for a tragedy *Ulysses auf Phäa* reminiscent of Homer and things Homeric. But Goethe's knowledge and recollection of Homer was rather weak and vague at that time. He was conversant neither with the name of the island nor that of Nausicaa herself, as the fictitious name of Arete from the first draft revealed. Not until the intoxicating experience of Sicily in the spring of 1787 amongst the Mediterranean gardens and the ruins of Magna Graecia did he direct his attention again to Homer and the plan for *Nausikaa*. 'It all recalled to my senses and to my memory the island of the blessed Phaeacians', the *Italienische Reise* recorded. Not by chance were the first things to be mentioned 'the senses'. But the experience of the senses was ephemeral. While still in Palermo Goethe acquired a Homer text. Yet only two days later the entire plan was dropped in favour of 'another spectre', the 'Urpflanze'. Only on one other occasion did the name crop up again, admittedly at an expressly classical place, in Taormina, perhaps denoting no more than a vague recollection. Here for the first time a classical motif, Antiquity, would have been fashioned out in Homeric form instead of by the tragic poets. For the first time too a tragedy would have been shaped, which *Iphigenie* was not and which *Elpenor* was not to become.

The subject was conceived as an elaboration of that part of the *Odyssey* in which with magnificent naïvety the naked Odysseus, magically rejuvenated by Athene, meets the daughter of the king Alcinoüs and her maidens playing ball after his shipwreck on the Phaeacian island, is clothed and hospitably received. Homer restricted himself to that with archaic severity. Not so Goethe on Mediterranean Sicily. A decade later he clarified his ideas in a letter to Schiller (14 February, 1798):

Die Rührung eines weiblichen Gemüts durch die Ankunft eines Fremden, als das schönste Motiv, ist nach der Nausikaa gar

nicht mehr zu unternehmen. Wie weit steht nicht, selbst im
Altertum, Medea, Helena, Dido schon den Verhältnissen nach
hinter der Tochter des Alkinoos zurück.[9]

These words indicate a praise of Homer penned at a later stage.
However they are valid too for the extant draft of the *Nausikaa*
tragedy. If, as was earlier mentioned, *Iphigenie* signified a modern-
ising of Euripides, in so far as it produced the sentimentalising of
the classical theme, the same is then true of *Nausikaa*. Here Goethe
intended going beyond Homer in making the royal child fall
violently and passionately in love with the handsome stranger and
in the end take her own life, when she finds herself deceived. How
modern it is as an action brought about by subjectivity! For the
problem is one of 'emotion' and not 'compromise', as Goethe later
phrased it in the *Italienische Reise*. In the first instance everything
was more relaxed, more open, with original deftness true to the
genuine Italian situation. Here, in contrast to *Iphigenie*, the sensuality awoken in the South was apparent in fact at the outset.
Odysseus's monologue in the second scene may serve for us as a
painfully beautiful example of this candid feeling for style:

> Was rufen mich für Stimmen aus dem Schlaf?
> Wie ein Geschrei, ein laut Gespräch der Frauen
> Erklang mir durch die Dämmrung des Erwachens.
> Hier seh ich niemand! Scherzen durchs Gebüsch
> Die Nymphen? oder ahmt der frische Wind,
> Durchs hohe Rohr des Flusses sich bewegend,
> Zu meiner Qual die Menschenstimmen nach?
> Wo bin ich hingekommen? welchem Lande
> Trug mich der Zorn des Wellengottes zu?
> Ist's leer von Menschen, wehe mir Verlaßnen![10]

[9] The stirring of a womanly heart through the arrival of a stranger can no
longer be undertaken as the most beautiful theme after Nausicaa. How inferior to the daughter of Alcinous, even in antiquity, are Medea, Helen,
Dido inevitably, due to their circumstances.

[10] What voices summon me from sleep? Like a shriek, a loud conversation
between women resounded through the twilight of my awakening. I see
no one here. Do nymphs disport themselves among the shrubs? Or does the
fresh wind, as it moves through the high reeds, imitate human voices
to torment me? Whither have I come? To what land did the anger of the
god of the waves bear me? If it is desolate of humans, woe to me, the
abandoned!

K

This is a stylistic stage which *Iphigenie* had not yet attained, and which the other great stylistic example, the festival play *Pandora* of 1808 had already surpassed; a stage of candour, warmth, indeed an uplift to the point of intoxication, something which did not characterise Goethe's style in his old age at all and which never returned in the same way again. Even *Tasso* was harder, stylistically speaking.

Those parts of *Faust* which originated in Rome were still relatively close to the exaltation of *Nausikaa*. The completion work on *Faust* began with the 'Hexenküche' scene. It was no accident, since the theme of rejuvenation here dramatised can be understood as a direct parallel to the regeneration of the senses in Italy. Within *Faust* the scene serves to bridge that still harsh contrast which makes the figure of the hero in the *Urfaust* appear somewhat incongruous as a scholar and magician on the one hand, and on the other in the Gretchen-action a remarkably experienced *galantuomo*. The fact that Goethe should prefer to make an organic development of this sudden leap of the scholar into the Gretchen-action corresponded to his own development towards Classicism, and particularly in the sphere of his view of Nature. The theme of Faust's rejuvenation before he falls in love with Gretchen is therefore quite a natural result. Faust as a man of action thereby attains at the same time psychological credibility. There is one other point: The scene is the first grotesquerie that slips into the *Faust* plan. But it signifies too a powerful desentimentalisation of the emotional 'Storm and Stress' action. Further, the scene as erotica has much affinity to the *Römische Elegien* (*Roman Elegies*). Ultimately however it constitutes a stylisation of Faust according to classical standards, a pre-echo of the Helenact of 1800, an outmanoeuvring of the 'gothic' spectre by a Faust who can say apodictically 'I find wild magic repugnant', who condemns the long-tailed monkeys and the magic circle as 'in bad taste' and who instead of which can ask, in the thoroughly classical feeling for style, 'Has nature and has a noble spirit / not found some balm or other?' No wonder, when we recall that the *locus* for conception was the Borghese gardens in Rome, where later the Roman fountain poems of C. F. Meyer and Rilke were inspired. Indubitably Faust's taste has here become remarkably classical. And the same is true of the symbolism of the mirror motif. Faust's susceptibility for the beautiful image of woman, which the magic mirror reveals to him – perhaps a reminiscence of a Giorgione or a Titian – no longer corresponds to 'gothic' taste. At the same time it should be emphasised that Faust's rapture at the sight of the phenomenon is indeed no mere consequence of the magic potion. Before the magic rejuvenation it is evident as a kind of a sudden awakening of his senses. At the same time beauty is an ideal, a 'heavenly' image:

> Muß ich in diesem hingestreckten Leibe
> Den Inbegriff von allen Himmeln sehn?[11]

Already since Jakob Minor we know that the actual idealistic realism of this Faust awakened to sensuality (without the medium of magic) probably derived from the exchange of ideas with Karl Philipp Moritz:

> Wenn ich es wage, nah zu gehn,
> Kann ich sie nur als wie im Nebel sehn.[12]

Beauty as a perfect form assumes reality only at a distance, the coarse grasp of desire destroys it. Herein expressed is totally classical aestheticism, Winckelmannian, anti-naturalistic aestheticism. Mephisto's final words ironically parody this, indeed from the viewpoint of the naturalist, so to speak:

> Du siehst, mit diesem Trank im Leibe,
> Bald Helenen in jedem Weibe.[13]

But the cynicism here expressed is definitely that of the gothic devil, the very opposite of a classical spirit.

Besides the 'Hexenküche', the 'Wald und Höhle' scene also stemmed from this Roman period. Just as Faust's path outwards into the comprehensible world, a world understood by the senses, begins with the 'Hexenküche', so this intermezzo marks a contemplation and a way inwards, which invest Faust's character with a new dimension of profundity. Here the monologue comes into its own, in which Faust first thanks the 'sublime spirit' for the new reality of the closeness of nature:

---

[11] In this body stretched out before me must I see the epitome of all the heavens?

[12] If I dare to go close—I can only see her as if in a haze.

[13] With this potion in your body you will soon see Helen in every woman.

Gabst mir die herrliche Natur zum Königreich,
Kraft sie zu fühlen, zu genießen.[14]

The phenomena of this nature are for him a 'fraternal' experience. However this experience involves not only a 'coldly marvelling visit' but also a 'severe enjoyment afforded by contemplating'. This formula is already contained in the second expression of gratitude to the 'sublime' one. It is the thanks for self-knowledge in History, for the 'silvery figures of Antiquity'. Nature and History, the new conquests of Faust's soul, ensure both observation and self-contemplation and imagination. Here moments of self-reckoning are found, like the verses on insatiability attributed to the influence of Mephisto: 'Thus I reel from desire to enjoyment / and in the enjoyment I languish for desire', and the consequence of this, the nihilistic section in which Faust enters into judgement with himself. 'Am I not the fugitive? The homeless one? / The monster without purpose or peace', leaving the final word for a total vision of destruction. The presupposition was herewith created which was to lead to the expansion of the *Faust* conception into the Universal, the first product of which was to be the modified and completed *Urfaust*: *Faust. Ein Fragment* (*Faust. A Fragment*) (1790).

The lyrical harvest of the Italian journey can be termed small, at least as far as the range is concerned. The lyric had perhaps the least part to play in the upsurge of these years. This is certainly true if we regard the *Römische Elegien* (which belong anyway to the field of the lyric epic) as essentially a product of the post-Italian era, something we probably have to do on account of the close links which exist between them and the Christiane Vulpius experience.

On the other hand both the *Kophtische Lieder* (I and II) were *paralipomena* to the studies of Cagliostro's genealogical tree in which Goethe took pleasure in Sicily and which then in 1791 led to the comedy *Der Großkophta*. Originally destined for a comic operetta *Die Mystifizierten*, both 'Lieder' reflect the nature of a lofty play, a sense of life and power, in which one sees the exaltation of the days in Sicily still exerting an effect, although the stand taken is the imaginary one of the masonic charlatan ('coptic' observance). That is true of the moralising refrain of the

[14] You gave me glorious nature for a kingdom, strength to feel, to enjoy it.

one: 'children of sagacity, make fools / of the fools, as is right
and proper!', as well as of the other: 'You must rise or sink, / you
must rule and win / ... be anvil or hammer.'

Into the second Roman sojourn falls the poem *Amor als Landschaftsmaler* (published 1789), the inspiration for which was
the beautiful Milanese Maddalena Riggi. It does not belong to
Goethe's great poems, but numbers amongst his charming ones:
it describes how Amor conjures up for the painter before his
empty canvas the delectable landscape with the most beautiful
maiden; painted reality, which is then unexpectedly transformed
into natural reality. It is not by chance that the painting of the
boy Eros relates significantly to the theme of regeneration:

> Hell und rein lasiert' er drauf den Himmel
> Und die blauen Berge fern und ferner,
> Daß ich ganz entzückt und neu geboren
> Bald den Maler, bald das Bild beschaute.[15]

Historically we should not see the poem as an isolated phenomenon. It points to a willing acceptance on Goethe's part of the
erotic side of life which had already been anticipated in Weimar
but which now powerfully developed to the stage of the *Römische Elegien*. This receptivity stems from influence exercised by the
Dutch Humanist Johannes Secundus, the author of *Basia* (*Kisses*).
In the latter's work Goethe found a door already opened which
allowed this new sensuality entry into the field of appropriate
language. Directly after his return this development influences the
Christiane lyrics (*Morgenklagen, Besuch*) and runs parallel to the
freedom of the *Erotica Romana*, the originally intended title of
the *Römische Elegien*.

[15] Bright and pure he painted the sky on it, and the blue mountains afar
and more distant, that I, quite enraptured and born anew, now beheld the
painter, now the picture.

21 Reorientation in Weimar

If a portion of the poems that originated in Rome already combined the Italian experience and Weimar (on a new basis), the same is true of the completion of *Tasso* as well as of the work, commenced in Rome, on the *Elegien*. In a game of hide-and-seek with the reader, the mysterious Roman Faustina assumes the figure of the girl whom Goethe took into his house as his mistress (or 'bedroom sweetheart', in the words of Frau Aja) soon after his return to the Thuringian capital, to the horror of his old circle of friends and naturally Charlotte von Stein in particular, and whom he kept as his common-law wife until 1806, even after the birth of his son August. Not until he possibly owed his life to her courage at the time of the French occupation in 1806, did he legalise the relationship. There is hardly much sense in analysing psychologically the background to this behaviour, although a kind of anti-bourgeois defiant reaction had undoubtedly contributed, conditioned by the experience of 'indulgence' and freedom in the erotic sphere too, which he had enjoyed in Rome. The girl in question was Christiane Vulpius, from the humblest of backgrounds and with no intellectual interests at all; she was therefore no real equal in the marriage and basically continued in the role of a maid, indeed persisting in the use of his proper title and polite form of address towards her husband even when she was in fact later promoted to the rank of 'Geheimrätin'. It is therefore rather difficult not to view her in the same way as she appears in Thomas Mann's *Lotte in Weimar*: primitive, unrestrained, naïve, but charming in a sensual way and hence loved. At all events since becoming Goethe's companion in life in 1788 up to her death in 1816, Christiane had won such a decisive place in the poet's existence that he, notwithstanding all their incompatibility, broke down on her death, whilst he came to terms with the death of his mother and later that of his son in his usual way, that is in silence. In particular the ensuing period at the house on the Frauenplan would be inconceivable without Christiane. The house had been magnanimously granted by the Duke to Goethe following the latter's return from Rome and for a long time it became a focal point too for the intellectual élite of Europe.

In terms of literary history the critical factor is above all how far Christiane influenced the work of her husband. Actually neither the *Römische Elegien* in their final form completed in Weimar nor the Italian echoes of the *Venetianische Epigramme* are conceivable without her, not to mention the poems which directly concerned her.

It does not seem possible to differentiate between what devolved into the *Elegien* from Rome itself and what was a mere manufactured recollection under the subsequent impact of this new love. In October 1788 the first elegies were ready for distribution to the more intimate circle of friends. In the spring of 1790 the cycle was complete though it did not appear until five years later, and then not in fact in its full form. The change in the title from *Erotica Romana* to *Römische Elegien* did not only mark a stronger emphasis on the formal element. In terms of the relationship of the beloved to Christiane – a relationship that was transparent to everyone in the small town – it signified too a necessary distancing of the personal elements in the subject-matter. The old *Erotica Romana* now proved to be severe in terms of form, yet also playful in an elevated way. Their affinity to the more graceful poems in the manner of Johannes Secundus is already manifest at the close of the first elegy:

Eine Welt zwar bist du, o Rom; doch ohne die Liebe
Wäre die Welt nicht die Welt, wäre denn Rom auch nicht
Rom.[1]

If the lines are more strict and more exact in comparison with the earlier epigrams of Goethe, now metrically more competent through his recent study of the Roman elegiac poets, the content in images and allusions appears all the more relaxed, lighter, bolder in the 'worldly' sense. The satire too against the narrowness of the small

[1] Thou art indeed a world, O Rome; yet without love the world would not be the world, nor would Rome be Rome..

town and its citizens in the Second Elegy, including a self-paro-
distic jibe, can be interpreted along these lines ('Mother and
daughter rejoice over their Nordic guest, / And the barbarian
conquers Roman heart and body'). Only from the time of Italy
is such a trend conceivable, according to which no human element
should be alien to such poetry. This, and not the integrated
biographical matter, is the decisive factor. Without doubt the
Third and Fourth Elegies are a kind of mythical transfiguration
of free love. But the beauty of the poems is lost if we try to find
in them the all too human features. Passages like the contrafacture
to Herder's theory in the *Plastik* which Goethe attempted in the
Fifth Elegy would assume a distinctly lascivious undertone:

Und belehr ich mich nicht, indem ich des lieblichen Busen
  Formen spähe, die Hand leite die Hüften hinab?
Dann versteh' ich den Marmor erst recht: ich denk und vergleiche,
  Sehe mit fühlendem Aug', fühle mit sehender Hand.[2]

Really it is the theme of *Amor als Landschaftsmaler* that is here
taken up. Eros and artistic feeling condition each other. Feeling
for beauty arises only from the world that is understood with all
the senses. (Hence the *vis superbae formae*, which Goethe had
first noted in his Johannes Secundus, from the *Elegien* right to
Pandora). The moral idealism of *Iphigenie* has no place here.
Nausikaa would have been the intermediate stage between that
and the *Elegien*. In the *Elegien* there correspondingly predominates an extension of Winckelmann rather than a mere imitation.
In this context the central passage in the Thirteenth Elegy is
significant:

Du betrachtest mit Staunen die Trümmern alter Gebäude
  Und durchwandelst mit Sinn diesen geheiligten Raum.[3]

That is so to speak the Winckelmannian point of departure. But
it does not end there. The study of the Ancients is not everything:

  [2] And do I not instruct myself, as I attentively observe forms of the
lovely breast, run my hand down the hips? Then for the first time do I
really understand the marble: I think and compare, see with a feeling eye,
feel with a seeing hand.
  [3] With astonishment you observe the ruins of old buildings and wander
through this sacred area with your senses.

Denkst du nun wieder zu bilden, o Freund? Die Schule der
   Griechen
  Blieb noch offen, das Tor schlossen die Jahre nicht zu.
  Ich, der Lehrer, bin ewig jung . . .
  War das Antike doch neu, da jene Glücklichen lebten!
   Lebe glücklich, und so lebe die Vorzeit in dir!
  Stoff zum Liede, wo nimmst du ihn her? Ich muß dir ihn
   geben,
   Und den höheren Stil lehret die Liebe dich nur.[4]

That is a far-flung link between Classicism and Realism, which
embraces both the possibility of Iphigenie and Nausicaa as well
as Faustina-Christiane: even the understanding and the imitation
of the Greeks is conditioned by Eros. It is easy to see that in the
'Hexenküche' scene the position of the mirror motif shifted between the observation of beauty and erotic naturalism. In the
Elegien it is harder to define the limits of the *pura naturalia*.
Admittedly what is presented as aesthetic material is relativised
in the poems at the same time by roguishness and a gentle ironic
tone. The charm lies in the play with the risqué. What remains —
and one may extend this to cover all his output concerned with
erotic matters — is the High Classical attitude that a productive
relationship with Antiquity was only conceivable on the basis of a
full and developed sensuality. The high *cothurnus* of the idealistic
and solemn is abandoned; a mid-position between seriousness and
jest towards the classical world is adopted which can thus be
ironised and parodied. Even the High Classical Goethe warded off
Schiller's pathos.

If the *Römische Elegien* were projected as a total work of art
directly through the meeting of Goethe and Christiane, so that
this reflection of Rome so splendid in parts was indirectly due to
her, then on the other hand Goethe's relationship with Italy was
also indirectly affected by her: Goethe in fact went once more
for a short time to Italian soil, to Venice. But on that occasion
the omens were not favourable. The short trip which lasted from

[4] Are you now considering creative work again, O friend? The school
of the Greeks still remained open, the years did not close the door. I, the
teacher, am eternally young . . . antiquity was new, after all, when those
blessed ones lived! Live happily and antiquity will live within you! Material
for song, where do you get it from? I must give it to you, and only love
teaches you the more elevated style.

March to May of 1790 was not of his choice. Goethe was to await in Venice Anna Amalia of Weimar on her return trip from Rome (he had refused in any case to accompany her for the whole trip). Now however for the sake of courtly duty he had to leave the state of domesticity which he had just established with Christiane shortly after the birth of his son, and spent weeks waiting in the city he had once loved, ill-tempered, critical, entirely devoid of the earlier inspiration. The fruits of this were quite naturally the *Venetianische Epigramme* (*Venetian Epigrams*) (appearing 1796), from which, even though scraps from the work on the *Elegien* went into them, a real 'Book of Ill Humour' emerged. The bad temper with which Goethe reacted to this involuntary second Italian experience is obvious:

Das ist Italien, das ich verließ. Noch stäuben die Wege,
    Noch ist der Fremde geprellt, stell' er sich, wie er auch will.
Deutsche Redlichkeit suchst du in allen Winkeln vergebens;
    Leben und Weben ist hier, aber nicht Ordnung und Zucht.[5]

The just appreciation of earlier times seems to have vanished. Admittedly Goethe was experiencing a state of turmoil at that time: it affected faith (the anti-clerical complex in the epigrams!), his views regarding political organisation (1789!), and naturally too, his attitude towards aesthetic and natural scientific matters. All this complements the purely personal elements in the *Epigramme*, which no more than the *Römische Elegien* could have originated in terms of their total subject-matter on the spot in Italy.

At the same time there was a basis here too for *Torquato Tasso*, which just as much as *Iphigenie* and *Egmont* was conceived before Rome. The 'day of invention' was in fact 30 March, 1780. By 1781 two acts were in existence; it was in prose, probably corresponding to the style of *Egmont*. Goethe took this along with *Egmont* and *Iphigenie* to Italy, without however stopping in Ferrara on its account.

Instead Sicily was the place where he re-appraised it. An external stimulus was moreover provided in the study of a new publication on Tasso, the book by Antonio Serrassi (1785),

[5] That is the Italy I left. The roads are still dusty, the stranger is still cheated, whatever he does. German honesty you seek in vain in all the nooks and crannies. Life and activity is indeed here, but not order and propriety.

from which Goethe acquired the High Classical theme of the Tasso–Antonio conflict. That was the position up to his departure from Rome. Fascinated anew by it, he hastily sketched scenes in Florence. But the decisive work on the new verse version of *Tasso* was not accomplished until Weimar. The drama was ready in the spring of 1789. The work proceeded so to speak from the end to the beginning, since the Florentine impulse had directly influenced the final scenes. This clarifies the connection with Goethe's self-orientation resulting from the Italian experience. Or expressed in another way: the threat to the poet by the might of an undisciplined subjectivity and hence egocentricism now became the central motif for him. As in *Iphigenie* the verse drama that was completed in the spring of 1789 preserved the small classical cast of five people, preserved too the three Unities, the sole exception being the change of scene from Garden to Hall to Room to Garden, though the total setting is the *Lustschloß* Belriguardo. This formalistic classical note fully corresponds to the main theme, which in fact resolves the contrasts of disquiet and tranquillity, passion and moderation, pleasure and duty, content and form consistently in favour of the respective second idea. Its setting in the Renaissance court of the Muses, especially in its intensely stylised form, is not the result of the study of Serrassi, but of Goethe's view of Italy. The spiritualised Platonic sensuality is maintained somewhat more strictly than befitted the historical time of Tasso, being orientated more towards the preceding century. Without this strictness, which is clearly in contrast to the later picture of the Renaissance court as depicted, say, by Jacob Burckhardt and C. F. Meyer, there could have been neither a credible Antonio nor a Tasso who credibly compromises himself through his exorbitance. Even the Prince has little in common with the Renaissance hero of C. F. Meyer: superior, magnanimous, indeed even kind, the Duke of Ferrara appears humanistically related in spirit to Thoas, though in addition he has a passionate sympathy for the Arts. Also the two Leonoras, each in her respective way, do not lose control and direction for one moment, neither the Princess who is sentimental and reflective, nor the Countess who is sensual and naïve. They too are not only characters, but also the educated products of Humanism and are a match for the men. They are supposed to embody charm in a balanced form, not pretentiousness. In the disconcerting of the

Princess by Tasso we can nevertheless perceive the distinction too between the situation in Italy and the establishing of the new way of life in Weimar. The moment for an idealism of the kind conceived in *Iphigenie* was past. The play appears more psychological, more humanly profound, since the action of the gods is excluded, and therefore more sentimental. And the fallibility of the individual becomes thereby the greater, for all the characters, not just for the title figure. Even Antonio, who so to speak symbolically embodies this educated and cultivated world of the Court of Ferrara, which is very conscious of the fact that it is not barbaric, remains fallible in earthly matters. At the decisive moment he lacks a heart and with it kindness. For once the form here becomes gentlemanly inflexibility and coolness and thus human failure. A balance and not the extremes is what is intended. In this sense *Tasso* appears as an expression of admiration for Form, something which he acquired in Italy. (Already for this reason it is misleading to see it, from the *Ur-Tasso* on, in terms of his hopeless love for Frau von Stein within the context of Goethe's biography.) The finished *Tasso* is symbolic writing fully freed from the private sphere in favour of 'what is fitting' and not 'what is pleasing'. The Goethe of the post-Italian period aims ultimately at the indivisibility of the consciousness of Form in the broadest sense. It is against this that the self-centred poet Tasso transgresses and hence must suffer failure, both as a man and as a genius.

The other drama that originated before Italy and which Goethe sent from Italy to Herder, giving him permission to alter it where necessary, is *Egmont*. It is a piece that dates back to the earliest period of Goethe's development, originally pertaining to his personal attempts to escape from Lili (1775). Not until three years later was the draft sketched out. But then it required a further three years for a provisional form. The Roman version came in 1787 sufficiently in time to guarantee its appearance in the spring of 1788.

There is no reason to doubt that the problem of interpreting *Egmont* is closely related to that posed by Schiller's *Tell*. As with this latter play, so too here in *Egmont* the nationalistic overtones that are again and again flogged to death remain secondary to the moral law that encompasses the most personal level. For in this drama there emerges anything but a national hero as the title figure. Indeed there is not even that Kantian conflict of conscience which is the primary problematic concern in *Tell*. We know the controversy between Goethe and Schiller over the question of Egmont's character. We know that Schiller was not easy about Egmont's 'indulgence', which was however for Goethe a positive value, one of the values that had not been properly manifest to him until Rome. And so this drama shows, possibly more convincingly than anything else, how the original 'Storm and Stress' conception could be at one with the rejuvenation of the senses in Italy, without a visible break between the two phases of development. Egmont's individualism, including his 'indulgence', could hold its own even against the standards of the Italian Goethe, because both in the 'Storm and Stress' period and in the Classical, a moral and national hero embodied for Goethe something that was too bourgeois – one of the reasons, incidentally, why, in contrast to Schiller, he could never become the favourite poet of the national-liberal bourgeoisie of the nineteenth century. Despite his departing words uttered in the manner of a 'Storm and Stress' freedom fighter 'I die for freedom, for which I lived and fought and for which I now sacrifice myself', the figure of Egmont is not that of a national freedom fighter (as such his action could only be called irresponsible), but that of a representative of personal freedom. Egmont wants to live and really not to die at all. The grandeur of his death is that of the great lord who conducts himself befittingly, not that of the martyr for the common cause of the Netherlands; the lord who does not 'haggle', 'when it is a question of the full value of life on which a price can not be set', who claims for himself the right of the somnambulist in life, sees even this life depreciated when it is taken far too seriously, and who in the same context in the Second Act expresses the famous sentences to the apprehensive secretary:

> Wie von unsichtbaren Geistern gepeitscht, gehen die Sonnenpferde der Zeit mit unsers Schicksals leichtem Wagen durch; und uns bleibt nichts, als mutig gefaßt die Zügel festzuhalten und bald rechts, bald links, vom Steine hier, vom Sturze da die Räder wegzulenken. Wohin es geht, wer weiß es? Erinnert er sich doch kaum, woher er kam.[6]

[6] As if whipped along by invisible spirits, the sun's horses of time stampede with the light-weight carriage of our fate and nothing remains

In times of his nation's needs no politician speaks in this way. Yet the context is to be understood neither nihilistically nor merely as aristocratic *désinvolture*. Besides it is all too related to the hymn *An Schwager Kronos*. Goethe had defended his *Egmont* against Schiller from the point of view of the 'demonic' in his hero. And surely rightly so, since the image of the stampeding horses relates to the total situation and existence of the hero: to his position amongst the people, his relationship with Klara, also to his love/hate relationship with Alba. Although, by the way, the folk-scenes point back to *Götz*, a distinction is nevertheless clear: Götz was 'all character', not conceived in the sense of being 'demonic' like the unsuccessful popular hero Egmont. The latter for his part is an individual with his own 'demon' in the classical sense, just as Alba is one within the context of his personal fate. The old, unequivocal love/hate relationship of the 'Storm and Stress' type can no longer be deemed valid, despite the early origin of the play. (Such a differentiated figure as Alba's son Ferdinand is not found in *Götz*.) Finally it is Orange, the really responsibly thinking national leader, who most of all is the tactician and intriguer, despite the appearance of Machiavelli. The fact that Goethe very decidedly retained the colourful Shakespearean list of characters and also continued to reject the three unities in the Italian *Egmont* as against *Iphigenie* and *Tasso*, is hardly fortuitous. As a Classicist he thus quite deliberately legitimised a 'Storm and Stress' concept. *Egmont* exemplifies that subordinating of a 'Storm and Stress' genius, seen as valid in its *élan vital*, to the classical 'demonic element' that is mentioned in his later poem *Urworte. Orphisch*; that is to say, *Egmont* is interpreted as 'minted form, which develops as it lives'. The fact that this aim was difficult to realise dramatically is shown too in that only the unequivocating hand of Schiller was able to help *Egmont* towards theatrical effectiveness.

for us but to hold firm the reins with courage and now to the right, now to the left, direct the wheels away from a stone here, from an abyss there. Who knows where it goes? He scarcely can remember whence he came.

22 Schiller's Aesthetic Contribution

Between the Schiller of the *Raphael-Julius-Briefe* and Schiller the Classicist now fully conscious of himself and his ability in the period of his friendship with Goethe, lay the years during which the poet incorporated Kant into his aesthetic-moral concept of the world. This assimilation took place on another basis from the one Heinrich von Kleist was to experience soon after the turn of the century. Kleist's hitherto optimistic concept of the world based on Enlightenment thinking was shattered to its very foundations by his acknowledgement of Kantian criticism. The consequence was an existential crisis from which Kleist never finally recovered. It was quite a different matter in Schiller's case. He saw in Kant's philosophy not the refutation, but the confirmation of that Enlightenment optimism to which he had given expression in the programmatic poem *Die Künstler*. Since, in contrast to Kleist, he saw Kantian ethics as a linch-pin in the process of reason, the great philosopher was bound to appear to him as the guarantor of the 'Classical' philosophy. What Goethe – minus Kant – had integrated between Weimar and Rome into his philosophy as the ethos of the Manly, had its counterpart, as far as Schiller's development was concerned, in the Kantian experience and its ethical premises through which reason, properly understood, found expression. And the fact that Schiller, also impressed by Shaftesbury's psychophysical harmony, interpreted the aesthetic question, which did not appear to him to be a contradiction to the ethical, in his own way, facilitated the affinity to Goethe's Classical concept of the world. From his observation of Nature the latter acquired that tolerance which Schiller could not possibly have gained from Kantian rigour without Shaftesbury's tempering influence. Of significance in this context was the treatise *Über Anmut und Würde* (*On Grace and Dignity*) dating from the year 1793 and therefore prior to the decisive meeting with Goethe, in which the latter sensed a debasing of 'Nature', whilst in reality – as against Kant – it signified the conscious transition from that ethical rigorism to an aesthetic 'latitudinarianism' (Egmont!). The concept of the 'Beautiful Soul' which Schiller adopted from Shaftesbury in practice, but not in theoretical terms, clearly testified to this greater receptivity. It was no accident that in the second edition of *Religion innerhalb der Grenzen der bloßen Vernunft* (1794) Kant made reference, in a mild form admittedly, to this contrast between ethical rigorism and the aesthetic harmony of the 'Beautiful Soul', which Schiller's essay on aesthetics sought to bring out. Indeed nowhere so clearly as here must the 'servile' aspect of Kant's moral philosophy have manifested itself in the consciousness of Schiller the Classicist as in the concept of the 'Beautiful Soul' which logically contradicted Kant's view of radical evil. On the other hand, Schiller's idea that a 'Beautiful Soul' can exist which refuses to be 'slavishly led by duties' was basically not at variance with Goethe's view on Nature. Save that Schiller conceded merely as an exceptional case in special circumstances what was based on the norm and not the exception, from Goethe's point of view on Nature.

For Schiller *Über Anmut und Würde* signified in the final analysis the attempt to advocate with and in the Kantian system human kindness stemming from the heart and from feeling, whilst Kant derived it from reason and will. This anthropological postulation encroached on the aesthetic (in the narrower sense). Yet it is the one outward form of human existence, i.e. beauty, on which Schiller wanted to construct the blissful moment of our aesthetic and moral existence. And in this he went beyond the Kantian scheme which saw Beauty and Grace resulting necessarily from Virtue. The aim of the essay constituted therefore an attempt at harmonisation of a typically Classical kind, and moreover a genuine step towards Goethe, who had long since reached a similar position based on his study of Nature. Schiller's much wider interpretation of the concept of human freedom was incompatible with the Kantian system. That was already manifested in the initial theme of human motivation, which for Kant appertained to the 'arbitrary'; for the Classical Schiller on the other hand it was a natural expression of freedom, no longer an act of will as for Kant, but an act of character. And character could also embody naïvety, as for example in the case of the Greeks, which had also provided the clue for Plato and Winckelmann. The introductory theme of Venus's girdle, 'which possesses the strength to bestow grace on him who wears it, and to win love', imputes to the Greeks a pre-rational 'tender feeling' of differentiation. Grace as a kind of magic gift (an aesthetic analogy to the genuine ring in the parable of *Nathan*) has its roots in the realm of the pre-rational. And for this very reason the blessed phenomenon of the 'Beautiful Soul' can be derived from this chain of thought as a possibility beyond the Kantian contradiction of duty and inclination. Since Grace is determined as 'changing beauty', as a momentary genuine outward form of charm, it becomes, as a prerogative of human existence, something which is, one might almost say, added to man. However it retains, in affinity with Kant, character as an expression of morality. That separates it from the 'architectonic beauty', which even a 'tiger-like' character might possess, since it is beauty of sheer outward appearance. His idea of beauty turns beauty into an inhabitant of two worlds – belonging as it does to the sensual world by birth, to the world of intellect by adoption.

We already can notice in this train of thought Schiller's approach to Shaftesbury's harmony:

> Und was in dem Reiche der Vernunft harmonisch ist, wird sich durch keinen Mißklang in der Sinnenwelt offenbaren.[1]

Schiller thereby arrives at his definition of Grace as 'beauty of form under the influence of freedom; the beauty of those phenomena which the individual determines. Freedom and the individual he conceives in the sense of Kant's morality, in express contrast to pure natural beauty, the 'architectonic', devoid of the influence of moral freedom. Grace is accordingly beauty upgraded to the level of humanity. This conception marks it off from the naturalism of the 'Storm and Stress'. But we must also not overlook how Kant's idea is modified. For the latter, freedom was unthinkable without controlled will: 'Only after enormous tasks have been performed does Hercules become Musagetes', he writes

[1] And what is harmonious in the realm of reason will manifest itself in the material world through its very accord.

in his critical remarks on Schiller's essay. Schiller on the other
hand wants Grace as instinctive nature: 'in short, the function
of control must become part of nature'. With reference to
Grace:

> Grazie hingegen muß jederzeit Natur, d.i. unwillkürlich sein
> (wenigstens so scheinen), und das Subjekt selbst darf nie so
> aussehen, als wenn es um seine Anmut wüßte.[2]

That is naturally a purely human phenomenon, for the plant and
the animal are 'a necessity', but not a 'person'. Man alone as an
individual out of all known creatures has the 'prerogative through
his own will to intervene in the process of necessity, which is
unbreakable for mere creatures of nature'. Quite definitely
Schiller is echoing Kant at this juncture. And Goethe's attack on
the devaluing of Nature as against the 'moral' factor is psychologically understandable, seen in this light. But we also have to
recall that Goethe the Classicist sought his idea of 'Humanität'
in the 'manly', which is not so far removed from Kant's 'freedom'
in Schiller's aesthetics. These in fact were already moving at that
time in the direction of recognising a 'mean' between the
extremes of a categorical ethical standpoint and a naturalism
based solely on sensuality. Even genius should not be a 'meteor,'
for that was indeed the mark of an untimely quest for originality.
True genius on the other hand is realised in the fulfilment of an
objective duty: it does this by taking matter (as a phenomenon
of Nature), and through organising it with the help of acquired
(moral) form, it gives it its full value. Schiller's definition of
Beauty signifies this 'mean':

> So wie die Freiheit zwischen dem gesetzlichen Druck und der
> Anarchie mitten inne liegt, so werden wir jetzt auch die
> Schönheit zwischen der *Würde*, als dem Ausdruck des herr-
> schenden Geistes, und der *Wollust*, als dem Ausdruck des
> herrschenden Triebes, in der Mitte finden.[3]

[2] Grace on the other hand must always be Nature, that is instinctive (at
least must appear so), and the individual must never appear conscious of
his grace.

[3] Just as freedom lies midway between law and anarchy, so shall we
too now find beauty midway between *dignity*, as the expression of the
dominant mind, and *voluptuousness* as the expression of the dominant
impulse.

Only the High Classical Goethe was to comprehend fully the Classicism inherent in this idea of an aestheticism based on the 'mean'. On the other hand Kant sensed the element of compromise in this only too well. He was interested in Reason and not in Classicism. For his part Goethe had first, so to speak, to overcome the concept adopted from Winckelmann of 'common nature', which seemed much too idealistic to his own natural scientific insight. But Schiller even more than Kant had accommodated this concept with his championing of the 'Beautiful Soul' on lines suggested by Shaftesbury:

> In einer schönen Seele ist es also, wo Sinnlichkeit und Vernunft, Pflicht und Neigung harmonieren, und Grazie ist ihr Ausdruck in der Erscheinung.[4]

That however is Platonic harmony *via* Shaftesbury and is no longer Kant's categorical ethics. Goethe gladly made use of it later in his own way, namely in the Sixth Book of *Wilhelm Meister*, in the *Bekenntnisse einer schönen Seele*. And he patterned it so closely that he demonstrated it too in a female character, something which Schiller himself preferred to advocate for his idea of the 'Beautiful Soul'. Only Schiller in fact did not think of the possibility which Goethe perceived, namely the development of the 'Beautiful Soul' from Christian neo-Platonism.

Corresponding to the character of the 'Beautiful Soul' as an exceptional case was a certain systematic retreat on Schiller's part over the definition of the counter concept of Grace, that is Dignity. This in fact is introduced with the assertion that Man's ideal task is 'to be ever a harmonising entity and to act with his total, undivided humanity'. 'Humanität' in the Classical sense is thereby advocated. Only it is shown as never being fully realisable ('simply an idea'). Again Schiller moves here clearly within the framework of Kantian morals from which he had deviated boldly with the aristocratic nature of Grace, just as later he was again to move away from them with his conceptual view of the 'naïve'. Basically he keeps within the sphere of the sublime, the expression of which is 'Dignity', and of the pathetic, where he felt himself to be on more familiar and surer ground (just as he in fact was to claim for himself not the 'naïve', but the 'sentimental').

[4] A Beautiful Soul therefore is such where sensuousness and reason, duty and inclination harmonise, and grace is its expression in outward form.

For this is the real realm of the will and freedom, of superiority over the impulse, which subjects the animal to necessity:

> Schon der *bloße* Wille erhebt den Menschen über die Tierheit; der *moralische* erhebt ihn zur Gottheit.[5]

From this point of view, the 'Beautiful Soul' must again find an affinity with the morally sublime. And this affinity occurs 'in the state of strong emotion', in which it is elevated to 'pure intelligence'. It therefore has to act and react in sublime fashion within the dimension of freedom.

With the combination of 'Dignity', the 'sublime', the proof of freedom of the spirit manifest in both of them, and the 'heroic' too, Schiller transposes the debate not only into the sphere of Kant again, but also into that of Winckelmann's interpretation of Laocoön. Indeed he embraces this latter as well as the Shaftesburian-Platonic doctrine of harmony with obvious sympathy much more strongly than Kant, for whom the idea 'It is the lawgiver himself, the *God* within us, who plays with his own image in the material world' would not apply.

Schiller concluded this train of thought with the attempt to protect his basic concepts against the danger of 'affectation' to which Grace and Dignity seemed equally exposed. This was necessary in order to define Grace as distinct from mannerism, Dignity as distinct from false pathos. Schiller felt himself compelled to do this simply because, partly simultaneously with *Über Anmut und Würde*, partly directly afterwards, he had devoted a whole group of minor aesthetic writings exclusively to the question of the Sublime, which basically was his particular domain. These were the essays *Vom Erhabenen* (*The Sublime*), the second part of which was entitled *Über das Pathetische* (*On the Pathetic*), *Zerstreute Betrachtungen über verschiedene ästhetische Gegenstände* (*Diverse Considerations on Various Aesthetic Subjects*), *Gedanken über den Gebrauch des Gemeinen und Niedrigen in der Kunst* (*Thoughts on the Use of the Common and the Base in Art*) and *Über das Erhabene* (*On the Sublime*). They share with *Über Anmut und Würde* the aim of rescuing and defending sensuality allied with freedom as the highest expression of

---

[5] Mere will already lifts Man above the animal kingdom, the moral elevates him to the divine.

'Humanität'. The path of the Classicist towards the 'mean' there-fore leads here *via* as wide an interpretation as possible of the Kantian system to the Goethean view of Nature. The Laocoön interpretation in *Über das Pathetische* is an example of this, since it emphasises the authenticity of the sensual in line with Lessing and Herder against Winckelmann. Schiller was here seeking a special position for German Classicism which would reach deeper than the motif of stoic suffering in Baroque and French Classicism.

Besides this differentiation, he was also anxious (e.g. at the close of *Über Anmut und Würde*) to determine genuine sensu-ality in contrast to the affected or merely 'moving'. This latter is one-sided and not human in the universal sense. The distancing too of the Classicist from music, which later Stefan George was to complete in his attempt at a new Classicism on the basis of Schillerian aesthetics, should be noted in this context. Music appears in *Über das Pathetische* as a direct example of 'merely tender emotions', where 'the mind is the loser'. If we think of Goethe's, Nietzsche's, George's, Thomas Mann's and at times also Rilke's reservations on ('romantic' sentimental) music, this defini-tion quite clearly appears to have been at all times an act of self-assertion by the poet. In particular with regard to classical trends it seems to be a matter of course to seek the mean between atar-axia (Baroque and Classicism) and sensibility (Sentimentality, Romanticism), between closed and open form. Here Goethe and Schiller were also in affinity on another subject, namely that of the presentation of suffering. Goethe's repugnance of the painting of martyrs and the Passion in Italy corresponds to Schiller's definition:

Eine Darstellung der bloßen Passion (sowohl der wollüstigen als der peinlichen) ohne Darstellung der übersinnlichen Wider-stehungskraft heißt gemein, das Gegenteil heißt edel . . . Nichts ist edel, als was aus der Vernunft quillt; alles, was die Sinn-lichkeit für sich hervorbringt, ist gemein.[6]

[6] A presentation of mere passion (both of the voluptuous and of the painful) without the portrayal of the metaphysical power of resistance is common, the opposite is noble . . . Nothing is noble save what springs from reason; everything that sensuality produces of its own volition, is com-mon.

Here is the total and real Schiller speaking, with whom Goethe agreed at first only with reservations. Schiller was however to push him along his own line of thought, though in fact this happened against Goethe's will. Naturally the *Gedanken über den Gebrauch des Gemeinen und Niedrigen in der Kunst* were projected pretentiously enough in order to make the 'base' appear as an aesthetic problem of form, not merely one of subject matter and motif. Nevertheless the great Netherland realism remained foreign to Schiller, who reproached it with the charge of 'vulgar taste'. It came more easily to him to recognise the greatness of the vulgar in the form of immorality. In these thought processes however the decisive factor remained the classical impulse towards an aestheticism which expressed and satisfied the universal human element and which on the other hand rejected the merely partial human factor. The act of sacrifice at Thermopylae was acceptable not as a national deed – as such it would be for Schiller merely an expression of an extremely limited human act – but pleasing both to reason and imagination because the aesthetic and the ethical combined in it.

Schiller wrestled with the problem and scale of aesthetic greatness in his own way too in the *Zerstreute Betrachtungen über verschiedene ästhetische Gegenstände*. Starting with the contrast between idyllic and heroic landscape, thus with Nature and not Man, he leads the discussion here and in the treatise *Über das Erhabene* straight into the specifically human, the effect of strength in death on the ethos which alone befits the human. It amounts to a consideration of the voluntary harmony of Man with Nature and hence too with death. It would be unworthy to suffer death as a violence done to us by Nature. It contains therefore not only one of the central motifs of Schiller's own later dramatic work, but also deals again with the limitation of the pathetic through the possibility of grace.

The closer Schiller's link with Kantian ethics proved to be – and that to a special degree was the case where it occurred in the sphere of dignity, the sublime and the pathetic –, the more there arose in the background the necessity to expand the personal ethical problems to include those of human co-existence. Thus the essay *Über die ästhetische Erziehung des Menschen in einer Reihe von Briefen* (*Letters on the Aesthetic Education of Man*) (1793–94) extended beyond the chance cause of its origin to the already mentioned classical disposition towards universality. The fact that the *Briefe*, which were published in *Die Horen*, were not fictitious, but were really addressed to the Duke of Holstein – Augustenburg (the originals were burnt in Copenhagen in 1794), whose generously supported stipendiary Schiller had been for three years, was certainly a happy coincidence. But Goethe had become aware of the problematic nature of the individual within the State *via* a different route, i.e. through the events of the year 1789. So the time simply appeared ripe for Schiller too. The letters – twenty-seven in number – had to concern themselves with the needs of the Prince in question, as to how in the period of 'Humanität' one could rule responsibly in conformity with the new concepts regarding culture. They compelled the author therefore to tackle the practical issues (not merely Kant's 'practical reason') in quite a different way to that attempted in the reasoning and aims of his previously mentioned writings. But we would be far from the mark if we wanted to suggest that Schiller had gone astray here. Ever since he had read Winckelmann, the guiding philosophical light of Classicism was Plato, not Kant. Certainly in Platonism there lies the universal tendency towards polity. Thus, although the *Briefe* began with a confession of allegiance to Kant, we can hardly arrive at an understanding of the 'classical' nature of this essay here without the other source, i.e. Plato and his mediator Shaftesbury. For basically it limits the validity of Kant's philosophy too. Before reason lies the 'moral instinct', 'which wise nature set as a guardian for man until pellucid insight brings about his maturity'.

The real practical, contemporary problems begin with the Second Letter. Their basis is the optimism of *Die Künstler*: 'I should not gladly live in another century . . .' That is the one side. The other is that of decadence, under whose influence art and education were constantly repressed: '*Profit* is the great idol of the age.' The task before the politician, and that means, practically speaking, the responsible Prince, is to aim at the unification of the two disparate sides, to balance reason and egoism. This balance must be achieved within the State, as the Third Letter declares. Since the State however signifies a pre-determined form of human existence which would be coercion, we must liberally interpret the historical fact. The idea of a moral society must be added to the existing 'physical' one. However in the latter instance it is a question of pure nature, in the former, one of complete independence from it. The law-giver cannot depend completely on either of the two mutually exclusive ideas. From this results the demand for a third form: 'a perceptible guarantee of invisible morality, a mediator between the power of nature and law'. It is clear that Schiller is already aiming at the aesthetic personality, again following the law of the classical mean. Yet it is a question not only of a process of harmonisation, but also of a task of education aiming at ennobling elevation (Fourth Letter). The task devolving on the Prince is, so to speak, that of an artist-pedagogue, whereby the aim of the State becomes synonymous with the representation of the human factor in the sense of natural and legal harmony. The point of departure for the following letters is hereby provided. In them the 'Present Age' is first of all declared incapable of unity, harmony and dignity. It is maintained that it only controls the 'balance of evil' as the sole barrier to the vacillation 'between perversity and barbarity'. The ideal embodiment of aesthetic harmony therefore cannot be attained by confused modern man. And there, in the important Sixth Letter, fully in accord with the spirit of Winckelmann and Goethe, the Greeks are introduced as representing the ideal classical concept of harmony:

> Zugleich voll Form und voll Fülle, zugleich philosophierend und bildend, zugleich zart und energisch sehen wir die Jugend der Phantasie mit der Männlichkeit der Vernunft in einer herrlichen Menschheit vereinigen.[7]

This Hellenism signifies the sole 'totality' historically realised, which Schiller had propounded merely as a desirable goal at the close of the Fourth Letter. The regaining of totality serves as the aim of education. The pedagogue for harmony or totality, however, is the artist – or the statesman who seizes his chances by passing laws in furtherance of such totality.

Again we must pose the question underlying the philosophy of history: is it cyclic or progressive? If the Greeks are or were absolute as representatives of everything that is human, then the path towards them would be a historically retrogressive trend,

[7] Both full of form and fulfilment, both philosophising and educating, both tender and energetic, we see them unite the youth of imagination with the manliness of reason in one splendid humanity.

thus romantic. Does Schiller however thereby abandon the idea of progress? Schiller senses this problem himself in the central Ninth Letter and there seeks to avoid the alternative of Either–Or. The timelessness of pure morality must be brought into accord with historical development. The medium is the aesthetic, art. A return of the Greeks on a new basis is rendered possible through art. It is the basis of the individual: in the very movement caused by the change in his condition. This movement 'shall externalise all the inner self and form all the external self' (Eleventh Letter). There then develops from this the definition of the three impulses: the sense impulse, the form impulse and the play impulse. Of these the first two correspond to the extreme possibilities within the human being: the physical being, which strives for material things, and, on the other hand, the self-assertion of the individual in the matter of pure moral freedom. The sense impulse is but temporal, the form impulse is outside of time ('time is in us with its total, never-ending sequence' – Twelfth Letter). Thus neither of these two impulses constitutes a harmonising of the historical with the absolute. It is only to be found in the third impulse, the play impulse, as defined in the Fourteenth Letter. Here alone is the attempt made to determine philosophically the essence of the Classical, to express the intended harmony of collective humanity. For in the play impulse alone dependence joins hands with the freedom of the sense impulse and of the form impulse. It alone is geared neither to life nor to form, but to the 'living form', to beauty (Fifteenth Letter). But what is meant here by the concept of play? It cannot mean anything other than the classical-harmonious balance of human forces:

> Der Mensch soll mit der Schönheit *nur spielen*, und er soll *nur mit der Schönheit* spielen. Denn, um es endlich auf einmal herauszusagen, der Mensch spielt nur, wo er in voller Bedeutung des Worts Mensch ist, und *er ist nur da ganz Mensch, wo er spielt.*[8]

In the symbolism of the Grecian world of the gods this 'play' had once been a reality.

From this standpoint the idea of the State can be taken up

---

[8] Man is to *only play* with beauty and play *with beauty alone*. For to put it in a nutshell, man plays only when he is a human in the full significance of the word, and *he is only fully a human being when he plays.*

again, bearing in mind that to the three impulses there correspond three conceivable forms of State: the dynamic State (based on the sense impulse), the ethical State (based on the form impulse), and the aesthetic State (based on the play impulse). The first two forms rest on compulsion (power and the rule of law); the aesthetic State alone rests on freedom (namely the play impulse). This alone constitutes the State of good taste and harmony serving both the individual and society. Admittedly it appears possible only where realised by 'select circles'. What Schiller offers therefore is an aristocratic solution and as such also an enticement to the princely recipient of the letters.

Schiller was, incidentally, aware of the possible misuse of the Beautiful, which is established in the Letters as the absolute norm. He pursued this point of view more or less at the same time in the *Horen* treatise of 1795, namely *Über die notwendigen Grenzen beim Gebrauch schöner Formen*. The aesthetic entails, he argues, the danger of going beyond its limits, and this would bring about perversion of the heart and nullity of action, moral hypocrisy and sensual affectation.

Schiller's great period of communion with Goethe, both communication and competition, then gave birth to the treatise *Über naïve und sentimentalische Dichtung* (*On Naïve and Sentimental Poetry*) (1795). Not by chance is it more down-to-earth, more historical, more topical than the other aesthetic works. Profound criticism of the age and culture is to be found in those too at various points. But here he stirs himself to provide, quite deliberately, a typological theory of classical poetry, on his and Goethe's most familiar home ground, the realm of literature, and that provides this crowning work of Schiller's with the lifeblood of personal experience. Here theory and history combine with aesthetic psychology to produce a true synthesis. Since the author had unquestionable greatness and authority, his insights are universal, still not 'historical' even today, that is they are still pertinent. Not only did George and his circle in this twentieth century draw their aesthetic principles from Schiller's 'doctrine of beauty'. The aesthetic-philosophically orientated literary science of our day too, with its frequently marked emphasis on the play-concept and its constant eye for the correlation between tradition and originality, cannot afford to disregard Schiller's aesthetics.

These proceed from the simple discovery that with history behind him, consequently 'in artificial relationships and situations',
man experiences emotion and surprise through the sight and
experiencing of Nature. Such experience is only possible when the
object is 'naïve' and thereby 'puts to shame' art and artificiality.
And to this pertains also the awareness that the object is 'Nature',
without which consciousness emotion could not arise at all. For
given exactly the same aesthetic effect, an imitation, however
perfect, would immediately destroy the sense of naïvety in question,
if the manner of imitation were to become conscious. In his
Kritik der Urteilskraft Kant illustrated this pattern of behaviour,
as is well known, in the example of the effect of a real and
an artificial nightingale (from which Hans Christian Andersen was
later to devise the beautiful symbolism of his fairy-tale *The Nightingale*). Like Kant, Schiller infers that it is not the objects which
are felt to be naïve, that are loved, but the 'idea represented by
them'. He then formulates his historico-philosophical and anthropological postulation directly on this observation:

Sie *sind*, was wir *waren*: sie sind, was wir wieder *werden sollen*.
Wir waren Natur wie sie, und unsere Kultur soll uns, auf dem
Wege der Vernunft und der Freiheit, zur Natur zurückführen.[9]

The naïve therefore is at one and the same time our beginning and
our goal. However as man, since his emergence from his original
state, has undergone a development, namely to reason with its
inherent self-consciousness, Schiller's historico-philosophical aestheticism is not restorative. It remains a synthesis of the cyclical
view of history and a linear view. It is not a question of a simple
retour à la nature. We are separated from our origin by history.
We have however retained the notion of our origin as an ideal.
We dispose of this continuity by symbols. We are affected by
Nature, but we also experience that emotion (indeed it is one produced by Nature) which affects us on meeting a child, for in it we
experience ever anew our lost original state. Spurious affected
sentimentality is thereby eliminated from the outset. Quite on
the contrary the attitude of modern man towards the child and to
childlike peoples must demonstrate the legitimate, sentimental

[9] They *are* what we *were*; they are what we *shall become* again. We
were nature like them, and our culture shall lead us back to nature along
the path of reason and freedom.

relationship. This relationship is sentimental, the object must be naïve. Justice is hereby done to Nature. 'Art' is seen as placed in the wrong by the naïve object, in contrast to the naïve way of thinking itself, for which the relationship between Nature and Art is reversed. Nature, childlike peoples, *the* child, indeed even genius, are 'naïve':

Naiv muß jedes wahre Genie sein, oder es ist keines.[10]

His guide is instinct, not rules: 'his ideas are divine inspirations'. Here the argumentation of *Über Anmut und Würde* is again taken up, since for Schiller naïvety and simplicity are expressed in Grace: 'Divine prophecies from the mouth of a child.' Every victory of quiescent nature over 'art' is naïve. Yet if man is to achieve this, it is a pre-condition that he should have attained to it through reason. Only on the basis of our commitment to reason can we think of naïve sentiment as longing for the happiness and perfection of Nature. Understandably pertinent here are the lines: 'The world is perfect everywhere / where man and his torment do not reach.' Nature is perfect in itself. It can only serve man as a source of strength for his existential task: as moral self-realisation. For:

Jene Natur, die du dem Vernunftlosen beneidest, ist keiner Achtung, keiner Sehnsucht wert. Sie liegt hinter dir, sie muß ewig hinter dir liegen.[11]

That is said above all for the benefit of those sentimental people who strive for a would-be return to the original state in the idyll. For Schiller no contemporaneity with the original seems any longer thinkable or morally tenable. Only by means of the sentiment of the perfection of Nature, by means of the beautiful illusion of the idyll, can the inherent naïvety of Nature become that legitimate source of strength to man who has irrevocably developed through the course of history.

Schiller therefore saw the difference between the Greeks and his fellow contemporaries founded on the unsentimentality of the Greek disposition. This struck him much more sharply than it did

[10] Every true genius must be naïve, else he is not one.

[11] That Nature which you envy the man devoid of reason is not worthy of any attention, nor any longing. It lies behind you, must for ever lie behind you.

Winckelmann and the pre-Kantian eighteenth century. The possibility of a return to the Greeks was then unreservedly taken for granted. Only Schiller's perception of the contrast between naïve and sentimental facilitated an appraisal of the real situation of modern man for the first time. The Greeks could be naïve, but could not 'sentimentally' experience the naïve, being 'at one with themselves and happy' (in the feeling of their humanity), they could not lament lost Nature at all. The contrast revolved around the formula 'they were naturally "sentimental"; we are "sentimental" towards what is natural'. That simply means that modernity in its feeling for Nature is equated with 'how the sick man feels about good health'.

And here another much clearer distinction between the Greeks and Romans becomes possible. Horace, 'the poet of an educated and degenerate age', represents for Schiller 'the true author of this sentimental style of writing'. The two sides were therefore already divided in antiquity itself. If the Greeks could still be naïve, the Romans already constituted sentimental antiquity. And from this point there developed that historical Western aestheticism, which, by means of a sometimes magnificent interpretation, forms the subject of the second part of the essay. It does not overstep the limit of, but rather translates into reality that system which Schiller had built up in the first part in accordance with Kantian standards, yet with the express design of making concessions to his great associate Goethe. The poet of Western tradition is either 'naïve' (Homer) or 'sentimental' (Ariosto). But what is Shakespeare? Admittedly in different circumstances, he is a genius of the first order. That corresponds roughly to Lessing's interpretation of Shakespeare, and it also makes possible the observation even in Goethe's *Werther* of the synthesis of naïvety and sentimental thinking and feeling towards the naïve. Corresponding to the basic system here is the analogy between the history of mankind and this typology of its poets: the way from the 'living present' to the 'ideal'. From the historico-philosophical point of view this too is a three-stage process:

> Die Natur macht ihn mit sich eins, die Kunst trennt und entzweiet ihn, durch das Ideal kehrt er zur Einheit zurück.[12]

[12] Nature makes him one with herself, art separates and divides him. He returns to unity through the ideal.

It is a pre-Hegelian triad: thesis, antithesis, synthesis. (This was also anticipated in Herder's philosophy of history.)

On this basis Schiller now establishes a kind of aesthetics in terms of the 'sentimental' genres: satire, the elegy and especially the idyll. The intrinsic starting point for all of them is the tension between the ideal and reality. Satire can be pathetic or mocking, in the first instance it is a matter of sublime souls, in the second, of beautiful hearts. Judged by this standard, Lucian as well as Aristophanes, Fielding and the Cervantes of *Don Quixote*, and in the last resort even Wieland, would more than pass the test; Voltaire, on the other hand, would not. The elegy is mourning for a lost ideal:

> Der elegische Dichter sucht die Natur, aber als eine Idee und in einer Vollkommenheit, in der sie nie existiert hat.[13]

From this standpoint, Schiller links Ossian with Rousseau, Haller, Ewald von Kleist and Klopstock. They are the ones who lend the concept of the 'sentimental' a precise definition. The large group of 'sentimental' Anacreontics and poets of the *Göttinger Hainbund* are merely mentioned, *Werther* on the other hand is interpreted as an example of 'how the naïve poetic mind treats a sentimental subject'.

Schiller conceives the idyll as the 'poetic presentation of innocent and happy mankind', as the pre-urban pastoral vision of mankind concerning its original state. Here, in his remarks on the elegy and the idyll, Schiller specifically touches upon his ambition — shared by Goethe — to produce classical poetry in these very genres. Yet he again consciously links his philosophy of history with the genre of the idyll, which he postulates as an attitude: the idyll not only exists in naïve form 'before the beginning of civilisation', but it is also the 'ultimate goal' of cultural development. That is a danger but contains at the same time the possibility of success. A danger insofar that here theoretically a retrogressive step is taken instead of a forward one in practice. And according to the insight into this twofold movement which lies in man's destiny, the 'sentimental' or the 'naïve' will determine the idyll; this means that the former can be seen as dominated by realism, the latter by a desire to idealise. For Schiller it is the con-

---

[13] The elegiac poet seeks nature, but as an idea and in a form of perfection in which she has never existed.

trast between Voss's idyll and that of Gessner. From this there follows with full logical justification the typology of the 'naïve' and 'sentimental' poet through the ages. Schiller sees the 'naïve' poet as 'leading mankind, which now can no longer return to *Arcadia*, as far as *Elysium*'. This strength and quality is — like Grace earlier — one of Nature's gifts. The solution therefore again has an aristocratic flavour. This, incidentally, also naturally applies to the 'sentimental' poet, who arrives at his poetic art by way of an unusual idealism, just as the 'naïve' poet does so through an unusual realism. Both types run risks and face limitations which arise from their natures as defined: the 'naïve' poet has to be on his guard against vulgar realism, which even a Homer, a Shakespeare and Molière have not completely avoided. The 'sentimental' poet, on the other hand, succumbs easily to the seduction of abstraction, one-sided saturation with personal ideas, of exaggerations in feeling. Haller, Wieland, Goethe's *Werther* can be seen here as such borderline cases. This cautious delineation of the limitations is not only proof of Schiller's intellectual honesty, but also a consequence of the trend towards harmonising on the part of Classicism with its aversion to every form of one-sidedness. Basically, the typology 'naïve-sentimental', through constantly obviating possible one-sidedness, already bears the stamp of the Classical spirit. This objective becomes even clearer if we include the conclusion towards which the already moderated and harmonised typology in the essay is ultimately working: the ideal of the amalgam of both characteristics in one person who then of course must have greatness. Ultimately there really remains of the antithesis merely a psychogenetic distinction: the poet sentimental by disposition and origin must acquire sensuousness and hence realism. The genius, who is by nature naïve, must strive for the standpoint of ennobling idealism in order to gain greatness. Everyone recognises the figure of Schiller in the first type, that of Goethe in the second. And we know that behind this essay lay Schiller's ambition to prove himself, the idealist, to be of equal rank and standing with the realist Goethe through the synthesis of 'naïve' and 'sentimental'.

PART VII

The High Period of Classicism: Development

23 The Collaboration of Goethe and Schiller

After he fell ill in 1791, Schiller was no longer able to return to his Chair of History. The great enterprise of the *Horen* was now to ensure him his existence as a writer as well as the intellectual impact which he hoped to make through it. And so he sought afresh a closer association with Goethe, who now no longer rebuffed his approach. Indeed, Goethe became a kind of co-editor and reader for the journal. The manuscripts that were submitted were passed to and fro between them for decision. The public announcement in 1794 expressly emphasised the corporate character of the editorship. Thus it was the *Horen* that first led to a consciously planned classical cultural circle centred on Weimar. And even though it was unable to last for long, since its level proved to be too high for the general public of the day, it nevertheless represented the first positive bond which brought Schiller and Goethe into a deliberately culturally-orientated association that was something rather more than a spontaneous collaboration. The journal linked names like those of Humboldt, Herder, Goethe's artist friend Johann Heinrich Meyer, also those of leading Romantics like Fichte and August Wilhelm Schlegel. It was the first enterprise of the High Classical period of Weimar which was backed by both poets and to be followed later by others such as Schiller's *Musenalmanach*, the *Propyläen*, the prize review of the Weimar artistic circle.

But there were more important, human and intellectual grounds for their personal association. These Goethe has recorded in the *Annalen* when reviewing the year 1794:

> In diesem Drange des Widerstreits übertraf alle meine Wünsche und Hoffnungen das auf einmal sich entwickelnde Verhältnis zu

Schiller; von der ersten Annäherung an war es ein unaufhalt-
sames Fortschreiten philosophischer Ausbildung und ästheti-
scher Tätigkeit. Zum Behuf seiner *Horen* mußte ihm sehr angele-
gen sein, was ich im stillen gearbeitet, angefangen, unternom-
men sämtlich zu kennen, neu anzuregen und zu benutzen; für
mich war es ein neuer Frühling, in welchem alles froh nebenein-
ander keimte und aus aufgeschossenen Samen und Zweigen
hervorging.[1]

Not only this passage is a living echo of that heyday in the style
of the ageing Goethe. The famous conversation too on the *Ur-*
pflanze, which provided the actual occasion marking the beginning
of their joint work, has been recounted in his reminiscences.
Schiller and Goethe, both of them repelled by the merely ana-
lytical way of looking at Nature, which had just left them dis-
satisfied at a meeting of the Society of Naturalists, discussed as an
alternative Goethe's concept of the *Urpflanze* as it had struck
him in Palermo. It was at this moment that Schiller formulated
this old favourite vision of Goethe's in the lapidary antithesis:
'That is not experience, that is an idea.' He thereby pinpointed the
difference in their ways of looking at things. And Goethe, who because of his personal view of Nature was initially put out and for
whom the *Urpflanze* was worthless if not experienced, had to
recognise in the ensuing conversation on the contrast between
Kantian thought and Realism, that even for him the meeting with
its clash of ideas was fruitful and stimulating. Schiller in fact has
formulated this most clearly of all in a letter to Körner (1 September 1794):

Ein jeder konnte dem andern etwas geben, was ihm fehlte, und
etwas dafür empfangen.[2]

[1] In this ferment of conflicting ideas the relationship that suddenly
developed with Schiller surpassed all my wishes and hopes; from the
first approach it was an irresistible development of philosophical education and aesthetic activity. For the benefit of his *Horen* he must have
attached great import to knowing, to stimulating afresh and to using
everything that I had quietly worked on, begun and undertaken; for me
it was a new Spring, in which everything joyfully sprouted in concert,
and sprung up and blossomed forth from the germinating buds.
[2] Each could give something to the other that he lacked and receive
something back in return.

A few days earlier he had similarly stated the standpoint of mutual complementation in words which already underlay the whole postulation contained in the *Horen*-treatise *Über naïve und sentimentalische Dichtung*:

> Mir fehlte das Objekt, der Körper, zu mehreren spekulativi-schen Ideen, und Sie brachten mich auf die Spur davon. Ihr beobachtender Blick, der so still und rein auf den Dingen ruht, setzt Sie nie in Gefahr, auf den Abweg zu geraten, in den sowohl die Spekulation als die willkürliche und bloß sich selbst gehorchende Einbildungskraft sich so leicht verirrt. In Ihrer richtigen Intuition liegt alles und weit vollständiger, was die Analysis mühsam sucht.[3]

This and the association which followed at this time with the three great reviews by Schiller on *Egmont, Iphigenie* and Bürger's *Gedichte*, realised the great coalition which was to last till Schiller's death.

From the *Horen* on, the co-operation of both Classicists was permanently established. Even when the journal had to cease publication, their joint collaboration in publishing continued. Schiller's experience in journalism was transferred to the fashionable form of the Muses Almanac, whose Weimar version lasted from 1796 to 1800. It facilitated the transposition of theory to actual writing and harvested the essential products of the lyric poetry, the ballad competition, above all the planning and arrangement of the *Xenien*. However the publishing balance between Goethe and Schiller was fully re-established with the *Propyläen*, which commenced after the *Horen* had proved to be no longer viable. Corresponding to the classical attitude already struck by the *Xenien* in the *Musenalmanach*, they became the expression of the consolidated artistic pedagogical role of Classicism, though not without an occasional over-conventionalisation of classical self-awareness. Here Goethe led the way, together with Johann Heinrich Meyer, his friend from Eastern Switzerland, whom he had brought to the

[3] I lacked the object, the substance for several speculative ideas, and you put me on the track of it. Your observing eye which rests so imperturbably and purely on things never puts you in any danger of wandering off on tangents onto which both speculation and the arbitrary and merely self-obeying power of imagination so easily stray. Everything that the analysing mind laboriously seeks lies in the compass of your accurate intuition, and in much more exhaustive form.

Weimar School of Arts. The competitions of the Weimar Patrons of the Arts followed as a form of practical education. Schiller could be regarded as a source of co-inspiration in a similar sense as Goethe had been with the *Horen*. When appraising this stage of the Weimar Classicism one must not overlook the degree to which the reliance on Classical Antiquity entered into their thinking. Indeed in the *Einleitung in die Propyläen* (1798) we read:

> Welche neuere Nation verdankt nicht den Griechen ihre Kunst-bildung? und, in gewissen Fächern, welche mehr als die deutsche?[4]

This confirms that the intention was to stray from 'classical soil' as little as possible. Schiller's influence becomes clear even in the later context of the Introduction. Without a doubt the views held by the Jena Romantics also contributed to a stiffening and greater severity in the classicistic attitude mentioned above. For the *Propyläen* passionately spoke out against 'the intermingling of the various forms of art', which they interpreted as decadence. The Classicists strove for a normative aestheticism that established the exact and comprehensible demarcations of the genres.

This propensity for the normative, for the ordered and classified is clearly perceivable in Goethe's own contributions to the *Pro-pyläen*. For example, in his apodictic introduction when he inter-vened in the discussion *Über Laokoon* (1798), where one clear-cut definition is followed by another (Ideal, Grace, Beauty, with Schiller's influence quite clear). It is here in *Winckelmann und sein Jahrhundert* (1805), that the stylized manner of interpreting which belongs to the epilogue of Weimar Classicism can be seen to begin. It is the style of 'it is', 'must', 'is to be', 'remains'. Far more significant on the other hand is Goethe's other contribution to the *Propyläen: Der Sammler und die Seinigen* (1798–99), which clothes rules, laws and classifications in epic-dramatic form by means of resorting to letters and dialogues, so that everything has a more personal and immediate effect. Here too the Fine Arts and not Literature form the subject-matter. Nevertheless an occasional pre-Stifterian note of pedantry is not lacking, although personal preferences and not theoretical aesthetics are in the fore-front. Indeed, many of the epistolary discussions are characteristic

[4] Which modern nation does not owe the Greeks its artistic training? And, in certain subjects, which more than the German people?

of the High Classical standpoint, the utterances of a cultural circle of distinction, opinions on the age-old problem of originality and imitation, imagination and rules.

The appearance is sometimes created in masterly fashion, partly achieved through the prevailing calm and moderation of the style, of an objective distancing, on the author's part, from the contending parties. It is as if both the pillars of the *Propyläen* were speaking in concert. As, for example, in the dialogue passage in the Sixth Letter between Self and Guest, in which the letter-writer (the 'I') expressly adopts the Schillerian theory of History and Beauty. The same occurs in the conclusion:

> Nur aus innig verbundenem Ernst und Spiel kann wahre Kunst entspringen.[5]

The hidden meaning of the essay is herein implied. It lies in the methodical approach, not in the compartmentalising bordering on the pedantic of the qualities and mannerisms of the artists. Compartmentalising is not an end in itself, but the means of recognising 'dangerous one-sidedness'. From the synthesis of the individual classifications stem the 'requisites for the perfect work of art'. Universality versus 'dangerous one-sidedness': that is the Classical essence, the ultimately common cause of the two friends. But we can also note Schiller's personal contribution in the *Einleitung in die Propyläen*. His thoughts on education from the *Briefe über ästhetische Erziehung* come through just as well as Goethe's organic view of Nature. Characteristically, right from the first sentence, a shift from youthful enthusiasm to the seriousness of the adult after the fashion of Wilhelm Meister is evident:

> Der Mann bemerkt, nach langem Umherwandeln, daß er sich noch immer in den Vorhöfen befinde.[6]

In this way reference was justly made to the title *Propyläen*. The fact that the organ was to be a joint venture of friends was established likewise straight from the start.

There also resulted from the *Propyläen* the organisational attempts of the 'Weimar Patrons of the Arts' to propagate the

---

[5] Only when the serious and the playful are in heartfelt union, can true art originate.

[6] After wandering hither and thither for a long time, the man notices that he is still only in the vestibule.

High Classical idea of culture: essay subjects and art exhibition competitions, for instance, which in fact were so narrowly circumscribed as to the aims to be pursued that even prior to Schiller's death they had to be discontinued, having failed to stimulate any work of genius. For indeed the *Propyläen-Einleitung*, the very essence of both Schillerian and Goethean aesthetics, limited right from the start the freedom of those participating when it demanded that 'art, favoured by circumstances, fortified by knowledge, aspiring to conformity to rules, seriousness and severity, should rise to its heights, whereby it would then finally become possible for the fortunate genius, who found himself surrounded by all these expedients, to produce works of art possessing charm and rounded perfection'. Schiller himself had defined this fortunate genius, a genius again naïve after progressing through the stages of consciousness and conformity to rules, as an aristocratic exception. Small wonder then that the attempt to find this genius through competitions and exhibitions attracted in the first instance well-intentioned mediocrities. Thus this organisational programmatic venture of Weimar High Classicism proved historically ineffective and soon became outdated, historically speaking. The emergence of the Romantics already saw to that. Yet it is pertinent for the completion of the picture of the Weimar circle up to the death of Schiller.

Criticism of the literature and of the Age in the most comprehensive and detailed sense was provided by the joint epigrammatic works of these years. *Xenien* and *Tabulae votivae*, closely connected with the ventures of both poets to make Weimar into a kind of headquarters of German Classicism, were to bring these critical attitudes before the public. They came into being in the years 1795 and 1796, and appeared in the *Musenalmanach* of the following year. Both collections testified to a degree of collaboration that led Schiller to state to Wilhelm von Humboldt:

> Es ist auch zwischen Goethe und mir förmlich beschlossen, unsere Eigentumsrechte an die einzelnen Epigrammen niemals auseinanderzusetzen, sondern es in Ewigkeit auf sich beruhen zu lassen.[7]

[7] It has also been formally resolved by Goethe and myself never to separate our copyrights to the individual epigrams, but to let things alone for all eternity.

Later however they did indeed hive off about a quarter as their own separate work. However the important thing then was the common standpoint which was obvious in the majority of these art- and culture-orientated epigrammatic verses, so that the individual authorship played no role. Characteristic of these epigrams was their polemic sharpness of tone, a total lack of any disposition to be fair. Persons as well as things were pitilessly taken to task, be they Kotzebue or Nicolai or former friends like Matthias Claudius, Lavater or the Stolbergs. With the same absoluteness, the Enlightenment and Romanticism were annihilated as subjects which were of merely temporal significance, naturally the Revolution too. The sarcasm occasionally went beyond the limits of tact. Yet behind the intention to caricature and expose opponents there more or less indirectly lay a classical *apologia*, the ethical and aesthetic norm. But in most instances we have to discover it indirectly, clothed as it is in such extraordinary polemics. For example, the XVIth *Xenie* (against Lavater) bemoans:

> Schade, daß die Natur nur *einen* Menschen aus dir schuf,
> Denn zum würdigen Mann war und zum Schelmen der
>   Stoff.[8]

That is indirectly classicistic anthropology, which cannot conceive the amalgam of the 'worthy man' and Till Eulenspiegel. Such indirect statements of this viewpoint occur in many variants, for example as national criticism just as much as a general criticism of the Age. Among the best known are the *Xenien* 85 and 86 on a Germany which did not exist politically, not even as a nation, though it did as a potential educational centre for free people and as a land of science. It is easy to detect the classical image of human greatness behind *Der Zeitpunkt* (*Xenie* 26):

> Eine große Epoche hat das Jahrhundert geboren,
> Aber der große Moment findet ein kleines Geschlecht.[9]

Truth, even decidedly partisan Weimar truth, can also take on epigrammatic form directly and without irony, as a philosophical programme (*Xenie* 51):

[8] It is a pity that nature created only one man out of you, because the material was there for the worthy man and for the rogue.

[9] The century has given birth to a great epoch but the great moment finds an insignificant race.

Wird der Poet nur geboren? Der Philosoph wird's nicht
　　minder;
Alle Wahrheit zuletzt wird nur gebildet, geschaut.[10]

But the fireworks which the *Xenien* showered on persons, groups,
types, works and problems, by far outweighed such self-presentation of Weimar High Classicism. The ingenious is mixed in with
the somewhat coarse and sometimes with the thoroughly un-
witty. As a triumph of the spirit the *Xenien* and the *Tabulae
votivae* were only a partial and limited success. They were no
more than a criticism of literature and the Age, where no punches
were pulled in making a point. It remains for the reader to determine whether elegance of wit was not to be found in the Romantics rather than in this joint effort of Goethe and Schiller.

An unusual form of the 'contest' waged between Goethe and
Schiller in connection with the classical aesthetics concerning
genres that they were jointly seeking, can be seen in the culmination of the ballad poetry around the so-called *Balladenjahr* of
1797–98. Schiller had hardly made any sort of name for himself
in this genre, since the few pieces in the *Anthologie* rather pointed
back to Bürger, who had meanwhile been written off in reviews.
Pieces like *Die Schlacht* or *Die Kindesmörderin* were moreover
psychological and socio-critical rather than epic. On the other
hand Goethe had, so to speak, organically assimilated and cultivated the ballad since the time of his contact with the folk-song
in Alsace, though admittedly influenced more by the general
trends in taste of the 'Storm and Stress' period: the feeling for
spirits, demons and the gloominess of the fates of Ossianic heroes.
To this category belong ballads and ballad-like poems such as
Der Fischer, *Erlkönig*, *Der untreue Knabe* and Gretchen's song of
the *König in Thule*. In the exposition of epic and dramatic
verse, Schiller now provided the key for the re-establishment on
the classical plane of this genre both for himself and for his friend.
For Goethe this stimulus led to the group of poems that date from
1797 to 1798 and begin with *Der Schatzgräber* and proceed to
Die erste Walpurgisnacht, the *Hochzeitlied*, the *Müllerin*-cycle,
Das Blümlein Wunderschön, *Ritter Kurts Brautfahrt* and on to
Der Zauberlehrling, *Die Braut von Korinth* and *Der Gott und die*

[10] Is the poet merely born? The philosopher is no less so; All truth in
the last resort is only created, perceived.

Bajadere. The earliest piece, *Der Schatzgräber* (May 1797), seems to be merely a Faustian theme. In reality it deals with the allegorical interpretation of an old illustration to Petrarch, which is verified for us by the diaries and which links the boy with the shining vessel to the theme of digging for, and finding treasure. Goethe saw this as an opportunity to transpose a subject permeated with romantic mystery to the classically pedagogical and hence into serene clarity of thought. The bearer of light becomes rather clumsily the bearer of the 'teaching' that the meaning of life consists of an alternation between competent, responsible work and sober-minded gregarious enjoyment of life. Despite the vision, magic is virtually removed from the tale of this ballad. It is not only moral in the Schillerian–Kantian sense, but furthermore almost a reversion to the morals of the Enlightenment.

This retrograde tendency applies even more strongly to *Die erste Walpurgisnacht*, which dates from the following month (June). Somehow Schiller's concept seems to have confused Goethe to begin with. This ballad is broken up, dramatically speaking, more than is reasonable into antiphonal cantos sung by the chorus of druids, the precentor, the voices of the people, the heathen and Christian guardians. It is almost a fancy-dress parade. Corresponding to the clear-cut nature of the individual roles is the distinctness of the rationalistic wealth of ideas presented here. The repelled heathens enact before the Christian guardians the witches' vigil as a piece of delusive theatre with the slogan:

> Diese dumpfen Pfaffenchristen,
> Laßt uns keck sie überlisten!
> Mit dem Teufel, den sie fabeln,
> Wollen wir sie selbst erschrecken.[11]

The witchcraft and devilry is therefore a strategem, and in reality these old Teutons do not indulge in black magic at all, but in a kind of masonic belief in light. We may very well query whether its connection here as in *Der Schatzgräber* with the very genre of the ballad is convincing, indeed even at all possible. The early, heavy, uncanny, larger-than-life-size aspect of Goethe's 'Storm and Stress' ballads has been sacrificed in favour of classical rational

---

[11] These dull clerics, let us boldly outwit them! Let us frighten them with the devil whom they have concocted.

clarity, in that the ballad now serves as a medium of ideas and viewpoints.

Yet there is a counterbalancing group of ballads in which the 'naïve-realistic' poet expresses himself at least in formal terms. *Ritter Kurts Brautfahrt* borders on the 'Moritat'. The story of the knight whom the Jews and the usurers cause to be imprisoned for debt, just as he is riding off to his bride (an anecdote from Bassompierre's memoirs), is perhaps classical in its imperturbable humour, though the conclusion in its pointedness smacks of the popular ballad. The subject-matter here is medieval, as it is in the song of the captured count, *Das Blümlein Wunderschön*, in the four *Müllerin*-ballads and in the *Hochzeitlied*. The form of the antiphonal and dialogue-ballad, which characterises four of these six pieces, likewise follows the pattern of the *Minnesang* in their old folk-song tradition. Yet in the three dialogue poems of the *Müllerin*-cycle above all, Goethe developed not only the folksong-like simplicity, but also the operetta-like ease (the source in fact being the just recently heard *Bella Molinara* of Paesiello); the arioso-character is brought out by making them sound almost like duets. In this cycle all the demonic under-currents of the ballad are dissolved into lucid playfulness. In this connection the *Hochzeitlied* delves deeper, not only in its real fairy-tale motif, the princely dwarf marriage, of which the count dreams, and which presents even linguistically dream and reality as interchangeable in masterly fashion. Its very verse form – dactyls with anacrusis – the onomatopoeia defining everything in terms of sound, the vocabulary ranging from the decorative to the grandiose, turn the whole into a naïve-charming linguistic *tour de force*. One could say: enraptured story-telling as an end in itself.

The three ballads of the year 1797 that belong together most closely in time are *Der Zauberlehrling*, *Die Braut von Korinth* and *Der Gott und die Bajadere*, the first two from classical, though late-classical sources, the third based on the recollection of an Indian book of travels. These three pieces together with *Hochzeitlied* are probably the purest that the High-Classical Goethe achieved within this genre. In all of them the magic-demonic element, which is indeed part of the ballad tradition, has been restored again to its rightful status. *Der Zauberlehrling* is the most dramatic of the poems, devoid of any tendency towards description. Everything is a monologue by the apprentice, the magic words, the call for help. The dialogue-ballad is outplayed, the subject-matter, taken from Wieland's translation of Lucian, appears to be transposed with an ingenious feeling for style to the medieval Faustian sphere. The rhythmic variation corresponds to this in the style.

If this poem is dramatic, then the other two are predominantly epic. *Die Braut von Korinth* transforms a late classical anecdote from the time of the decline of paganism (related to the almost contemporary *Die erste Walpurgisnacht*) into a classical philosophical ballad in affinity with Schiller: a philosophical poem with a pagan message. The girl, whose fatal embrace the youth enjoys on his would-be wedding-night, is in reality a victim of Christian asceticism. The other philosophical ballad *Der Gott und die Bajadere* is similar. It signifies a transfiguration of hetaerism reminding one of the Diotima-theme of the Early-Romantic Friedrich Schlegel: the courtesan proves to be the pure and selfless loving girl even unto death. The humanity that lies behind both these ballads is conceived as a symbol of the Classical humanitarian idea, and concedes a very great deal to Schiller's influence. At the same time however these philosophical ballads of Goethe are differently formed from those contemporary ones of Schiller. They preserve more of the magic of the early period of the German ballad and of Goethe's own 'Storm and Stress' period.

A comparison with Schiller elucidates this observation further. Schiller, a lyric poet of ideas pure and simple, also a lyrical propagandist of Classical Antiquity, but hitherto never an epic poet of the closed form, drafted two-thirds of his ballads (in the strict sense of the genre) in his 'contest' with Goethe in the years 1797 and 1798. The rest date from 1801 to 1804. Yet these last ones are merely *parerga* for *Tell*. If we consider the ratio of medieval and classical themes to each other here, we can establish that they are almost equally divided. In any case the balance is established when we perceive the idea of *hubris* in *Der Taucher* (1797) and that of fate in *Der Gang nach dem Eisenhammer* (1797) as classical themes clothed in medieval costume. Moreover *Der Ring des Polykrates* (1797) and *Die Kraniche des Ibykus* (1797), *Das eleusische Fest* (1798), *Die Bürgschaft* (1798), *Hero und Leander* (1801), *Kassandra* (1802) and *Das Siegesfest* (1803) are unequivocally classical in subject-matter. Besides the two mentioned philosophical ballads with medieval subject-matter but classical motifs, *Der Handschuh*, *Ritter Toggenburg* and *Der Kampf mit dem Drachen*, also stemming from the 'Balladenjahr' of 1797–98, enter into the medieval world, as do *Der Graf von Habsburg* and the *Tell*-pieces (1803–4), among the later ones. If we look back from this point of view to Goethe's ballad production, we grow aware that this Classicist who was influenced far more by original Classical Antiquity did not create one single ballad with genuinely classical subject-matter. For neither *Der Zauberlehrling* nor *Die Braut von Korinth* can be regarded as such.

Goethe's affinity to Schiller certainly does not lie here then. It lies more in the formal aspect, in so far as Schiller's fusion of didactic idea and ballad genre, as has been pointed out, rubbed off on Goethe too at this time. For it is a characteristic of all of Schiller's ballads that they do not trifle, but give expression at least to an idea, if not a downright moral. In *Der Taucher* and in *Der Ring des Polykrates* it is *hubris*, in *Die Kraniche des Ibykus* the inability to conceal guilt, in *Hero und Leander* the fate of tragic love, in *Kassandra* the relationship between reality and illusion, in *Die Bürgschaft* the idea of the sacrifice of which friendship is capable. In the ballads with medieval subject-matter *Der Handschuh* provides the idea of the vulnerability and invulnerability of the individual, *Der Gang nach dem Eisenhammer* the restoration of the rule of law victorious after the machinations of intrigue, *Der Kampf mit dem Drachen* the problem of obedience, *Ritter Toggenburg* the problem of earthly and heavenly love, *Der Graf von Habsburg* and *Der Alpenjäger* the idea of humanity realised. The steady integration of an idea into an originally epic-lyrical genre is precisely what has, at all times, produced the tension which again and again has provoked parodying of Schiller's un- usually 'pathetic' ballad style on account of its didactic note. This has scarcely been the case with Goethe. Not by chance is the dis- tinction between the 'naïve' and the 'sentimental' poet revealed specifically in the tone and the style of the ballads. Hence all the more admirable is his virtuosity in the tense narrative style which Schiller attains despite the didactic tendencies. Through this he succeeds more than once in making us forget whether the theme is a classical or a medieval one. That applies both to *Der Taucher* and *Der Kampf mit dem Drachen*, to *Die Bürgschaft* as well as to *Hero und Leander*. The process can classicise the medieval as well as medievalise the classical. There is the theme of the temptation of the gods in both subject ranges, as well as that of love and loyalty of friendship. It is precisely this universal validity however that is characteristic of Schiller's ballads dating from the time of the 'contest' with Goethe. The pieces from Swiss history dating from the nineteenth century (*Der Graf von Habsburg, Der Alpenjäger*) are inferior in quality, if only because sentimentality and morality render the interchange with classical motifs impossible. Nevertheless one stands time and again dumbfounded before the fascination exercised by presentation and description, the result too of a wealth of forms over which Schiller here shows mastery, on a par with his work at that time on *Wallenstein*. Here he staked part of that ambition to match Goethe in realistic writings. Thus the 'Balladenjahr' led to a decisive clarification of the individuality of both Goethe and Schiller. The more pronounced feeling for style which sees the traditional ballad genre as a special epic form of the *Lied* lay with Goethe. He allowed himself to be enticed into the world of the philosophical–didactic in but few poems. Schiller did not make an equivalent concession to the *Lied* element. Without doubt, for Schiller the ballad became a form of expression suited to the needs of Classical didactic poetry. The emphasis on classical subjects and motifs, which Goethe tended to avoid, can only confirm that, of the two friends Schiller was the more classicistic. The effect of his ballads however exerts its own fascination which is in no way inferior to that of Goethe's song-, dialogue- and dramatic ballads.

In these same years Goethe's first novel since *Werther*, namely *Wilhelm Meister*, matured to its Classical form of *Wilhelm Meisters Lehrjahre* (*Wilhelm Meister's Apprenticeship*) (1795–96). For the Early Romantics it became the epitome of great literature (though for Novalis later a source of annoyance too). Yet the great prose work had by no means begun in this form. Since the missing 'Urmeister' came to light in 1910 in Switzerland amongst the estate of Bäbe (Barbara) Schulthess, we no longer know the early version of *Wilhelm Meisters theatralische Sendung* (*Wilhelm Meister's Theatrical Mission*) merely by its title. Since the copy belonging to Bäbe Schulthess has bequeathed to us only six books of the planned first part that originated between 1777 and 1785, we cannot determine with any certainty where the original conception would ultimately have led. At all events, one thing is clear, namely that the title 'Theatralische Sendung' narrows the theme more than the title 'Lehrjahre' does for the Classical version (and 'Wanderjahre' for the post-Classical). The hero in the later versions is the subject of a process of education through life itself, where experimenting with the theatre formed but one stage. In the original version the theatre was the focal point, irrespective of how far the non-extant continuation might have negated the theme of the 'theatrical mission'. It was a *Künstlerroman* therefore in accordance with the originally planned genre, from which there later emerged an *Erziehungsroman* of universal application.

The Weimar friends, amongst them notably Herder, well acquainted with the 'Urmeister', received the Classical version with coolness, even regret. In Herder's case for example this was not primarily due to what can be defined as the 'trend' displayed in the *Lehrjahre*, since its 'manly' and educative core could not be at all repugnant to him. It stemmed to a large extent from the 'playing about' with the form. The 'Urmeister' depicted in a historically continuous epic sequence the development of the hero beginning with his childhood. The *Lehrjahre* now shifts the historical-temporal element (analogous to the style of the great English novelists and reflected in Jean Paul's works too at the time) in such a way that Wilhelm Meister's childhood is only brought up later in his account to Mariane. Herder's criticism of the Classical version expressly argued this point. The change in the principle of the epic form constituted for him rather an incrimination of the hero and his later moral debauches, as the reader was no longer familiar with his childhood. The historian must further note that the Classical stage of *Wilhelm Meister* originated, so to speak, under the critical eye of Schiller, no longer under that of Herder, so that Herder's jealousy of Schiller was an additional factor for consideration. But the extension of the theme of the *Künstlerroman* into a treatment of the problem of universal education (with obvious integration of Schillerian–Kantian maxims into the Goethean ethos of manliness) actually provided the conception with a broader basis. This is proved not only in the Sixth Book of the Second Part, that is in the adoption of the idea of the 'Beautiful Soul', but also in the demand for an experiencing of nature and the world as the medial prerequisite for education into manhood, an experience that restricted subjectivity. Herder leapfrogged, so to speak, this stage of development by means of his theology, at all events in his later period. In the new conception of *Wilhelm Meister* however it was humanistically legitimised, as it were, by the acquiescence of Goethe the observer of nature in Schillerian ethics. In this connection Friedrich Schlegel, the immediately contemporary critic of the *Lehrjahre*, in which he saw his and Novalis's 'Universalpoesie' realised, has shown a different kind of understanding of the transition from the 'Urmeister' to the *Lehrjahre* in his *Versuch über den verschiedenen Stil in Goethes früheren und späteren Werken*:

> Die erste [Idee] war bloß die eines Künstlerromans; nun aber ward das Werk, überrascht von der Tendenz seiner Gattung, plötzlich viel größer als seine erste Absicht, und es kam die Bildungslehre der Lebenskunst hinzu, und ward der Genius des Ganzen.[12]

In fact, the new Classical conception of the novel found specifically with the Romantics that reception which it had not encountered with Wieland and Herder.

From Goethe's point of view, it would be possible to make a whole series of causes responsible for the Classical conception of *Wilhelm Meister*. The constant contact with Schiller has already been mentioned. The change of style which Italy effected for Goethe should be added. But even the motif of the theatre now rested on a different philosophical basis to that of the time of the 'Urmeister'. Goethe had in the meantime learned to combine the functions of theatrical producer and director (*Euphrosyne*) and had consequently acquired experience in theatre matters, which had been absent from the amateur theatricals of Weimar in the eighties. That enabled him here to subordinate and integrate the Hamlet and strolling players motif into a new and comprehensive educational theme, so that Wilhelm Meister, no longer now the artist but the dilettante in the serious sense of the word, experiences his transitional and developmental stage within the theatre, though his aim is to become a man and a human being in the fullest sense. Admittedly we do not know exactly what purpose the theme of the beautiful, unknown girl, Natalie, was to have served, that was accorded the final word at a decisive moment

[12] The first idea was merely that of a *Künstlerroman*; surprised by the trend of this genre, the work now however became suddenly much greater than its first intention and the educative teaching on the art of living was added and became the presiding spirit for the whole.

in the early version (in the 'Urmeister'). Was it already in accord with the first conception to introduce the elevation of Wilhelm from the sphere of the theatre to a chivalrous-worldly level? For here indeed we find the real link between the *Künstlerroman* and the universal *Entwicklungsroman* of Classical form. The *Künstlerroman* provided the story of Wilhelm's bourgeois youth (which only his happy love-relationship with Mariane later elicited from him), the rupture with the bourgeois atmosphere of the rich merchant's house, the adventures with the actors in the period of his dubious relationship with the Countess, the involvement in the fate of Mignon and the Harper, the unexpected attack by the robbers after leaving the castle, in which Wilhelm is wounded and receives the help of the 'Amazon', finally Wilhelm's resolve to join forces with Serlo's theatrical troupe as partner and producer, after he had become master of his own fortune through the death of his father. In that period Mariane, the Countess, Mignon, Philine and Aurelie had significantly entered his life, yet all of them through the medium of his passion for the stage. Only Natalie, still nameless in the 'Urmeister', remained independent of this environment.

All these factors appear in the *Lehrjahre* in an essentially richer and also more complex form, in that the old lines of action are expanded or linked and interwoven with new ones. The framework of the earlier action assumes with this expanded conception both a different educational and corrective importance. One can well understand that Schiller, involved with the new manuscript from the third book on, was still most uneasy when, in a moment of productive criticism in the July of 1796, he tried to track down the unity of the new conception, although he admitted that he was aware of its 'consistency'. Yet he appears to have been overwhelmed by the artistic quality of the eight books he looked over:

> Wie sehr mich die Wahrheit, das schöne Leben, die einfache Fülle dieses Werkes bewegte . . . ruhig und tief, klar und doch unbegreiflich wie die Natur, so wirkt es und steht es da, und alles, auch das kleinste Nebenwerk, zeigt die schöne Gleichheit des Gemüts, aus welchem alles geflossen ist.[13]

[13] How very much the truth, the beautiful life, the simple wealth of this work moved me . . . tranquil and profound, clear and yet inconceivable like nature, this is and remains its effect, and everything, even the most minor incidental theme, shows the beautifully balanced mind from which everything has issued forth.

This assessment would not possibly have been valid for the 'Urmeister'. The new version, however, shows in fact the development of a man for whom his artistic inclinations clearly signify now henceforth only a transitional stage in his development. What in the 'Urmeister' grows simply in accord with the 'Storm and Stress' style, becomes in the *Lehrjahre* an austere education through experience, which is both the means of acquiring culture as well as of self-correction. This feature also turns out to be eminently Classical. The Classicist is not afraid of the 'moral' element: that is the existential responsibility of man towards the principles of 'Humanität'. That includes the transition through misguided inclinations and an honest acknowledgement of past errors. A complementary or diametrically opposed kind of world had therefore to arise from the world of the theatre: the sphere in which the uncle and the 'Beautiful Soul' are at home, the world of Lothario, Therese and Natalie, the world of pedagogic free-masonry incorporated therein, as the 'Society of the Tower', with Jarno and the Abbé, operates it. There finally grows within Wilhelm Meister a much more intensive feeling of responsibility for the fate of Felix, his later acknowledged son by Mariane, together with the deepened concern for Mignon and the Harper. All this constitutes the demands of the objective world over against the 'Storm and Stress' subjectivity from which Wilhelm Meister's very being originally sprang. He gains personality and character in the Classical conception only through crises from which results his 'education'. And that in essence is the new theme as against the subjective one of the *Theatralische Sendung*. If we picture to ourselves the comprehensiveness of the critical themes in respect of their function for Wilhelm's development, we should have to proceed from the tension felt by the merchant's son regarding the middle-class atmosphere of his background. It finds its clearest mirroring perhaps in the relationship between Wilhelm and his friend Werner. It also imparts to the motif of the theatre – downgraded in comparison to its treatment in the *Theatralische Sendung* – a new significance by contrasting idealism with philistine lack of imagination. Thus the *Lehrjahre* contains a clear questioning of subjectivity. Hence originality is limited once again on the basis of Classical ethos. What springs from youthful enthusiasm is not yet art *per se*; dilettantism must be clearly recognised for what it is. Finally: the goal which results, already in the re-interpretation of the theatre-motif as a longing for harmony, is the ideal of a harmonious education, for the development of which the *Hamlet*-analysis can serve too. Goethe lets all the significant representatives of one-sidedly introverted humanity fail or perish: Werner, Aurelie, Mignon, the Harper. In the view of the Classicist, only the universal is viable. The hero is drawn to this end in his own educative responsibility (to Mignon, Felix) through the conflict of duty and inclination (thus under Schiller's influence) – in the literal sense too, for his encounter with fate is manipulated to a large degree: through the 'Society of the Tower', that affects his life from afar and without whose approval Wilhelm could not even at the end have been united with Natalie, the tranquil, the 'Beautiful Soul' as fully envisaged by Schiller.

The theme, in which all this is specifically brought out, i.e. the *Bekenntnisse einer schönen Seele* – admittedly already prepared in 1793 prior to his association with Schiller – is interpolated in Book Six of Part Two. The correspondence with Schiller over the *Bekenntnisse* contains Goethe's observation in the July of 1796:

Das Prädikat der schönen Seele wird auf Natalien abgeleitet.[14]

This modification took place after the dispute between the two friends about Book Six concerning which Schiller had expressed some regret because it anticipated the theme of the 'Beautiful Soul' as incorporated in the character of Natalie. This argument typifies the different meaning which the two friends gave to Shaftesbury's 'moral grace'. Goethe unhesitatingly makes this, in the *Bekenntnisse*, the attribute of the woman who walks with God (Natalie); Schiller, however, alienated from his own pietistic childhood, interpreted the concept of the 'Beautiful Soul' in a purely aesthetic sense, both here and in his essay *Über Anmut und Würde*. For Goethe, however, the *anima pia* could represent that overcoming of the contradiction of duty and inclination from his own experience. It must have been distressing for Schiller that his historico-philosophical path from originality through consciousness and culture to a new guilelessness ('naïvety') should find its exact religious-pietistic counterpart in the *Bekenntnisse*. For that reason he pressed for the transfer of the criterion of the 'Beautiful

[14] The criterion of the 'Beautiful Soul' is transferred to Natalie.

Soul' to the character of Natalie. In this matter Goethe showed himself to be obliging. Nevertheless Book Six remains significant as a testimony of his own personality that was kept intact even in his friendship with Schiller. Goethe had in fact not invented the basic life story, but had used and elaborated on the posthumous autobiographical papers of Susanne von Klettenberg, the pietistic friend of his youth. The original material was therefore already historically provided.

But Goethe selected decisive elements from the autobiographical documents used. What emerged from those was a psychological tale in which subjectivity developed into a total synthesis between duty and inclination in the course of the gradual coming-to-terms with external incidents and necessities. It achieved this, remarkably enough, by virtue of a particular development of imagination and observation through early illness. From this sprang a confused turning towards God which intensified with the first love to a 'pull' towards God. Contact with the courtly world and in it with Narcissus, her fiancé, led to increasing friction with the 'world'. Corresponding to that was the inner (counter-) development of the soul, which deepened and, following the failure of the secular plan of marriage, soared to a superior feeling where God's nearness meant everything, while secular society meant less and less. Thoughts of Hell and feelings of sin in the manner of the Halle missionary pietism were abandoned, and with them fear. Death became something more and more familiar, serenity and tranquillity something more and more influential. The formula 'pure feeling in my soul', characteristic of the affinity to the Moravian mysticism of the Cross, introduces the last phase of the story of the soul. It shows both an affinity to, and a distancing from Moravia, a working with the 'antennae of the soul'. Everything culminates in an original, unschematic religiosity which is broad and free enough to maintain 'neutrality' within the conventicle confusions at that period, whilst resolutely preserving its own central belief in Christ. The symbolic autobiography, which incidentally is linked not for nothing with the theme of the aesthetic uncle and his castle, is summed up in the following:

Ich erinnere mich kaum eines Gebotes, nichts erscheint mir in Gestalt eines Gesetzes, es ist ein Trieb, der mich leitet und mich

immer recht führet; ich folge mit Freiheit meinen Gesinnungen
und weiß so wenig von Einschränkung als von Reue.[15]

Schiller's lyric poetry in the last decade of his life adds also
essentially new notes to the old ones. In part it is admittedly
philosophical poetry as before, especially an expression of aesthetic
views too. Thus, for example, *Die Macht des Gesanges* (1795)
echoes the philosophy of history of the aesthetic writings: the
return to nature by means of poetry after the transitional stage
through consciousness. *Die Ideale* and *Das Ideal und das Leben*
(both also dating from 1795) are historico-philosophical as well.
The latter poem is most closely linked with Schiller's aesthetic
view of history which wants to advance into the realm of 'pure
forms' without any concession to the moral sphere. It is the poem
with the characteristic basic theme:

> Nehmt die Gottheit auf in euren Willen,
> Und sie steigt von ihrem Weltenthron.[16]

Stylistically speaking, that is all still very much the old Schiller,
coming alive through the pathos of the rhyme and the message of
the strophe; in terms of content it constitutes the conquest of the
natural-physical world by the spirit. In competition with the
Goethe of the *Elegien* we find Schiller's numerous distich poems
of this period such as *Der Tanz, Der Genius, Der Spaziergang*
(all 1795) and *Pompeji und Herculanum* (1796). In them Schiller
attained a symbolic stylisation which he had not previously
mastered. The basic theme of *Der Tanz*: 'And a quiet law directs
the playful character of all transformations' recalls Goethe; 'Each
a ruler, free, obeying only his own heart' derives from the Schiller
of the 'Beautiful Soul'. The same motif, its validity extended
from the artistic genre to originality *per se*, appears in *Der Genius*,
but this time in contra-distinction to systematic knowledge; there
genius rules with its own freedom and in its innocence, over which
laws cannot exercise compulsive power. The splendid final penta-

---

[15] I scarcely recall a commandment. Nothing appeared to me in the
shape of a law. It is an impulse which directs me and leads me always
along the right path; I freely follow my views and know as little of restraint as of repentance.

[16] Receive the Godhead into your Will, and it will descend from its universal throne.

meter recapitulates it: 'Simply and peacefully you pass through the conquered world.'

The highest achievements in elegiac form are probably *Der Spaziergang* (1795) and *Nänie* (1799). In these is expressed an unprecedented linguistic and formal advance: German High Classicism in poetry of the most sublime order. In the earlier poem, life in all its rich texture and change; in the latter, in compressed form, the theme of death. *Der Spaziergang* is in its opening and its close an idyll, in the central portion a charming presentation of Classical philosophy in which ordered life in state and city with their cultural acquisitions is associated with the idyllic. Here, in the central portion, Schiller goes characteristically dithyrambic, the pathos turns to passion. The affinity to Goethe is clear. This holds true too for the standpoint taken, which is anti-revolutionary and in favour of the eternally lasting law, the 'quiescent pole in the flight of phenomena'. Through this attitude the experience of the Greeks is eternally renewed for him: 'And Homer's sun, see, it smiles on us too.' Yet this merely reiterates the picture of evolution and history contained in *Über naïve und sentimentalische Dichtung*. A more decisive factor is the gain in creative formal strength, which restrains the purely reflective element and effects a sovereign stylisation of sensual reality. On the other hand, the mastery in *Nänie* lies in the concentration of the elegiac ethos which turns the lament for Achilles and Adonis, the most beautiful of the 'Beautiful', directly into the symbol for the concluding lines:

Siehe! da weinen die Götter, es weinen die Göttinnen alle.
    Daß das Schöne vergeht, daß das Vollkommene stirbt.
Auch ein Klaglied zu sein im Mund der Geliebten ist herrlich,
    Denn das Gemeine geht klanglos zum Orkus hinab.[17]

We should also try to approach Schiller's possibly most popular poem, *Das Lied von der Glocke* (1799) from the point of view which led us to interpret the philosophy of history in *Der Spaziergang* as something that one might call a morphology. Neither the aphorism that Schiller had borrowed from the still preserved bell in

[17] Look, the gods are weeping and all the goddesses too, weeping that beauty must pass, that perfect things must die. There is splendour even in this – to be a lament in the mouths of those we loved, for what has no distinction goes down to Orcus unsung.

Schaffhausen, nor the rather unfortunate *Biedermeier*-like familiar interpretation actually produce the proper point of view. This lies more in the analogous element of the destiny of the bell and human fate and in the morphological view of history therein concealed, which becomes for that very fact more than just an allegorical observation. This comprehensive poem is better than its reputation, even with regard to the flexibility of form and tempered nature of the pathos. Schiller's lyric poetry of this period, taken as a whole, also proves to be a mirror of assurance, of self-realisation, indeed of serene turning towards the world of sensual reality. Manifestly as a result of the friendship with Goethe, a mood developed, from which song-like poems such as *Sehnsucht* (1801), *Die Gunst des Augenblicks, An die Freunde, Die vier Weltalter* (all 1802), and the symbolism of 'Kairos' in *Punschlied* (1803) could arise. This is the one side of the coin. For Goethe it was a matter of course, for Schiller it was a necessity. The other side of the Classical coin, that of resignation, is expressed in *Der Antritt des neuen Jahrhunderts* (1801), since this poem opens with the lines 'The century has departed in a storm. / And the new one opens with murder' and concludes with a withdrawal into subjectivity, which links it with *Nänie*:

> Freiheit ist nur in dem Reich der Träume.
> Und das Schöne blüht nur im Gesang.[18]

A spreading-out from the ideal to the sensual world, more comfortable and more confident traits in earthly terms, a self-limitation in resignation, above all in relation to the theme of death – all this can be regarded as the Classical direction of Schiller's lyric verse in terms of content. In this poetry such expressions as 'We, we *live*! The time is ours. / And the person alive is right' (*An die Freunde*) range alongside the thought of transitoriness (*Die Gunst des Augenblicks*) and the demand to hazard everything unconditionally (*Sehnsucht*).

[18] Freedom is only in the realm of the dreams, and Beauty blossoms only in song.

24 Neptunism and Vulcanism

The 'Wald und Höhle' scene in *Faust* which originated in Rome had already added the formula 'severe enjoyment of contemplation' to Faust's 'brotherly' views on all living creatures, which could have been interpreted too in the sense of early Goethean pantheism. Expressed therein was Goethe's striving – already initiated prior to Italy – for a comprehension of nature that was both universal and responsible in the cognitive sense. Here in the Classical period the dilettante note receded behind the determination to observe exactly and to classify what had been observed. Schiller had mentioned to him with the utmost clarity *àpropos* the subject of the 'Urpflanze', that in Goethe's natural scientific work of this Classical period the eye and the other senses not only determined the 'severe enjoyment of contemplation', but also that pleasure in the idea was at work. For this very reason we may be able however to explain Goethe's polemical resentment of traditional natural science, which in his opinion did not take him seriously enough. He regarded himself as a pure empiricist. But it was Schiller, the thinker, who had the clearer cognisance of the amalgam of observation and ideal preconception which was peculiar to his friend. For all that however Goethe's self-interpretation remained subjectively the genuine and authoritative one as far as he was concerned:

> Willst du ins Unendliche schreiten,
> Geh nur im Endlichen nach allen Seiten.[1]

For the methodological approach of the two friends was different. It was based on the contrast of induction and deduction. Goethe's original aversion to Schiller was not unjustified from that point of view. Schiller deduced Nature's laws from Nature. From Nature

[1] Should you wish to step into Infinity, just walk to every perimeter of the finite.

Goethe induced her substance, working from an idea. In Goethe's eyes, Schiller necessarily underrated Nature, given this hypothesis. For Schiller, Goethe necessarily attributed too high a value to pure observation, without regard to a possible deception of the senses, as described only too clearly in Kant's *Critiques*. Yet even prior to his association with Schiller, Goethe had himself encountered Kant, as his own significant comment *Der Versuch als Vermittler von Objekt und Subjekt* (1792) shows. Proceeding from the manner of looking at things with reference to the subject, which can become the source of 'a thousand errors', it recognises its inapplicability to the objects of Nature ('Investigate what is and not what pleases'). Here the 'even peaceful gaze of objectivity' is demanded, the experiment appears as a genuine mediator, not as a confirmation of theses ('an idea too hastily conceived'), but rather as a corrective to the inner enemies, 'power of imagination, impatience, rashness, self-complacency, stiffness, formalism of thought, preconceived opinion, indolence, levity, fickleness'. All that is the cause of precipitous deductions and also of a misuse of the experiment. The correct approach lies in the determination and in the power of the observer to synthesise the details. And so there result 'experiences of the higher kind', which are analogous to the mathematical method and must be honestly acquired and comprehensibly expressed. This too is Classical ethos.

The treatise has a close inner connection with the sketch *Erfahrung und Wissenschaft* (1798), which similarly relates to the example of Goethe's work on the theory of colours. The exchange with Schiller is here visible nevertheless in the concession that the 'pure phenomenon', the 'Urphänomen', which had already fascinated Goethe with his conception of the 'Urpflanze', was an idea, 'a kind of ideal'. In terms of Goethe's natural scientific work, it depended on these methodically conceptual views and clarifications, in which an organic view of the world (view in the literal sense) is reflected, not on the tough and bitter struggle with Newton and his adherents which Goethe began with his *Beyträge zur Optik* (1791–92) and which concluded with the *Zur Farbenlehre* (1810). In the course of his work on these he arrived at the fundamental principles of a Classical doctrine of Nature, and these essentials are: type, metamorphosis, intensification, polarity, morphology, pure phenomenon ('Urphänomen'). The contrast with Newton rested purely and simply on the insistence of an 'Augenmensch' on his experience as against that of the professional scientist. With his discovery of the intermaxillary bone the dilettante appeared to have been proved right in spite of the scepticism expressed by traditional scientists. After all, everyone was allowed to take sides in the dispute between the two factions of geologists, i.e. the followers of Vulcanism or Neptunism. However the individual contribution of the Classical Goethe lay in the development of the above-mentioned fundamental principles right up to the poetically condensed form they found in *Urworte. Orphisch.* The decisive factor for literary history is here not the 'science', but the 'dilettantism' in the higher sense of the term as the mature Goethe himself established it. It is here we find the synthesis of experience and idea seriously venturing beyond every form of specialisation into the wide open spaces of the theory of shapes and forms, without which his Classical work would not be fully understandable, since it was both its inspiration and result. In the *Versuch, die Metamorphose der Pflanzen zu erklären* (1790) the essence of observation is epitomised in the formula:

> . . . so werden wir auf den regelmäßigen Weg der Natur desto aufmerksamer gemacht, und wir lernen die Gesetze der Umwandlung kennen, nach welchen sie einen Teil durch den anderen hervorbringt und die verschiedensten Gestalten durch Modifikation eines einzigen Organs darstellt.[2]

The account relates to the botanical object. It expresses however Goethe's observant attitude towards Nature in general. The poem in elegiac metre, *Die Metamorphose der Pflanzen* (1799), shows this relationship once again in a fascinating way. 'Shape' and 'law' here point to 'a sacred enigma' of growth and decay in the midst of 'perfection':

> Und hier schließt die Natur den Ring der ewigen Kräfte;
> Doch ein neuer sogleich fasset den vorigen an.[3]

Plant, animal and human all appear subject to transformation and metamorphosis. All that is law, is life in formation and develop-

[2] . . . and thus we are made the more attentive to the regular path of nature, and we get to know the laws of metamorphosis, according to which it generates one part through another and displays the most varied shapes through modification of a single organ.

[3] And here nature completes the circle of the eternal forces. Yet a new one immediately links on to the previous one.

ment and constant intensification towards higher forms. The miracles of Nature however serve the structure of the being, contain decay merely for a higher purpose, are altogether a purification of forms and shapes. However what Goethe was ill-equipped to understand was the thoroughly destructive element, the senseless element, which he saw in the concept of violence and destruction. Almost all his work of the Classical period served to refute what he must have felt to be un- or counter-natural.

Goethe underwent *the* decisive historical experience immediately following his return from Italy, if one includes the Venetian journey as well: the French Revolution. It extensively stamped Goethe's poetry in the succeeding period as well as the development of his natural scientific outlook. It may be appropriate to make some anticipatory remarks at this point: the whole philosophy of Classicism, (already preluded by Winckelmann) was based on the organic, on evolution. With Winckelmann it was the conception of the history of art, which rested on the gradual causal connection of ages with the history of mankind. Such a view was also propounded by Herder. The Classical idea of universality could not disregard natural history. 'Minted form which develops as it lives' – in these orphic words of Ancient Wisdom this found its appropriate formula at a later stage. In keeping with this is Goethe's attitude towards the great geological dispute of the age. This revolved around the theories on the origin of the earth; whether by eruption of volcanoes, through, so to speak, historic-terrestrial 'Revolution', or through 'Evolution'. 'Vulcanism', the acknowledgement as 'progress' of an earth created through eruption, meant therefore the recognition of Revolution. The element involved here would be fire. The counter-theory of Neptunism presupposed the development of the earth in organic ways, instead of in inorganic ones, through gradual sedimentation whose developmental stages would necessarily have been conditioned organically by the prehistoric oceans. The element here would be water. The elderly Goethe with his well-known aphorism on the New World: 'America, you are better off / than our continent, the old one. / You have no ruined castles / And no basalt', reduced the philosophy of history and natural philosophy to a common denominator, so to speak. What he had argued since 1789 appeared quite logical still in symbolical terms to the Goethe of the time of the genesis of *Faust II*. But already in his High-Classical period he had adopted his position as was clear to everyone: for him, the earth had originated organically not through the violent and eruptive element of fire but rather through the slowly shaping element of water. This concept also involved siding with the history of mankind, as the Classical Herder had conceived of it being something organic in the *Ideen*, the genesis of which Goethe had been able to follow in Italy through an exchange of manuscripts.

Goethe's position *vis-à-vis* the French Revolution was influenced by all this. It could not be positive as in the case of the young Schiller or the ageing Klopstock. It could appraise *the* political event of the century only as an encroachment upon the organic principle. Not the politics of the day, but the philosophical standpoint determined his judgment here. It was therefore no accident either that Goethe put down his most searching definition and consideration of the word 'classical' in an essay which linked the political with the literary already in its very title: *Literarischer Sansculottismus* (1795). The inner connection, in which the meaning and importance of the Classical factor were here imbedded, is exactly the same as in the *Unterhaltungen deutscher Ausgewanderten*. Classicism appears as a consequence of national unity and historical greatness. Subjectively it is the capability of genius to 'sympathise with the past as with the present'. That means, the Classicist could not be a revolutionary. Rather had he to be a man of continuity. This emphasis on organic development could lead here to the almost paradoxical sentence:

> Wir wollen die Umwälzungen nicht wünschen, die in Deutschland klassische Werke vorbereiten könnten.[4]

Therefore even here (politically) we find anti-Vulcanism, where (intellectually) the possibility of a new classical art was at stake.

Small wonder therefore that the Goethe of the High-Classical period maintained a sceptical, indeed hostile attitude in his lyric verse, epic poetry and dramas towards this revolutionary event — as a 'Neptunist' in fact. Even his theoretical views on social life, as found in the *Unterhaltungen deutscher Ausgewanderten* (*Conversations among German Emigrants*) of 1795 were decidedly conservative. The lament of the Baroness over the lack of self-

---

[4] We would not wish for the Revolutions which could pave the way for Classical works in Germany.

control which had broken out in society since the Revolution finds expression in these sentences:

> Wir suchen recht eifrig jede Gelegenheit, wo wir etwas vor-bringen können, das den andern verdrießt und ihn aus seiner Fassung bringt. O laßt uns künftig, meine Kinder und Freunde, wieder zu jener Art zu sein zurückkehren! [5]

The Tasso-theme, though amply accounted for when seen as the product of earlier personal development, now merged smoothly into Goethe's anti-revolutionary attitude. Moderation, order and tradition collapse under the social incursions of the Revolution. Thus Goethe's reaction was less concerned about the political organisation of the State than about the individual. Much later, in the essay *Bedeutende Fördernis durch ein einziges geistreiches Wort* (Vol. II of the *Beiträge zur Morphologie*), he reminiscently established the relationship between his work during the nineties and the French Revolution:

> An eben diese Betrachtung schließt sich die vieljährige Richtung meines Geistes gegen die französische Revolution unmittelbar an, und es erklärt sich die grenzenlose Bemühung, dieses schreck-lichste aller Ereignisse in seinen Ursachen und Folgen dichter-isch zu gewältigen. [6]

The elderly Goethe was to look back on this period of development as being 'unprofitable' in the bitter knowledge that the great dramatic trilogy which was to have formed the zenith of his anti-Revolution works had only progressed to the extent of the first piece – *Die natürliche Tochter* – and that had been a failure on the stage too. Nevertheless there were works of significance originating from that period.

To begin with, there were the two comedies *Der Großkophta* and *Der Bürgergeneral*. They still belonged to the time prior to the association with Schiller. *Der Großkophta* was written in 1791 and is really more symbolical than is appropriate to a comedy. Origin-

---

[5] Quite zealously we seek every opportunity where we can present some-thing which annoys the other person and makes him lose his composure. O let us in future, my children and friends, return to that former state.

[6] The trend of my thinking against the French Revolution over many years is directly linked to this very conception, and it explains my boundless efforts to come to terms, in poetic form, with the causes and effects of this most terrible of all events.

ally for Goethe the figure of the charlatan and pseudo-Count Balsamo-Cagliostro provided a psychological motif, just as *Der Geisterseher* did for Schiller. Subsequently however it developed in the process of creation into the symbol of the corruption of society on the eve of the Revolution. Added to that was the shattering impression of the Rohan necklace affair[7] in which Marie Antoinette herself was involved. Against his will Goethe had to see society compromised in such phenomena of the age and thereby see the hidious Revolution justified as a volcanic natural event. The usurped dignity of *Der Großkophta* (resulting from the historical prototype Cagliostro) was a genuine dignity of the *Magic Flute* period, with the same background of Egyptianised freemasonry rites. Hence the poetic image was also topical. Whether or not of course this criticism of the age and of society was too serious anyway for a comedy is debatable. At all events there emerged that rather unfortunate combination of comedy and dramatic presentation of morals, a hybrid rather, in which the names themselves already symbolise ranks and types in abstract fashion: *the* Canon, *the* Count, *the* Knight. Such type-casting is justifiable, since it does not introduce a discordant note, in the later centenary festival play *Paläophron und Neoterpe* or in *Faust II.* In comedy however (in accordance with the class convention) only the servants were allowed to have names, as is the case in fact in *Der Großkophta.* It disturbed the necessary concrete nature of the comic spirit. The fact that the real action takes place in a class setting between the amorous, gullible Canon and the Marchesa as well as the pseudo-Count, whose pawn he becomes, is no more comic than the theme of superior swindling can rank as criticism of the era. (Otherwise Thomas Mann's *Felix Krull* could also be counted as a novel of social criticism.) The sinister power of the *tiers état* should have been clearly demonstrated if Goethe's work had intended to bring out this aspect. However this was by no means acceptable to Goethe, for that aspect constituted the direct contradiction of the Classical concept of order.

The reason for the Third Estate and the people in *Der Groß-*

---

[7] In an incident at the court of Louis XVI in 1785, Cardinal de Rohan was duped through court intrigue, involving Marie Antoinette herself, over his attentions to the queen and an expensive necklace he wished to give her as a present. There was a trial the following year, but Rohan was acquitted. (*Translator's note*)

kophta not being able to get an adequate opportunity to speak becomes clear once again from the comedy of the year 1793, *Der Bürgergeneral*. Goethe had just (in 1791) taken over the superintendence of the Weimar Theatre. These comedies on the Revolution were written for it. A mediocre French comedy, which was nevertheless successful as a play, served as a source for *Der Bürgergeneral*. The question of the qualities to which this Revolution play of Goethe's owed its success, is pertinent. An eminently stageworthy light comedy, *Der Bürgergeneral* had the advantage, over against *Der Großkophta*, of being pure in terms of genre. Familiar types of the village comedy are shown on the stage. Realistic prose reigns supreme, again in contrast to the Rococo-like earlier Goethean musical comedies. The types are pre-cast: the good, honest peasant Görge, who is madly jealous over his young wife Röse, then Röse's father Merten, the distrustful, sly, inquisitive peasant-type, and the village braggart Schnaps, a drunken liar who is hoisted with his own petard. The innocuous legal squabble of the village is presided over by the nobleman, a good-natured, patriarchal figure but an over-zealous judge. As Goethe identifies the *braggadoccio* Schnaps with the primitive propagandist of the new freedom and equality, he turns the comedy into a revolutionary satire in which the representative of the new order is exposed to the full scorn of ridicule through being contrasted with patriarchal attitudes which have the quality of permanence. 'Revolutionary' ideas are in this way presented only as a caricature and are hardly taken seriously enough.

In the same year he planned a 'political drama', *Die Aufgeregten*. Goethe was going to rely here on the early comedy of the great Danish writer Holberg, *Der politische Kannegießer*, from which he even borrowed by name the main character, the barber-surgeon Breme von Bremenveld, except that he turned this figure topically into a negative image of the revolutionary-vulcanic idea. Only through this did he treat the theme of the Revolution seriously and not in a superficial satirical-polemical fashion. In Holberg's play the would-be politician who sees himself to some extent as the leader of the Third Estate, immediately runs headlong into the trap which had been so gracefully laid by his patrician opponents, namely his rigged election as mayor. The defeat of the village braggart at the hands of the representatives of tradition was never in any doubt as far as Holberg was concerned. Goethe however turns the incitement of the peasants by the village surgeon into a not illegitimate action, since true justice is withheld from the revolutionaries. Through his admission that injustice is being suffered here and that only the use of force can produce justice, Goethe offers no longer only the feudal viewpoint as hitherto, but rather – and in more penetrating fashion – Luther's advocacy of non-violence in solving legal issues which occur between people and authorities. To be sure, a real change of position on Goethe's part is hardly noticeable. That would have been improbable already in view of the simultaneous appearance of *Der Bürgergeneral*. The injustice that is done to the people is blamed upon a deceased person, the old Count, and on the deceitful magistrate. The morality and integrity of the Countess as the contemporary representative of (feudal) order however outshines all other figures. The regenerative capability on the part of the old ruling class which is willing to atone for its lapses is therefore introduced as a theme. Through the discernment of the latter, the peasants' revolution in Act V becomes unnecessary and is hence robbed of its legitimacy. Though the motif therefore appears to have received more penetrating treatment, the change is merely relative.

A further dramatic fragment about the Revolution, *Das Mädchen von Oberkirch* (1795–96), falls into the period following his association with Schiller. This was already the time of the planned trilogy on the Revolution, that progressed only to the extent of the one lifeless piece *Die natürliche Tochter* (1803). Under Schiller's influence at that time the plans were expressly directed towards tragedies. It seems a characteristic feature of Goethe that he should not only make a fresh start on several occasions, but that in turning from genre to genre he should become more serious and more comprehensive each and every time. Only the first two acts of *Das Mädchen von Oberkirch* were completed. This time it did not deal with background and long-term effects resulting from the theme of revolution, but with the events in revolutionary France itself. For the first time they affect the very heart of the old aristocratic class. The Revolution becomes therefore a dangerous opponent. The political attitude of the young Baron and his wooing of a child – a distinguished child incidentally – of the people point to Goethe's attempt to build a bridge from the old to the new. The motivation of the love of the Baron for Marie that transgresses class and rank is spelt out clearly enough here:

M

Und warum? weil sie alle Tugenden besitzt, die uns anderen . . .
eine Revolution . . . wünschen ließen.[8]

Yet this so to speak organic process of evolution proceeds from
individuality to individuality. 'The monstrous tyrant, the mob, or
rather this or that tyrant who leads and directs the monster' does
not gain in legitimacy in the process. This seems the real reason
why the 'political drama' remained but a fragment. The Neptune-
organic factor was not to be reconciled with the Vulcanic-
destructive urge ('the masses want to destroy'). For then in
accordance with Goethe's plan Marie, the beloved child of the
people, would have to have died violently at the hands of the
people, when she refused to represent the goddess of Reason at
the State celebration in the Minster at Strassburg. Indeed Goethe did
venture further and further into the intrinsic problems of the theme
of revolution, yet humanity and violence were not to be reconciled.
Deciding against the new tyranny meant, now in genuine tragic
form, deciding one's own downfall. We may see Goethe's later
respect for Napoleon being based in the final analysis on the fact
that he viewed the Emperor's historical role in the elimination of
this alternative and hence in the reimposition of the human
element, in the organic principle and not the eruptive.

The inability to reconcile revolution and evolution seems once
again manifested in the second drafted tragedy *Die natürliche
Tochter*. The trilogy was to have been the zenith of Goethe's
dramatic endeavours on the theme of revolution. The laborious
task had stretched over almost five years (1799–1803). But once
more Goethe downed his pen before he was able to bring the
tragic plot of an individual's fate to a genuine dramatisation of
historical forces. For the Eugenie-drama, stimulated by the
memoirs of an illegitimate Bourbon lady (1798), provided a personal background, but not the confrontation of the forces of the
great Revolution itself. The court intrigue, going back to the
seventies, in which, for reasons of inheritance and politics, the
illegitimate daughter of the Duchess of Mazarin was abducted
immediately prior to her legitimization by the King and forced
into a bourgeois marriage, was after all simply a family feud and
only linked with the theme of revolution in a very general socio-

---

[8] And why? Because she possesses all the virtues which make us others
wish for a revolution.

critical fashion, no more even than the Cagliostro theme. Corresponding to this cautious contemporisation was the formal side of Goethe's drama, which must be termed classicistic rather than classical. Here too we again meet the symbolic stylisation: King, Duke, priest, governess appear unnamed as representatives of classes and professions. And even in the case of the central figure who could not very well be cloaked in anonymity, the historical name of Stephanie was changed into the name Eugenie (the well-born), symbolically parodying the theme contrary to the original draft. The consequence of this stylisation is a phantom-like character that caused Madame de Staël, who was accustomed to stylisation and pathos, to pass judgement on the drama to the effect, not without reason, that it created a 'noble ennui'. Indeed, what is lacking is a lively sense of immediate history which should in fact have increased from play to play in the trilogy, as Goethe's own plan makes only too clear. After the forced marriage of his heroine to the Justice of the Peace Goethe had wanted to depict the Rütli-oath[9] of the three pro-revolutionary classes (solicitors, soldiers, craftsmen) and let it founder on the rock of general selfishness. Through this selfishness the Justice too was to have compromised himself, in a personal tragic way at the very moment when through his intellectual superiority he wins Eugenie's affection hitherto denied him. The Goethean picture of history would therefore here be: dissolution of an old world quite rightly going to rack and ruin in favour of a new world which however, in its turn, is also corrupt. One of the drafts expresses this view quite clearly. After a pitiless depiction of absolute despotism with the inevitable consequence of 'ferment from below', the key passage continues:

Aufgelöste Bande. Der letzten Form. Die Masse wird absolut. Vertreibt die Schwankenden. Erdrückt die Widerstrebenden. Erniedrigt das Hohe. Erhöhet das Niedrige. Um es wieder zu erniedrigen.[10]

---

[9] A reference to the central scene in Schiller's *Wilhelm Tell* where representatives of the Swiss people meet to swear an oath of allegiance in defence of their human rights. (*Translator's note*)

[10] Dissolved ties. The form of the last stage. The mob becomes absolute. Drives out the vacillating. Crushes those resisting. Debases the noble. Elevates the vulgar. In order to debase it in turn.

The shadow of a deep senselessness of the historical process becomes manifest in the background. Only the ethos of the Classicist can preserve Goethe from nihilistic resignation. And this occurs too in the famous couplet in the same draft, which has a Schillerian ring to it:

> Nach seinem Sinne leben ist gemein,
> Der Edle strebt nach Ordnung und Gesetz.[11]

As in the dramatic work, so too in verse and prose epics Goethe's output following his return from Italy is widely stamped by the intrinsic confrontation with the theme of evolution and revolution. Already in 1792 there emerged the fragments of a travelogue novel, *Die Reise der Söhne Megaprazons*. The island of the Monachomanes (France) disintegrates and its pieces carry into the ocean the catastrophic events brought about by the Revolution, the consequences of its bogus principle of electoral majority and freedom of speech which leads to the chaos of conflicting opinions:

> Ein wilder Schwindel ergriff die Brüder, von ihrer Sanftmut und Verträglichkeit erschien keine Spur mehr in ihrem Betragen . . .[12]

Die Reise would have become an anti-revolutionary novel on the 'fever of the age' with clear reference to the Vulcanic character of the revolutionary historical event. The basic principle underlying the work is further illustrated in the image of the quarrel of the sons as a medical crisis and attack of madness. Shades here of Rabelais and Thomas More!

Unequivocal escapism – escape from a history seen merely as a threat – is seen too in the *Unterhaltungen deutscher Ausgewanderten*, published in 1795 in the *Horen*. In terms of the form they already belong – like the formal model, the *Decamerone* – to that literature which seeks either to overcome the pressure of contemporary historical events or to resolve it by means of diversion, entertainment, cheerfulness, in the playfulness of literary imagination. And that attitude prevails far beyond this particular work. Thus in the *Campagne in Frankreich* (*Campaign in France*) Goethe

[11] Living one's own way is common.
     The noble person strives after law and order.
[12] A wild dizziness seized the brothers and there was no longer any trace of their cheerful temper and conciliatory spirit in their behaviour.

has expressly described the link between his reluctant involvement in the battles of the year 1793 and his work on *Reineke Fuchs*:

> So war es nun wirklich erheiternd, in den Hof- und Regenten-spiegel zu blicken: denn wenn auch hier das Menschenge-schlecht sich in seiner ungeheuchelten Tierheit ganz natürlich vorträgt, so geht doch alles, wo nicht musterhaft, doch heiter zu . . .[13]

'The unfeigned brutishness', with which the campaigner unwillingly came into daily contact, emerges transfigured in the humour of the old fable and is thereby made tolerable. In Goethe's *Unterhal-tungen* on the other hand this sovereignty has not yet been attained. It is sharp and politically unequivocal. The framework motif is provided by the 'noble' family which emigrates across the Rhine to Germany 'in order to escape the oppressions with which all the distinguished persons were threatened, for whom it was made a crime to remember their fathers with joy and hon-our . . .' That is decidedly aristocratic or, on the other hand, bourgeois-conservative. Freedom in the sense of the Revolution is talked of in terms of a 'dazzling beauty' that 'seduces' men. At the same time Goethe's disposition in this appears Classical in the sense of a rejection of the Revolution as being an expression of passion and lack of humanity.

> . . . er hatte die Willkür der Nation, die nur vom Gesetz sprach, kennengelernt und den Unterdrückungsgeist derer, die das Wort Freiheit immer im Munde führten.[14]

Thus Goethe compiles the experiences of the old Privy Councillor who supports the emigrants. The consequence of the more or less natural consensus among the circle is the banning of all discus-sion of the politics of the day. From the dangerously formless, the intentional move is to the most formal mode of expression – the cultivated conversation through the *Novelle*. As once in the

[13] And so it was now really exhilarating to look into the mirror of courts and rulers, for even if here the human race presents itself quite naturally in its unfeigned brutishness, everything still goes on, if not in exemplary fashion, nevertheless serenely.
[14] He had got to know the arbitrariness of the nation which spoke only of the law, and the spirit of oppression of those who always had the word free-dom on their lips.

Decamerone, having recourse to this genre amounted therefore to a form of escapism. The motivation and definition of this genre that was still hardly used at all in Germany and then only in a qualified way, prove to be strongly sociological: the stories that are told are based on the social function of 'news'. And here the poet himself appears in the first instance not as a subjective genius, but as an exponent of the social niveau (as against the *Werther*-period).

Fragen Sie sich selbst und fragen Sie viele andere: was gibt einer Begebenheit den Reiz? Nicht ihre Wichtigkeit, nicht der Einfluß, den sie hat, sondern die Neuheit. Nur das Neue scheint gewöhnlich wichtig, weil es ohne Zusammenhang Verwunderung erregt und unsre Einbildungskraft einen Augenblick in Bewegung setzt, unser Gefühl nur leicht berührt und unsern Verstand völlig in Ruhe läßt.[15]

The *Novelle* is defined as a genre both of tension and repose, the application of the play instinct in humans, and in essence even the later *Falke* of Paul Heyse, the *one* motif, is therein contained under the concept of the 'moment'. With reference to the French Revolution, the *Novelle* signifies 'entertainment' as a release from the pressure of a barbaric present, and perhaps too a future, for *one* magic moment. It is a consciously aristocratic solution:

. . . aber lassen Sie uns wenigstens an der Form sehen, daß wir in guter Gesellschaft sind. Geben Sie uns zum Anfang eine Geschichte von wenig Personen und Begebenheiten, die gut erfunden und gedacht ist, wahr, natürlich und nicht gemein, so viel Handlung als unentbehrlich und so viel Gesinnung als nötig, die nicht still steht, sich nicht auf *einem* Flecke zu langsam bewegt, sich aber auch nicht übereilt, in der die Menschen erscheinen, wie man sie gern mag, nicht vollkommen, aber gut, nicht außerordentlich, aber interessant und liebenswürdig. Ihre Geschichte sei unterhaltend, solange wir sie hören,

[15] Ask yourself and ask many others: what is it that gives an event its charm? Not its importance, not the influence that it has, but the novelty. Only the novel generally appears important, because devoid of any context it arouses astonishment and stirs our power of imagination for a second, only gently touches our emotions and leaves our understanding completely undisturbed.

befriedigend, wenn sie zu Ende ist, und hinterlasse uns einen stillen Reiz, weiter nachzudenken.[16]

In this guise, therefore, the *Novelle* appeared in Germany as a literary genre *à la* Boccaccio. It was an accentuatedly cultivated prose epic genre, the definition of which was far removed from the time of *Werther*. The basis was political; for both public and storyteller were seen as anti-revolutionary, consciously classically aristocratic. How far anecdote and *Novelle* really differ here when considered in the stricter sense which the Romantics and the nineteenth century gave to them, must remain an open question. Both genres could in fact be an illustration of the supernatural. The series of stories in the *Unterhaltungen* takes that line in particular. The tale of the Neapolitan singer and the remarkable posthumous jealousy of her deceased lover is followed by another, but hardly more than anecdotal attestation to the supernatural: the report of the poltergeist that could be disciplined by threats, and after that the tale taken from the historical memoirs of the Marshal Bassompierre, of the plague and the night of love that Bassompierre spent with the unknown shopkeeper's wife, which Hofmannsthal was to refashion a century later (probably because here the supernatural and the spine-chilling are strangely identical with what is possible). The procurator's tale adapted from the *cento novelle antiche* and originally considered by Goethe to be a piece by Boccaccio corresponds most readily to the definition of the *Novelle*. It is the old stock theme of the rich man who marries in his old age; worrying about his young wife remaining at home all alone, he grants her with remarkable liberality a lover whilst he is absent, provided that he is no loathsome youngster but is really worthy of her. This superior condition imposed in making allowances for the demands of nature leads in fact to nothing reprehensible occurring at all.

[16] . . . but let us at least see by the form that we are in good company. To start with, give us a story involving few people and few events, which is well invented and thought out, true, natural and not vulgar, as much action as is indispensable and as much contemplation as is necessary, which is not static, does not mark time on *one* spot too slowly, but does not go too quickly either, in which people appear as one likes them, not perfect but good, not extraordinary but interesting and amiable. Your tale should be entertaining for as long as we hear it, satisfying when it is finished, and should leave us with a quiet inducement to meditate further.

The conclusion to the *Unterhaltungen* is provided by the tale of Ferdinand, which renounces all supernatural and spine-chilling elements. It is the story of a young man from a respectable merchant family who, led astray by the extravagant courting of his would-be bride, secretly taps his father's cash-box, but at the end pulls himself together off his own bat, makes good the loss, sends the demanding bride away and instead brings home a simple, hard-working girl. It is more a moral family portrait in narrative form after the model of the contemporary theatre.

In contrast to the tales which make it seem that the French Revolution had never occurred and yet cannot divorce themselves from it, the final piece belongs to another genre: *Das Märchen* is by no means apolitical, though one might well expect that here. In the pure play of fantasy in the *Märchen* however, Goethe takes up and ensures for himself a symbolic position *vis-à-vis* revolutionary change as a historical phenomenon. There have been countless attempts at interpreting this composite work of art and the number should not be augmented here. At all events the dream of a Utopia is fashioned in the *Märchen* too. This was not to be influenced by the concept of violence expressly embodied in the bronze king among the three statues. The newly dawning kingdom (with its *leitmotif* 'the time has come') was rather to be aligned with the three reawakened forces. According to the text the golden and the silver king signify wisdom and splendour (i.e. content and form). Only with them together can the bronze king, violence, enter the new Age. But he can only be a guarantor of the eternally necessary order, no longer a tyrant. The kingdom that emerges is a kingdom of change, yet visibly of metamorphosis and not Vulcanic revolution. In the symbol of the *r*eawakened kings the flashback to historical continuity prevails and the action of the snake which initiates the new kingdom is symbolically intended self-sacrifice – an act of love, not of violence. Its symbol is the bridge, an evolutionary and not a revolutionary symbol. Further Goethe could not and would not go in the assimilation of this subject that moved him so passionately. The Humanist and Classicist within him would not permit it.

In the *Vier Jahreszeiten*, a *parergon* to the *Xenien* and printed with them in Schiller's *Musenalmanach* of 1797, this humanistic-classical basis of Goethe's viewpoint finds expression in a piece which originally bore the title 'Revolutions' (No. 62):

Franztum drängt in diesen verworrenen Tagen, wie ehmals
Luthertum es getan, ruhige Bildung zurück.[17]

This is undisguised polemics that the symbolism of the *Märchen*
expresses: civilisation is peaceful, not revolutionary and Vulcanic
as the Reformation had been. There are many attestations of this
viewpoint in the Goethe of the nineties – already in the *Venetiani-sche Epigramme*, in the *Xenien*, in the epigrammatic secondary
stream of the *Weissagungen des Bakis*. Here we find the bitter
polemic against Klopstock's enthusiasm for the Revolution (No.
11):

Einen seh ich! Er sitzt und harfeniert der Verwüstung;
Aber der reißende Strom nimmt auch die Lieder hinweg.[18]

However sheer aristocratic arrogance lies behind epigrams like
Number 26, in which all kinds of lower forms of existence, para-sites and rodents, represent the mob, or Number 53 of the
Venetianische Epigramme, which is expressed in direct and current
political terms:

Frankreichs traurig Geschick, die Großen mögen's bedenken!
Aber bedenken fürwahr sollen es Kleine noch mehr.
Große gingen zugrunde: doch wer beschützte die Menge
Gegen die Menge? Da war Menge der Menge Tyrann.[19]

That Goethe's classical verse epics like the *Unterhaltungen* are
also literary expressions bordering on or held against the back-cloth of that Vulcanic period, does not emerge so obviously from
them in fact as from the politically orientated epigrams. Yet in-deed they at least share the polished, refined, High-Classical dac-tylic form. And the remoteness of their thematics from the con-temporary scene remains but an optical illusion, as the reference
to *Reineke Fuchs* showed. *Hermann und Dorothea*, the continu-ation of the idyllic elegiac poetry, and finally the High-Classical

[17] Gallicism, as Lutheranism had formerly done, represses peaceful civil-isation in these days of confusion.

[18] One I see! He sits and plays the harp to destruction;
But the impetuous current drowns even the songs.

[19] France's tragic destiny, let the Great reflect on it!
But the insignificant should in fact reflect on it still more.
Great men perished: but who protected the crowd
Against the crowd? There the crowd was tyrant of the crowd.

attempt to follow Homer in *Achilleis* are not to be divorced from the events of the day. It is no mere chance that this series of works is moreover of decisive importance in the history of the assimilation of classical verse by Goethe. The process involved in the genesis of these works, wherein he made use of the advice offered by Herder, Knebel, Schiller, Voss, August Wilhelm Schlegel in turn and also of literature on metrics like the *Elementa metricae* of Hermann, may be interpreted as a conscious return to the classical, to the traditional and non-revolutionary. The unity of solace and Classical self-knowledge in the work on the 'profane world bible' *Reineke Fuchs* had been recorded by Goethe himself in the *Annalen* for 1793, in the same context moreover as the continuation of the *Farbenlehre*. The background situation is that of the Campaign in France, in the midst of the 'symbols of contemporaneous world history' and amongst which Goethe for his part 'clung to these studies as to a plank in a shipwreck':

> Denn ich hatte nun zwei Jahre unmittelbar und persönlich das fürchterliche Zusammenbrechen aller Verhältnisse erlebt.[20]

The problems of form confronting the Classicist, natural science, personally experienced history, the old allegorical beast epic used in an attempt to deal with them on the literary level – Goethe saw them expressly as one and the same thing.

The Classicist's resigned view of the world and the natural scientist's sceptical one determine in the background the work on the 'mirror held up to courts and rulers' in *Reineke Fuchs* (1794). Goethe himself was conscious that the hexameter form signified an experiment. One can indeed not use 'Domino placebo' or 'Kardinal' as openers, so to speak, for hexameters. Yet for all that, Goethe had on his side both Schiller's and Herder's enthusiastic judgement on the Homeric-naïve element in the work. And with reason: for Flemish-like rough and ready situations and robust figures, home-truths occasionally bordering on obscene quips were made possible and legitimised for literary purposes through the Homeric epic form.

Between *Reineke Fuchs* and the expressly idyllic *Hermann und Dorothea* came Goethe's association with Schiller. This is in fact observable in the work itself. Not only because it originated under

---

[20] For I had now experienced for two years directly and personally the terrible breakdown of all conditions of life.

Schiller's eye, so to speak, in Jena in a week in September 1796
(and the conclusion of the work followed then in the autumn of
1797 under the same circumstances), but because Schiller's theory
of the 'naïve' lies behind it. Goethe latches this theme on to a
historical event from the year 1731, an episode from the history
of the Protestant emigrants from Salzburg. But he relates it to the
context of the *Unterhaltungen* and thus to the contemporary universal significance of the Revolution. He thereby achieves the
physical contemporaneity of the citizens of the peaceful little
town on the German side of the Rhine who are unaffected by
events as well as the actuality of the sufferings of the refugees.
Immediate historicity and High-Classical stylisation exemplify
the merit of this idyll. Nine cantos after the number of the Muses
and superscribed with their names cushion the all-pervading
immediacy of the subject in masterly style. Goethe's letter to
Johann Heinrich Meyer dates the action very specifically to August 1796, and then continues:

> Ich habe das rein Menschliche der Existenz einer kleinen
> deutschen Stadt in dem epischen Tiegel von seinen Schlacken
> abzuscheiden gesucht und zugleich die großen Bewegungen und
> Veränderungen des Welttheaters aus einem kleinen Spiegel
> zurückzuwerfen getrachtet.[21]

Only this is a classical idyll, more so than Voss's *Luise*: it is
historical – not peaceful existence in isolation which ignores the evil
age – a deceptive security of life amidst the gleam of the flaming
torches across the river. In *Reineke Fuchs* there was still a kind of
desperate irony of the all-too-human at work. In *Hermann und
Dorothea* however, we notice *àpropos* the human element the influence of Schillerian idealism – an influence now dating back
more than three years. Yet Goethe now recognises too the limits
of the human existence. This finds shattering expression in
Dorothea's recollection of her first fiancé being engulfed in the
whirlpool of the Revolution:

> Lebe glücklich, sagt' er. Ich gehe; denn alles bewegt sich
> Jetzt auf Erden einmal, es scheint sich alles zu trennen.

[21] I have sought to separate in the epic crucible the purely human aspect of
life in a small German town from its dross and at the same time endeavoured to reflect the great movements and changes in the universal
theatre in miniature.

Grundgesetze lösen sich auf der festesten Staaten,
Und es löst der Besitz sich los vom alten Besitzer,
Freund sich los von Freund: so löst sich Liebe von Liebe.
. . . Uns gehört der Boden nicht mehr, es wandern die Schätze;
Gold und Silber schmilzt aus den alten heiligen Formen;
Alles regt sich, als wollte die Welt, die gestaltete, rückwärts
Lösen in Chaos und Nacht sich auf und neu sich gestalten.[22]

Never had Goethe faced up to the picture of human historicity from the standpoint of a revolutionary so positively as here. And just as he makes the revolutionary into an evolutionary morphologist, correspondingly he ventures to treat the idyllic bourgeoisie not only as representing order against chaos, but also to circumscribe it in terms of its narrowness, its shallowness, its torpidity. Hermann, the child of this bourgeois world, needs Dorothea in order to sustain his enthusiasm. For without doubt her experience signifies an element of unrest for the firmly established world of the family, of the community, of order, of morality and of sound hard work. The idyll is thereby stripped of its all too easy tendency towards escapism. It becomes historical, and indeed, by means of contact with another historical law, for which the subject of revolution is legitimised by Goethe. Never before had he ventured forth in so far-reaching and, above all, superior and relaxed a manner.

The rapid and happy success of *Hermann und Dorothea* owed, according to Goethe's own view, much to his study of F. A. Wolf's *Prolegomena ad Homerum*. The great philologist in nearby Halle had early on anticipated for Homeric criticism what Lachmann, following in his footsteps, did too for the *Nibelungenlied* at the time of the Romantics. Wolf had ignored the personage of the poet Homer and declared the epics that were attributed to his name to be a collection of songs by various hands. Fascinated by this thesis, the Classical Goethe then extolled it as an excellent idea to be but a 'Homerid' too. As against the 'Storm and Stress'

[22] Farewell, he said, I'm going; for everything is now in motion on earth. Everything seems to be coming apart. Basic laws of the most stable States are being broken, and possessions are being taken from the original owners, friend is separated from friend: and thus love is dissolved from love . . . The very ground belongs to us no longer, treasures change hands; gold and silver are being melted from the original sacred forms; Everything is astir as if the world, the established world, wanted to turn back the clock into chaos and night and fashion itself anew.

with its enthusiasm for the one Homer, this acceptance was an act of resignation. But resignation meant too in this case wanting the possible instead of the unattainable. Such a decision seemed more appropriate to the weaker powers of modern man. Only this inner transformation made possible Goethe's attempt to be a 'Homerid' in *Achilleis*. Two cantos compressed into one had their genesis in the spring of 1799, yet the plan dated back to the year in which *Hermann und Dorothea* was conceived. The conception was linked with the definition of the very essence of the epic and the dramatic that was jointly sought after by Goethe and Schiller, with the concern for the limitations of the genres at a time when the Early Romantics were just beginning to loosen these distinctions. Just as *Nausikaa* was intended to plug, in dramatic terms, a 'gap' in the *Odyssey*, so likewise in *Achilleis* something which had been left out of the Homeric songs in Wolf's opinion, namely the fate of Achilles from the death of Patroclus up to his own death, was to be rectified in a separate classical epic. Goethe's plan, as formulated to Riemer, was as follows:

Achill weiß, daß er sterben muß, verliebt sich aber in die Polyxena und vergißt sein Schicksal rein darüber, nach der Tollheit seiner Natur.[23]

There were some 650 lines in all: these covered the depiction of the gods' decision on the imminent death of Achilles and his conversation of comfort with Athene, who afterwards approaches him in the form of his friend Antilochus. Yet the fact that even this poetry stamped with myth remote in time can be linked with the contemporary myth of revolution, is shown by Athene's speech to the gods:

Ach! und daß er sich nicht, der edle Jüngling, zum Manne
Bilden soll! Ein fürstlicher Mann ist so nötig auf Erden,
Daß die jüngere Wut, des wilden Zerstörens Begierde
Sich als mächtiger Sinn, als schaffender, endlich beweise,
Der die Ordnung bestimmt, nach welcher sich Tausende richten.

[23] Achilles knows that he must die, but he falls in love with Polyxena and completely forgets his own fate in the process, in accordance with the extravagance of his nature.

Nicht mehr gleicht der Vollendete dann dem stürmenden
   Ares.
Dem die Schlacht nur genügt, die männertötende! Nein, er
Gleicht dem Kroniden selbst, von dem ausgehet die
   Wohlfahrt.
Städte zerstört er nicht mehr, er baut sie: fernem
   Gestade
Führt er den Überfluß der Bürger zu; Küsten und Syrten
Wimmeln von neuem Volk, des Raums und der Nahrung
   begierig.[24]

A comparison of this hexameter style with the almost contemporaneous one of *Hermann und Dorothea* could prove informative.
Voss's formal emphasis is repressed in *Achilleis*, the pathos is more
uniform and lofty than in Voss's Homer translation. Admittedly,
whether it would have continued to be tolerable in a completed
epic must remain an open question.

Goethe's classical hexameters can be found not only in the
more grandly planned epics and idylls, but also in the less ambitious elegies of the nineties which appeared in Schiller's *Musenalmanach* in the years 1796 to 1799. They represent the stylised
continuation of the *Römische Elegien*, whilst also being related
to *Hermann und Dorothea* through strong idyllic elements. The
first piece, *Alexis und Dora*, originated in fact in the same year
as the classical idyll, namely in the May of 1796; Schiller was
enchanted by its 'simplicity', its 'profound depth of sensitivity'.
Indeed, the stylistic design is that of the 'naïve' in the Winckelmannian and Schillerian sense of the word. The temple walk of the
lovers or the parting gift of the finest fruits to Alexis may be interpreted in this light. The fact that the Classicists themselves did not
perceive the occasionally almost Klopstock-like sentimentality is

---

[24] Alas, that he, the noble youth, shall not mature to manhood! A princely
man is so necessary on earth, that the more youthful rage, the eager desire
for wild destruction may finally show itself as a powerful mind, a creative
mind, which determines the order according to which thousands direct their
steps. No longer then does the accomplished man resemble the impetuous
Ares, for whom only battle suffices, battle the killer of men! No, he resembles a true son of Kronos himself, from whom well-being proceeds. He
no longer destroys cities, he builds them: to distant shores he leads the
overflow of citizens; coasts and sandy bays teem with new people eager for
space and nourishment.

perhaps understandable (as elsewhere too). Lines like those in the farewell scene when the young sailor has to leave his bride behind alone, are however truly sentimental (even sentimentalising):

> ... Da floß
> Häufig die Träne vom Aug' mir herab, du weintest, ich weinte,
> Und für Jammer und Glück schien uns die Welt zu vergehn.[25]

And sentimental too is the theme of jealousy at the close, which incidentally Schiller immediately criticised as an insufficiently motivated interruption. Schiller's objection was still vexing Goethe in 1825 (*Gespräche mit Eckermann*, 25 December). The individuality of the two friends found paradigmatic attestation here: the idealist Schiller wanted the idyll 'naïve' in terms of pureness of style; the realist Goethe defended the 'sentimental' on psychological grounds. The next of these 'Elegies Book Two', *Der neue Pausias und sein Blumenmädchen* (1797), becomes a regular interchange of 'He' and 'She' strophes, each of which numbers only one distich. The form leaves one cold, because it produces an artificial impression. The distichs, isolated as they are, sometimes encroach upon the epigrammatic form, nearer to the *Xenie* than to the style of an elegy.

However the finest and most impressive of these elegies is undoubtedly *Euphrosyne* (1797–98), the splendid elegiac lament over the death of Christiane Neumann, the Mignon-like child actress, whose development Goethe had passionately promoted since he had encountered her as a thirteen-year-old. The human shock here produces a tone akin to Hölderlin's *Heimkehr*:

> Auch von des höchsten Gebirgs beeisten zackigen Gipfeln
> Schwindet Purpur und Glanz scheidender Sonne hinweg.
> Lange verhüllt schon Nacht das Tal und die Pfade des Wandrers,
> Der, am tosenden Strom, auf zu der Hütte sich sehnt.[26]

---

[25] ... Then the tears flowed copiously from my eyes, you wept, I wept, and the world seemed to us to dissolve in woe and happiness.

[26] Even from the highest mountains' frozen jagged peaks the crimson and splendour of the departing sun disappears. For a long time already night has enveloped the valley and the paths of the wanderer who, by the roaring current, longs for the sanctuary of the cottage.

Even in its conclusion this elegy seems to be one of the most convincing things fashioned by Goethe in his High-Classical period. The very subject, the vision of the dead friend in the cloud as she appeared in her last role (albeit graphic rather than plastic), is allegorically classical through and through. Still more so is the conclusion, the result of the closest affinity to Schiller's *Nänie*, the last lines of which coincide in essence with the end of *Euphrosyne*:

> Laß nicht ungerühmt mich zu den Schatten hinabgehn!
>   Nur die Muse gewährt einiges Leben dem Tod.
> Denn gestaltlos schweben umher in Persephoneias
>   Reiche, massenweis, Schatten vom Namen getrennt;
> Wen der Dichter aber gerühmt, der wandelt, gestaltet,
>   Einzeln . . .[27]

Seen in conservative and aristocratic terms, only the relative deferment of death through the extolling of poetry, the surviving form, here remains of the theme of revolution or preservation. It is a would-be aesthetic and hence classicistic solace, which already led to Goethe and Schiller raising themselves and each other above their own stature. This is true too of the language which, with its vocabulary ranging from 'significant, gratifying, pleasing, comfortable, respectable, honest, worthy, sound, witty, serene' to 'develop, cultivate' and 'structure, law, moderation', does not cover the Vulcanic aspect at all. The same holds good even for the real elegy of passion amongst these pieces, *Amyntas* (1797). It does however bring the counter-complaint:

> Aber, ach! das Wasser entstürzt der Steile des Felsens
>   Rasch, und die Welle des Bachs halten Gesänge nicht auf.
> . . . Und so spricht mir rings die Natur: Auch du bist, Amyntas,
>   Unter das strenge Gesetz ehrner Gewalten gebeugt.[28]

[27] Let me not descend to the Shades uncelebrated! Only the Muse affords some life to Death. For shapelessly Shades divested of names hover around in Persephoneia's kingdom in large numbers; he, however, whom the poet extols, wanders, created as an individual.

[28] But, alas! the water plunges rapidly down the steep rock, and the ripple of the stream is not arrested by poems . . . And thus nature all round speaks to me: And you too, Amyntas, are subject to the harsh law of immutable forces.

Even where elemental force is reintegrated, as Goethe the realist wanted, it is subjected to the law (nature or fate). And
we already hear too pre-Romantic Epimetheus-sounds in the
theme of excessive indulgence of lovers who in their enjoyment do
not consider the requirements of their personal lives. That is
not Schillerian Classical ethics. It is the integration of excess into
the universal concept even of Goethe the Classicist; this was a
realistic element rooted within him, as *Pandora*, *Selige Sehnsucht*
and the Marienbad *Elegie* were later to confirm. It was this very
urge to venture even to the point of self-sacrifice that raised
Goethe above Winckelmann, Herder and even Schiller in this
High-Classical period. The preponderance of Neptunism was thereby tempered, and the possibility of mistaking the idea of an
organic development for the tempered moderation of Enlightenment, though not excluded, was nevertheless reduced.

Pure lyric poetry rather receded into the background in the
years of High Classicism as far as Goethe's literary output was
concerned; in this he differed from Schiller. His chief form of
poetic expression was the epic lyric verse of elegies and ballads
or the satiric, programmatic utterances in didactic and epigrammatic verse. Lyric poetry in the narrower sense of the term
originating between his return from Italy and Schiller's death
flowed in a weaker trickle. Even so poems of high merit can be
found such as *Meeresstille* and *Glückliche Fahrt* (both about 1795),
twin poems in both of whose short forms there is a concentration of tranquillity and movement, systole and diastole. Rhythmically speaking, *Nähe des Geliebten* has a similarly enthralling
effect; the poem is a contrafacture to a strophic model of Friederike Brun,[29] which in fact surpassed her average standard.

In addition however, the most significant material is characteristically found in the philosophical lyric verse – Schiller's genre
and home territory, so to speak. One of these pieces, *Dauer im
Wechsel* (1803) presents in its own style Goethe's personal
Classical problems together with those of his friend: transitoriness
of Nature and of Man: – 'alas, you will never swim a second time
in the same river'. In thought the end of the poem is close to
Schiller with its stress on oneness into which beginning and end
must contract. Only Art creates immortality:

[29] A very minor lyric poet (1765–1835). (*Translator's note*)

Danke, daß die Gunst der Musen
Unvergängliches verheißt,
Den Gehalt in deinem Busen
Und die Form in deinem Geist.[30]

The other, probably somewhat earlier (1802?) philosophical poem *Weltseele* already presupposes the confrontation with the Romantics, above all with Schelling. It is therefore natural philosophy in the narrow sense, an orgy of realities which arise beyond time and space, organology transfused into something hymnic, geo- and anthropognosticism, a return to the pantheistic vitalism of his early period in the sense of the line 'And every speck of dust is alive' or of the last line 'From the Universe back to the Universe'. Schiller would not have produced such poems on the growth of the colossal cosmos and the first insignificant pair of human beings in it in but a few strophes. Only the Neptunist Goethe, the pupil of Herder, could see and give poetic form to the macro- and microcosm in this way.

[30] Give thanks that the favour of the muses promises what is imperishable – the import in your breast and the form in your spirit.

25 Schiller's Classical Dramas

History, aesthetics, ballad and philosophical poetry, the critical epigrammatic verse of the *Xenien* conceived jointly with Goethe, his publishing activities: all this had fully occupied Schiller since his entry into the Weimar circle. Since *Don Carlos*, therefore, there had been no further dramatic writings on his part. And not without reason. The subjectivity still prevailing in *Don Carlos*, its unclassical essence, and hence too its different stylistic bent must have been evident to the Classical Schiller. What in the meantime had emerged as a problem of human historicity to Schiller the philosopher had to leave its mark in a new type of drama too. This had to be neither predominantly social criticism as in *Die Räuber* and *Luise Millerin*, nor simply philosophical programmatic pieces like *Don Carlos*.

The *Wallenstein*-trilogy was the first slowly elaborated result of Schiller's dramatic work from a Classical standpoint. His starting point was his involvement in that work of art which belonged to the realm of historiography, his *Geschichte des Dreißigjährigen Krieges*. At that time, in the summer of 1791, Schiller got to know too the historical places in Bohemia where Wallenstein's fate had been decided. But that merely formed part of the background which was then supplanted by his Kantian experience. The first drafts were only to come three years later. Then the prose stage developed, that too being a sign of the Classical desire for objectivisation. Also characteristic was the awareness of responsibility for an overall plan, and the new relationship to the subject-matter. Earlier, Schiller had dramatised subjects which inspired him. Now responsible aesthetic insight distanced him from his material, which he approached with strict calculation and mature understanding. Inevitably the weaknesses of the dramatic works of his youth had to impress themselves on him now that he had dis-

covered a new feeling for style and taste. An added factor was the
self-interpretation of his individuality as a predominantly sentimental poet, the result of his meditative self-consciousness in
comparison with Goethe. The conclusion of the essay *Über
naïve und sentimentalische Dichtung* advanced, however, the ideal
demand for a synthesis of both these components. So from self-
limitation and self-consciousness grew now the ambition to provide for himself personally the proof of this synthesis, which meant
that as a sentimental poet, he aimed to present realistic subject
matter in such a way that a dramatic work of Classical universality
should emerge. Thus it was that the plan for *Wallenstein* developed
into the phase of actual elaboration and completion only from
1796 on through a process of sharp self-reflection. A characteristic of this phase, according to the communications with Körner
above all, was now a conscious approach on the part of the poet
towards his subject matter on the basis of a 'disinterested pleasure'
derived from Kantian objectivity. The subject matter leaves him
ostensibly cold and indifferent: the only enthusiasm left to the
artist is that experienced in his work on it. And it was with this
very attitude that the Wallenstein theme was energetically taken
up as the first work – despite the plan for *Die Malteser*. The
Wallenstein-conception of 1796 refers therefore more to a
questionable greatness of the hero, which as a mixture of good and
evil had by its very nature a more repulsive than sympathetic
effect, but which could become sublime greatness through its inherent tragic nature. To develop this however from the fullness
of material on which Schiller the historian had conscientiously
worked proved difficult. To make Wallenstein's end appear to be
a consequence of his weakness of character did not produce
tragedy in itself. This insight Schiller acquired about the turn of
the year 1796–7. The reading of Shakespeare and Sophocles and
the confrontation with Goethe over epic and dramatic poetry
decisively influenced the new shift from the motif of character
to that of fate. As a result the Prologue was freed perforce from
the mass of material, and subsequently from five acts overloaded
with material there emerged ten acts ready for the stage, that is
just two plays, and which, together with the Prologue, form the
trilogy. At the same time in place of prose there now was verse,
whereby the all too accentuated realistic ambition was cast into the
mould of universal literature under the influence of Goethe and

the Early Romantics and thus at the same time idealised in the classical sense. This too was true of the *Knittelvers* in which the Prologue now appeared as *Wallensteins Lager* (*Wallenstein's Camp*). And the question of balance caused a further vacillation on Schiller's part with regard to the demarcation lines to be drawn between *Die Piccolomini* (*The Piccolomini*) and *Wallensteins Tod* (*Wallenstein's Death*). In the October of 1798 the first part was ready for the stage; at the beginning of 1799 *Die Piccolomini* and in the Spring, *Wallensteins Tod*.

The meaning of *Wallensteins Lager* extends beyond the nature of a mere exposition for the two following five-act plays. First of all it excludes the unhistorical constructed manner of *Don Carlos*. Through its very objectivity and its realistic form, *Wallensteins Lager* is both a limitation of the later pathos as well as its precondition, because it includes the development of the historical forces with their trend towards the pathetic. For here is presented – intrinsically – the play of forces which are driven, and – excentrally – the play of forces which motivate. In this way Schiller gives import from the outset to the question 'What is the driving force and what or who is being driven?' He poses the historical question – carefully without providing an answer – which the Prologue written for the first performance of *Wallensteins Lager* relates to the hero:

> Von der Parteien Gunst und Haß verwirrt,
> Schwankt sein Charakterbild in der Geschichte.[1]

The aim of the drama can but be to make this ambiguity aesthetically meaningful and thereby to provide a characterological possibility of interpreting the ambivalent figure of the hero in the oneness of person and fate. Yet this occurs still excentrally in the *Vorspiel*. The fundamental, class-structured groups of people appear on a broad base of reality. The historical situation is mirrored on the plane of the 'naïve', in the actions of the soldiers, citizens and peasants. As Schiller lets the people's words and deeds be contiguous with history through their enthusiasm for the Commander-in-Chief, he provides the 'Volk' with a historical role. Herein lies the transfiguration and ennoblement which Schiller the aesthetician set as a task for Schiller the poet. It is therefore

[1] Confused by the favour and the hatred of the factions, the picture of his character has vacillated in the course of history.

no mawkish idealisation, but an emergence from the gloom into the light of historical self-awareness. Hence the politicising words of the first marksman:

> Und der Geist, der im ganzen Korps tut leben,
> Reißet gewaltig, wie Windesweben,
> Auch den untersten Reiter mit.[2]

It is the same marksman who can shortly afterwards say of Wallenstein that he is not at all motivated by his duty to the Emperor, but by the intoxication of power ('to venture and to undertake all'). The basic tension of the historical truth already finds expression here on the level of the 'naïve'. This army seems to be free, that is broad-minded, independent, indeed with traces of the noble, but only towards Emperor and citizens. In reality it is the creation of the Commander-in-Chief. For his part he believes himself to be free, but is just as much the pawn of history on whose high-staked game he has embarked. The Capuchin's sermon already hints at this dialectic in primitive form. It then becomes quite obvious in *Die Piccolomini*.

In this first of the two main parts Schiller turns with obvious relief again to the sphere of the 'sentimental' in which he felt at home. Initially it is to be seen in terms of the subject matter, through its transposition from the 'Volk' to the level of the 'ruling class'. The historical question of power now becomes a matter of tactics and diplomacy. Questenberg's commission from Vienna to render the army harmless through splitting the ranks provokes on a higher plane ambivalent and unequivocal voices for and against. The course of intrigue on the part of the old Piccolomini commences and reveals at the same time the weakness or even the intrinsic shallowness of Wallenstein's position, as his powerful personality is represented directly to the spectator for the first time. The question which was merely broached in *Wallensteins Lager*, namely which was the driving force and which the driven, is here partly answered. The external forces with which Wallenstein has to deal emerge from the darkness; at the same time he has to deal with the internal ones. The 'vacillating' character portrait now becomes intelligible to a considerable degree. Wallenstein proves to be a 'mixed' character in accordance with Schiller's

---

[2] And the spirit, which lives in the whole corps, like a gust of wind, violently sweeps along even the lowest cavalryman.

aesthetic prescription. The self-revelation (Act II, Scene 5) is impressive. On the one hand there are the pathetic words to Terzky about the Swede:

> Es soll nicht von mir heißen, daß ich Deutschland
> Zerstücket hab, verraten an den Fremdling,
> Um meine Portion mir zu erschleichen.[3]

That would be indubitably idealistic, did not his subsequent words cast doubt upon his integrity:

> Und woher weißt du, daß ich ihn nicht wirklich
> Zum besten habe? Daß ich nicht euch alle
> Zum besten habe? Kennst du mich so gut?
> Ich wüßte nicht, daß ich mein Innerstes
> Dir aufgetan – [4]

That is again extremely realistic, as indeed Schiller intended it to be as the main quality in his conception of his hero. Noblemindedness and a shrewdness that never betrays the most secret thoughts at one and the same time – that is the amalgam. It prohibits the possibility of interpreting Wallenstein as a common criminal on the one hand and as a great criminal on the other. Luther's 'Si peccas, pecca fortiter' has no place here. For Wallenstein oscillates not only before the eyes of his contemporaries as an unfathomable hero, he also vacillates subjectively within himself. The sureness of instinct appears to be broken in him. He is no longer sufficiently the product of nature for that. The superiority of his intellect clashes with his faith in the stars again. He therefore does not yet embody pure reason to a sufficient degree. These are obvious limitations, and it appears to be an essential task in this part of the trilogy to throw them into bold relief time and again through the suggestive impact of Wallenstein's character. Initially, awareness of a mission and doubt counterbalance each other. The oft-cited line 'In your breast are the stars of your fate' is spoken by Illo, not Wallenstein. And it is Illo too and Terzky who play the dialectic game with Wallenstein, who for his part believes he is

---

[3] It shall not be said of me that I have dismembered Germany, betrayed it to the foreigner, in order to surreptitiously obtain my portion.

[4] And how do you know I am not making a fool of him? That I am not making a fool of you all? Do you know me so well? I would doubt that I had revealed my innermost being to you –

playing with them. With the proposed deceit in falsely obtaining the signatures of the generals — by secretly extracting the clause referring to loyalty to the emperor — Wallenstein is really no longer the master but the pawn of his own creations. As the final pointer, that in reality Wallenstein is even the tool in the machinery of history, whose manipulator he in fact believes himself to be, we can look to the beginning of *Wallensteins Tod* (Act I, Scene 3). When his envoy, sent to the Swedes following the obtaining of the generals' signatures, is captured by the Imperial forces, Wallenstein himself too now knows he is the driven man:

> Wie? Sollt' ich's nun im Ernst erfüllen müssen,
> Weil ich zu frei gescherzt mit dem Gedanken?
> Verflucht, wer mit dem Teufel spielt![5]

And the monologue in the following scene provides the complete self-revelation:

> Wär's möglich? Könnt' ich nicht mehr, wie ich wollte?
> Nicht mehr zurück, wie's mir beliebt? Ich müßte
> Die Tat *vollbringen*, weil ich sie *gedacht* . . .
> Beim großen Gott des Himmels! Es war nicht
> Mein Ernst, beschloßne Sache war es nie.
> In dem Gedanken bloß gefiel ich mir;
> Die Freiheit reizte mich und das Vermögen.[6]

We should recall that these scenes were still part of *Die Piccolomini* at the first performance. And in them in fact Wallenstein's true nature at one with his real historical position is realised. It is freedom as temptation. But the temptation historically occurs as a motif, which at the same time subordinates subjective freedom to necessity. Thus the ambivalence of the character portrait merges with the higher ambivalence of the historical figure, which keeps subjectivity and the Super-Ego in constant lively and moral tension. In this way an ethical decision in the Kantian sense is given a

[5] What? Am I supposed to fulfil this idea now in all seriousness, because I toyed too freely with the thought? Accursed he who plays with the Devil!

[6] Would it be possible? Could I no longer do as I wanted? No longer retreat as it suits me? I would have to *complete* the deed, because I *conceived* it . . . Great God in Heaven! It was not my serious intention, my resolve it never was. I merely took pleasure in the thought; the freedom attracted me, and the power.

chance to operate. Indeed, without this tension such a decision would not be possible at all.

The purpose of *Die Piccolomini* however is also to mix the (historical) realism of the figure of Wallenstein with the 'sentimental' and idealistic element through the Thekla–Max action, and thereby invest it with a new essentiality. The pure and innocent love which Max feels for Thekla is carefully preceded by his selfless devotion to, and vehement trust in Wallenstein, to whom Max holds fast, undeterred even by his own father. Up to the final decision in the third play, Max and Thekla are both unequivocally 'Beautiful Souls', to whom Thekla's famous line 'The impulse of the heart is the voice of fate' applies. Yet in her love too is embodied the highest level of sentimentality. That holds good not only for the external action, as concentrated in Thekla's song on the lute ('I have lived and loved'), but also for the clear echo of the Julius-figure from the *Philosophische Briefe*, which characterises Max's nature:

> Auch für ein liebend Herz ist die gemeine
> Natur zu eng, und tiefere Bedeutung
> Liegt in dem Märchen meiner Kinderjahre
> Als in der Wahrheit, die das Leben lehrt.
> Die heitre Welt der Wunder ist's allein,
> Die dem entzückten Herzen Antwort gibt . . .[7]

Here to some extent is Julius speaking before the awakening by Raphael. Refuted by cruel reality, Max has no other choice left than death in battle, just as there is no other choice for Thekla than to spend her life in mourning at the grave of her beloved. The possibility of a compromise with the reality of life must remain alien to this world in which duty and inclination cannot be separated. This stands in stark contrast to Wallenstein, the realistic tactician, who is nevertheless paralysed by his belief in the stars when it comes to action and on whom this very daughter of his and this young innocent friend indirectly bestow something of their idealistic significance. It is an aesthetic, not a moral significance, in contrast to his fellows and opponents who swarm around

---

[7] Even for a loving heart common nature is too narrow, and a deeper meaning lies in the tale of my youthful years than in the truth which life teaches. It is only the serene world of miracles which gives an answer to the enraptured heart.

him. As a man thus ambivalently characterised, he matures towards his hour of death. The purpose of the last play of the trilogy is to make this manifest as being a consequence of character and fate.

In this third part Wallenstein appears with absolute clarity as the man of action and at the same time the man paralysed through his own belief in fate. The whole business of the character's responsibility here comes into question, precisely in that the sinister element of magic gains in importance. This balance is not fully resolved by Schiller. The character of the hero remains a mixture of antipathetic and sympathetic traits: of calculation, coldness, artfulness and contempt for his fellow men on the one hand, and of practical and human superiority, a capacity for friendship, humanity, sometimes even a heart, on the other. Yet over both there ultimately rules an egoism that is never abandoned. The fact that his character is that of a realist with sentimental admixture prejudices the aesthetic effect of greatness, since neither the immorality of the absolute man of action nor the rigour of the absolute moral person really come into conflict here. The motif of astrology can also not establish greatness. Indeed, it imparts the mysterious breath of magic. But what emerges from the attempt to link classical thoughts on fate with a romantic subject-matter? Illusion and self-alienation. The effect of Wallenstein's path towards destruction hardly lies in his being struck down by the gods. It is more a matter of superstition contributing decisively to render him at variance with himself and to destroy what seems to be important to him, namely the leader instinct. How is Seni's final warning consistent with the extraordinarily propitious horoscope earlier? That is more a magic motif than the classical idea of fate. And in this sense in fact the Romantic fate tragedy has later pointed back with some justification to *Wallenstein* as being its great precursor.

The effect of the last play of the trilogy, in which too the public of the Napoleonic Age could recognise itself, lies nevertheless not so much in the ethical/ideal sphere perhaps as in the realistic/psychological. Wallenstein is finally forced to a decision which for so long he endeavoured to avoid. He becomes more desperate from one stage to the next and falls a victim to the twist of history, that is to the forces he himself had provoked. The decisions of Octavio and Butler encircle him, the mercenary leaders desert him one by one. Indeed, even Max and Thekla abandon him. At the end his catastrophe is brought about perhaps less by the weapon of the murderers than by the terrible loneliness in which he already finds himself, before his last faithful friends, who are equally desperate, fall, and he himself in their wake. The realist is overcome realistically too. But since the power which overwhelms him is the reality of history, Wallenstein's struggle does not remain a private one. Significance and dubiety, which are both his lot, also underlie the fate and character of his antagonists. Octavio has to pay for the elevation to Princedom with the death of his only son. Wallenstein's inevitable demise is more merciful than Octavio's continued existence. This very contrast restores to Wallenstein his dignity which he had largely forfeited as a vacillating pragmatist. The despairing tactician Octavio remains a lonely figure on the stage. Universal history is here also universal judgement. The protagonist, inconceivable outside this context, can realise his individuality by decision or non-decision only in that light. With Goethe, the 'naïve' person, this aspect of the Super-Ego would produce more features of a life of greater vitality. We need think only of *Faust*. For Schiller, the first great dramatic project of his Classical period is only secondarily the proof that he can be a realist too. In the first instance however it is testimony of his individuality as a 'sentimental' poet. The inclination towards distancing oneself from the subject-matter (which signifies anti-subjectivity at the same time) and the universal standpoint are Classical.

Wallenstein commences the series of Schiller's historical dramas that then stretch from *Maria Stuart* to *Die Jungfrau von Orleans* and *Wilhelm Tell* and right up to the *Demetrius* fragment. It was whilst working on the last that Schiller passed away. They all bear one common characteristic which marks them off from the majority of historical dramas of the nineteenth century. They are neither 'Ritterstücke' nor portrayals of an age, nor even historical fate dramas, *Die Braut von Messina* notwithstanding. Admittedly, history is also 'fate' in them, but rather as a means to an end, namely as a linchpin for human tragedy. This however arises only through the confrontation of human freedom and historical necessity, not, as in the Romantic fate drama, through mysterious pitiless facts whereby an anonymous fate strikes down its victim. Schiller incorporated his Kantian thought in the whole of the rich dramatic creations of his last years, and indeed a stricter version of it than he had used as the basis for *Wallenstein*. After that play there was no longer to be in Schiller's dramas any Thekla nor in the true sense any Max, that is 'Beautiful Souls' being destroyed in the supra-personal tragedy that is history. Duty and inclination would clash in keeping with Kantian ethics, and the main dramatic figures were to reveal themselves thereby. The only drama that lacks the tragic conclusion, namely the last completed one, *Wilhelm Tell*, is perhaps even the most personal drama of decision in the ethical sense. Its moral tension clearly outweighs the 'national substance', with the optimistic victory of good at the end.

Maria Stuart, which was not written until 1799 to 1800, had already been conceived as far as plan and motivation were concerned about fifteen years prior to *Wallenstein*. Schiller had already been collecting historical data on this subject in 1782 in Bauerbach. However *Don Carlos* supplanted his interest in *Maria Stuart*, and it was not until after the great test of the *Wallenstein*-trilogy that Schiller the Classicist dared to come to grips with the theme again. From the start, the idea of sentimental compassion is put at a distance: 'My Mary shall arouse no soft, effeminate mood . . .' He is not concerned with 'tenderness' but with 'violent passions'. At the same time, however, it is also a question here of historical necessity, of integrating passion and suffering into the conflict of emotions and high politics in general, to which in fact not the character, but certainly the actions of the heroes and their antagonists are subjected. With classical balance, guilt is shared by Mary and Elizabeth, and so greatness is not only on the side of Mary. This is the poetic conception, but it was born of the comparative study of English, French and German versions of history. In contrast to *Wallenstein*, but allied to the subsequent *Jungfrau von Orleans*, *Maria Stuart* is a 'drama of purification', which is concerned not with the catharsis of the spectator, but of the main character herself. Law (also seen as the law of history) and subjectivity are in this way equated, here again in contrast to *Die Braut von Messina*, where the workings of fate with its classicistic overtones inevitably prevented a theatrical effect such as that produced by Schiller's other historical dramas. In *Wallenstein* the dramatic hero appears as a person, as a whole, as a character in the literal sense already indirectly through the *Vorspiel*. Similarly in *Maria Stuart* this happens in the First Act through Mary herself and the sufferings inflicted on her. The queen is superior to the cruelty of the chicaneries not only through her bearing; as far as the essence of her character is concerned her real greatness reveals itself – right in the middle of the situation prior to the sentence of death, which is in effect expected – in the consciousness of her earlier misdeeds and guilt. Without this the dignity which Schiller would like to bestow on the queen, despite all the questionable aspects of her erotic and political conduct, would not be credible. Without the past as a burden on her conscience the dignity would be void. And so for Mary her 'husband's spectre, demanding revenge' is an inner reality, as it also arouses in her the thought of unpalliated atonement. This possibility and reality exists in the concept of the character from the outset. But Schiller did not want to have the queen resign herself in sackcloth and ashes. She bears the judgement as expiation when it is inevitable. But only when it has become a necessity. She has neither cut herself off from life, nor does she stand above it in the real sense. We note that immediately in her conversation with Mortimer, in her spontaneous reaction to the magnificent picture of Rome, to the possibility of liberation which seems to present itself to her, even if it be with the aid of Leicester. It is this very line of development which alone can lead to the catharsis and hence to the perfect inner greatness of Mary Stuart. When she stands before the scaffold (after the communion-scene in Act V), she stands truly above life without any trace of bitterness or vindictiveness and ready to forgive all. In exactly the same measure Schiller has developed her counterpart Elizabeth with great artistry into a morally questionable figure, yet she is no less significant. Admittedly she hardly owes that to her character, but to her historical position which compels the Queen of England – and herein lies her tragedy – to act without a clear division between actual necessity and jealousy and vindictiveness, which constitutes her personal plight. Abandoned and deserted on all sides, Elizabeth remains alone and afflicted with indelible shame on the historical scene. This too is seemingly not without greatness, even if not the greatness of inner surety with which her opponent made her exit, but rather the greatness of despair.

We can scarcely accept that in the all-decisive scene of the confrontation of Elizabeth and Mary, Schiller had in mind the famous dispute of the queens from the *Nibelungenlied*. Yet he provides something very closely related, though only on the basis of the 'sentimental'. The meeting arranged with good intention is the *peripeteia*, though not for the reconciliation but as the moment of decision for Mary's end. If *Wallensteins Lager* was supposed to be a test of Schiller the 'Realist', a similar function was being served in *Maria Stuart* by the dispute of the queens in terms of the psychological differentiation. The catastrophe occurs no longer on political grounds but because the women here mortally offend one another as women. That is a modern motif; it is Shakespeare, not Sophocles. Even the vacillating figure of the double-dealing lover Leicester in his function of court intriguer and diplomat shows himself as belonging utterly to the modern world in his inability to reach a decision. The same is equally true, in the last resort, of Mortimer, whose youthful fanaticism is presented equivocally enough; he is capable of personal sacrifice, but is also dominated by impulses which are partly checked by sentiment. These figures too belong to 'Realism' under the definition of the 'naïve and sentimental' poet, as contained in the treatise on Goethe's *Werther*. And the incorruptible Eckhart-like personality of the old Shrewsbury is required as a contrasting figure. If the historical drama were also to be interpreted at the same time as a drama of ideas, then the possibility of purification, of which greatness is capable and which makes it triumph over the course of historical events, must be seen as the idea around which the drama revolves. In contrast however to Baroque drama, self-conquest derives not from Christian stoicism, on the plane of principles involved, but from an intrinsically human historicity, on the plane of subjective moral freedom of decision. It is this which leaves the antagonist Elizabeth in the tragic greatness of isolation.

The subject matter too of *Die Jungfrau von Orleans* (*The Maid of Orleans*) had already stirred Schiller in his pre-Classical period. He had himself published it in his German edition of Pitaval's *Causes célèbres*. Yet the serious plan for a drama of his own on this subject did not get under way until the middle of 1800. The work on it, right through to the conclusion, went on in the one uninterrupted flow from the September of 1800 to the April of 1801. Although by that time Schiller had already been long at variance with the Romantics, he nevertheless gave his new drama the subtitle 'A Romantic Tragedy'. Naturally we must not think here of the definitions of 'Romantic' of, say, Novalis and Friedrich Schlegel. The designation is to be taken conservatively, more in the sense of Herder: the material is romance-like, from the age of chivalry. A treatment of the theme on the basis of Voltaire's *La Pucelle* must have been far from Schiller's mind. Voltaire had consciously compromised the figure of the 'Maid of Orleans' together with the Church and a belief in miracles. It virtually signified a challenge to transpose it again to a serious form whilst renouncing irony. Although Schiller the Classicist was anything but a Christian believer in miracles, he was able to interpret the visions of Joan as the key to both her historical role and also her tragic downfall. In this way he is merely continuing the course from *Wallenstein* to *Maria Stuart*. How he does this is perhaps shown most clearly in the Schillerian deviation from Joan's historical end at the close of the drama. In George Bernard Shaw's *Saint Joan* the emphasis lies specifically on the trial with the historically true fatal outcome and its backlash on the Inquisitors. Schiller however completely ignores Joan of Arc's historical death at the stake and substitutes the highly sentimental motif of Joan's miraculous self-deliverance from Isabeau's chains and the final battle which is decided by her intervention but in which she is mortally wounded. As a result she dies with visionary words on her lips, 'raised up in freedom', with the standard surrendered to her in her hand under a sky 'illuminated with a roseate hue'. The longer and the more removed it is from Classicism, the stronger the impression of a character virtually on the borderline of sentimental *kitsch*. The flag which covers the dead woman, the 'muted emotion' of the survivors as they stand round the heroine, the flags of the victorious army laid over her at the behest of the king: all combine to form a pathos that suits the conclusion of neither *Wallenstein* nor *Maria Stuart*. Schiller has carefully avoided the historical reality which has Joan of Arc die as a condemned heretic at the stake. The theatrical effectiveness of the play in any non-pathetic age, above all at the present time, is thus open to question. Indeed the High-Classical pathos has even provoked parodies since the time of Naturalism. The question which would then have to be posed would be whether the excessively sublime conclusion can be accepted as still contributing to the convincing effectiveness of a grand ideal concept shaped with such great artistry. For the pathos of the dramatic conclusion arises from the desire to assimilate the sublime aspect of an extraordinary human fate with her rise, fall and return to her true self. The precondition of Joan's victories, which were to procure the Imperial crown for a king who was 'inactive', is her immunity to human love. In her aberration over Lionel, she herself is guilty of breaking this condition, which in real Schillerian fashion identifies her human subjectivity with her historical destiny. The consequence being Fall and Atonement. Yet this coming-to-terms with herself again must be accomplished in a different way from that of Mary Stuart. The queen had had an earlier history that was not subject to any condition. Joan's path however is unequivocally predestined for victory or for downfall. Her appearance on the historical scene was not due to birth but was the result of her inner voice. This is the kind of duty that excludes inclination. Grace is alien to this destiny. For her there remains only dignified self-assertion, but the expression of this dignity is pathos. Schiller the 'Realist' cannot prove his mettle in such a dramatic heroine. He is diverted into presenting the Court, the army and its battles. Only the pathos of the 'sentimental' poet remains for the 'heroine'. But this appears consistent in its fashion. It can scarcely consider Joan as a passive victim of a trial for heresy that leads to the stake. After the precipitous downfall only the dignity of the standard was left, not the realistic suffering of death through fire.

The result can also be perceived in the language. With a certain legitimacy Joan herself can indeed speak the language of rhetoric as the mouthpiece of her voices. It is something else, however, when Raimond, a *peasant* and her wooer from the same village, declaims on this level:

> Ich staune über euch, ich steh erschüttert,
> Im tiefsten Busen kehrt sich mir das Herz!
> O gerne nehm ich euer Wort für Wahrheit,
> Denn schwer ward mir's, an eure Schuld zu glauben.
> Doch konnt' ich träumen, daß ein menschlich Herz
> Das Ungeheure schweigend würde tragen![8]

The tension between reality (of the peasant) and idealism (of the language) can hardly be missed. The peasant who stands 'shaken',

[8] I am amazed at you, I stand shaken, my heart turns deep within my breast! O gladly do I take your word for the truth, for it was hard for me to believe that you were guilty. Yet, how could I dream that a human heart would bear something so atrocious in silence!

who 'dreams', and from whose lips abstract terms ('truth', 'guilt', 'atrocity') fall effortlessly, loses credibility. But even the King does not speak according to his character, which is irresolute, passive, vacillating, a little dissolute, when suddenly in the final scene he fluently masters the pathos of a preacher:

> Sie ist dahin – Sie wird nicht mehr erwachen,
> Ihr Auge wird das Ird'sche nicht mehr schauen,
> Schon schwebt sie droben, ein verklärter Geist,
> Sieht unsern Schmerz nicht mehr und unsre Reue.[9]

Schiller had obviously given little thought to all this. His re-emergence on the dramatic scene with *Wallenstein* and the sense of competition with the 'naïve' genius Goethe in the realism of *Wallensteins Lager* did not last long in practise. The same remark can later be made with reference to *Wilhelm Tell*. The matter may be discussed here as an example of Schiller's dramatic technique, because it helps to explain the later effects of this style: the often empty rhetoric of the epigones[10] and the difficulty for post-Naturalist modern literature to overcome the stumbling-block of the high sententious tone. The fact that this can be overcome with historical awareness is hardly open to question, yet it is no legitimate means of comprehension. Today it can only impress us adequately if we decide to be receptive to the intended and achieved unity of the sublime language, the pathos of the tragic motif, to which Schiller subjects heroes and kings, peasants and soldiers on *one and the same* plane. The Winckelmannian aversion to 'common nature' only on occasion permits Schiller to choose the middle course of a Shakespearian realism, which is not in keeping with his theory, but certainly in line with his natural disposition. So there emerges that solemnity which can only then be effective when the overpowering element of total pathos facilitates a genuine and not merely a historistic contemporaneity. Where it is attained, a dramatic stylistic unity of extraordinary quality certainly asserts itself time and again.

For all that the key to the understanding of the pathetic style remains history, that is history in which the individual finds him-

---

[9] She has departed – she will no longer awaken, her eye will no longer gaze upon the earthly. Already she hovers above, a transfigured spirit, and no longer sees our pain and our remorse.

[10] *Vide* Glossary.

self cast, which debars him from the idyllic and demands from him that he should fulfil himself as a genuine personality capable of renouncing the quest for private happiness and good fortune. In Joan's decisive monologue at the start of Act IV, which reflects her seduction by Lionel's beauty, that is to say the real catastrophe whereby she incurs guilt, we find a passage that is valid for the basic problem of Schiller's dramatic work:

> Kümmert *mich* das Los der Schlachten,
> Mich der Zwist der Könige?
> Schuldlos trieb ich meine Lämmer
> Auf des stillen Berges Höh',
> Doch du rissest mich ins Leben,
> In den stolzen Fürstensaal,
> Mich der Schuld dahinzugeben
> Ach! es war nicht meine Wahl! [11]

This need only be taken as one example. It could be complemented by the consciousness of an overwhelming fate in utterances of Wallenstein, of Tell, not to mention *Die Braut von Messina*.

Die Braut von Messina (*The Bride of Messina*), Schiller's next drama, originated in part at the same time as *Wilhelm Tell*, yet was completed before it. The play shows how a popular 'Storm and Stress' dramatic theme can reach a High-Classical level in keeping with Winckelmannian Classicism. The discord between brothers that leads to fratricide is well known as a typical 'Storm and Stress' theme through Leisewitz and Klinger. Yet in the earlier period the theme served, as has been shown, as an extreme expression of emotional genius. In so far as it is a fate tragedy, it remains something supernatural, not moral. The Classical Schiller was to incorporate both his knowledge of Kant and his recent study of Sophocles' *Oedipus*, about which he corresponded with Goethe in 1799. Yet a gestatory period elapsed before the real composition, which occurred in the second half of 1802. *Die Braut von Messina* is the only drama by the Classical Schiller which is not a historical drama – for good reason – but is drama based on legend. What he had envisaged would not have been realisable in

---

[1] Does the lot of battles worry *me*, the discord of kings? Innocently I used to drive my lambs to the heights of the silent mountain. Yet you dragged me into the midst of life, to the proud Prince's Hall, to make me guilty. Alas! It was not my choice!

a figure or group of figures taken from modern history, however extensive the poetic licence. He could hardly combine oracles in an equivocal psychological sense (unlike in *Wallenstein*) or in the visionary 'Romantic' sense as befitted the traditional picture of Joan of Arc, with historical heroes of modern times. Still less could one have associated the chorus in its ancient classical role, that is as commentator and didactician, with historical events which had already been invested with a predestinational character through dreams and oracles. With its meditations and moralising interpretations, the chorus regularly interrupts in fact the 'action' in the modern drama sense. But it was with this very venture that Schiller was concerned. What makes Schiller differ from Sophocles is that in the former's case the choruses were the mouthpieces of the parties involved to a much greater degree than in Sophocles. At all events they represent a formal venture on Schiller's part which the Romantics, and foremost amongst them the author of *Alarkos*, Friedrich Schlegel, rightly interpreted as an experiment in their direction. Even the Late-Romantic fate-drama of Zacharias Werner and his epigones still echoed *Die Braut von Messina*, but Early Romanticism looked above all to the choice of form as well as the theme. Schiller had justified this in the essay *Über den Gebrauch des Chors in der Tragödie*, in a one-sided fashion from the idealistic perspective of his own aesthetics. Reflection devolves on the chorus, reflection which in no way has to serve the catharsis here, even the poetic catharsis of emotion which is assigned to the 'dull passion of the masses'. Moreover here Schiller was coming round to the path taken by Goethe and, from the point of view of the essay, *Die Braut von Messina* is one of the thoroughly anti-Revolutionary pieces of writing in High Classicism.

In thematic terms it constitutes the bold attempt to combine 'Storm and Stress' subject matter with classical problematics. Don Manuel and Don Cesar stand in opposition to each other, rival brothers temporarily reconciled by their mother at the beginning of the play. Yet the dream of the dead father lives on, the interpretation of which, fatal for the whole princely House of Sicily, foretold as inevitable the killing of the third child Beatrice. Neither of the two brothers knows of the existence of their sister, whom the mother had secretly saved and had brought up in a convent. And yet they both know Beatrice 'by chance'. In this way the incest motif from *Oedipus* is introduced. Both brothers love their unrecognised sister in innocent guilt. The mother's attempt to circumvent the dream oracle cannot exorcise fate. It can only lead to fraternal discord in which Don Cesar stabs Don Manuel in a fit of jealous passion because of Beatrice and then finally kills himself. The oracle is thus literally fulfilled.

The blows fall in rapid succession here, and they fall predestinedly. Here it is not Wallenstein's vacillation, Mary Stuart's struggle for her higher Self, or that of Joan for regeneration following her downfall. The father's dream of the lily, from which a flame emerges that engulfs the house, necessitates, in keeping with the thinking of those naïve times, the order to kill this dangerous daughter. The order in turn necessitates that the secret of the continued existence of the daughter her mother has saved, be carefully kept. This secret then effects the fatal double passion which inevitably leads to the catastrophe. None of Schiller's dramas therefore is less a drama of character and more a didactic drama than *Die Braut von Messina*. The choruses which take up and reflect the emotions portrayed are merely a formal symptom of the didactic drama that Schiller was venturing to offer to a theatregoing public which admittedly had also been educated in an enthusiasm for the world of Greece. We can hardly suppose that he had taken into account the sociological uniqueness of dramatic composition. The sudden shift from the classical to the uncanny idea of fate was much too easy for that, as the highly sentimental mode of the fate-drama confirmed even into the 1820s. In that mysterious fate was reduced to the level of poltergeists, goblins and spectres. Such a result could in fact not have been Schiller's intention. He intended the theme of fate in *Die Braut von Messina* as a suggestion of the greatness of destiny still, not as a mere source of stimulation through the medium of magic. And this is confirmed by the level of pathos in the style, which proves utterly unsuccessful in the Romantic fate-drama.

Schiller returned to the historical drama with *Wilhelm Tell* (1804), which the sick poet managed to complete though with difficulty, and with the more adventurous of his plans, *Demetrius*. The fact that the 'national subject matter' as well as the individual in *Tell* attracted him has produced the misuse of this great achievement for the theatre as a national festival play right up to the present day. It is based however on a misunderstanding. *Wilhelm Tell* was not conceived on the same plane as *Die Her-*

mannsschlacht (*The Battle of Arminius*)[12] but on the plane of Kantian moralism, and this too in more definitive and impressive fashion than in the earlier dramas. The basic idea is not primarily inspiring victory or admonitory downfall of a people, that is nationalistic/romantic, but the moral assertion of the individual in the raging torrent of history.

The genesis already points to this. Schiller had got the suggestion for the Tell-theme from Goethe, who had toyed with it from the time of his third visit to Switzerland (1797). Schiller himself had never been to Switzerland. But even Goethe's picture of it was subject to changes. The youthful enthusiasm of 1775 gave way to the maturely objective view he obtained on his journey with the Duke in 1779, which was then in turn replaced by the sceptical realism of his last Swiss journey. Between 1779 and 1797 however there emerged the fictitious letters of Werther from Switzerland, letters of depressing and bitter criticism of egotism and petit-bourgeois narrowmindedness, of 'gossip', which supposedly scandalise his Werther. We have to bear this in mind in order to understand the conception of Tell 'the carter' (not Tell the free huntsman), as the idea passed from Goethe to Schiller. For Goethe formally relinquished the theme to his friend. There was nothing inspiring in it, not even in the national 'pathetic' sense. Schiller could have found this dimension to his hero only too easily in the spirit of his own age, as cultivated especially in Germany under the Napoleonic despotism. How near in time Kleist's *Die Hermannsschlacht* was to *Tell*! However Schiller had quite obviously not intended this line of approach. For the 'Nationalstoff' which he added to Goethe's early conception was not intended to be topical and was thus not anti-Napoleonic.

We can glean from Eckermann Goethe's plan for *Tell*:

Den Tell dachte ich mir als einen urkräftigen, in sich selbst zufriedenen, kindlich-unbewußten Heldenmenschen, der als Lastträger die Kantone durchwandert, überall gekannt und geliebt ist, überall hilfreich, übrigens ruhig sein Gewerbe treibend, für Weib und Kinder sorgend und sich nicht kümmernd, wer Herr oder Knecht ist.[13]

[12] Heinrich von Kleist's play, written in 1808. (*Translator's note*)
[13] Tell I thought of as a very powerful heroic figure, contented in himself, with a child's unconsciousness, who wanders through the Cantons, by trade

If we take Goethe's comment at face value, it holds the key too for Schiller's figure of Tell. It shows in fact the decisive isolation of Tell from the real patriots, which point has been disregarded time and again when interpreted in national terms in Germany and Switzerland. Of similar significance is the fact that Schiller relied not on the popular tradition of the Tell theme which he knew, but rather turned to his oldest source from the sixteenth century, the *Chronicon Helveticum* of Ägidius Tschudi (using the edition of 1734–36). The rustic performance of *Tell* in Keller's *Der grüne Heinrich* (*Green Henry*) provides a version of Schiller's play along the 'Volksspiel' traditional lines. There the Rütli-scene forms the conclusion with all its exuberant national enthusiasm. Schiller however has carefully held to Tschudi's historical sequence of events, which makes the apple-shooting and the murder of the tyrant occur *after* the Rütli oath. This choice however is in exact accord with Goethe's conception. Schiller's Tell is an individual and lonely figure amongst the patriots and so is he intended to be. He is missing from the Rütli oath; only when he is confronted personally by Gessler acting in inhuman fashion, does he decide to act. His is not the executive hand carrying out the will of the people; primarily he is the image of the responsible family father who takes the general welfare of the people in his stride, so long as the tyranny does not disturb his private circle. Baumgarten, Melchthal, indeed even Attinghausen and Rudenz understand the events from the point of view of national liberation before he does. The great controversial monologue before the killing of Gessler and the Parricida-scene that Iffland already criticised at the time are Schiller's justification for Tell's solitary course of action as he intended it, as inspired by Goethe and carefully confirmed in the reliance he placed on Tschudi. The monologue provides the scruples of conscience of an Ego, moral in the Kantian sense, whose measure is not national tub-thumping enthusiasm, but moral decision, the categorical imperative. This is the yardstick of Schiller's Wilhelm Tell, in contrast to the 'Volksspiel' tradition. Everything points to the fact that Goethe would have wished to keep him just as individualistic, acting only from an instinctive force, something however which was impossible for Schiller. His Tell

a carter, known everywhere and loved everywhere, helpful, but quietly pursuing his own business, caring for wife and child and not at all worrying who is master and who is servant.

is only initially a natural human being at one with himself. He must not and cannot remain so, for that would be unhistorical. Like Joan of Arc, he has to recognise that the destiny of a man demands a role of historic significance when he finds himself enmeshed and forced into action, which really runs counter to his nature and his inclination. Schiller's confrontation with Iffland over the monologue and the Parricida-scene expressly proves once again the intentional nature of Schiller's motivation:

> Gerade in dieser Situation, welche der Monolog ausspricht, liegt das Rührende des Stücks, und es wäre gar nicht gemacht worden, wenn nicht diese Situation und dieser Empfindungs- zustand . . . dazu bewogen hätten.[14]

The insertion of the Parricida-scene however does not serve the idea of patriotism, but rather the dramatic exposition of the dis- tinction between the criminal act of murdering the Emperor, 'the bloody guilt of a quest for honour', and the 'just self-defence of a father' who has merely 'avenged sacred nature' with his deed. Tell's deed is to be understood not as an act of patriotism, but as an act of humanity. Schiller was concerned with this as a moral problem. We may recall that he had drawn a strict line at literary material of a patriotic, political nature already in his *Briefe über ästhetische Erziehung* and even earlier had expressed it plainly in correspondence with Körner:

> Es ist ein armseliges, kleinliches Ideal, für *eine* Nation zu schreiben; einem philosophischen Geiste ist diese Grenze durch- aus unerträglich.[15]

In the same letter, the nation for him is but a 'fragment'. For Kleist's *Die Hermannsschlacht* and related plays it is the goal. With this point established, we may freely admit that though the Rütli-oath and consciousness of patriotic unity are to be separ- ated from Tell as a person, they nevertheless also signify more than merely one side of the 'local colour' on which Schiller again places as much importance here as in *Wallensteins Lager*. He does

---

[14] It is in this very situation which the monologue expresses that the pathetic nature of the play lies, and it would not have been written at all, if this situation and this emotional state had not induced it.

[15] It is a paltry, trivial ideal to write for *one* nation. To a philosophical mind this restriction is thoroughly intolerable.

not allow the enthusiasm displayed on the Rütli to become the 'driving force', to be subordinated to 'nature'. The outcome of the Rütli-scene is, in the last resort, the product of circumspection and moderation.

Wilhelm Tell is a play, not a tragedy as are all the other dramas of Schiller. It is certainly a drama of ideas. Yet the idea proves to be an ethical one in the Kantian sense and not nationalistic and political. If we were to draw a comparison with Lessing, then Schiller's last drama would relate not to *Philotas* in terms of plot – despite tantalising possibilities of comparison – but to Lessing's last play, *Nathan der Weise*. Nathan too strays unintentionally from the role of the caring father into the mainstream of history. And for him too as for Tell, this experience signifies a test of character and mental outlook. And his personal history does not end in tragedy either. Yet he does what duty and inclination demand of him. The idea is based on the optimism of the Enlightenment. The idea in *Tell* however is grounded in the vigour of Kantian ethics. Optimism is manifest in the action of the people, not in Tell's own deed. The fact that it does not end in tragedy lies in the characteristically Schillerian touch that here – and only here – the force of historical necessity for once does not include the compulsion to self-estrangement on the part of the moral individual, but lets him attain his very Self and highest potential. From the point of view of the subjectivity of the hero of historical drama, we would here think, first of all, of Goethe's Egmont, even if Egmont does have to pay with his life; only for a time does Tell pay with his peace of mind and concern for his reputation (the Parricida-scene). There thus emerges a drama presenting the highest moral challenge, yet no tragedy. The fact that it does not come to this is effected through the integration of Tell's character and conscience and their attendant problems into the action of the 'Volk'. It is this which provides the solution to the subjective moral problem, but it can only do so because it has no revolutionary character of its own, only *mâze* (moderation), as the Rütli-scene shows. But this reserve is characteristic of both classical conception and classical style. For this reason alone no discordant note is sounded when the finale claims Tell as the liberator and saviour of the national cause.

Besides a large number of abortive or only embryonic dramatic projects, Schiller also left some more significant fragments, of which the earliest, *Die Malteser*, was a side- or subsidiary product of *Don Carlos*. But there are only a few lines extant, though they do in fact include a completed chorus of the Knights of the Order, in addition the draft scheme and interesting reflections on the motivation. The motif would have been the self-sacrifice, as it were, of two generations in favour of a spiritual rebirth of the degenerating Order of Knights.

From the research on *Maria Stuart* grew the plan for a drama *Warbeck*, of which Schiller apprised Goethe in the August of 1797. It was to be the tragedy of a false pretender to the Crown of England in the course of the Wars of the Roses. Warbeck, a puppet figure manipulated by the House of York against the House of Lancaster, was finally unmasked and executed. Schiller proposed (in writing to Goethe) to illustrate from this theme how in fact the writer of historical dramas should adopt only the general circumstances of the age and naturally the historical figures as the inspirational basis, and 'invent all the rest with poetic freedom'. He would let the hero appear 'as if born into his role':

Es müßte ganz so aussehen, daß der Betrug ihm nur den Platz angewiesen, zu dem die Natur selbst ihn bestimmt hätte.[16]

That indeed was a major project and Schiller did not even go beyond the draft and completion of the First Act. Not only because the project, which was regularly resumed, found itself crowded out as a stop-gap between the major dramas, or because the self-imposed task proved greater than his powers, but because of the fact that in the course of the year 1804 the theme of the false pretender to the throne was concentrated in a profounder and mightier conception, namely in the plan of *Demetrius*. The historic and the 'fictitious' Warbeck remained a cheat through and through, who for a short time came to the fore thanks to the intrigue of a political party. With *Demetrius* however the theme of the Crown Pretender is transferred to the twilight zone of psychology and treated from the viewpoint of the irony of history, as in *Wallenstein*. More experienced than he was at the time of his first Classical drama, Schiller wanted to make the lofty interplay of illusion and reality work once again. This turning to a new sub-

[16] It would have to appear entirely as though the deception had merely pointed out to him the place to which nature itself would have destined him.

ject matter, though the motif remains the same, can be biographic-
ally ascribed to the occasion of the Russian marriage of the Weimar
Crown Prince, which, incidentally, introduced Schiller the historian
to the history of Russia. The resolve to write the *Demetrius*
tragedy, equal in significance to the *Warbeck* project, dates from
the March of 1804, after the burden of the *Tell* drama had been
removed. But it was not granted to Schiller to work on the great
project uninterruptedly. Not only advancing illness and weakness,
but also other intervening plans kept interrupting. The elaboration of the first two acts occupied the last months of his life.

With *Demetrius* a fate-drama again emerges; again too it is
reminiscent of Oedipus. For Demetrius's stars are not in his
breast, they are a fateful inheritance, of which he cannot be at all
conscious. His awareness of a mission is not a crime subjectively.
The tragedy of his involvement and the final unmasking of the
hero in his innocent guilt is all the more terrible. In *Warbeck*
Schiller had wanted to provide the reduction of the hero through
deceit to the position to which he was destined by Nature. In
Demetrius he lets this materialise, as it were, through the cunning hand of fate. Originally Schiller wanted to begin with the rise
of his hero from vassal to the individual suddenly addressed as
Czarevitch; it was therefore markedly 'pathetic'. His love for the
'Polish woman of humble origin', who terminates the recognition
of Demetrius as the son of Ivan, was also to be pathetic. The later
version rejects all that, and begins with the ruler Demetrius at
the Imperial Diet at Cracow. There he is already involved in history and entangled by fate, behind a mask, of which he himself
knows nothing but which has fitted him as if it were nature. It is
not only a Greek classical mask from the point of view of fate,
but is also a *persona* in the literal sense. Subjectively the Pretender on the Czarist throne is here still at one with himself.
Demetrius only ceases to be at one with himself – like Wallenstein with his vacillation between faith in the stars and his own
'demon', after realising that he can no longer turn back – at the
point when, enlightened as to the truth of his illegitimacy, he continues in the role into which he has grown. A victim of his fate, but
a usurper of a title that does not belong to him in the final
analysis, he becomes guilty simply by virtue of his office. With the
failure of the moral being – again as in *Wallenstein* – Demetrius's
historical downfall is also adequately motivated for Schiller.

Demetrius would have been the counterpart to the dramas of purification: it would have become the first tragedy of desperate *hubris* in Schiller's writings, something which *Wallenstein* had only half been, and which had not even occurred in the Gessler-action in *Tell*. Yet this is a thoroughly classical aspect: the tragedy of *hubris* is pre-eminently Greek. And it also corresponds to *Faust*. The psychological differentiation of the moral problems admittedly appears modern. It was the same too with Tell, Joan of Arc and Mary Stuart. And so even in the last great project of the Classical dramatist, the drama with the superimposed idea of justice which would have been ultimately revealed in the future legitimacy of the Romanovs, there remain the 'naïve' and the 'sentimental', the realistic and the idealistic in that amalgam which Schiller the aesthetician had envisaged in his essay.

German Classicism has been termed 'Late Classicism' (by Karl Scheffler) and that in the sense of 'belated' in comparison with the Classicism of the other great European nations which was based directly on the Renaissance. It was not by chance that France and England – following their literary Classicism and by virtue of it – then became the countries in which Enlightenment originated. Indeed German Classicism was belated, if we take into account the fact that it did not even follow on directly from the *Aufklärung*, but was based on an intervening phase of irrationalism, in part in the shape of the same representatives (Herder, Goethe, Schiller). To this phase Classicism then appeared as a kind of backlash, almost as much a re-action as action. Its duration was fairly limited in terms of time. Between Winckelmann himself and Goethe's *Winckelmann und sein Jahrhundert* (1805) there was a time-span of but fifty years. The High-Classical period proper lasted however hardly more than a decade, if we put as its limits Goethe's association with Schiller and Schiller's death. In fact Goethe's picture of Winckelmann in 1805 was already a terminal point and valediction, since it already signified the transition into a Classicism which then soon led to the epigones, whilst Goethe's greatness enabled him to tear himself away from it once more.

All the more astonishing therefore is the achievement which this short historical interlude produced in its degree of concentration, its profundity and scope ranging beyond temporal and national frontiers; beyond too the purely literary, into philosophy and the pictorial arts, education and human self-understanding, assimilating its own age and thereby at the same time assuming lasting values. The formal importance too of Classicism for subsequent periods proved admirable: joy in experimenting with the classical heritage of form, which manifests too a high-minded sense of continuity; for Antiquity and Humanism were integrated and new ways of expression were thereby created for the German language which remain unsurpassed even today. Rilke's *Duineser Elegien*, George's and Hofmannsthal's poetry, indeed even the later works of Gottfried Benn are all inconceivable, if there had been no period of Classicism. Alternating Goethe and Schiller 'renaissances' mark our course up to the present day – and these have by no means simply taken the form of centenary celebrations in recent decades. The finest and the most concentrated works of German Classical writers are still a source of fascination.

Glossary

Entwicklungsroman *Erziehungsroman* *Bildungsroman*	Terms given to the characteristically German types of novel dealing mainly with the development of the hero's character to the point of maturity at which he is ready to assume a responsible position in human society.
	The term *Entwicklungsroman* may be taken in a more generic sense as depicting the stages in the development of a personality.
	The *Erziehungsroman* is frequently understood to refer more specifically to novels in which the hero is guided towards his goal by a process of education. Thus it is a didactic pedagogic novel.
	The *Bildungsroman* is sometimes seen as synonymous with the *Erziehungsroman*. But fundamental to the *Bildungsroman* is the idea of the hero's essentially inner development and growth.
Künstlerroman	The *Künstlerroman* comes within the general genre of the *Entwicklungsroman*, but here emphasis is placed on the growth of artistic awareness within the hero, in the course of which he becomes increasingly estranged from common life and values.
Staatsroman	A novel frequently utopian in nature, that centres on the affairs and welfare of the State.
Schlüsselroman	Or *roman à clef*. A novel frequently satirical in nature, in which real persons appear under fictitious names.
Epigone	A term more common in German literary criticism than in English denoting the late-

	comer who inherits and exploits a literary tradition; it may imply a certain lack of original creative power.
Fastnachtspiel	Late medieval Shrovetide play popular in Nuremberg and other German towns.
Knittelvers	A sixteenth-century German doggerel verse form popularised by Hans Sachs, consisting of rhymed couplets with four stresses and eight (or nine) syllables.
Minnesang	The German medieval poetry of courtly love.
Moritat	An artless song for popular consumption in which a street singer recounts some terrible or unusual event in a moralising poem set to very simple music.
Rondeau	A French fixed verse form characterised by a refrain and the use of only two rhymes, and consisting of thirteen lines, usually arranged in two five-line stanzas split by a three-line stanza. The first half of the opening line forms the refrain which is found at the end of the second and third stanzas. aabba aabC aabbaC.
Sprachgesellschaften	A movement dating from the early seventeenth century for the reform and embellishment of language, consisting of so-called 'language societies' based on the Florentine model. The earliest was the 'Fruchtbringende Gesellschaft'.
Tagelied	A song of the parting of lovers at the break of dawn. It became a distinct variant of the medieval courtly love poem.

Chronological Table

The first column lists historical figures and events of significance. The second column contains the major literary events and works covered by Professor Kohlschmidt. The third column comprises contemporaneous occurrences of literary interest.

1730		Gottsched, *Critische Dichtkunst*
1733		
1740	Frederick the Great of Prussia (1740–86) Maria Theresia of Austria (1740–80)	Breitinger, *Critische Dichtkunst* Bodmer, *Abhandlung von dem Wunderbaren*
1744	Duke Karl Eugen of Württemberg (1744–93)	
1748		Klopstock, *Der Messias, I–III*
1749		
1755	Lisbon earthquake	Lessing, *Miß Sara Sampson*
1756–63	Seven Years War	
1758		
1759		Young, *Conjectures on Original Composition*

Second column entries:

Hamann born	
Wieland born	
Herder born	
Goethe born	
Winckelmann, *Gedanken über die Nachahmung der Griechischen Wercke*	
Hamann's conversion in London; *Gedanken über meinen Lebenslauf*	
Hamann, *Sokratische Denkwürdigkeiten* Schiller born	

1760	Wieland, 'Kanzleidirektor' in Biberach	Macpherson, *Ossian*
1762	Hamann, *Kreuzzüge des Philologen*; Wieland, *Komische Erzählungen* (1762–65); translation of Shakespeare (1762–66)	
1763		Jean Paul born
1764	Winckelmann, *Geschichte der Kunst des Alterthums*; Wieland, *Don Sylvio von Rosalva*	
1765	Goethe in Leipzig	Percy, *Reliques of Ancient English Poetry*
1766	Herder, *Uber die neuere Deutsche Litteratur. Fragmente* (1766–67); Gerstenberg, *Briefe über Merkwürdigkeiten der Litteratur* (1766–67)	Lessing, *Laokoon*; Death of Gottsched
1767	Füssli, *Remarks on the Writings and Conduct of Jean Jacques Rousseau*	Lessing, *Minna von Barnhelm*; *Hamburgische Dramaturgie* (1767–69); A. W. Schlegel born
1768	Wieland, *Musarion*; Gerstenberg, *Ugolino*; Goethe, *Die Laune des Verliebten*	

1769	Herder, *Kritische Wälder;* his voyage to France: *Journal meiner Reise im Jahre 1769*	
1770	Herder and Goethe in Strassburg (1770–71) Claudius, *Der Wandsbecker Bote* (1770–75)	Lessing, librarian in Wolfenbüttel Hölderlin born
1771	Wieland, *Der neue Amadis* Herder, *Über den Ursprung der Sprache* Lenz in Strassburg	Klopstock, *Oden*
1772	Founding of the 'Göttinger Hainbund' Goethe in Wetzlar; Wieland in Weimar	Lessing, *Emilia Galotti* Novalis and F. Schlegel born
1773	Wieland, *Der teutsche Merkur* (1773–89) Herder, *Von deutscher Art und Kunst* Goethe, *Götz von Berlichingen* Bürger, *Lenore* Schiller at the Karlsschule	Wackenroder and Tieck born
1774	Wieland, *Die Abderiten* Herder, *Auch eine Philosophie der Geschichte zur Bildung der Menschheit; Älteste Urkunde des*	

1774—cont.		*Menschengeschlechts* (1774–76) Goethe, *Clavigo*; *Die Leiden des jungen Werthers*: Lenz, *Der Hofmeister*; *Anmerkungen übers Theater*	Nicolai, *Freuden des jungen Werthers*
1775	Duke Karl August of Weimar (1775–1828)	Goethe's first Swiss journey; goes to Weimar Lavater, *Physiognomische Fragmente* (1775–78) Jacobi, *Eduard Allwills Papiere* Klinger, *Otto; Das leidende Weib*	
1776	American Declaration of Independence	Herder invited to Weimar Goethe, *Stella* Lenz, *Die Soldaten* Leisewitz, *Julius von Tarent* Klinger, *Sturm und Drang; Die Zwillinge* Wagner, *Die Kindermörderin* Miller, *Siegwart* Müller, *Faust* (1776–78)	E. T. A. Hoffmann born
1777		Jung-Stilling, *Heinrich Stillings Jugend* Herder, *Plastik*	Nicolai, *Feiner Kleiner Almanach* Kleist born
1778		Herder, *Stimmen der Völker in Liedern* (1778–79) Hippel, *Lebensläufe* Bürger, *Gedichte*	Brentano born

1779		Jacobi, *Woldemar*	Lessing, *Nathan der Weise*
1780	Joseph II in Austria (1780–90)	Wieland, *Oberon* Klinger, *Plimplamplasko*	Lessing, *Erziehung des Menschengeschlechts* Frederick the Great, *De la littérature allemande*
1781		Pestalozzi, *Lienhard und Gertrud* (1781–85) Schiller, *Die Räuber*	Death of Lessing Kant, *Kritik der reinen Vernunft*
1782		Hölty, *Gedichte* Schiller's flight from Stuttgart	
1783		Schiller, *Fiesko*	
1784		Schiller, *Die Schaubühne als moralische Anstalt; Kabale und Liebe* Goethe, *Uber den Granit* Herder, *Ideen zur Philosophie der Geschichte der Menschheit* (1784–91) Voss, *Luise*	
1785		Schiller, *Rheinische Thalia* (1785–86), *Thalia* (1786–91), *Neue Thalia* (1791–93) Jacobi, *Spinoza-Büchlein* Moritz, *Anton Reiser* (1785–90)	
1786–88		Goethe's Italian Journey	
1786		Schiller, *Philosophische Briefe*	

1787		Goethe, *Iphigenie auf Tauris*; Schiller, *Don Carlos*; *Der Geisterseher* (1787–89); Herder, *Gott*; Heinse, *Ardinghello*; Schubart, *Kaplied*	
1788		Goethe, *Egmont*; Schiller, *Abfall der Niederlande*	Kant, *Kritik der praktischen Vernunft*; Eichendorff born
1789	French Revolution	Schiller, Professor in Jena; Bräker, *Der arme Mann im Tockenburg*; Jung-Stilling, *Heinrich Stillings häusliches Leben*; Goethe, *Tasso*	
1790		Goethe, *Faust. Ein Fragment*; *Metamorphose des Pflanzen*	Kant, *Kritik der Urtheilskraft*
1791		Schiller, *Geschichte des dreißigjährigen Krieges*; Goethe, Director of the Weimar Theatre; *Der Großkophta*; Klinger, *Fausts Leben*; *Medea*	Grillparzer born
1792		Goethe in France	
1793		Goethe, *Der Bürgergeneral*; Schiller, *Über Anmuth und Würde*; *Über das Pathetische*	

1794	Goethe–Schiller friendship begins Goethe, *Reineke Fuchs*	Fichte, *Wissenschaftslehre*
1795	Goethe, *Wilhelm Meister* (1795–96); *Unterhaltungen deutscher Ausgewanderten*; *Römische Elegien* Schiller, *Ästhetische Briefe*; *Uber naive und sentimentalische Dichtung* (1795–96); *Die Horen* (1795–97)	Tieck, *William Lovell* (1795–96)
1796	Goethe, *Alexis und Dora*; *Venetianische Epigramme* Goethe and Schiller, *Xenien*	Jean Paul, *Siebenkäs*
1797	Goethe and Schiller, *Balladen* Goethe, *Hermann und Dorothea* Schiller, *Uber epische und dramatische Dichtung*	Wackenroder, *Herzensergießungen* Tieck, *Der gestiefelte Kater* Hölderlin, *Hyperion* (1797–99) A. W. Schlegel's translation of Shakespeare (1797–1810) Schelling, *Ideen zu einer Philosophie der Natur*
1798	Schiller, *Wallenstein* (1798–99); settles in Weimar Goethe, *Propyläen* (1798–1800)	Tieck, *Franz Sternbalds Wanderungen*; *Die verkehrte Welt* *Das Athenäum* (1798–1800) Schelling, *Von der Weltseele* Death of Wackenroder

1799			F. Schlegel, *Lucinde* Schleiermacher, *Reden über die Religion* Novalis, *Die Christenheit oder Europa*
1800		Schiller, *Maria Stuart*	Novalis, *Hymnen an die Nacht* Schelling, *System des transzendentalen Idealismus* Jean Paul, *Titan* (1800–1803)
1801		Schiller, *Die Jungfrau von Orleans; Über das Erhabene*	Brentano, *Godwi* Death of Novalis
1802		Schiller, *Die Braut von Messina*	Novalis, *Heinrich von Ofterdingen*
1803		Goethe, *Die natürliche Tochter* Death of Herder	Death of Klopstock
1804		Schiller, *Wilhelm Tell*	Death of Kant Jean Paul, *Vorschule der Ästhetik; Flegeljahre* (1804–05)
1805		Death of Schiller Goethe, *Winckelmann und sein Jahrhundert*	
1806	Battle of Jena. Defeat of Prussia		Arnim and Brentano, *Des Knaben Wunderhorn* (1806–08)

Bibliography

The following list of suggested titles for further reading has been deliberately restricted, with the interests of the English reader in mind, to works in English. It does not claim to be exhaustive.

I GENERAL

Boesch, B. (ed.), *German Literature: A Critical Survey* (tr. R. Taylor: Methuen, 1971)

Bruford, W. H., *Germany in the Eighteenth Century* (C.U.P., 1935)
—— *Culture and Society in Classical Weimar 1775–1806* (C.U.P., 1962)

Menhennet, A., *Order and Freedom: German Literature and Society 1720–1805* (Weidenfeld & Nicolson, 1973)

Pascal, R., *The German 'Sturm und Drang'* (Manchester University Press, 1953)

Ritchie, J. M., *Periods in German Literature*, vol. 1 (Wolff, 1966)

Stahl, E. L., and Yuill, W. E., *German Literature in the Eighteenth and Nineteenth Centuries* (Cresset, 1970)

II AUTHORS AND SUBJECTS

Abbé, D. M. van, *C. M. Wieland: A Literary Biography* (Harrap, 1961)
—— *Goethe: New Perspectives on a Writer and his Time* (Allen & Unwin, 1972)

Clark, R. T., *Herder's Life and Work* (University of California Press, 1955)

Fairley, B., *A Study of Goethe* (O.U.P., 1947)

Friedenthal, R., *Goethe: His Life and Times* (Weidenfeld & Nicolson, 1965)

Garland, H. B., *Schiller* (Harrap, 1949)
—— *Schiller: The Dramatic Writer* (Blackwell, 1969)

Gillies, A., *Herder* (O.U.P., 1945)

Graham, I., *Schiller's Drama: Talent and Integrity* (Methuen, 1974)
—— *Schiller: A Master of the Tragic Form* (Pittsburgh, 1974)

Hatfield, H. C., *Aesthetic Paganism in German Literature* (Harvard, 1964)

Leppman, W., *Winckelmann* (Gollancz, 1971)

Mainland, W. F., *Schiller and the Changing Past* (Heinemann, 1957)

O'Flaherty, J. C., *Hamann's 'Socratic Memorabilia'* (Baltimore, 1967)

Peacock, R., *Goethe's Major Plays* (Manchester University Press, 1959)

Stahl, E. L., *Friedrich Schiller's Drama: Theory and Practice* (O.U.P., 1954)

Wilkinson, E. M., and Willoughby, L. A., *Goethe: Poet and Thinker* (Arnold, 1962)

Index of Names

406   *Index of Names*

Shakespeare, William—*cont.*
    219, 252, 294, 309, 311, 364, 374, 377
Shaw, George Bernard, 375
Socrates, 7, 8, 199, 214, 215, 278
Sophocles, 142, 205, 364, 374, 378, 379
Spinoza, 3, 31, 60, 63, 66, 67, 79, 125, 236, 241, 242, 244, 246, 247, 248, 250
Stadion, Anton Heinrich Friedrich von, 211
Stäel, Mme de, 347
Stäudlin, Gotthold Friedrich, 193
Stein, Charlotte von, 57, 141, 188, 224, 228, 229, 234, 235, 269, 270, 271, 272, 274, 276, 286, 292
Sterne, Laurence, 117, 118
Stifter, Adalbert, 202, 208, 318
Stolberg, Christian von, 33, 35, 47, 167, 180, 321
Stolberg, Friedrich Leopold von, 33, 35, 38, 39, 40, 45, 47, 167, 180, 321
Streicher, Andreas, 187
Sulzer, Johann Georg, 85
Swift, Jonathan, 118

Tasso, Torquato, 132, 290, 291
Tauler, Johannes, 56
Teniers, David (the Younger), 213
Theocritus, 64, 162
Thomas à Kempis, 56
Thorvaldsen, Bertel, 202
Tieck, Ludwig, 82, 97, 127, 135, 166
Tischbein, Johann Heinrich Wilhelm, 160, 273
Titian, 135, 275, 283
Tobler, Georg Christoph, 235, 236
Tschudi, Ägidius, 382

Uz, Johann Peter, 42, 106, 258

Veronese, 135
Vinci, Leonardo da, 205
Volpato, Giovanni, 273
Voltaire, 3, 11, 24, 30, 80, 158, 211, 263, 310, 375
Voss, Johann Heinrich, 33, 34, 35, 36, 37, 38, 39, 45, 47, 102, 106, 311, 354, 355, 358
Vulpius, Christiane, 57, 224, 240, 284, 285, 286–9, 290

Wackenroder, Wilhelm Heinrich, 97, 128, 160, 161, 202, 208
Wagner, Heinrich Leopold, 4, 78, 80, 145, 151, 157–8, 159, 161
Waldner, Henriette von, 140, 144
Watteau, Antoine, 212
Werner, Zacharias, 379
Wieland, Christoph Martin, 3, 37, 86, 89, 90, 108, 109, 132, 144, 146, 153, 159, 167, 186, 199, 200, 201, 210–20, 221, 222, 223, 224, 228, 229, 230, 231, 239, 253, 258, 260, 261, 271, 279, 310, 311, 325, 329
Willemer, Marianne von, 57
Winckelmann, Johann Joachim, 5, 12, 15, 16, 52, 90, 132, 161, 173, 199, 200, 201–10, 212, 213, 220, 224, 227, 228, 230, 231, 237, 240, 241, 242, 244, 245, 259, 261, 263, 269, 271, 273, 275, 277, 278, 283, 288, 297, 299, 300, 301, 303, 304, 309, 318, 340, 358, 361, 377, 378, 387
Wolf, Friedrich August, 201, 356, 357
Wolff, Christian, 102
Wolzogen, Henriette von, 187

Young, Edward, 16

Ziegler, Luise von, 65, 222
Zimmermann, Johann Georg, 170, 171